Accession no.
36201591

LIVING NARRATIVE

LIS LIBRARY

Date	Fund
15/7/14	Cwr-Che

Order No

2534836

University of Chester

LIVING NARRATIVE

Creating Lives in Everyday Storytelling

Elinor Ochs and Lisa Capps

HARVARD UNIVERSITY PRESS
Cambridge, Massachusetts
London, England

Copyright © 2001 by the President and Fellows of Harvard College

ALL RIGHTS RESERVED

Printed in the United States of America

First Harvard University Press paperback 2002

Library of Congress Cataloging-in-Publication Data

Ochs, Elinor.
Living narrative / Elinor Ochs and Lisa Capps.
p. cm.
Includes bibliographical references and index.
ISBN 0-674-00482-5 (cloth : alk. paper)
ISBN 0-674-01010-8 (pbk.)
1. Storytelling. 2. Discourse analysis, Narrative.
I. Capps, Lisa. II. Title.

GR72.3 .O35 2001
808.5'43-dc21   00-054074

ACKNOWLEDGMENTS

The first draft of this volume followed the familiar path of our collaborations. With the computer placed between the two of us, together we composed the chapters. The writing of *Living Narrative* grew out of our research on the relation of ordinary narratives of personal experience to emotional and physical well-being. Fusing Lisa's interest in psychopathology and Elinor's background in discourse and ethnography, the manuscript allowed us to develop a perspective on why and how people recount events in their lives. Completion of the first draft flowed smoothly, despite the challenges of geographical distance and family and professional callings. Lisa, in particular, squeezed writing trips to Los Angeles between caring for her brand new son Walter and his older brother David and the activities associated with her recent appointment as assistant professor in the Department of Psychology at the University of California, Berkeley.

Receiving apt, demanding, and inspiring comments on the first draft from Jerome Bruner and anonymous reviewers, we were issued a challenge to be concise, forthright, and more theoretical in our essay on quotidian narrative. Lisa and I took a deep breath and began to meet this challenge, fueled by an optimism that we could push our horizons much farther. Then, just as we began revamping the manuscript, Lisa was diagnosed with advanced lung cancer. Just under a year later, on February 7, 2000, Lisa died.

This period evidenced an ever more gallant Lisa. With great spirit and courage she managed therapy, family life, and research enterprises, among which this volume held an important place. The final draft of

Living Narrative has Lisa's touch on every page. This possibility is a direct outcome of loving members of the Brostrom and Capps families, who managed the exigencies of Lisa's health and household, freeing her to ponder how narrative helps human beings to cope with the absurdities of life. In addition, the medical community, dear friends, members of the Epworth United Methodist Church, colleagues, and students augmented and inspired Lisa's creative life through heartfelt support. In the course of this intense period, we conversed at length, read a lot of literary philosophy, and mapped the theoretical blueprint for this volume. As her illness progressed, Lisa brought ideas on narrative and illness to the work; Elinor drafted a perspective on narrative that addressed its variable realizations and functions.

A number of our colleagues influenced the direction of *Living Narrative* at different points in its production, especially Patricia Baquedano-Lopez, Jerome Bruner, Susan Ervin-Tripp, Carol Feldman, Gelya Frank, Linda Garro, Candy Goodwin, Chuck Goodwin, John Heritage, Janet Hoskins, Dacher Keltner, Mary Lawlor, Nancy Lutkehaus, Mary Main, Cheryl Mattingly, Dan Slobin, Manny Schegloff, Bambi Schieffelin, John Schumann, Dan Siegel, Marian Sigman, and Carolyn Taylor. Our graduate student co-workers, especially Tami Kremer-Sadlik, Angela Nonaka, Karen Sirota, Olga Solomon, and Laura Sterponi at UCLA and Molly Losh, Eve Muller, and Lisa Rasco at UCB, generously contributed ideas and lent emotional and practical support. Completion of the volume relied heavily on Laura Sterponi, who performed amazing feats in editing and readying the manuscript for publication, saving us from scholarly gaffes, and fine-tuning the thread of our argument. Actress-writer Mary Jo Deschanel infused the work with her unique sense of life as theatre.

At Harvard University Press a flow of e-mail messages from our editor Elizabeth Knoll sustained the writing process, especially in the wrenching months of the past year. Elizabeth gave priority to expediting the publication of this work, offered substantive commentary, applauded chapter completions, and generally held Elinor's hand through the drama of producing the final draft a few days before Lisa's death.

The conceptualization and writing of *Living Narrative* was supported by the Spencer Foundation for Education and Related Research. Spencer is an unusually creative organization, promoting interdisciplinary reflections on human learning wherever it takes place. The book relies upon narrative analyses developed across three Spencer-funded projects, most recently a study of the everyday narrative skills of high-functioning children with autism (Elinor Ochs and Lisa Capps, co-principal investigators).

Beyond the realm of acknowledgment is our gratitude for the strength that each of our spouses and children lent to us in our respective households. Lisa sounded out different ideas with Nathan, as did Elinor with Sandro. These soundings were invaluable to our thinking. Nathan and Sandro gave priority to sustaining our creative spirit, clearing the way for hours and sometimes days of collaboration. In the middle of writing, we often would pause to reflect on our good fortune in husbands. The voices and insights of Elinor's children—David Keenan and Marco Duranti—and Lisa's children—David and Walter Brostrom—opened our eyes to the power of narrative in shaping the course of human experience.

During the last week of Lisa's life we endeavored to write these acknowledgments together, but that was not to be. From her hospital bed Lisa mused to her mother, Lois, the wording of a dedication, reproduced with great feeling here: *Living Narrative* is dedicated to our boys and their fathers.

CONTENTS

Transcription Conventions

Notational conventions employed in the transcribed excerpts examined in the book include the following:

.   The period indicates a falling, or final, intonation contour, not necessarily the end of a sentence.

?   The question mark indicates rising intonation, not necessarily a question.

,   The comma indicates "continuing" intonation, not necessarily a clause boundary.

:::   Colons indicate stretching of the preceding sound, proportional to the number of colons.

-      A hyphen after a word or a part of a word indicates a cut-off or self interruption.

<u>word</u>   Underlining indicates some form of stress or emphasis on the underlined item.

WOrd   Upper case indicates loudness.

° °   The degree signs indicate the segments of talk which are markedly quiet or soft.

> <   The combination of "more than" and "less than" symbols indicates that the talk between them is compressed or rushed.

< >   In the reverse order, they indicate that a stretch of talk is markedly slower.

=   An equal sign indicates no break or delay between the words thereby connected.

(( ))   Double parentheses enclose descriptions of conduct.

(word) When all or part of an utterance is in parentheses, this indicates uncertainty on the transcriber's part.

(   ) Empty parentheses indicate that something is being said, but the transcriber could not hear it.

(1.2) Numbers in parentheses indicate silence in tenths of a second.

(.) A dot in parentheses indicates a "micropause"; hearable but not readily measurable, ordinarily less than two tenths of a second.

[Separate left square brackets, one above the other on two successive lines with utterances by different speakers, indicates a point of overlap onset.

hhh The letter "h" indicates hearable aspiration.

→ The arrow in the margin indicates the lines of the transcript relevant to the point being made in the text.

word Boldface indicates forms relevant to the point being made in the text.

LIVING NARRATIVE

1

A DIMENSIONAL APPROACH TO NARRATIVE

For decades Buddy Levy's drugstore served as the hub of intellectual and political life for liberal-minded Annapolitans. During the week, Elinor's dad and others in the community found excuses to stop by and chat, and on Sundays a cadre of doctors, lawyers, professors, store owners, and others would regularly congregate at Buddy Levy's, ostensibly to pick up the *New York Times* at one of the few places it was delivered. The regulars would linger, some at the lunch counter with the paper folded or spread out in front of them but not eating, and others, like Elinor's dad, leaning his elbow on the pharmacy counter, his head close to Buddy's in intense dialogue. Wherever they rested themselves, they carried on extended, animated exchanges about political happenings. These Sunday experiences served as the analog of a church service for townsfolk as they told each other what they knew, what they believed, what they felt, and what they wished to be happening. Although often irreverent and challenging, the stories of the congregants cemented their moral positions about political events and about one another.

The scene at Buddy Levy's drugstore is emblematic of the social life of narrative. Acquired in childhood, personal narrative is ubiquitous. Whether in a store, along the road, at work, play, home, or other community settings, when people are together, they are inclined to talk about events—those they have heard or read about, those they have experienced directly, and those they imagine. Their talk about such events often takes the form of personal narrative. In *Living Narrative*, we examine this central proclivity of humankind.

Narrative Proclivities

Personal narrative is a way of using language or another symbolic system to imbue life events with a temporal and logical order, to demystify them and establish coherence across past, present, and as yet unrealized experience.[1] *Living Narrative* focuses on ordinary social exchanges in which interlocutors build accounts of life events, rather than on polished narrative performances. The narrators are not renowned storytellers, and their narratives are not entertaining anecdotes, well-known tales, or definitive accounts of a situation. Rather, many of the narratives under study in this volume seem to be launched without knowing where they will lead. In these exchanges, the narrators often are bewildered, surprised, or distressed by some unexpected events and begin recounting so that they may draw conversational partners into discerning the significance of their experiences. Or, narrators may start out with a seamless rendition of events only to have conversational partners poke holes in their story. In both circumstances, narratives are shaped and reshaped turn by turn in the course of conversation.

The difference between telling a story *to* another and telling a story *with* another is an important one. Everyday recountings of incidents, especially those that happened recently and those half-forgotten or repressed, often look like rough drafts rather than finished products. Narrators have something to tell, but the details and the perspective are relatively inchoate; they are still in the middle of sorting out an experience. People who routinely converse with one another sometimes narrate personal events they have recounted many times, but more typically those who keep in touch tend to relate fresh or forgotten events that have not been fixed into a received narrative configuration.

Under these circumstances, the activity of narrating with a family member, friend, neighbor, or perhaps a healer serves as a prosaic social arena for developing frameworks for understanding events. Narrative activity becomes a tool for collaboratively reflecting upon specific situations and their place in the general scheme of life. In assays of this sort, the content and direction that narrative framings take are contingent upon the narrative input of other interlocutors, who provide, elicit, criticize, refute, and draw inferences from facets of the unfolding account. In these exchanges, narrative becomes an interactional achievement and interlocutors become co-authors.

In this sense, conversational narratives of personal experience crystallize literary philosopher Mikhail Bakhtin's notion that "the life of the text, that is, its true essence, always develops *on the boundary between two consciousnesses, two subjects.*"[2] Bakhtin considered readers to be authors and the act of reading to be a dialogue between a text already produced and a reactive text created by a reader. In conversational narrative, Bakhtin's ideas about literary dialogue are realized more intensely in that actual, continuous dialogue allows interlocutors to go beyond responding to an already inscribed ("ready-made") text to collaboratively inscribe turn by turn one or more narrative texts. Moreover, interlocutors do not necessarily take on fixed roles of teller and listener, but rather may shift back and forth, sometimes telling and sometimes apprehending a narrative detail or perspective.[3]

Everyday conversational narratives of personal experience might be regarded as the country cousins of more well-wrought narratives. Why then devote a book to discerning their character? In addressing this question we are reminded of the work of archeologist Nicholas Toth, who revolutionized the understanding of Stone Age tools. Prior to Toth's studies, the received perspective was that early hominids chipped a cobble in such a way that it could be used as a pick or hand axe. Researchers considered the splintered flakes as waste products and examined them for information about techniques used to shape the stone core tool. While others were analyzing the morphological shapes and cognitive correlates of the chipped cores, Toth, in a radical turnabout, discovered that the flakes were the primary tools and that the large stone was an incidental by-product, possibly a secondary tool. The flakes turned out to be "extremely effective cutting tools"[4] for animals, wood, hides, and other work. In this book, we posit that like stone flakes, mundane conversational narratives of personal experience constitute the prototype of narrative activity rather than the flawed by-product of more artful and planned narrative discourse.

As what Bakhtin calls a "primary genre," conversational narrative is central to narrative broadly speaking, if only because it is the most common form of narrative the world over and the ontogenetic starting point of performance and literary genres of narrative ("secondary genres").[5] Bakhtin argues that secondary genres (e.g., the novel) "absorb," "digest," and otherwise transform everyday, primary genres. To understand the life of narrative, i.e., narrative as a discursive and creative activity, it is vital to examine prosaic as well as artistic realizations.

Moreover, ordinary narrative crafted in everyday social encounters elaborately evidences the central tension that drives human beings to narrate. All narrative exhibits tension between the desire to construct an over-arching storyline that ties events together in a seamless explanatory framework and the desire to capture the complexities of the events experienced, including haphazard details, uncertainties, and conflicting sensibilities among protagonists.[6] The former proclivity offers a relatively soothing resolution to bewildering events, yet it flattens human experience by avoiding facets of a situation that don't make sense within the prevailing storyline. The latter proclivity provides narrators and listeners with a more intimate, "inside" portrayal of unfolding events, yet narrators and listeners can find it unsettling to be hurtled into the middle of a situation, experiencing it as contingent, emergent, and uncertain, alongside the protagonists.

Literary critics such as Mikhail Bakhtin, Michael Bernstein, Lawrence Langer, and Gary Morson, and historian Hayden White among others argue that literary and historical narratives overwhelmingly give in to the first proclivity. Comparing literary and oral narrative, Langer notes: "A written narrative is finished when we begin to read it, its opening, middle, and end already established between the covers of the book. This *appearance* of form is reassuring (even though the experience of reading may prove an unsettling challenge). Oral testimony steers a less certain course, like a fragile craft veering through turbulent waters, unsure where a safe harbor lies—or whether one exists at all!"[7] White offers a similar comment on historical narrative: "I have sought to suggest that this value attached to narrativity in the representation of real events arises out of a desire to have real events display the coherence, integrity, fullness, and closure of an image of life that is and can only be imaginary . . . Does the world really present itself to perception in the form of well-made stories with central subjects, proper beginnings, middles, and ends, and a coherence that permits us to see 'the end' in every beginning?"[8]

Linear, coherent narratives generally have a plot structure that depicts a sequence of temporally and causally ordered events organized around a point, with a beginning that situates a significant, i.e. unexpected and hence tellable, incident and moves logically towards an ending that provides a sense of psychological closure. According to Morson: "Narratives, which often turn earlier presents into mere pasts, tend to create a single line of development out of a multiplicity. Alternatives once visible disappear from view and an anachronistic sense of the past surreptitiously infects our understanding."[9]

Such narratives gain a sense of unity through techniques such as *foreshadowing* and *backshadowing*. In foreshadowing the narrator considers "the present not for itself, but as the harbinger of an already determined future."[10] The narrator knows what will follow and casts characters and events in terms of this future trajectory. "Backshadowing," according to Bernstein, "is a kind of retroactive foreshadowing in which the shared knowledge of the outcome of a series of events by narrator and listener is used to judge the participant in those events as though they too should have known what was to come."[11] Thus, for example, knowledge of Nazi atrocities during World War II is used to cast Jews who remained in Austria during the late 1930s as naïve or somehow responsible for their suffering and annihilation. Here again the narrator is more knowing than the unwitting protagonists in the tale. In both foreshadowing and backshadowing, life is treated as structured, orderly, and goal-directed. The narrative itself is coherent and amenable to formal and thematic analysis.

Less commonly, literary and historical narratives cast events as ambiguous, conflictual, unstable, subject to constant revision, perhaps even unknowable. Those that follow this proclivity use a technique that Bernstein and Morson call *sideshadowing*.

> By restoring the *presentness* of the past and cultivating a sense that something else might have happened, *sideshadowing* restores some of the presentness that has been lost.[12]

> Against foreshadowing, sideshadowing champions the incommensurability of the concrete moment and refuses the tyranny of all synthetic master-schemes; it rejects the conviction that a particular code, law, or pattern exists, waiting to be uncovered beneath the heterogeneity of human existence. Instead of the global regularities that so many intellectual and spiritual movements

claim to reveal, sideshadowing stresses the significance of random, haphazard and inassimilable contingencies, and instead of the power of a system to uncover an otherwise unfathomable truth, it expresses the ever-changing nature of that truth and the absence of any predictive certainties in human affairs.[13]

Dostoevsky, Tolstoy, and Musil, among others, revolutionized literary narrative by exquisitely capturing the polyphonic and indeterminate quality of human events and non-events. The rub is that the formal architecture of these works is difficult to systematically describe; they tend to be temporally and causally nonlinear and oscillate back and forth between perspectives, which may conflict. In brief, these works resemble more closely the contingent quality of human experience itself. This quality is at once a literary achievement and a formalist's anathema. In narratives like these, the boundary between life and art is blurred, and narrative can no longer be categorically distinguished from other genres. Those seeking a set of defining formal criteria for narrative, such as posited for classic narrative (exhibiting streamlined beginnings, middles, and endings), are faced with either excluding modern texts that exhibit sideshadowing or accepting that (1) the boundaries of narrative are fuzzy and (2) that narrative along with other forms of discourse allows authors and protagonists to imagine possibilities, weigh alternatives, shift mindsets, and act without knowing what lies in the future.

To be sure, when conversationalists informally recount incidents, they too are pulled between the proclivity to cast what happened in terms of comforting schemata and the proclivity to air doubts and alternatives in an effort to regain the authenticity of the experience. And so too are conversationalists more disposed to shape events into a common-sensical and socially affirming trajectory of intentions, wills, fates and outcomes and to depict protagonists in terms of cultural typifications. Yet conversation with familiar interlocutors in a wide range of communities affords open-ended storytelling. Let's consider why casual conversation among familiars promotes narrative exploration:

Open-endedness is an inherent property of conversation. Conversation is informal discourse, which characteristically displays a contingent orderliness. According to sociologists Harvey Sacks and Emanuel Schegloff, conversation is locally organized.[14] That is, the direction of conversation can be loosely anticipated inside of a conversational turn (e.g., conversational turns have orderly ways of beginning and ending, which allow interlocutors to overlap at predictable moments) and from one turn to the next turn (e.g., certain types of conversational turns and moves project possible next speakers and next turns). Generally, however, the order of acts and speakers and thematic content of extended stretches of conversational discourse cannot be even loosely anticipated at the outset. Rather, the flow of talk lies in the hands of the interlocutors; it is a moment-by-moment, emergent "interactional achievement."[15] The absence of a *Robert's Rules of Order* or other formal canon for determining who can say what, when, and how in everyday conversation means that interlocutors, even those of lower social rank, have opportunity to insert their knowledge and evaluate narrated events, protagonists, and even another interlocutor's view or manner of telling the events. Although such repartee can lead interlocutors to reaffirm a dominant, status quo perspective, it also provides a stage *par excellence* for envisioning actual and possible events through alternative voices.

Conversation is the most likely medium for airing unresolved life events. When people hear about or are directly involved in an unexpected situation, they often don't have a clear sense of what transpired and why. They also may not grasp possible implications of an experience. In still other cases they may understand events in ways that diverge from and challenge prevailing narrative accounts. The events to be recounted also may not be earthshaking or of wide interest but rather fall into the category of minor incidents. In other cases, the events may be painful and difficult to articulate coherently. Under these circumstances, people tend to relate events—large or small—not as a tidy narrative package but as incomplete and unresolved, and informal conversation with those one knows or trusts rather than more formal genres is the medium of choice. Akin to the virtual dialogues that take place in a writer's head in the throes of drafting a story (and which later become invisible),[16] conversation lays bare the actual dialogic activity through which different versions of experience are aired, judged, synthesized, or eliminated. In this manner, conversational interaction realizes the essential function of personal narrative—to air, probe, and otherwise attempt to reconstruct and make sense of actual and possible life experiences.

Conversational involvement is a hallmark of familiarity. Informal conversation is the communicative glue that establishes and maintains close relationships in many communities. This does not mean that close relationships require continuous talk, but rather that commiserating, gossiping, philosophizing, exchanging advice, and other informal discourse interlaces lives and builds common ways of acting, thinking, feeling and otherwise being in the world. In their analysis of family narrative activity, Elinor Ochs, Carolyn Taylor, and their colleagues observed that Caucasian American family members tend not to listen politely to one another's narratives, but rather to contribute substantially.[17] They supply and elicit relevant pieces of the setting, events, psychological responses, and outcomes. Indeed, the family member who initiated a narrative contributed approximately 60 percent of the narrative components, while other family members contributed the rest.[18] Ochs, Taylor, and colleagues posited that active narrative involvement defines what it means to participate in a mainstream American family. Family members dive into one another's narratives, even when they have no direct experience of or privileged access to the events, in part because they do usually have background knowledge concerning the protagonists or the events and in part because they have the right to intervene as a family member. The authors suggested that, at least among Caucasian Americans, similar funds of background knowledge and rights to narratively intervene obtain in other relationships, for example, among friends and close colleagues. Indeed, active narrative participation may be a hallmark of familiarity in this community and others, and more passive narrative conduct (e.g., supplying only minimum feedback cues such as "hmm") may signal that an interlocutor is taking social distance. When interlocutors become centrally involved in the telling of a narrative, there is no guarantee of narrative coherence or predictability. In the narratives recorded by Ochs, Taylor, and colleagues, for example, family members routinely challenged perspectives and details of narrated events. In this manner, conversational tellings of personal experience can manifest an open-ended assemblage of narrative possibilities.

To illuminate the contingent, open-ended quality of conversational narrative, we turn to a personal narrative.[19] Collaboratively recounted by wife (Marie) and husband (Jon), the narrative involves Marie, who runs a daycare center, and Bev, the mother of one of the children who attend. Having decided to pull her daughter out of daycare, Bev paid Marie

$320 she believed she owed. At the outset of the narrative, Marie casts the $320 as overpayment because her account book showed Bev owed only $80:

> Marie: Bev walked up? (and/she) handed me three twenty?
> Jon: mhm
>> (0.6 pause)
> Marie: And I <u>thought</u> she only owed me eighty. (.) and she said she
>> didn't want a receipt (.) and I went in and got the: receipt book
>> n: she only owed me eighty=
> Jon: =hmmhm.
>> (0.4 pause)
> Marie: n she was real happy about that
>> (1.0 pause)
> Marie: She says "No no no no no:: <u>I</u> don't need a receipt."
>> (0.8 pause)
>> . . .
>> (and just hands me three twenty)
>> (2.0 pause)
> Marie: I took my <u>book</u> out though (.) cuz she hardly <u>ever</u> (.) makes
>> mis<u>ta:h:kes</u> [I thought maybe I wrote it wrong
>> [((laughing))
>> but I went back and got three receipts and they all were
> Jon: mhm
> Marie: in- you know (.) what do you call that?
>> . . .
> Jon: consecutive order?=
> Marie: =Yeah

The narrative to this point has a coherent storyline in which a mistake is corrected and Marie is cast as a scrupulous professional. Jon offers only minimal feedback, passively affirming his wife's rendition of events. The incident appears abandoned when Marie starts recounting how Bev received money from a false insurance claim and John responds with disgust. In the middle of this implicit comparison of Marie's honesty with Bev's duplicity, however, Marie suddenly mentions that Bev had not given her the required two weeks' notice prior to pulling her daughter out of daycare:

Marie: you know what thou:gh (.) I started questioning was (.)
the fact she gave me (.) <u>no notice</u>. (.) she just called up after the
accident and said.
Jon: Yeah ["I'm not coming anymore"
Marie: ["That's it" (.) no (.) no two weeks' pay (.) not

In this outburst Marie opens up the narrative to the possibility of alternative perspectives. She tells Jon, "I started questioning . . . the fact she gave me (.) <u>no notice</u>." With the airing of this information, however, Marie's original version of the $320 incident is cast into doubt. Jon recasts the $320 as the stipulated penalty for withdrawing a child without two weeks' notice:

Jon: (Marie?)
Marie: no: consideration- (whe [ther I had to make/without ever)
Jon: [She did <u>a:ll that</u> when she paid you
three hundred and twenty dollars.
She didn't do that by mistake. (.) She wanted to see how <u>you</u> felt
about it n she felt she <u>owed</u> you

In this manner, over the course of conversational turn-taking, a story and a counter story emerge. Originally, Marie's coherently crafted "Overpayment" story is supported by Jon (who seems only half-listening). But emergent information ushers forth Jon's countering "Two Weeks Notice Payment" story. How does Marie react? She resists:

Marie: No: wa:y (.)
[no: [nonono (.) no
[((shaking head and hand))
Jon: [Oh no?
You don't think so?
Marie: No [<u>she</u> thought she had not paid me for the month of June
Jon: [Oh
[((lightly))
Marie: and she's <u>pay</u>ing me fro:m
Jon: eh
Marie: the <u>fi</u>[rst week of Ju:ne

Jon: [I would read it
           Oh [(eh/yeah)
Marie: [to:: the- the ending (.) the third of . . .

Jon tries to rally evidence for his perspective, but Marie holds her own, and Jon reluctantly caves in:

Jon: You had <u>said</u> that she never made a mistake in the past? though
       (didn't you)
       She was always very good about that
Marie: [<u>No</u>
       [((*with index finger pointed*))
       she she's made <u>one</u> mistake in the past
Jon: oh oh [huhuh
         [((*slight nod*))
Marie: [but her <u>record</u> i:s (.) very few mistakes?
       [((*raised finger moves horizontally to indicate Bev's record over time*))
Jon: [hmhm (okay)
      [((*nodding yes*))

In this conversational exchange, Jon shores up his counter story by citing behaviors that contradict Marie's narrative perspective that Bev had made a *mistake* when she paid $320, but Marie contradicts him with a background detail ("she's made <u>one</u> mistake in the past"). It should be noted, however, that Marie does not entirely preclude Jon's point of view, because she also notes "but her <u>record</u> i:s (.) very few mistakes." That is, there is no definite closure to (demystification of) this life experience.

Later in the conversation, the narrative "theory," as Ochs, Taylor et al. call it, is reopened to scrutiny. In contrast to her earlier portrayal of herself as a virtuous businesswoman, Marie is now cast negatively, as lacking the necessary assertiveness for the head of a daycare center. In this return to the incident, Marie plunges into the existential presentness of the affair. She begins to agonize over her handling of the $320 incident, then her husband fans the flames of her self-rendering by pontificating about what he would do under the circumstances:

Marie: [You know (.) Jon I verbally did tell Bev two weeks' notice.
  [((head on hand, elbow on table))
  Do you think I shouldov stuck to that?
  or (to have/just) done what I did
  (0.8 pause)

Jon: When I say something I stick to it. unless she: (.) s- brings it up.
  If I set a policy (.) (you know/and I) and they accept that
    policy (.)
  .h unless they have reason to change it and and say something?
  I do not change it. I don't automatically assume .h "We:ll it's not
    the right thing to do." If I were to do that e- I would be saying
    in the first place I should never have mentioned it. I should
    never have set the policy if I didn't believe in it. (.) If I thought
    it was (.) a hardship on people I shouldn'a brought it up?
  shoulda kept my mouth shut (.) .h If I: say there's two weeks'
  notice required (.) I automatically charge em for two weeks'
    notice
  without thinking twice about it. I say and I- "If you- you need (.)
  your pay will include till such and such a date because of the two
  neek- weeks' notice that's required."
  [I:f THE:Y feel hardship it's on thei:r part
  [((gesturing emphatically with his hands))
  it's (.) THEIRS to say "Marie I really? (.) you know I didn't expect
  this to happen 'n I'm [sorry I didn't give you two weeks' notice
                        [((softly))
  but it was really un- avoidable" (.) a:nd you can say "We:ll, okay
    I'll
  split the difference with you (.) (it's har-) a one we[ek's notice"

Marie: [see you know
  in o[ne way wi- in one (instance)

Jon: [and then they (st- if) they push it

Marie: [she owed me that money
  [((pointing to Jon))
  but I just didn't feel [right taking it on that (principle because)

Jon: [well you're (.) you

Marie: She (wanted) she thought she was paying it for something [that (she didn't   )

Jon: [You: give her the money and then you let it bother you then (.)
you (.) then you get all ups-set
[(You'll) You'll be upset for weeks

Marie: [No no no
I'm not upset (.) it's just
(0.4 pause) ((Marie raps knuckles on table))
I guess I just wish I would have s:aid (.)
I'm not upset with what happened. I just wanted (.) I think I (.)
would feel better if I had said something

The narrative is left dangling at this point, without clear closure. Marie
and Jon conflict over the moral perspective to adopt regarding Marie's
stance and actions during her encounter with Bev. In addition, Marie
herself wrangles with her inability to satisfy both her desire to be honest
and accommodating in financial matters and her desire to voice her true
point of view to Bev ("she owed me that money . . . I just wanted (.) I
think I (.) would feel better if I had said something"). While her spouse
proffers a ready-made counter narrative for this type of life encounter,
Marie's inclinations remain bathed in the language of uncertainty ("I
guess," "I just," "I think").

Is narrative exploration of this sort unique to mainstream American
society? We believe that it is not. Consider, for example, the following
narrative interaction between a Samoan chief (Tāvō) and his compan-
ions (Fonotī and Paito). In this excerpt, the narrators build two possible
accounts of what happened to Tāvō's missing watch. Tāvō at first provides an account that explains the disappearance of his watch in terms
of theft:[20]

Tāvō: *Ke iloa le mea malie Fogoki*
Do you know the funny thing Fonotī

lea e kupu iā a'u?
that happens to me?

Fonotī: *'O le a?*
What is it?

Tāvō: *I le pō fo'i ga kākou kalagoa kalagoa*
In the night (when) we talked and talked

(kou-) 'o a'u moe
(you) I sleep

ga'o a'u
only me

→   *ae 'ave (e) le kagaka la'u uaki.*
and *((advers.))* someone takes my watch.
(1.0 pause)

→ Fonotī: *'Ave lau uaki?*
Take your watch?

→ Paito: *'Ave le uaki.*
Take the watch.
(1.0 pause)

Instead of stopping at this point and considering the issue resolved, however, Tāvō goes on to formulate an alternative possibility, namely that he might have accidentally dropped it in his hurry to catch his ride home:

    Tāvō: *'O lo'u a la magaku,*
                What I really thought

              ua fo'i ga sau pō ā Ie'u,
              because Ie'u also came very early,
              (1.0 pause)

              lo'u a magaku
              What I really thought

              uo'u- (0.2 pause) *sau ā oso le ka'avale*
              I had come and jumped (in) the car

→   *'a la'e pa'ū la'u uaki i fale,* (0.2 pause) *ā,*
              but my watch was dropped at the house (over there), y' know?

   Fonotī: *'o:* ( )
              oh

    Tāvō: *'O le mea gā sa'u magaku i ai.*
              That's what I thought.
              (2.2 pause)

The narrative continues with suggestions as to how to find the watch and finally a restatement of competing versions of past experience:

→ Tāvō: *ga pa'ū 'ese ma lo'u lima*
(it) dropped off my wrist

go'u o'u moe,
while I was asleep,

→ *po'o le mea 'ua kakala e kagaka i lo'u lima*
or it was that someone took it from my wrist

'a 'ou moe.
when I sleep.

This exchange illustrates how narrative activity in a Polynesian village provides a platform for entertaining diverse construals of life events. In addition, it displays how narrative may leave the meaning of events unresolved. The narrator launches the account in a search for closure—indeed he inspires others to look for the missing watch—but the narrative stops before closure is achieved. Here the emphasis is on narrative activity as a sense-making *process* rather than as a finished product in which loose ends are knit together into a single storyline.

Is narrative exploration of this sort limited to adults? We believe not. Consider, for example, linguistic anthropologist Marjorie Harness Goodwin's analysis of narrative activity among nine- to fourteen-year-old African-American neighborhood girls.[21] The girls often recounted stories in which a girl not present offended a girl who is present. The storytelling involved the girls in evaluating different moral perspectives concerning a past incident. A characteristic feature of these exchanges is that the girls rallied behind the perspective of the offended girl in their midst and critiqued the perspective of the offending absent party. In one exchange, for example, twelve-year-old Julia draws her interlocutors Barbara and Bea into probing through narrative an incident in which Kerry (not present) did not include her name on a hall pass allowing a group of girls to go to the bathroom at school. In the course of the exchange, Bea reports that Kerry said that she did not want Julia's name on the pass, because Julia was "acting stupid" around some girl:

Bea: SHE said, <u>SHE</u> said that um, (0.6 pause) that (0.8 pause) if that

GIRL wasn't there=<u>YOU</u> know that girl that always makes those funny

jokes, Sh'aid if that <u>GIRL</u> wasn't there <u>YOU</u> wouldn't be actin'
(0.4 pause) a:ll <u>stu</u>pid like that.

[°Sh-

→ Julia: [But was I actin stupid w[ith them

  Bea: [Nope, no=and

she- and she said that <u>YOU</u> sai:d, that

"<u>AH:</u> go tuh-" (0.5 pause) somp'um like [that

Julia: [°No I didn't,

  Bea: She's- an uh somp'm like THAT. She's-

  Barb: <u>Kerry</u> <u>AL</u>ways say somp'n .

Here Julia calls into question Kerry's interpretation of past events, specifically Julia's comportment. She asks, "But was I actin stupid with them," whereupon two narrative versions of events are entertained in tandem, one from Kerry's perspective (recounted by Bea) and one from the perspective of Julia, supported by Bea and Barbara.

These narrative interactions illuminate how sometimes one narrator entertains multiple storylines, as does Marie in recounting the $320 transaction and Tāvō in recounting events surrounding his missing watch; sometimes co-present narrators oppose each other's narrative renderings, as do Marie and Jon; and sometimes co-present narrators coalesce around a storyline that starkly contrasts with an absent party's purported perspective on events, as do Julia, Bea, and Barbara in opposition to Kerry's version of the hall pass incident. In each conversational interaction, a prevailing narrative meets resistance through a counter narrative, which in turn may be adopted or resisted.

The airing of alternative narrative renderings is not exclusive to conversational narrative. All narrative activity has this potential, from literary to oral performance to elicited interview narratives. An interview, for example, may at first yield a tidy story that subsequently disintegrates. Psychoanalyst Roy Schafer treats such shifts in narrative perspective as a core feature of the therapeutic process:[22]

> People going through psychoanalysis—analysands—tell the analyst about themselves and others in the past and present. In making interpretations, the analyst retells these stories. In the retelling, cer-

tain features are accentuated while others are placed in parentheses; certain features are related to others in new ways or for the first time; some features are developed further; perhaps at great length . . . The analyst's retellings progressively influence the what and how of the stories told by analysands. The analyst establishes new, though often contested or resisted, questions that amount to regulated narrative possibilities. The end product of this interweaving of texts is a radically new, jointly authored work or way of working.

Schafer's comments offer insight into everyday conversational narrative as a site for working through who we are and how we should be acting, thinking, and feeling as we live our lives. Familiar conversational partners, recruited or uninvited, are likely to recall relevant background events, ask questions, raise issues and possibilities, and otherwise provoke further thinking about an incident. Such sustained collaborative reflection can destabilize a person's prevailing interpretation of the self and others, leading the way for alternative ways of remembering the past and inhabiting the present.

Just as narrative exploration is not limited to conversational narrative, so conversational narrative does not consistently manifest the airing and evaluating of alternative possible understandings of past events. As noted, conversation is also an avenue for soothing, conventional reconstructions of incidents. Our point is that narrators everywhere are confronted with the desire for a stable reconstruction of our remembered past and the desire for an authentic reconstruction of the past, and that conversational narrative is particularly suited to satisfying the latter. Stable narratives that lack authenticity are ultimately vulnerable to conscious or unconscious resistance; alternatively, authentic narratives that promote possibility and relativity may render one unable to choose among possible courses of action or diverse ways of thinking about life experience.

Depending upon community and circumstance, then, narrators are pulled in the direction of formulating a tightly organized storyline with a beginning and an end or in the direction of probing what transpired. The dialectic generated is a condition that is basic to narrative as a human genre. Vaclav Havel writes,[23] "The world seems (among other things) to grow out of an eternal struggle between two fundamental tendencies of Being: its will (entropic) to make things uniform, to dissolve and blend together all of its particular expressions and homogenize itself entirely; and its creative or creatorial (antientropic) will to defend, strengthen, and cultivate the uniqueness of all its richly varied manifestations and to develop them in the direction of ever higher (more structured) forms." Havel's point is that creative will overcomes simple uniformity by "cultivating" complexity and building an "ever higher" philosophy that tries to comprehend wider horizons of the human condition. Writing these and other passages during his years in prison for political resistance, Havel was well aware of how uniformity backed by institutional power silences the creative will: "The final effect in each case is silence: the silence of the half-mad man who is constantly writing appeals to world authorities while everyone ignores him; and the silence of the Orwellian citizen."[24]

Narrative Dimensions

As such, narrative bows to no simple generic blueprint that sets it apart once and for all from other forms of discourse. More tightly organized narratives, with coherent thematic progression of actions, reactions, and resolutions, are more amenable to formal analysis, but even these narratives overlap with other kinds of discourse. Narrative is a cognitively and discursively complex genre that routinely contains some or all of the following discourse components: *description, chronology, evaluation,* and *explanation* (Figure 1.1a). Settings, for example, are built from *descriptions.* Classic plots depict both a linear or more complex *chronology* of unfolding events and an overarching *explanation* of why a particular event transpired at a particular point in the narrative sequence. And, from its inception, the narrative is imbued with a moral and aesthetic *evaluation* of actions, emotions, thoughts, and worldly conditions.

Once we turn to conversational narratives, other conversational acts and genres of discourse penetrate. Conversational narrative routinely involves *questions, clarifications, challenges,* and *speculations* about what might possibly have transpired (Figure 1.1b). In other words, narrative is a host genre that draws upon commonly used text structures. The structure that is the best candidate for distinguishing narrative is chronology, in that temporal sequencing of two or more events is considered by many to be a hallmark of narrative. But even this property is not universally recognized. In his book *What Stories Are,* literary critic Thomas

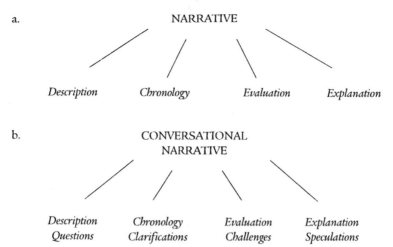

Fig. 1.1. Discourse components of (a) *narrative, and* (b) *conversational narrative*

Leitch does away with plot configurations of chronology and causality as necessary to narrative:[25] "The constitutive feature of narrative development is the sequence of the audience's perceptions, projections, and reintegrations of the story, typically following a line of development from illusion to disillusionment, and for this purpose plot in the sense of a temporal or causal sequence of events is clearly not necessary . . . Story is possible without plot."

We believe that narrative as genre and activity can be fruitfully examined in terms of a set of *dimensions* that a narrative displays to differing degrees and in different ways. Rather than identifying a set of distinctive features that always characterize narrative, we stipulate dimensions that will be always *relevant* to a narrative, even if not elaborately manifest. In this book, we focus on dimensions of relevance to narratives of personal experience. Candidate dimensions of relevance to personal narratives are shown in Table 1.1. The dimensions pertain both to narrating as activity and to narrative as text. Each narrative dimension establishes a *range* of possibilities, which are realized in particular narrative performances. We use these dimensions and their fields of possibilities to analyze how different interlocutors shape the telling of a narrative and how life events are structured through narrative form. A cluster

Table 1.1. Narrative dimensions and possibilities

Dimensions		Possibilities	
Tellership	One active teller	→	Multiple active co-tellers
Tellability	High	→	Low
Embeddedness	Detached	→	Embedded
Linearity	Closed temporal and causal order	→	Open temporal and causal order
Moral stance	Certain, constant	→	Uncertain, fluid

of narrative possibilities may characterize whole narratives. Alternatively, the configuring of possibilities may shift in the course of a single narrative's telling.

The default narrative of personal experience analyzed in the social sciences tends to exhibit a cluster of characteristics that fall at one end of these continua:

one active teller,
highly tellable account,
relatively detached from surrounding talk and activity,
linear temporal and causal organization, and
certain, constant moral stance.

Such narratives are generally easy to identify, have inherent appeal, and are amenable to systematic analysis. They are often related during interviews with a researcher or facilitator. Anthropologists, folklorists, psychologists, historians, and linguists characteristically initiate interaction with community members to record rich accounts of memorable past events. In some cases, the interviewer makes an explicit request, such as the question posed by linguist William Labov asking subjects to recount an experience in which they came close to death.[26] The following excerpt from a well-crafted, coherent narrative dominated by one primary teller, for example, was elicited in the course of an interview between educational ethnographer Lucila Ek and an African American teacher concerning children's understanding of racial and cultural diversity:[27]

Teacher: One >little boy little girl< came up °to me: (0.2 pause) uh::
          yesterday

        (0.4 pause)

        you know

        (0.6 pause)

        and this has been my <u>o</u>nly incident

        (0.4 pause) ah:: (.) Miss Ek is (0.4 pause) sh- (.) little black girl came up,

        she said "Would you please tell that boy to stop calling me a <u>nigger</u>"

        (0.6 pause)

        [and

→   LE: [Mm hm

Teacher: so I said (.)

        a::nd <u>it</u> was <u>some</u>body from my <u>cla:::ss</u>?

        (0.2 pause) so I was like "<u>oh my gosh:::</u>"

        (1.0 pause)

→   LE: °Mm hm

Teacher: Uh:: so:: I asked him

        I said you know (0.2 pause) "Why would you call her that.

        So (0.4 pause) d- do you talk about <u>me</u> like <u>th</u>at when you get home"

        And [this kind of thing

→   LE: [Mm hm

Teacher: He said >no=no=no<

        Well I said it to her because she's been saying "<u>f- you</u>" (0.4 pause) to <u>me::</u> [all the time

→   LE: [Oh::

Teacher: So [she had a part in it

→   LE: [Mm hm

Teacher: He had a part in it

        He admitted that had (.) <u>done it</u>

        She admitted her part

        And today I saw them playing together

        (0.4 pause)

        [A:nd we talked about when I got the two of them <u>together</u>

→   LE: [Mm hm

Teacher: how (0.4 pause) you know those name calling and saying ugly things

        to each other

"Why were you doing that?"
(0.4 pause)
It turned out because they were in first grade together
and had a problem two years ago
(0.6 pause)

→   LE: Mm hm

Teacher: And so wu- I (0.6 pause) that kinda (0.8 pause) got resolved

As primary teller, the teacher portrays a linear sequence of events in which she handily and impartially solves a potentially explosive racial incident by bringing both parties together and airing grievances. The narrative establishes a single overarching storyline in which specific events are framed as causing other events and maintains a consistent psychological stance of certainty and competence in discerning right and wrong.

Similarly, a visit between an ethnographer and a community member can serve as a catalyst for a member to relate a font of well-formed stories. The following exchange between folklorist Katharine Young (accompanied by friends) and an elderly English man (Algy) illustrates the way in which periodic visits inspire elaborate storytelling:[28]

Algy: I like the story about [a

Katharine: [ha see?
He always tells a story

Algy: No go on (give him)

MF: [((*chuckles*))

Algy: [When [((*chuckles*))

Katharine: [((*chuckles*))

Algy: Is it ((*tape recorder*)) on?

Katharine: Of course it's on let's see

Algy: All right I'll- This is my final thing.
I was (.) had a drink or two
and I was walking back from Newton Abbot to Ashburton
And (.) in the wintertime.
And I was tired. I thought I saw a car coming.
In fact it did come. Slowly overtook me.
I thought I don't know it's got no lights.
Anyhow opened the door jumped in passenger side.

Thought um anything special (in the thing)?
And sat there you see and when we got to a corner great hairy
    hand comes round

Katharine: Hm.

    Algy: moves the steering wheel and on we go.

Katharine: *((Coughs))*

    Algy: Then I nodded off (.) went to sleep

((The story continues for extended series of turns))

The opening turns of this exchange suggest that Algy and Katharine are oriented to storytelling performance. We imply this from Algy's comment, "I like the story about a . . .," from Katharine's confirming remark, "Ha see? He always tells a story," and from Algy's and Katharine's attention to the tape recording of the story ("Is it *((tape recorder))* on?" "Of course it's on let's see"). Algy then proceeds with little interruption to carefully craft a dramatic story filled with suspense.

Much less is known about narratives whose characteristics fall at the other ends of the continua on the chart of narrative dimensions:

multiple, active co-tellers,
moderately tellable account,
relatively embedded in surrounding discourse and activity,
nonlinear temporal and causal organization, and
uncertain, fluid moral stance.

Full of hesitations, queries, and consideration of alternative perspectives, such narratives are generally difficult to demarcate and systematically analyze. *Living Narrative* brings these narratives to analytic light. We examine how conversational narratives are launched in ordinary social exchanges among interlocutors, how interlocutors move back and forth across time to make sense out of events, how causes and effects are stitched together only to fall apart when narrators are reminded or informed of inconsistencies.

Yet, *Living Narrative* does not focus exclusively on these narratives. Rather, the volume considers narratives of personal experience that span the continua of tellership, embeddedness, tellability, linearity, and psychological consistency. In addition to examining a diverse array of narratives, we explore how a given narrative can shift along these con-

tinua as it unfolds. Examining the spectrum of narrative possibilities
helps us to fathom the essence of personal narrative, namely the oscilla-
tion between narrators' yearning for coherence of life experience and
their yearning for authenticity. That is, narrators contending with life
experiences struggle to formulate an account that both provides an
interpretive frame and does justice to life's complexities. This tension fuels narrative activity and accounts for much of the social life of
narrative.

TELLERSHIP

The dimension *tellership* refers to the extent and kind of involvement of
conversational partners in the actual recounting of a narrative. Tellers
are what sociologist Erving Goffman calls "animators."[29] They bring a
set of reportable events to life through a range of communicative resources including talk, print, visual representation, gesture, body orientation, movement, and facial expression among other modalities. Possibilities range from a teller who basically recounts a narrative in front of
a relatively passive audience (as is the case in the teacher interview on
racism) to a set of active *tellers* who collaboratively supply and elicit information and stances relevant to events that have transpired (as in the
case of Marie and Jon's telling of the daycare payment incident). There is
considerable variation across social groups and situations concerning
the extent to which tellership resides in the hands of one teller or is dis-
tributed across several. Discourse analyst Janet Holmes, for example,
found that New Zealand interlocutors of Maori descent provided one
third less feedback and were more reluctant to ask questions in the
course of the telling of a narrative than were interlocutors of European
descent.[30]

The role of teller is distinct from that of author.[31] Even the quietest
conversational partners can be active co-authors of a narrative, as is
strikingly apparent in the largely silent psychoanalyst's powerful role
in shaping the analysand's life story.[32] Yet the authorial shaping of a
storyline is not the same as physically telling a story.[33] As noted by literary philosopher Mikhail Bakhtin, a teller may be influenced by the
thoughts and words of others who are not present and may assimilate
these absent voices while recounting events.[34] Sometimes others' voices
are explicitly quoted, as in the narrative exchange among African American girls that we saw earlier:[35]

Bea: SHE said, <u>SHE</u> said that um, (0.6 pause) that (0.8 pause) if that
GIRL
wasn't there

A teller may even incorporate several voices through embedded quotes.
As noted by Marjorie Goodwin, a teller (A) may report to a co-present
addressee (B) what an absent party (C) said to A about what B said:

(A)　　　(C)　　　　(B)
↓　　　　↓　　　　↓
Bea: and she said that <u>YOU</u> sai:d, that
"<u>AH:</u> go tuh-"

In other narratives the incorporation of authorial voices into the telling
of a narrative is less clearly marked, as when, in the narrative excerpt below, Dad paraphrases the words of someone's advertisement:[36]

→　Dad: I got to <u>tell</u> you what they were advertising in Glenview (.)
on Glenview Boulevard on the way home
　Sean: *((looks at Dad))*
　Beth: *((looks at Dad))*
　Mom: What. *((anxiously))*
→　Dad: WE could <u>have</u> a:: <u>pit bull</u> [and <u>shepherd</u> and part <u>rottweiler</u>
puppy
　Mom: 　　　　　　　　　　　　[*((jerks back away from Dad))*
　Dad: HA HA HA HA ha ha ha ha ha
　Mom: Oh yeah
　Beth: Pit bull shepherd and rottweiler
　Mom: Who needs a <u>gun</u> with a dog like that

And in yet other cases, the influence of others' ideas on the shape of
the narrative is invisible. Taking the logic of revoicing to the extreme, every word, expression, and genre we employ in a narrative has been co-
authored in the sense that they have been developed and used by others
before us.[37]

As noted by sociologist Jennifer Mandelbaum, listeners vary their involvement in the actual telling of a narrative from cursory displays of attentiveness to posing probing questions to supplying narrative details.[38]

As represented in our chart of narrative dimensions, relatively *low involvement* in co-telling is characteristic of narrative interactions in which one teller prevails in the telling and conversational partners maintain the role of relatively passive listeners. Relatively *high involvement* characterizes narrative interactions in which, although one person may be positioned as primary teller, substantive narrative contributions are made by more than one interlocutor.[39] Interlocutors can display relatively high involvement in a conversational narrative *vocally* through utterances and *nonvocally* through culturally appropriate eye contact, head moves, body orientation towards the speaker, or expressive facial and somatic reactions.[40]

Narratives of personal experience that emerge in formal interviews often evidence low involvement in co-telling. That is, often the narrative interaction consists of an interviewee telling a narrative to an interviewer, who provides minimum feedback. This tellership profile characterizes the start of the teacher interview excerpt, wherein the interviewer provides primarily continuers[41] ("Mm hm") that signal attentiveness and encouragement to the storyteller to proceed but otherwise does not contribute substantively to the telling of the emergent narrative, as in:

Teacher: So [she had a part in it
→　　LE:　　[Mm hm

But even in interview contexts, tellership can move from relatively passive to more active involvement. In the remainder of the teacher interview, for example, the researcher becomes more involved in the narrative when she shifts from using mainly "Mm hm" to offering assessments that empathize with the teacher's predicament and provide support for her handling of the situation:

Teacher: It turned out because they were in first grade together
　　　　　and had a problem two years ago
　　　　　(0.6 pause)
→　　LE:　Mm hm
Teacher: And so wu- I (0.6 pause) that kinda (0.8 pause) got resolved
　　　　　But I mean I was (0.8 pause)
→　　LE:　Yeah:: (0.6 pause) [that's scary
Teacher:　　　　　　　　　　[((*coughing with laughter*))
　　　　　(0.4 pause)

→ LE: It's scary because then what do you do?

Teacher: Right

→ LE: And how do you °know how to help them

Teacher: <u>And</u> I know other:: (0.4 pause) I'm sure (0.4 pause)

Not to pat myself or anything but probably some other teacher
would have just said, you know "Go sit down (.) I don't I don't
want to hear it"

(0.4 pause)

→ LE: Yeah

Teacher: and not dealt with it at all

→ LE: Exactly (.) <u>exa:ctly</u>

In this excerpt, the researcher first offers affect-laden agreement through a drawn out "Yeah::" then appreciation of the magnitude of the problem ("that's scary . . . It's scary because then what do you do? . . . And how do you °know how to help them"). Finally, when the teacher compares herself favorably to how others might respond, the interviewer strongly aligns ("Yeah . . . Exactly (.) <u>exa:ctly</u>").

Sometimes conversational partners are *coaxed* into the role of highly involved co-teller. For example, in the above excerpt, the teacher encourages the interviewer to take a more active tellership role by inviting her to complete an utterance left dangling:

Teacher: And so wu- I (0.6 pause) that kinda (0.8 pause) got resolved

But I mean I was

(0.8 pause)

→ LE: Yeah:: (0.6 pause) that's scary

(0.4 pause)

When the teacher says "But I mean I was," then allows a long pause to transpire, she signals that she is not eager to resume narration and encourages the researcher to take the floor and complete the unfinished proposition.[42] In drawing the interviewer more centrally into the narration, the teacher effectively shifts the relatively formal interview narrative into a more conversational narrative interaction between the two of them. Using a similar strategy, in the beginning of the narrative (excerpted earlier) concerning a $320 payment for childcare, Marie coaxes her initially passive husband into the storytelling by asking him to supply the expression she is searching for:

Marie: I took my <u>book</u> out though (.) cuz she hardly <u>ever</u> (.) makes
mista:h:<u>kes</u> [I thought maybe I wrote it wrong
[((*laughing*))
but I went back and got three receipts and they all were
Jon: mhm
→Marie: in- you know (.) what do you call that?

. . .

Jon: consecutive order?=
Marie: =Yeah

A subtle form of coaxing consists of using a *euphemism,* which invites
conversational partners to supply the more explicit meaning.[43] The use
of a euphemism becomes a source of possible misunderstanding and
initiates attempts to clarify or repair the misunderstanding.[44] In the
narrative excerpt below young Beth is irritated that her math teacher
says "Oh God." Rather than actually uttering the word "God," however,
Beth spells out "G-O-D" then grunts "OH UH" instead of "OH GOD."[45]

Beth: My math teacher? I don't <u>like</u> her.
She's always- she'll go
"I know you're (.) when you look at this math problem,
→   you're probably thinking 'Oh my G-O-<u>D</u>'" ((*brassy tone*))
(0.4 pause)
Lisa: Your math teacher [says that?
Beth: [Yeah, she says it a lot.
(0.4 pause)
→   Or- or when she's <u>upset</u> or something
she'll go "OH ((*grunts*)) UH"

Following Beth's circumlocutions, Beth's mother offers a candidate interpretation of what Beth means:

→ Mom: "Oh God?" ((*soft, tentative tone*))

In this interaction, Beth manages to involve her mother more actively in
the telling of the narrative. Specifically, she succeeds in getting her
mother to actually formulate the word "God" as it was used in the blasphemous context of her teacher's interjection. Once the taboo interjection is uttered by her mother, Beth begins to incorporate the explicit interjection in the continuation of her story:

→ Beth: She'll go "Oh Go:d" *((scornfully))*
   Mom: Yeah, that's not very (0.6 pause) good.

This practice of relying upon conversational partners to fill in information as a means of sharing responsibility for information is widespread across languages and social groups.[46]

Interlocutors can be drawn into active co-telling when a storyteller asks for help, even though it is not strictly necessary.[47] In the following family interaction, for example, Oren and his mom have been recalling an incident in which Oren accidentally ate a chili pepper in a restaurant. When Oren asks his Mom how old he was when this happened, Mom relays the question to a heretofore uninvolved Dad, who in turn provides an answer:[48]

→ Mom: *((looking to Dad))* How old was he Don? when that [happened?
   Dad: [Two

While this appears to be an innocent request for information, Mom immediately challenges Dad's answer:

→ Mom: Was he even two?
   (1.0 pause) *((no noticeable affirmation from Dad))*

Mom's query suggests that she views herself as the greater authority and that her request for help in recalling details of a narrative incident may have been primarily a pretense for recruiting Dad as an active teller.

Conversational partners don't have to be cajoled or otherwise enticed into taking an active role in the telling of a narrative. Depending upon social circumstances, they may spontaneously jump into the ongoing narration to offer a psychological reaction:[49]

   Mom: Judy Wilson broke her wrist on the ski trip
→ Dad: Oh no:: *((leans back in chair, looks at Mom))*

They may request elaboration:

   Mom: Judy Wilson broke her wrist on the ski trip
   Dad: Oh no:: *((leans back in chair, looks at Mom))*

```
        Mom:  Hm hm hm
   →    Dad:  What was she doing?
```

They may request clarification: [50]

```
        Dad:   I'd be afraid to have it (.) to have that dog around the kids
   →    Beth:  What dog?
        Sean:  [Pit bull
        Dad:   [The pit bull
   →    Beth:  Oh. across the street?
        Mom:   No
        Dad:   No
        Beth:  OH
        Mom:   [Any-
        Dad:   [Joe and Charlotte's
        Beth:  Joe and Charlotte's
        Mom:   Any pit bull actually
```

They may elaborate:[51]

```
        Marie:  My (.) my point is that (.) the response that would have made me
                feel like my effort had been worthwhi::le would be (.) uh
                "Gee: thanks (.) you know the: (.) I rilly could use the day off. It's
                    nice to have a break" whatever whatever
        Jon:    Yeah of course (she should be thankful=)
        Marie:  =Bu:t (.) she turned it around like "You [owe it to me=
        Jon:                                            [Right
        Marie:  =This is something [.hh you owe me"
        Jon:                       [Yeah
   →            "I'm a-"
                Yeah
   →            "It's about time you gave me something
                I've been waitin (to see how)"
```

Or they may disagree/deny:[52]

```
        Jon:    ('f) Janie had come out and said to me
                "Dad will you tell M:Mommy where the films (.) are from the
                    pictures," I would have said "Yes Janie"
```

Marie: Well [when she's about eight or nine I bet she'll be able to do
            that
  Jon: [Janie came out

            . . .

  Jon: <u>YOU:</u> are over eight or nine are you not?
Marie: Ye:s (.) and that's exactly what I told her to say?
  Jon: That's right?
Marie: is to find out where the negatives were . . .
            so I could give them to Susan
            (0.2 pause)
  Jon: I see (.)
            Well she didn't she di- she didn't give me your message

            . . .

            in the form you asked it
Marie: B[ut (.) did you know Susan was <u>here?</u>
  Jon: [(you know)
            <u>No:?</u> (.) I didn't know <u>who</u> was here Marie
            I didn't know <u>what</u> was going on. (.) I was busy with <u>plumb</u>ing

In these and other ways, sensitive to local cultural narrative rights,
conversational partners contribute significantly to the shaping of the
storyline.

Eager conversational partners sometimes *take over* the telling of a narrative from its initiator. In some instances, the takeover is invited—as
when one interlocutor forwards a story to another to continue.[53] Carolyn Taylor illuminates this dynamic in the parent-child narrative interactions wherein the child designates a parent as his or her "proxy voice."
In the segment below, for example, Mom encourages Sharon to continue telling her siblings about her new molar, but Sharon designates
Mom as her proxy:[54]

  Mom: Oh <u>tell</u> them
            I bet they don't know the good news
Rhoda: <u>I:</u> do.
→ Sharon: ((*pointing to Mom with both hands*)) <u>You</u> tell.

Alternatively, a conversational partner may attempt to take over the telling uninvited, as when a conversational partner disputes or claims
superior knowledge or rights to tell the narrative.[55] Taylor notes that

Caucasian American middle-class children often fail in their attempts to assert their knowledge and right to assume the telling of a particular set of events, while parents' attempts are more likely to succeed.

Active co-telling assumes another form when conversational partners expand on a narrative by *launching a parallel story episode*. That is, the telling of one narrative touches off other tellings.[56] As noted by sociologist Harvey Sacks, "the teller of the second [story] is in some way concerned to produce a recognizably similar story to the first."[57] After Beth initiates a story that bemoans her math teacher's use of "Oh God," for example, her mother launches an account of her own experience with blasphemy:[58]

> Mom: I remember once-
>   I don't know where it was, somewhere in my church-going
>   experience
>   I- (0.2 pause) was told that you should never take-
>   to say "Oh my God" unless you're really <u>talking</u> to God.

Touched-off tellings such as this are understood to be part of a series of related stories.[59] Each telling is shaped by earlier narratives, thematically and structurally. Reciprocally, each telling shapes earlier accounts by providing either comparable or contrasting experiences and perspectives. The touched-off narrative about Mom's church-going experience, for example, gives further credence to Beth's moral perspective concerning her math teacher who swears. Mom confirms that this conduct should never be condoned.

In summary, telling a personal narrative is a social activity that varies in breadth and type of participation of interlocutors. In the words of Charles Goodwin: "Within conversation participants are able to not only comment on what they have heard in a variety of ways, but rapidly become speakers themselves so that the party they were audience to now becomes audience to them. Such possibilities are frequently not available at more formal performances, such as a play, at which members of the audience do not have the option of becoming performers in their own right."[60] While typically one person prevails in telling a personal experience, other interlocutors contribute to the shaping of the narrative: Listeners' vocal and nonvocal displays of attention give tellers the go-ahead to continue recounting. Further, interlocutors may elicit or provide information and perspectives on the events under narration, affirming or challenging the prevailing storyline. A particularly elaborate realization of active co-tellership transpires when interlocutors initiate additional narratives that shed light on a previous narrative of personal experience.

TELLABILITY

In a remarkable, ground-breaking essay, "Toward a Speech Act Theory of Literary Discourse," literary critic Mary Louise Pratt dissolves the distinction between literary and oral narrative. She argues that both are "display texts," in the sense that both are designed not so much for utilitarian purposes to inform as to elaborately display highly tellable circumstances and incidents "in such a way that the addressee will respond effectively in the intended way, adopt the intended evaluation and interpretation, take pleasure in doing so, and generally find the whole undertaking worth it."[61] The blurring of boundaries between literary works and oral accounts of personal experience resonates with our view that personal narrative has properties characteristic of other genres.

We view oral narrative of personal experience, however, not as a homogeneous genre but rather as varying in relation to certain narrative dimensions (as laid out in Table 1.1.). In particular, personal narratives vary in their quality as tellable accounts, that is, in the extent to which they convey a sequence of reportable events and make a point in a rhetorically effective manner.[62] Highly tellable narratives are of such interest that they can be told again and still be appreciated. Discourse specialist Amy Shuman analyzes the following narrative told by an adolescent girl (Stacie), who retells a story she had read in the newspaper to her friend Marie:[63]

Stacie: Oh. I want to tell y'all about something else
      This lady, her baby
      She had um (.) she had a little girl
      She dressed her little girl up
      Oh, it was Eastertime
      She dressed her little girl up in pretty clothes
      So the father could come and take her out
      Because the parents were separated
      And do you know what she did?

> She put the (.) she beat the girl up and started stabbing the little
> baby and everything
> And then she put it in the oven?
> Marie: Oh!

While the events reported above are particularly gruesome, *tellability* is related not only to the sensational nature of events but also to the significance of events for particular interlocutors and the way in which events are rhetorically shaped in narrative. While not restricted to any topic in particular, narratives of personal experience typically report human events that touch our lives. They are personal narratives in that they imbue events with personal relevance. The narratives excerpted in this chapter—about the $320 for childcare, a lost watch, being snubbed at school, a racial insult, a pit bull in the neighborhood, an annoying math teacher, a friend who broke her wrist, a spouse's failure to locate family photos—involve events that impinge on the well-being of the tellers or those about whom they care.

A highly tellable narrative of personal experience relates events of great interest or import to interlocutors. The events may be unknown to interlocutors. Or an unknown or known event may have bearing on their future lives, lending great value to the narrative account. In addition, a narrator may use rhetorical skills to transform even a seemingly prosaic incident into a highly tellable account. Pratt and other literary scholars note that listeners and readers often evaluate narratives in these terms, judging whether the account is worth listening to, tedious, involving, and so on.

In everyday social interaction, personal narratives take on the qualities of both high and low tellability. A narrator may relay an unusual incident that captures the audience's interest and appreciation and draws them into his or her perspective. Alternatively, in other conversational narratives, conversational partners are grilled about their day's activities and reel out what happened reluctantly, without bothering to dress up the events as particularly important.[64] We would say that such narratives relate barely reportable incidents. Another low tellability scenario consists of a narrator launching an account hesitantly and awkwardly. These tellings are not the practiced and polished works of professional performers. The tellers search for words:[65]

→ Mom: She wasn't skiing she was ah
  Sean: *((looks up))*
  Mom: Judy Wilson was on the ski trip and she was uh (0.3 pause)
        I don't know what they call it- snowboarding?

They cut off sentences, and then restart them, sometime repetitiously:[66]

→ Oren: Mommy - <u>wasn't it funny?</u> when - wh-
       Wasn't it funny when you - thought that thing was a pickle? and
       I ate it?

And sometimes they revise their initial claim or perspective:[67]

Daughter: I found this *((holds up letter))*
       (0.4 pause)
       Or Mom and I found this . . .

Tellers aren't always certain where their stories are going:[68]

  Marie: [You know (.) Jon <u>I</u> verbally <u>did</u> tell Bev two weeks' notice
       [*((head on hand, elbow on table))*
→   Do you think I shouldov stuck to that?
       or (to have/just) done what I did

And sometimes they leave threads of the tale dangling without resolution. Unevenness is emblematic of the dynamic nature of narrative as a sense-making activity. When interlocutors meet and chat, they often recount narratives they have never told before or never told in quite the same way. Conversation among friends, neighbors, family members, work mates, team mates and other acquaintances creates an opportunity to launch a personal narrative whose storyline is not resolved. While these narratives concern events deemed worthy of telling, those who introduce an account may be unclear about the details. In addition, what makes an incident tellable may not yet have been discerned by the initial teller. In the narrative excerpt concerning the $320 payment for childcare, for example, Marie seems unsure whether the payment was an error on the part of the client or compensation for not giving Marie two weeks' notice before taking a child out of care. This issue determines whether the narrative is about Marie's honesty or lack of business acumen. Marie does not initially craft the narrative as a tantalizing incident. Instead, she relates events as a springboard for engaging her spouse in collaborative problem-solving. Rather than letting one version rest, she keeps reopening the storyline to scrutinize the protagonists' motives, actions, and reactions. The resulting narrative lacks the character of a display text.

The orientation to high or low tellability may be partly linked to the organization of tellership. Personal narratives that recount highly significant human events in a rhetorically effective manner are often told by a teller to a relatively passive audience, e.g., the danger-of-death narratives collected by Labov or narratives performed by skilled storytellers in front of an appreciative (or critical) audience.[69] Sometimes engaging, rhetorically elaborate narratives are co-told by multiple tellers, using, for example, call and response and other interactional formats in which interlocutors repeat the lines of a principal teller.[70] When multiple interlocutors take over the telling of a narrative, however, taking it in directions not intended by its original teller, turning back to a prior event, or bringing up an irrelevant point, a narrator's storyline and rhetorical punch often (but not always) suffer.

From one point of view, such narratives might be judged as failures. Our view is that such narratives rank low on the tellability dimension but are not infelicitous narratives. They simply constitute personal narratives that are geared less to narrative as performance and more to narrative as a social forum for discovering what transpired and/or piecing together an evaluative perspective on an incident, including its implications for the future.

EMBEDDEDNESS

Narratives of personal experience vary in terms of their *embeddedness* in surrounding discourse and social activity. The extent to which a personal narrative is an entity unto itself, separate from prior, concurrent, and subsequent discourse, is related to turn organization, thematic content, and rhetorical structuring. Relatively *detached* narratives may, for example, recount an experience in one or more lengthy conversational turns. This turn format sets a narrative apart from the generally briefer turns that characterize conversational interaction. In addition, relatively detached narratives may relate thematic content that is unrelated to the current topic or focus of attention. As noted by Pratt, detached narratives also relate reportable events in a distinct rhetorical format from that of surrounding discourse.[71]

Alternatively, relatively *embedded* narratives of personal experience do not have a distinct turn-taking format. Rather than occupying long turns dotted by minimal feedback from the listener, these narratives are recounted over turns of variable length, similar to those that precede and follow. In addition, embedded narratives are thematically relevant to a topic under discussion or activity underway. These personal narratives illustrate a point, make a comparison, support an argument, or otherwise elaborate a focus of concern. The rhetorical format of embedded narratives also takes on discourse features of the surrounding discourse. Specifically, narratives embedded in prayers, explanations, disagreements, and other speech activities are organized by those activities.

Extended *turn length* by a principal teller is a distinguishing feature of many personal narratives, a point that has been noted by conversation analysts.[72] Lengthy turns characterize, for example, Algy's mysterious narrative about getting a car ride while drunk, the teacher's narrative of a racial incident, and Stacie's narrative about the mother who dressed her baby for Easter then put her in the oven. Turn length sets this kind of talk off from the surrounding flow of conversational turn-taking. Yet the shift into this turn organization is generally not abrupt. Rather, taking up the floor for an extended period to narrate is often negotiated between would-be tellers and interlocutors before the actual narrative is initiated.[73] Sometimes tellers get a go-ahead to initiate a narrative, as in the following conversational exchange among friends:[74]

> Julia: Um: Guess what happened last night.
> → Shannon: What.
> Julia: Um I went u, okay. Last night, um my brother um, my b-
> Okay my dad said, "Julia you gotta pick up, by yourself,"
> And ( ) I said, "Well, if my brother doesn't have to" and so
> me and my dad got into a big fight and everything y'know?
> And u:m, oh god. And I bit him. I couldn't <u>believe</u> it. Oh
> god!

And sometimes they get a similar go-ahead in more formal institutional interactions:[75]

→ Police: So *you* can start telling me a bit what happened that evening
             and what the reason was . . . for what you did
Suspect: Mm. (2.0 pause) Yeah.
             We were going to go down . . . and check out.
             We had heard that there was a party going there then . . . on the
                beach in Norrby.
  Police: Mm
Suspect: And so we drove out there.
             I think, but I don't remember whether it was a Thursday or
             what it was (2.0 pause)
             I have an idea it was a weekday.

Other narratives of personal experience, however, are recounted over a series of relatively brief turns, often by more than one active co-teller. In some exchanges, more than one person is familiar with the incident, such that no sooner does one teller begin to recount events than another chimes in. In the following excerpt analyzed by Charles Goodwin, three interlocutors recount to a fourth the narrative of Jim and Nadine's three weddings:[76]

Nadine: You remember Father Denelland that mar- Well *yeah*
           We *were* married three times. Y[ou knew that story.
   Anita: [I didn't know ever hear that
Nadine: Yeah well we were married in-
→   Jim: That's why [I'm hooked!
Nadine: [We-
→   Jim: [I can't get out!
Nadine: [When we- When we were youngsters we elo:ped,
           and were marr[ied in *Ma*ryland:,
→   Jim: [Went to Elkton.
Nadine: to Elkton Maryland,
    Jim: ·hh
→   Then we got [married in Jamaica,
Nadine: [The- the *se:*cond time we had
           all s[orts of (0.1 pause) property and everything

→   Jim: [Then we got married in Saint Pa:t's.
Nadine: We thought we should be married again
            because of c:ivil papers and all that
            were ma(h)rried [in *Long* Island.
  Anita: [I never heard this.
→   Fred: And then in Saint Pat's . . .

In this excerpt, Jim is as eager to tell the story as Nadine, and he and Nadine overlap each other in bids to reveal the succession of events, rationales, and psychological responses.

Personal narratives also assume a relatively short turn or variable length format when interlocutors unfamiliar with the incident recounted make assessments, request clarification, ask information questions, provide background information, and otherwise provide substantial narrative elements. Examples of such narratives are provided in the earlier discussion of tellership. These narratives are characteristically indistinct from the turn-taking organization of routine conversational interaction.

Relative embeddedness is also tied to *thematic* and *rhetorical* integration with surrounding conversation. Narratives of personal experience can be initiated abruptly, with no link to current concerns, such as Marie's story of the $320 payment for childcare, which is initiated out of the blue, and Algy's story of the creepy car ride, told to a folklorist at the outset of her visit. Many other narratives, however, are interwoven with what interlocutors are thinking and doing. Conversation analyst Gail Jefferson notes that would-be narrators go to great lengths to make their stories appear relevant (even when they are not), acting as if something said has touched off the recounting of an incident.[77] And frequently, narratives of personal experience are launched precisely to further a point made in the surrounding discourse. For example, as noted earlier, in the middle of Marie's story of the $320 payment, she launches a related story that casts the protagonist of the first story as dishonest. This story then provokes her spouse to narrate a hypothetical scenario that amplifies Marie's moral stance towards the protagonist. We can say that each successive narrative is thematically and rhetorically organized by the earlier narrative(s) and that, complementarily, the successive narratives lead the co-tellers to look at prior narratives from a new perspective.

Narratives can be intertwined not only with other narratives, but with other forms of discourse as well. For example, as will be discussed in Chapter 7, personal narratives may be embedded in a prayer. Prayers are not always highly formulaic; there are also personal prayers, many of which contain narratives of personal experience. Prayers for divine intervention may recount worrisome events, and prayers for forgiveness may contain confessional narratives of sinful personal experiences.[78] The narratives are rhetorically organized by the prayer context in the sense that cultural expectations surrounding prayer influence the tellers' psychological perspective and choice of grammar and lexicon.

Similarly, personal narratives may be part of a disagreement. The narrative may be used to buttress a position or to dispute facets of an account. For example, an earlier narrative excerpt captures a marital dispute over who was responsible for finding missing photo negatives. The verbal interaction is both a narrative and a disagreement, each fueling the other: one version of the incident casts one of the spousal protagonists on morally higher ground than the other, leading to a counter narrative that promotes an alternative point of view.

In these and other ways, narratives of personal experience vary in the degree and kind of integration with surrounding discourse. While narratives of personal experience are generally analyzed as self-contained forms of discourse, in this book we consider as well how they are constrained by the form, content, and purpose of ongoing social activities. This view is consequential for the analysis of narrative as genre in that it considers discourse to be often if not usually multi-genred, for example, both narrative and prayer, or narrative and disagreement, or narrative and conversation, and so on. As such, personal narrative is one facet of a socially and linguistically complex interaction, and genre is one facet of a stretch of discourse.[79]

LINEARITY

A narrative of personal experience may organize events across a lifetime, as in an autobiography. Or it may organize life events that transpire within a more limited timespan, for example, a brief encounter, an illness, a festivity, and so on. Narratives of lifespan scope are rare in everyday social interaction. Rather, conversational narratives of personal experience tend to focus on more circumscribed events. These pervasive, quotidian personal narratives form the focus of this book.

While all narratives of personal experience organize events in terms of time and causality, they do not uniformly thread events into a unilinear time line and cause-effect progression. The dimension of *linearity* concerns the extent to which narratives of personal experience depict events as transpiring in a single, closed, temporal, and causal path or, alternatively, in diverse, open, uncertain paths. Relatively linear narratives depict an overarching progression of events in which one event temporally precedes or causally leads to a subsequent event:

$$Event_x \rightarrow Event_y$$

The following excerpt from an adolescent fight story analyzed by Amy Shuman depicts a highly linear sequence of events. Prior to this excerpt it has been reported that Mary called Joan a whore in front of Joan's sister. The excerpt begins with her sister's response:[80]

Joan: It was me and Mary
      We had a fight and right
      Yesterday
      My sister went over to her
      and she grabbed her
      and she pulled her
      and she say that "You want to fight my sister?"
      She said "Go do it"
Linda: By your place?
Joan: So I went over to her
      and then she wants to fight me
      so then I walked away.

The primary teller, Joan, recounts to her friend, Linda, a teleological progression of events in which Mary's insult leads Joan's sister to fight Mary and taunt her to fight Joan. This sequence of events in turn leads Joan to face off with Mary ("So I went over to her"), provoking Mary's desire for a fight ("and then she wants to fight me"), which in turn causes Mary to walk away ("so then I walked away").

As discussed by Morson and Bernstein, foreshadowing is a common rhetorical device in linear narratives. Foreshadowing dominates the following passage from a testimony analyzed by Holocaust scholar and literary critic Lawrence Langer:

> Every roll call was a selection: women were sent to the gas-chamber because they had swollen legs, scratches on their bodies, because they wore eyeglasses or head kerchiefs, or because they stood roll call without head kerchiefs. Young SS men prowled among the inmates and took down their numbers and during the evening roll call the women were ordered to step forward, and we never saw them again. Maria Keiler, a childhood friend and schoolmate, died that way. She had a scratch on her leg and an SS man took her number. When they singled her out at roll call, she simply walked away without even nodding goodbye. She knew quite well where she was going, and I knew it, too; I was surprised at how little upset I was.[81]

In relatively nonlinear narratives, however, the way in which one event relates to another temporally and causally is open-ended:

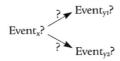

Did $Event_x$ take place? Did $Event_{y1}$ take place? Did $Event_x$ anticipate and/or cause $Event_{y1}$? Did $Event_{y2}$ occur? Could it be that $Event_x$ anticipated and/or caused instead $Event_{y2}$? In recounting relatively nonlinear narratives, tellers display various reasons for blurring the relation of one event to another, including confusion, disagreement, and memory lapses.

Confusion: →   Marie: you know what thou:gh (.) I started
                              questioning was (.)
                              the fact she gave me (.) <u>no</u> <u>notice</u>. (.)
                              she just called up after the
                              accident and said.
                       Jon: Yeah ["I'm not coming anymore"

Marie: ["That's it" (.) no (.) no two
weeks' pay (.) not

Disagreement: Jon: She did a:ll that when she paid you
three hundred and twenty dollars
She didn't do that by mistake. (.) She
wanted to see how you felt about it
n she felt she owed you

→ Marie: No: wa:y (.) [no: nonono (.) no
[((shaking head and hand))

Memory lapses: → Male Informant: I'm afraid I can't remember anything
about the actual event.

Interviewer: Mmm . . . Could you tell me what you
actually remember?

Male Informant: Yeah, I remember us arguing . . .
I got very upset.
I must have got a black-out,
→ because I didn't remember anything
until I found my wife bleeding on the
floor.
It was . . . it was really a terrible
experience both of us . . .
I had to help her . . .[82]

In some nonlinear narratives, tellers lose track of links they have posited between events. They start off building one logic of how events are related, then abandon this logic. In a study of agoraphobia, we found that narratives about panic attacks have this character: the teller articulates a set of circumstances (e.g. being overburdened with holiday preparations) that anticipate a panic attack, but, rather than linking it causally to these antecedent circumstances, the teller instead relates the attack to the immediate setting of the attack (e.g., a traffic jam).[83] In these narratives, the teller becomes drawn into the drama of the attack itself, losing track of how the attack fits into a coherent storyline, with a beginning, middle, and end:[84]

Meg: And we got halfway back to the church and
then I started when I started having (0.6 pause) those weird just
ph- pure physical anxiety.

> I began to feel shaky inside, like a (0.6 pause) like a (0.5 pause) like a
> motor was vibrating inside me.
> I just felt shaky inside, like you would
> if- if you were really afraid of something.
> I could almost feel like my teeth were going to chatter
> if I didn't get this (0.3 pause) feeling of shakiness under control . . .
> And then I felt (0.4 pause) uh like an urge to run
> or g- or (0.4 pause) uh to escape.
> But I didn't know what it was I was supposed to be escaping.

The teller's absorption in the details of the panic attack and the disjunctive shaping of these narratives mirrors and perpetuates the sense that the sufferer is caught in the vortex of a world spinning out of control, which in turn is symptomatic of this panic disorder.

In other nonlinear narratives, tellers entertain hypothetical alternative scenarios about a life experience:

→   Jon: ('f) Janie had come out and said to me
             "Dad will you tell M:Mommy where the films (.) are from the
             pictures," I would have said "Yes Janie"

These hypothetical narrative alternatives as well as confused, conflictual, half-forgotten, and fragmented accounts exhibit what Morson and Bernstein call sideshadowing, wherein the contours, rationale, and consequences of incidents are flexible and/or envisioned from diverse logics. As Bernstein notes: "To acknowledge the validity of sideshadowing is not merely to reject historical inevitability as a theoretical model. Far more important, it means learning to value the contingencies and multiple paths leading from each concrete moment of lived experience, and recognizing the importance of those moments not for their place in an already determined larger pattern but as significant in their own right. This is what I have called a prosaics of the quotidian, and it is fundamentally linked to the historical logic of sideshadowing."[85] Many of the narratives exchanged in everyday conversation have this quality. They often dwell upon details of events, take topical detours, or dissolve into squabbles rather than move swiftly towards a climax and resolution.

The dimension of linearity lies at the heart of the tension that drives

LIBRARY, UNIVERSITY OF CHESTER

human beings to tell narratives of personal experience. On the one hand, tellers seek the clarity and coherence that linearity offers. As captured by novelist Robert Musil in a passage from *Man without Qualities,* linear chronology lends an irresistible orderliness to human experience: "It struck him that when one is overburdened and dreams of simplifying one's life . . . the law one longs for is nothing other than that of narrative order, the simple order that enables one to say: 'First this happened and then that happened . . .' Lucky the man who can say 'when,' 'before,' and 'after'! Terrible things may have happened to him, he may have writhed in pain, but as soon as he can tell what happened in chronological order he feels as contented as if the sun were warming his belly."[86] In this passage, Musil's anti-hero pays tribute to the power of narrative to cast temporal order on the cacophony of daily life. Linear narratives channel events into a temporal flow, thereby making even "terrible things" somewhat comprehensible.

On the other hand, humans are questioning beings, as Vaclav Havel notes.[87] Indeed, we are the only species who have the capacity and will to question ourselves. Constructing highly linear narratives leaves little room for such proclivities. Nonlinear narration opens narration to multiple truths and perspectives and the realization that certain life experiences resist tidy, ready-at-hand interpretive frameworks.

MORAL STANCE

Narratives of personal experience do not present objective, comprehensive accounts of events but rather perspectives on events. Literary critic Kenneth Burke sees narratives as selections rather than as reflections of reality.[88] Central to narrative perspective is the *moral stance* assumed by tellers and protagonists. Rooted in community and tradition, moral stance is a disposition towards what is good or valuable and how one ought to live in the world. Human beings judge themselves and others in relation to standards of goodness: they praise, blame, or otherwise hold people morally accountable for their comportment. Philosophers from Aristotle to Alasdair MacIntyre propose that moral judgments are based on standards for social roles, practices, and the good life in relation to person and community.[89]

While moral understandings are transmitted through a variety of cultural forms such as proverbs, laws, maxims, advice, songs, and visual representations, everyday narratives of personal experience elaborately encode and perpetuate moral worldviews. Personal narratives generally concern life incidents in which a protagonist has violated social expectations. Recounting the violation and taking a moral stance towards it provide a discursive forum for human beings to clarify, reinforce, or revise what they believe and value.[90] In this sense, personal narrative is akin to prayer in that both imbue experience with moral direction. In Chapter 7, we elaborate this point, suggesting that personal narrative provides a secular, interactive means of building a moral philosophy of how one ought to live.

Across time and communities, people recount a personal narrative to instantiate a moral point of view. This rhetorical practice is illustrated in the following exchange in which a teacher (Mrs. Collins) initiates a narrative to illuminate a principle for the students in her cosmetology school:[91]

Mrs. Collins: Okay, the best interest of the client should be your fir::st (4.0 pause) The best interest of the client your should be your first consideration . . .

→   You know I was in a grocery store yesterday in Summerville. I was at Winn Dixie shopping and bo::y it was two ladies standing at the (.) two black ladies standing at that
counter. I don't know who this cosmetologist was or you know that they go to to get they hair done but boy they was dogging her the name in the grocery store

Class: Heh hehe

Mrs. Collins: O::h (.) I was like WOW ma::n. I mean, "and she do this and she gave me a french twist" (.) and talking all LOUD up in the grocery story in broad daylight yesterday!

Class: O:::h

Mrs. Collins: And she gave me a french twist and she didn't do this and girl you know I ain't going back and I got to sit in the salon so hour
. . . ((narrative continues))

Tina: Word of mouth can either make you or break you

Mrs. Collins: Make you or break you that's way that's right so you need to if don't have but one client

Lynn: You need to give a:::LL you got to that one client . . .

As analyzed by linguistic anthropologist Lanita Jacobs-Huey, the excerpt begins and ends with the same emphatic moral point that failure to prioritize the client can motivate a client to ruin the reputation of a hair stylist. Mrs. Collins recounts the incident at Winn Dixie grocery store as a horror story, using negative affect markers such as "bo::y," "dogging," "WOW ma::n," "I mean," "all LOUD," "broad daylight," along with negatively cast reported speech and repetitions that highlight facets of the clients' bad-mouthing.

Narrators of personal experience evaluate protagonists as moral agents, whose actions, thoughts, and feelings are interpreted in light of local notions of goodness. Narrators often shape the narrative to make their own comportment appear morally superior to that of another protagonist. This predilection is what discourse analysts Elinor Ochs, Ruth Smith, and Carolyn Taylor call the "looking good" principle.[92] Folklorist Richard Bauman has analyzed a collection of stories recounted by Texan dog traders, for example, that highlight their integrity. In the following exchange, the trader (Moore) backs up his reliability with a narrative about a time he himself was duped by a trader:[93]

Byers: He run with a pack good?
Moore: Oh yes, oh yes.
And he'll stand . . . he'll stand three nights out a week.
Has did that and took off (.)
ain't seen him waitin' behind that. ( )
He'll stand three nights out a week.
I've known that to happen to him
(pause)
I try to be fair with a man 'bout a dog.
Tell the truth about a dog, tell you what he'll do.
If there's any fault to him, I wanna tell the man.
If I get a dog from a man, if there's any fault to him,
I want him to tell me.
→ I bought . . . we bought some puppies from a man,
we asked him, said, "they been vaccinated?"
Said, "now we gonna buy the puppies,"
say "now if they been vaccinated,
we wanta know if they ain't."
Say "now, what we's gettin' at,

if they ain't been vaccinated distemper's all around."
We wanted 'a vaccinate 'em.
And he swore they was vaccinated
and after we bought 'em they died, took distemper and died.
    Then he told a friend o' ours,
he say he hate that he didn't tell us
that the dogs, the puppies, wasn't vaccinated . . .

Bauman notes that the dog traders are well aware of one another's proclivity to stretch the truth and that part of the enjoyment and challenge of trading is one-upsmanship in the realm of gullability.

The "looking good" principle is also evident in a narrative we saw earlier, in which the primary teller, Marie, laces her narrative with linguistic forms that contrast her truthfulness with the unethical conduct of the mother of a child in her daycare center. After depicting herself as a scrupulous businesswoman, Marie portrays the mother as violating daycare policy:

Marie: you know what thou:gh (.) I started questioning was (.)
        the fact she gave me (.) <u>no no</u>tice. (.) she just called up after the
        accident and said.
Jon: Yeah ["I'm not coming anymore"

Here Marie presents a key piece of the narrative, namely the background information that the mother "gave me (.) <u>no no</u>tice" before pulling her daughter out of Marie's daycare center. Marie carefully couches this information in the language of certainty: she uses the expression "You know what," which marks what is coming up as news,[94] and then casts the news as "the fact." This "fact" becomes a basis for discrediting the mother, whose actions are further belittled with the adverb "just" in "she just called up after the accident." In this manner, language becomes a palette for constructing moral portraits.

Similarly, in the narrative excerpted earlier between an interviewer and a male informant accused of beating his wife, the informant shades his narrative in tones of exculpability:

Male Informant: . . . I remember us arguing . . .
               I got very upset.

> I must have got a black-out,
> because I didn't remember anything
> until I found my wife bleeding on the floor . . .

The teller uses the cognitive verb "remember," which frames the information that follows as relatively certain. But how are the remembered events portrayed in moral terms? First, the teller diffuses his responsibility for the argument with his wife through use of the plural pronoun "us" in the phrase "us arguing." The teller next uses the verb "got" twice. This verb positions the protagonist (who is also the teller) as one who passively experiences two unpleasant conditions—being "very upset" and blacking out. The verb "got" is typically used to make a protagonist look like a victim in a situation that calls for accountability. [95] The teller amplifies his portrayal of self as blameless by further claiming that he "didn't remember anything" and that he merely "found" his wife bleeding on the floor. Using these and other linguistic forms, tellers construct moral frameworks for interpreting incidents. [96]

It is also common for tellers to collaboratively affirm their own moral stance in opposition to a rival moral perspective. [97] Recall, for example, the narrative co-told by a group of pre-adolescent African-American girls, in which a classmate (Kerry) did not put Julia's (one of the tellers') name on a hall pass, because Julia was "actin stupid." At one point Julia asks, "But was I actin stupid with them," to which one conversational partner responds "Nope, no" and another disparages Kerry with the remark, "Kerry always say somp'n," meaning that Kerry is always going around saying bad things about people. Similarly, in the interview narrative about a school racial incident, interviewer and teacher agree that the teacher's handling of the problem was much better than what other teachers would have done:

Teacher: <u>And</u> I know other:: (0.4 pause) I'm sure (0.4 pause)
           Not to pat myself or anything but probably some other teacher
           would have just said, you know "Go sit down (.) I don't I don't
           want to hear it" (0.4 pause)
→   LE: Yeah
Teacher: and not dealt with it at all
→   LE: Exactly (.) <u>exa:ctly</u>

While all narratives of personal experience are laced with moral stance, in some narratives the moral stance is presented as relatively *certain* and remains *constant* throughout the telling, while in other narratives it is *uncertain* and *fluid* as the narrative progresses. The narrative initiated by Mrs. Collins to her cosmetology students, for example, clearly and consistently inculcates the moral tenet that they should put the interests of their clients above all else. Similarly, the story we saw earlier about the math teacher who says "Oh my God" illustrates how tellers adhere with certainty to a moral perspective. Throughout the story the teacher is portrayed as blasphemous and failing to meet the moral standards the tellers set for that social role: Beth, the primary teller, can't even bring herself to utter the deprecation produced by the teacher ("she'll go . . . 'Oh my G-O-D' . . . she'll go 'OH UH'"); her interlocutor Lisa expresses shock ("Your math teacher says that?"), and Beth's mother follows with an explicitly negative moral judgment ("that's not very (0.6 pause) good").

Alternatively, the moral stance in narratives of personal experience may be *indeterminate* and *unstable*. As sociologist Zygmunt Bauman comments, "Moral life is a life of continuous uncertainty. It is built of the bricks of doubts and cemented with hours of self-deprecation. Since the dividing lines between good and evil have not been drawn before, they are drawn in the course of action; the outcome of these efforts at drawing lines is akin to a string of footprints rather than a network of charted roads."[98] Bauman describes the fragmentation of authoritative codes and beliefs that mark the postmodern condition. Yet human beings throughout time have questioned and pondered what constitutes good and bad comportment. According to MacIntyre, goodness is a quality that must be learned and achieved through reflection and physical effort: "The systematic asking of ['What is the good for me?' and 'What is the good for man?'] and the attempt to answer them in deed as well as in word . . . provide the moral life with its unity. The unity of a human life is the unity of a narrative quest."[99]

The pursuit of goodness in the course of narration is not a matter of locating the whereabouts of a set of ready-made moral tenets, as on a treasure hunt. Rather, it is the pursuit itself, what MacIntyre calls the "narrative quest" that builds virtue: "The medieval conception of a quest is not at all that of a search for something already adequately characterized, as miners search for gold or geologists for oil. It is in the course of the quest and only through encountering and coping with the various particular harms, dangers, temptations, and distractions which provide any quest with its episodes and incidents that the goal of the quest is finally to be understood. A quest is always an education both as to the character of that which is sought and in self-knowledge."[100]

A virtuous person is thus one who queries, seeks, and in so doing, learns what is good. Everyday narration of life experience is a primary medium for moral education, in that each recounting involves piecing together the moral meaning of events. The temporal and causal structure of narrative, philosopher Charles Taylor reminds us, builds a moral framework for understanding human comportment: "Making sense of my present action, when we are dealing with . . . the issue of my place relative to the good, requires a narrative understanding of my life, a sense of what I have become, which can only be given in a story."[101] Even when tellers adopt a secure, recognized moral grid for interpreting experience, they may be initially uncertain and arrive at their moral perspective incrementally through dialogic construction of what transpired, when, and why.

Further, tellers who initially appear certain may find their moral stance unravel as the telling proceeds. In some cases, certainty dissolves into uncertainty through emergent self-doubt, as when Marie questions her competence as a good administrator of her daycare center. Marie's initially clear portrayal of herself as honest and efficient gives way to hesitancy about the way she handled the payment by the mother who abruptly took her child out of the daycare center: she asks her husband if she should have brought up the two weeks' notice requirement or kept silent: "Do you think I shouldov stuck to that? or (to have/just) done what I did?"

In addition to self-doubt, moral stance becomes destabilized when it is directly or indirectly challenged by another co-teller. In the daycare story, for example, Marie's self-doubts are fanned by her husband's subsequent critique of her comportment: he contrasts what *he* would have done in similar circumstances to Marie's less adequate response. In this interaction, Marie invites her spouse to pass judgment, but in other narrative interactions, challenges to a teller's moral stance are uninvited. A carefully narrated complimentary portrayal of oneself, for example, may fall apart when someone spontaneously narrates contradictory information. In the following excerpt, Federico, a high-school dropout, recounts why he lasted only a week at one school before being expelled.

Initially, Federico presents himself in a good light, as a victim of another gang's aggression:[102]

Federico: I lasted only for a <u>week</u> there
 Manny: a week . . .
Federico: Our neighborhood started having shit with that neighborhood
         down there?
        So I went over there to the bus
        so they came an' hit me up
        I said my neighborhood
        and they said fuck that
→   so they socked me?
→   <u>E</u>verybody rushed me.
        Hn. Then the next day we,
→   we and the homeboys went down (0.5 pause)
→   and they got me.
        So that's it.

As analyzed by researcher Betsy Rymes, Federico uses a number of linguistic strategies to make himself look good by mitigating his responsibility in the gang fight. He positions the other gang ("they") as the aggressors and himself as victim ("so they came an' hit me up," "so they socked me," "<u>E</u>verybody rushed me"). The reprisal the following day is presented as a logical consequence ("Then the next day . . .") , and Federico's role is blended in with the whole group ("we and the homeboys went down").

Rymes, however, goes on to ask Federico if he started the gang fight:

Betsy: Did you start the fight, er-
Federico: No, <u>they</u> (.) they did.

Curious about the explicit denial, Rymes probes further:

Betsy: So how did you get kicked out.

At this juncture, Federico's classmate, Manny, challenges the moral portrait that Federico has been building, and Federico caves in:

→ Manny: 'Cause [the next day <u>he</u> started it.
  Federico: [Cause the next day I went down.
→   The next day I started a fight.

In this narrative, one co-teller explicitly debunks another's claim to virtue. In other narrative interactions, the challenge to moral superiority is more subtle. In the following excerpt, for example, it is a younger brother's (Chuck's) reminder that reverses the moral fortunes of his older sister's (Lucy's) version of events. Briefly, the narrative concerns the upsetting actions of a girl who pulled up the dress of Lucy's friend in front of a group of boys. The narrative begins with Lucy's complaint that her school principal was overly lenient with the girl:[103]

  Lucy: I don't think Mrs um Andrews is being fair
        because um . . . when we were back at school um (.)
        this girl? (.) she pulled um (.) Vicky's <u>dress</u> up t'here *((gestures with hand high on chest))* in front of the boys
  Mom: mhm?
  Lucy: She only (.) all she did was get a <u>day</u> in de<u>ten</u>tion

This moral high ground is augmented when Mom proposes a punishment that Lucy might consider just, and Lucy deems it the minimal acceptable response:

  Mother: mhm? (.) <u>you</u> think she should have gotten suspended? (0.6 pause)
  Lucy: at <u>LEAST</u>

This virtuous self-portrait, however, falls apart when Lucy's younger brother Chuck reveals an earlier event that casts Lucy in a negative light. He discloses that Lucy herself was given one day's detention at an earlier time:

  Chuck: Lucy? (.) you only ever went to it <u>once</u> (.) right?
  Father: *((clears throat))* (1.0 pause) *((Lucy arches her back, eyes open wide, looks shocked, starts shaking her head no once; Father looking at her))*
  Mother: <u>You</u> can tell us can't you?
  Father: I'm lis<u>ten</u>ing
  Lucy: *((low to Chuck, glaring))* thanks (0.4 pause)

Lucy: *((louder))* [yeah that was
Mother: [she was in it once?
        (0.6 pause)
Lucy: Once.

This turning back in time unearths information that alters the meaning of Lucy's indignation. Once we know that Lucy herself has been detained one day after school, her motives appear rooted in indignation that the principal has treated her misconduct on a par with her classmate's vile transgression. In this and other narratives of personal experience, the telling lurches forward and back in time, as interlocutors recall or dispute various details, some of which may have been buried or skewed in an attempt to portray a protagonist in a morally positive light.[104]

Summary

Our overarching message is that narratives of personal experience cover a range of discourse formats, running from virtuoso verbal performances to more prosaic social exchanges. Because personal narrative is so varied and, more to the point, because it is a ubiquitous feature of ordinary conversation, it resists delineation in terms of a set of fixed, generic, defining features. Instead, in *Living Narrative* we propose narrative dimensions that account for the ways in which narratives of personal experience are realized in everyday social life around the world. These dimensions—tellership, tellability, embeddedness, linearity, and moral stance—celebrate the breadth of narrative activity in that each dimension can be variably realized.

The dimension of tellership, for example, focuses on narrative as a social activity involving certain participants who position themselves as more or less active tellers. Tellership varies across social groups, situations, and even across the telling of a single narrative. It ranges from one primary teller recounting to a relatively passive audience to a group of active co-tellers who collaboratively build a storyline. Narratives told in informal conversation often have multiple tellers who ask questions, react, and otherwise contribute what they know, believe, or feel about some life incident. The active participation of conversational partners means that no one person holds control over the direction a narrative may take. On the one hand, highly collaborative tellings facilitate status quo interpretation of a narrated experience, as interlocutors offer familiar scenarios and conventional wisdom. On the other hand, the distribution of telling across interlocutors means that a storyline may be taken in unexpected directions and even overturned.

These interactional practices are central to the narrative process. They also may be narrative's most enduring product: an existential locus where memory and anticipation are co-authored into the autobiographical record. This is not to idealize conversational narrative as a democratic forum for making sense out of experience. To the contrary, the dialogic character of everyday narrative activity allows personal experience to be shaped by those participating in the interaction. When an interlocutor relates an experience, the experience becomes the object of public discourse. The experience is given shape and meaning, with certain interlocutors exerting authority in this process. In this book we illuminate a central paradox: the practice of rendering personal experience in narrative form entails de-personalization. Though the experiences may be unique, they become socially forged. Idiosyncratic experiences become co-narrated according to local narrative formats, recognizable types of situations and people, and prevailing moral frameworks, which inevitably constrain representation and interpretation. It is in this sense that narratives of personal experience are at the same time narratives of impersonal experience.

The dimension of tellability acknowledges that narratives of personal experience present reportable events, but that some are more notable than others. Or, to put it another way, some tellers craft their accounts as dramas worth listening to, while other tellers are less mindful of rhetoric. Tellability also attends to variability in criteria for rhetorically successful narrative. More or less tellable narratives may be related to a teller's goals rather than to his or her rhetorical skills and social sensibilities. In particular, while certain tellers appear to recount a sequence of unusual events primarily for an interlocutor's interest, other tellers do so primarily to gain insight into events, recruiting their interlocutors to build a perspective.

Attention to rhetorical style is related to the dimension of embeddedness in that rhetorically elaborate narratives of personal experience are often recounted as performances and are stylistically and thematically distinct from surrounding discourse. Alternatively, other personal narratives are enmeshed in the flow of social interaction, as part of a larger topic under discussion or larger activity undertaken. This dimension acknowledges that the boundaries between personal narrative and other forms of discourse are often permeable; that, for example, narrative may be woven into prayer, classroom instruction, or informal arguments among scientists trying to understand the physical world. Narrative is not merely situated in but shaped by other forms of discourse. For this reason *Living Narrative* explores how narrative influences and is influenced by these genres. Each laminated genre reveals another facet of the life of narrative. Chapter 7, in particular, presents an innovative perspective on the relation of narrative to prayer, suggesting that when personal narrative penetrates prayer, highly ritualized prayer gives way to more personalized ways of praying. Further, the interpenetration of prayer and personal narrative yields insights into secular narrative, especially the quotidian need to develop a moral framework for living.

The dimensions of linearity and moral stance address a central opposition that drives human beings to narrate life experience—the desire to sheathe life experience with a soothing linearity and moral certainty versus the desire for deeper understanding and authenticity of experience. Imbuing an experience with a linear causal and temporal structure and conventional moral stance is the goal of many narrative interactions. Yet, autobiographically and historically, these narrative formats may not resonate with actions, conditions, and mindsets of tellers or, more important, those participating in a set of life events. Some tellers resist prevailing versions of events, disagree with one another, or begin to doubt their own memories and sensibilities.

The conversational narratives analyzed in this volume are generally unrehearsed renderings of events close to the time of the telling. These events are fresh in mind but the details, background, orderliness, and significance are not necessarily in hand. While some interlocutors are more rhetorically skillful than others, the narratives of such events look like works in progress: they contain hesitations, unfinished thoughts, interruptions, and, often, contradictions. They relate a moment in time, then fill in background circumstances. A narrative may be interrupted by a related story or a plan of action. In developmental research, narrative consistency is a hallmark of competence.[105] Yet the conversational narratives of adults and children alike analyzed throughout this volume are typically *inconsistent* in temporal reference, plot structure, and stance.

Narrative scholarship has centered on narratives with the following qualities:

> A coherent temporal progression of events that may be reordered
> for rhetorical purposes and that is typically located in some past
> time and place.
> A plot line that encompasses a beginning, a middle, and an end,
> conveys a particular perspective, and is designed for a particular
> audience who apprehend and shape its meaning.

Narratives of this sort have been the focus of literary philosophy,[106] folklore,[107] sociolinguistic studies,[108] and cognitive approaches.[109] These rhetorically developed narratives provide one model of narrative as text and performance.

Understanding narrative, however, compels going beyond these exemplars to probe less polished, less coherent narratives that pervade ordinary social encounters and are a hallmark of the human condition. These narratives have the character of rough works in progress, because interlocutors use narrative to grapple with unresolved life experiences. In this book we demonstrate how these everyday narratives of personal experience are interactionally constructed accounts of a temporal progression of events, whose contents and ordering are subject to dispute, flux, and discovery; whose boundaries reach beyond the past to concerns in the present and possible future. The plot line of these narratives may or may not encompass a beginning, middle, and end, given that the plot is what interlocutors are attempting to craft and that life events are not necessarily coherent nor immediately resolvable. Such narratives collaboratively build one or multiple perspectives, which may conflict.

These everyday conversational narratives realize an essential function of narrative: a vernacular, interactional forum for ordering, explaining, and otherwise taking a position on experience. People apprehend their lives through the filter of narrative and build communities through the co-authoring of narrative; inversely, collaborative probing and redrafting of events propels, shapes, and keeps narrative alive. Although our research lies in the interface of linguistics, anthropology, and psychology, *Living Narrative* also incorporates literary and philosophical reflections on self, text, and social life. In this sense, the book forges a hybrid perspective—part social science and part humanities—to fathom the intricate and potent properties of the narratives that live within and among us.

2

BECOMING A NARRATOR

The impulse to narrate likely has roots in certain kinds of communicative exchanges within other species.[1] Bees, for example, display narrative-like practices when they depict through dance the location and potency of nectar. The bee dances are instinctual, highly conventionalized, and confined to the topic of nectar.[2] Certain primates, such as vervet monkeys, signal the proximity and type of predators (e.g., eagles, leopards, snakes), strangers, and other possible threats through a series of conventionalized alarm calls and grunts, which elicit an array of conventional responses. Though the symbolic status of such calls remains in question (i.e., whether they are symptoms of arousal or referential communication), they indicate affect—generally some degree of distress—towards some noticed event.[3] The signals also primitively encode particular past and future events in that they indicate an occurrence and imply a course of action.[4]

Human narrative reflects these evolving communicative competencies. Like bees and monkeys, humans use narrative to recount meaningful experiences that impact the well-being of conspecifics. Talk about past discoveries deemed good or bad informs present and future conduct and instills logical schemata for daily living. Further, akin to the ritualized accounts produced by other species, human narratives conform to a conventional structure for gaining attention, delineating events, and assigning positive or negative valences thereto.

Yet human narrative diverges significantly from these proto-narratives. Human narrative encompasses a rich array of motives and topics. Human beings narrate to remember, instill cultural knowledge, grapple with a problem, rethink the status quo, soothe, empathize, inspire, speculate, justify a position, dispute, tattle, evaluate one's own and others' identities, shame, tease, laud, and entertain, among other ends. Further, these ends are not necessarily secured at the onset of narration but rather emerge over the course of a narrative's telling. The emergent content and significance of narratives are an outcome in part of the contributions of other interlocutors. As linguistic anthropologist Richard Bauman notes: "Every [narrative] performance will have a unique and emergent aspect, depending on the distinctive circumstances at play within it. Events in these terms are not frozen, predetermined molds for performance but are themselves situated social accomplishments in which structures and conventions may provide precedents and guidelines for the range of alternatives possible, but the possibility of alternatives, the competencies and goals of the participants, and the emergent unfolding of the event make for variability."[5] While the alarm call accounts of vervet monkeys may be influenced by others' responses or lack thereof, human interlocutors probe, provide counterpoints, bring up missing details, display a vast range of emotions, and demonstrate alignment or nonalignment with another teller's rendering of events. Further, human narrators draw upon complex linguistic and stylistic repertoires. Humans' narrative palette includes not just one but several dialects' or languages' resources for representing events and saturating them with evaluative hues. Human narrators draw from grammatical, lexical, phonological, and discursive forms available to mark time, causality, modality, assign responsibility, and take a stance towards narrated events.

The genres of personal narrative found across speech communities are so plentiful that they alone constitute a staggering diversity of formats, including gossip, instigating stories, prayers, lamentations, reminiscences, agendas, plans, parables, jokes, eye-witness testimonies, confessions, reports, broadcasts, toasts, ballads, and certain forms of poetry.[6] While all of these genres display temporal sequencing of events, their organizational features are distinct. Each speech community establishes expectations about the parameters of a given genre of narrative. Competent speakers know how to nuance tellings to meet these criteria and to organize their tellings in relation to their perception of settings and interlocutors.

Children's Narrative Competence

The study of how and when young children participate in conversational narratives of personal experience is limited in at least three ways. First, most developmental studies of narrative examine how children (re)tell or comprehend "once upon a time" or picture-book narratives rather than their ability to narrate personal experience.[7] Second, the concept of narrative used in developmental studies tends to rely upon only one pole of the dimensions of tellership, tellability, embeddedness, linearity, and moral stance. In addition to interpretive skills, narrative competence is generally viewed as the ability to recount a narrative by oneself (one active teller), in a rhetorically effective manner (high tellability), which is relatively self-contained (detached from surrounding discourse), with a coherent and progressive beginning, middle, and end (linear organization), and a consistent moral stance. In other words, the model of narrative has the features of what Pratt calls a "display text," a form of discourse crafted for drama and performance before an audience.[8] As noted in Chapter 1, display texts characterize many literary and interview-elicited narratives.

Display texts are cognitively demanding in that they require attention to the unity and plan of the narrative. Each condition, action, thought, and feeling of a protagonist is interrelated into a thematic pattern and a temporal and logical trajectory of events. The display text model is an important one for children to appropriate. In many communities, there are occasions when a member is expected to recount a fluent and coherent story on his or her own over a single stretch of extended discourse to a relatively passive audience. In this sense, developmental studies are justified in visualizing this model as an endpoint of competence. The model also has the added advantage that this genre is relatively distinctive and amenable to structural analysis.

What most developmental studies of everyday personal narrative fail to acknowledge, however, is that the shape and function of personal narrative varies in the social worlds of adults. Few studies, for example, relate children's narrative skills to the proclivity of adults to jointly tell narratives of personal experience as a way of fathoming the social and moral meanings of events. Where collaborative sense-making (rather than performance) is the business at hand, narrators may dialogically probe alternate, sometimes conflicting, versions of what (could have) transpired, and attempt to piece together moral perspectives on events.

As delineated in Chapter 1, narrative activity of this sort breaks up the temporal and causal progression of circumstances and events. Narrators may suddenly return to incidents already recounted to dispute or add beliefs, knowledge, or emotions. Or an interlocutor may elaborate on a point and take the narrative in an unexpected direction. Moreover, plunging into the details of a narrated situation may leave narrators with a sense that events do not fit easily within a single logical progression or cannot be easily explained in terms of a comprehensive story logic or evaluated in terms of a single moral paradigm.

Rather than being inelegant and flawed renditions of display texts, these nonlinear narratives adhere to an aesthetic that calls for openness to contingency, improvisation, and revision. In the context of everyday conversation, such narratives also require skillful collaboration with interlocutors who may desire soothing coherence, but may yield to the quest for experiential complexities and alternative possibilities.[9] This aesthetic is critical to narrative competence, yet we know little about children's skill at the roles of problem-raiser, explorer of possible worlds, and moral philosopher. What we do know comes largely from contributions to a volume edited by Katherine Nelson that analyzes the narratives of a young child named Emily, as she lies in her crib at night.[10] As will be discussed in later sections, Emily's narratives grapple with the contingent, the unexpected, and the possible in her event-filled world.[11] Their often disjunctive character is reflective of this important narrative activity and Emily's willingness and ability to engage in it.

A third major weakness in developmental research on young children's narratives of personal experience is that it is culturally skewed, based primarily on White middle-class, English-speaking populations. Although Ruth Berman and Dan Slobin's cross-linguistic study of children's renditions of a picture-book narrative stands as an exception, systematic cross-linguistic and cross-cultural comparisons of how young children talk about life events in everyday social life are limited.[12] Fifteen years after Shirley Brice Heath's *Ways with Words,*[13] only a handful of studies document when and how culturally distinct conversational narrative practices and skills emerge in early childhood.[14] These studies range in focus from the socialization of tellership and moral stance to the acquisition of temporal, logical, and referential continuity in personal narrative.

In her stunning 1985 keynote address to the Stanford Research Child Language Development Forum, Heath laid out reasons for the dearth of cross-cultural studies on children's acquisition of everyday narrative genres.[15] They included the necessity of sustained ethnographic fieldwork, intimate knowledge of the language, documentation of genres children hear and are expected or not expected to initiate, and the role of other interlocutors in verbally shaping children's narrative practices. That all normal children eventually become narrators of personal experience is undisputed. It is also undisputed, however, that normal children growing up in different communities are variably oriented to particular genres, styles, and interactional tellings of life events. Compelling evidence that young children organize their narratives in different ways, responding to a plurality of cultural expectations, comes from a study of children's narrative practices in school. Heath details how mainstream American pedagogy privileges a narrow range of narrative practices that are not congruent with the valued narrative practices of working-class African-American and White families. As will be discussed below, this inconsistency, combined with the power asymmetry of teacher and child, can disenfranchise the knowledge bases that certain children have been socialized to respect. It may also interfere with their access to school-ratified genres of communication: "Researchers and schools are a long way from understanding that it is first necessary to understand what people do in language, before we try to decide what institutions want to make them do."[16]

Discussions of narrative socialization, including socialization *into* narrative practices and socialization *through* narrative practices, utilize the concept of apprenticeship. Elaborated by developmental psychologist Barbara Rogoff, this concept positions the child as part of one or more communities and as actively and appropriately interacting with more experienced persons in socially organized ways that by accident or design facilitate the child's competence in cultural practices critical to membership in these communities.[17] Although apprenticeship is essential to cultural continuity, it does not guarantee the child's success as an apprentice. Motivation, talent, and access organize the path of apprenticeship. Moreover, the organization of apprenticeship varies across situations and communities. The extent to which and the contexts in which more experienced persons clarify, highlight, repeat, intervene, or otherwise accommodate to children is embedded in local expectations about childhood, learning, communication, and social order more broadly.[18]

The following sections bring together ethnographic and psycholinguistic research that bears upon children's developing abilities to participate in narratives of personal experience. The methodology in these studies varies from longitudinal to cross-sectional and from qualitative, in-depth analyses of a limited corpus of data to quantitative studies of children's narrative competence. Further, while some studies examine the socialization or acquisition of particular narrative structures, other studies focus on the use of narrative to instill valued ways of thinking, feeling, and acting. In this chapter, children are considered as acquirers and apprentices in relation to four of the five dimensions of narrative practice presented in Chapter 1: tellership, tellability, linearity, and moral stance.

Tellership

Tellership is a narrative dimension that attends to the organization of participation in the actual telling of a narrative of personal experience. Tellership runs from one primary teller recounting to a relatively passive audience to multiple active co-tellers who respond with reactions, queries, or relevant narrative details. Young children are aware that narratives of personal experience require at minimum the continued attention of others and actively recruit interlocutors. Katharina Meng found that German three- to six-year-old children attempted to recruit a conversational partner when initiating a narrative:[19] "In one third of the event presentations, the 3-year-olds . . . started the event presentation with a minimal statement, waited for the partner's reaction, and pursued the event presentation after the partner had demonstrated a willingness to listen or had at least not used the opportunity to take over the speaker's role." The four-and-a-half and six-year-old children routinely sought out listeners, signaling to them that they wanted to have an extended conversational turn space to continue their narrative.

Meng's exceptionally thorough study also documents developmental trends in the German children's role as narrative listeners. The three-year-olds were highly competitive and unwilling to give one another extended turn space for narration. Once one child began to narrate, another rushed in to relate a comparable event. The four-and-a-half-year-olds were also competitive but allowed others to spin out their narratives in alternate turns; i.e., your narrative event$_1$ → my narrative event$_1$ → your narrative event$_2$ → my narrative event$_2$ and so on.

The German children's developing skills in co-narration are echoed in the narrative interactions of five-year-old Canadian children recorded by Alison Preece.[20] In their daily carpool conversations, these children were active tellers who not only elicited narrative involvement for their own narratives but also contributed to narratives initiated by others. The children prefaced their narratives with bids to tell:[21]

Kepmen: Hey, who wants to hear a story?

defended another's right to tell:[22]

Bronwyn: KEPMEN, let . . . Kepmen, let Heather say this . . . her little tiny
                one ((story))

invited one another to narrate:[23]

Heather: ((to Kepmen)) Tell what happened!

repaired one another's perceived errors:[24]

Heather: D'you know what?
                It (.) um (.) at our house you should (0.4 pause) should smell,
                it smelled like poop from the subject tank!
Bronwyn: No not "subject tank" (.) um (.) um (.) what's it called?
                It's not subject tank (.) um (.) um (.) subject (0.3 pause) septic
                (0.3 pause) SEPTIC tank.
Heather: Well Dad and Mum call it the subject tank.
Bronwyn: Well, it's not that. It's a SEPTIC TANK, right Mum?

provided elicited information and confirmation:[25]

Heather: And he um and he um, he always (0.3 pause) hurt things,
                and everytime, what is Angus did to you, Bronwyn?
Bronwyn: What?
Heather: What does he always do to you Bronwyn?
Kepmen: He KICKS her, and one time he even threw her down on the
                ground.

offered sound effects and gestures to enhance rhetorical effect, elaborated on narrative details, and where events were co-witnessed, the narratives were intricately co-authored turn-by-turn.

Even though young children are active contributors to peer and family narrative activity,[26] their contributions are organized according to family and community expectations and worldviews. In some communities, for example in certain working-class Euro-American families, young children are expected to recount stories only when directed by an adult; in other areas, like the working-class African-American community of Trackton, children are encouraged to initiate stories on their own in a manner that sustains attention and interest.[27] In some groups, children are permitted to ask questions during the telling of a personal experience; in other groups, children cannot interrupt the flow of a story. Pueblo Indian children of the American Southwest, for example, are expected to provide only periodic minimal vocal feedback as a sign of respect.[28] Athapaskan Indian families also discourage eliciting information in the course of narrating events by both children and adults.[29]

A number of studies document the extent to which and how family members engage young children as co-tellers of personal narratives.[30] Peggy Miller and her colleagues found that American and Chinese families involve young children in co-telling past experience with roughly the same frequency: "Both telling stories with children and telling stories about children in their presence occurred several times per hour in Chinese and American families."[31] Cultural differences lay in how families cast the children as moral protagonists, with the Chinese emphasizing the child as transgressor and the Americans highlighting the child's positive qualities.

Alternatively, in a comparison of middle-class American and Korean mother-child interaction, Mary Mullen and Soonhyung Yi found that American mothers engaged their young children in talk about past events three times as much as did Korean mothers.[32] Furthermore, American mothers were far more active than Korean mothers in getting their child to talk about himself or herself, especially thoughts and feelings.[33] Mullen and Yi attribute this difference in part to differences in socialization goals and cultural values, especially the American mother's use of narratives of personal experience to promote a sense of the child as an individual.

Similarly, a comparative study of family storytelling by Shoshana Blum-Kulka and Catherine Snow indicates ethnic and class differences in how often children participate in the recounting of personal experience.[34] In working-class Caucasian and African-American families and middle-class Caucasian-American families, children were active contributors to the majority of narratives (80–87 percent). In contrast, in Israeli middle-class families, children participated in only 55 percent of the narrative exchanges. American middle-class children were encouraged to initiate narratives and prevail as primary narrator, as the excerpt below illustrates:[35]

→   Child: mommy, to who will I tell how my day goes?
→ Mother: Okay let's hear your day.
     Child: well, I play puzzles and ( ) and ( ) and I made ( )
  Mother: A what?
     Child: a shoe-print.

American working-class children (especially preschoolers), on the other hand, contributed primarily when adults elicited information about past events:[36]

→ Mother: What did you do?
     Child: and then we made a funky monkey
→ Mother: You made a funky monkey?
            Oh the monkey that you made huh?
            (pause)
            That's a cute monkey.
→   Where is it anyway?
            (pause)
            I think we left it in Roy's by um by accident
            when we were there.
     Child: hunmm mommy it's under. it it's under your coat.

These findings support Heath's observations of family narrative activity in the working-class White Piedmont Carolina community of Roadville. Roadville children were expected to tell personal narratives primarily when directed by an adult. Usually the narratives centered on the child's misdeed, and children were expected to stick to the facts of the events.

In the excerpt below, for example, babysitter Sue directs five-year-old Wendy to tell her mother about her foolish mistake of climbing while holding Easter eggs. In the co-telling, the adult takes on the role of truth police:[37]

→   Sue: Tell yo' mamma where we went today.
   Wendy: Mama took me 'n Sally to the Mall.
          Bug Bunny was=
→   Sue: =No, who was that,
          That wasn't Bugs Bunny.
   Wendy: Uh, I mean, Peter, no, uh a big Eater bunny was there,
          'n we, he, mamma got us some eggs=
→   Sue: ='n then what happened?
   Wendy: *((turning her head to one side))* I don't 'member.
→   Sue: Yes, you do,
          What happened on the climbing=
   Wendy: =me 'n Sally tried to climb on this thing,
          'n we dropped, I dropped, my eggs, some of 'em.
→   Sue: Why did you drop your eggs?
          What did Aunt Sue tell you 'bout climbin' on that thing?
   Wendy: We better be careful.
→   Sue: No, 'bout the eggs 'n climbing?
   Wendy: We better not climb with our eggs, else 'n we'd drop 'em.

This narrative interaction suggests that adults shape children's narratives in several ways. The *elicitation* of the narrative itself ("Tell yo' mamma where we went today"), for example, organizes the thematic content of the child's narrative. In this case, the elicitation orients the child to a particular moment of the day Aunt Sue has in mind.

In their study of Euro-American family dinner narratives, Ochs and Taylor also found that children had little control over when they narrated their personal experiences. Table 2.1 displays the extent to which fathers, mothers, and children introduced narratives about their own and others' experiences. In this sample, both adults and children do not introduce most narratives about themselves. Children, however, are more subject to this practice than adults. Slightly under half of the narratives about the experiences of the mother or father were introduced by other family members, whereas two-thirds of the stories that centered

Table 2.1.   Who introduces whom? To what extent did family members
introduce the narratives about themselves as opposed to having
"their" narratives introduced by others?

Protagonist (# narrs)	Who introduces (elicits or initiates):		
	Self (%)	Other (%)	*Which* other (%)
Father (24)	54.2	45.8	M = 33.3
			Ch = 12.5
Mother (28)	53.6	46.4	F = 35.7
			Ch = 10.7
Children (72)	33.3	66.7	M = 34.7
			F = 19.4
			Sib = 12.5
> 6 yrs old (31)	45.2	54.8	M = 25.8
			F = 22.6
			Sib = 6.5
~ 5 yrs old (33)	24.2	75.8	M = 42.4
			F = 18.2
			Sib = 15.2
< 4 yrs old (8)	25.0	75.0	M = 37.5
			F = 12.5
			Sib = 25.0

Ochs and Taylor (1992, p. 321). This analysis is based upon 100 narratives drawn from
videotaped family dinner interactions in seven two-parent middle-class Euro-American
families, each with a five-year-old child and at least one older sibling.

on the experiences of a child in the family were introduced by others—
primarily the mother. Further, younger children have less control over
introducing a narrative about themselves. Children over the age of six
get to introduce nearly half of the stories about themselves, while children five years old and younger introduce only a fourth of the narratives
in which they are the protagonists.

In addition to eliciting narratives, adults recruit children's participation and exert control over the telling by *questioning* them about past
events or their attitudes towards them.[38] For example, Aunt Sue makes
sure that Wendy gets to the point of the day's events through questions
such as "'n then what happened?," "What happened on the climbing?,"
"Why did you drop your eggs?," and "What did Aunt Sue tell you
'bout climbin' on that thing?" This practice is culturally widespread.
Katherine Demuth recorded similar questioning among the Basotho
people of South Africa, as illustrated in the following exchange between
26-month-old Hlobohang and his grandmother:[39]

Grandmother	Hlobohang
→ *U n´o ile ke maobane?*	
You went where yesterday?	
	E?
	What?
→ *U n´o ile kae?*	
You went where?	
	E?
	What?
→ *U n´o ile tlininking?*	
(Did) you go to the clinic?	
	M.
	yea.
. . .	
→ *O il´a u fang?*	
She you gave what?	
	li - jo
	food.

Similarly, in the excerpt below, a Caucasian-American middle-class mother asks her 19-month-old daughter Allison about past events:[40]

Mother	Allison
	((*A putting hand to head*)) Car.
	Car.
→ What?	
	Car.
→ Who was in the car?	
	Mommy.
→ Mommy what?	
	Car.
→ What was Mommy doing?	
	Drive.

Questions may be designed rhetorically to get the child to recount what the adult already knows, or they may lead the child to recount events unfamiliar to the questioner. Heath reports that this distinction has cultural weight in that the working-class white children of Roadville were routinely exposed to leading questions such as those used by Aunt Sue with Wendy, while the working-class African-American children of Trackton were less likely to be asked such questions in the course of recounting a personal narrative.[41] Indeed, Trackton children were socialized to be discerning, even wary, of questions directed at them, especially when interacting with unfamiliar adults. This cultural orientation has created difficulties for Trackton children upon entering the public-school classroom, where most of the teacher's talk consists of questions. One Trackton mother summarized the culture clash as follows:[42]

> The teachers won't listen.
> My kid, he too scared to talk,
> 'cause nobody play by the rules he know.
> At home, I can't shut 'im up.
> Miss Davis, she complain 'bout Ned not answerin' back.
> He say she asks dumb questions she already know 'bout.

Another common strategy for encouraging and controlling narration involves *prompting* children as to what to say. For example, in a final attempt to get Wendy to recount the warning that Aunt Sue had given her about climbing with the Easter eggs, Aunt Sue prompts her, "No, 'bout the eggs 'n climbing?" Children can be prompted not only to make narrative assertions but also to elicit information from others concerning their past actions. Anthropologist Bambi Schieffelin analyzes a triadic adult-child-child interaction among the Kaluli of Papua New Guinea, in which the mother (M) prompts 26-month-old Wanu (W) to question his older sister Binaria (B), who has eaten more than her share of pandanus.[43] In a number of languages, prompts are grammatically marked by morphological constructions that direct the child to repeat. In Kaluli the prompt is followed by ɛlɛma, which means "Say it!"

    M to B: What was left of yours
                from yesterday?
→ M to W to B: Where did you put it? ɛlɛma,
        W: where

Later Wanu's older cousin Mama (Ma) tells him to ask Binaria:

→ Ma to W to B: Did you pick it?! ɛlɛ ma

Although he ignores them, his mother and his cousin continue to urge
Wanu to recount:

→ M to W to B: My grandmother picked it! ɛlɛ ma
→ Ma to W to B: My grandmother picked this! ɛlɛ ma

This practice of directing children to query others and make claims
about actions has been observed throughout the Pacific Islands, Eu-
rope, America, and Africa.[44]

Sometimes children are *corrected* after they produce an utterance that
is inappropriate or incomplete. An Athabaskan Indian man, for example, recalls this practice in his childhood:[45]

> My grandfather say, "In-chee'!,"
> he mean, not right, like don't brag?
> Boy say, "I kill moose today!"
> Man say, "In-chee'! Don't say that!
> Say, instead, maybe today I see moose."
> Boy say, "I cross river now."
> My grandfather say "In-chee'!
> Maybe you fall in river down you say that.
> Say, instead, maybe I try cross river today."

Scollon calls this practice "glossing" in that the elder person provides
a culturally acceptable translation of the child's utterance.[46] In communities like the Athabaskan and Kaluli, children are directed to imi-
tate culturally appropriate topics, stances, and words to say in a social
situation.

In some communities, co-tellers routinely and elaborately repeat all
or part of what their conversational partner recounts to them. Linguistic anthropologist Penelope Brown has analyzed the prevalence of conversation repetition among Tzeltal Mayan Indians.[47] In polite Tzeltal social interactions, adults may engage in up to eight turns of repetition of
one another's utterances. Adult-child interactions, including narrative

exchanges, are similarly marked by extensive repetition, and it is not always the child who repeats what the adult says. In the following exchange between X´an, who is two years and one month old, and her mother Con, it is primarily the adult who repeats and elaborates what the child is saying:[48]

    X´an: *tzi´*
          dog

→ Con: *tz´i´*
          dog

    X´an: *ja´*
          It is

→ Con: *ya´ maj tz´i´*
          You hit (a) dog.
          ((guessing child's reference))

    X´an: *jo´*
          yeah

     Con: *bi xi a´baji*
          Where did it go?

    X´a n: *bej*
          trail

→ Con: *ta´ bej*
          onto the trail

    X´an: *jo´*
          yeah

→ Con: *lɔk´ bel ta bej.*
          It went away on the trail.

    X´an: *naj.*
          house

→ Con: *bajt ta snaj.*
          It went to its house

    X´an: *jov.*
          yeah

     Con: *aj*
          Ah
          (8.0 pause)

→ X´an: *naj xi*
          house, he/she said

→ Con: *bajtix ta sna*
　　　 it tzi ´i ´i
　　　 The dog has gone to its house.

These repetitions serve a wide range of pragmatic functions that exceed mimicry, including maintaining topic of attention and displaying agreement, empathy, or tentative understanding.

In addition to repetitions and glossings of children's utterances, adult co-narration may provide a *model* for young children's subsequent narrative efforts. In the following Caucasian-American working-class parent-child exchange analyzed by Peggy Miller and Linda Sperry, 19-month-old Amy reproduces part of her mother's ongoing narrative, which her mother in turn affirms through paraphrastic repetition:[49]

　　　 Mother: She pulled a little sneaky the other day,
　　　　　　　　 went out the back door
→ 　　　　　　　 and fell down the back steps
　　　　　　　　 and busted her back all up
Investigator: Oh!
　　　　 Child: *((drinking from cup, nods head))*
　　　 Mother: Mm *((nods head))* Say 'yes'
　　　　 Child: *((puts finger into Mother's glass))*
　　　 Mother: Get yours out of there!
　　　　　　　 ((Mother shares her Coke with child, elicits 'thank' from
　　　　　　　　 child, child drinks))
→ 　　 Child: me big fall down. *((lifting up dress))*
→ 　 Mother: You fell down, yeah *((smiling))* You hit your back

In the Miller and Sperry study, children's *imitative* narratives declined with age and increased in mean length of utterance. Imitative narratives characterized about 17 percent of the personal narrative corpus when the mean length of the children's utterances was less than 2.5 morphemes. Once the children produced utterances above 2.5 morphemes per utterance, the proportion of imitative narratives dropped to 5 percent.

In Judith Hudson's case study of the autobiographical memory of a 21–28-month-old English-speaking child named Rachel, maternal scaffolding of children's narrative recall shifted over developmental time.[50] The proportion of questions decreased, while contributions of new information and verifications of the child's contributions increased. In line with this trend, Rachel's contribution shifted from minimal or no responses to more expansive responses to inquiries and more spontaneous narrative assertions. As Hudson notes, "This seems to indicate that Rachel was treated as a more equal participant."[51]

While such interactions suggest that adult elicitation of narratives, questioning, prompting, repeating, glossing, and modeling provide the collaborative groundwork for narrative development, *adult co-telling of narratives of personal experience may not necessarily be facilitative*. Carol Feldman's analysis of one Euro-American toddler's personal narratives indicates that those the child produced on her own were far more complex than ones co-produced with her parents at the same age. Although the narratives produced by the child alone in bed and together with her parents both link events temporally, only those produced alone revolve around problematic events and link events causally: "She seems to invent the problem-solving narrative herself, and it appears first in, and for nearly a year thereafter exists almost entirely in, speech for herself. The problem-solving narrative, then, seems to begin as private speech."[52] This observation suggests that while conversational narrative activity provides models for launching and co-telling narratives, such activity is not necessarily the optimal nor the exclusive environment for other narrative skills to flourish. Young children may use private speech to explore more complex forms of relating events in narrative.

Feldman's findings resonate with the observation by Robyn Fivush and her colleagues that children recalled more information about autobiographical events when talking with a stranger than with their mother.[53] This observation leads to a reassessment of proposals to the effect that elaborate maternal co-narration enhances autobiographical memory, a notion that we consider more fully in Chapter 4.[54] Fivush and colleagues suggest that children's narration is curbed by parental narrative goals. In contrast to strangers, the Caucasian-American middle-class mothers in the study discouraged the children from elaborating story events of their own determination, and, instead, encouraged them to supply specific information, as in the following excerpt:[55]

→ Mother: What did Aunt Susie buy you?
    Child: Glasses.
  Mother: She bought you glasses,

→		and did she buy you anything else?
→		. . . It was a particular type of truck.
→		What kind of truck was it?
	Child:	A green truck.
→	Mother:	I wasn't talking about the color.
→		What was the type of truck?
		It was for the sand.
→		What kind of truck was it?
	Child:	Dump truck.

This observation suggests that heightened emphasis on factivity and specificity is highly controlling and may be a disincentive to children's narrative involvement. In their study of family dinner narrative activity, Ochs and her colleagues found that the children of parents who pressed their children for details and challenged their narrative accounts often avoided narrative activity.[56] Some of the five- to nine-year-old children pretended not to hear, leading their parents to repeat a narrative inquiry; others responded monosyllabically or inaudibly, or tried to leave the dinner table as soon as possible. Thus, co-tellership in itself does not necessarily enhance children's narrative exploration.

Tellability

Tellability is a narrative dimension that varies from a rhetorical focus on a highly reportable breach of expectations and its eventful consequences (high tellability) to reporting relatively ordinary events (low tellability). Tellability also ranges from an orientation to narrative as performance (high tellability) to an orientation to narrative as dialogic sense-making (low tellability). While children initiate and participate in narratives of personal experience that span the tellability continuum, cultural expectations and children's social and cognitive skills impact the frequency, complexity, and rhetorical shape of personal narratives.

On the basis of existing cross-cultural data, it appears that the capacity to produce tellable narratives of personal experience that center around a notable event emerges *early* in the communicative development of normal children. The roots of highly tellable narratives may be located in children's awareness of unexpected events. For example, while walking with his mother and eyeing a tree, 18-month-old David commented, "Hi tree!," then as he passed by: "Bye tree!," and a few steps later: "No tree!," shrugging his shoulders and holding out the palms of his hands to convey his stance toward this state of affairs.[57] In this rudimentary quasi-personal narrative, David, a Euro-American child, articulates a sequence of reportable events that tracks the appearance and somewhat bewildering disappearance of a tree. Two-and-a-half-year-old Lem, an African-American child, formulates a more complex narrative that recalls the sound of a bell that impressed him at church:[58]

Lem: Way
  Far
  Now
  It a church bell
  Ringin'
  Dey singing'
  Ringin'
  You hear it?
  I hear it
  Far
  Now

Studies of children like David and Lem suggest that even very young children are compelled to narrate particularly striking, surprising, or perplexing events.

Heath notes that communities like the working-class African-American community of Trackton place a premium on the ability to narrate highly tellable personal experiences. Trackton's children are not saturated with fictional "Once upon a time" stories. Nor are their narratives of personal experience peppered with adult questions, prompts, and corrections that keep the telling close to the facts. Rather, even very young children are encouraged to tell interesting personal narratives that amuse or otherwise impress an audience. In other words, children are expected to narrate with style and to draw upon a range of communicative resources to this end. Trackton children like Lem rely heavily upon sound effects, gesture, alliteration, and exaggeration to enhance audience appreciation and involvement.

The narration of unexpected events assumes some degree of awareness of what is normative and expected in everyday life. Young children's acquisition of such knowledge is central to their competence as members of families, play groups, schools, neighborhoods, and other community institutions. Narratives of personal experience may well facilitate the acquisition of such knowledge by providing a genre in which young children can voice and reflect upon the temporal and causal ordering of canonical events in their lives.[59] In contrast to narratives performed primarily to captivate an audience, these narratives are recounted primarily to clarify basic routines of import to the child, including variations in daily activities. For the child narrator the events are charged with reportability in that they are not quite ingrained in the child's mind as routines. As Katherine Nelson notes, the child is preoccupied with what happens when.[60] The excerpts below from the bedtime monologues of a toddler named Emily illustrate early narrative representations of routine events:

Emily, 22 months:[61] when Daddy comes then Daddy come and
get Emmy then, when Daddy done getting
Mommy pretty soon then gets Emmy up
Daddy comes and play with me when up.

Emily, 24 months, 4 days:[62] I can't go down the basement with jamas on.
I sleep with jamas.
Okay sleep with jamas.
In the night time my only put big girl pants
on.
But in the morning we put jamas on.
But, and the morning gets up . . . of the room.
But, afternoon my wake up and play.
Play with Mommy, Daddy.

While normal children begin narrating particular and habitual experiences roughly at the same developmental age (two years or younger),[63] children's earliest personal narratives depict routine rather than particular, novel events.[64] In addition, when young children recount *routine, scripted events,* their narratives tend to be more detailed than those depicting less common incidents.[65] Children appear drawn to such narratives, because they are concerned with the ordering of events and narration helps solidify socio-culturally sanctioned templates for living in the world.

As Emily and other children rapidly master a wide range of routines, however, the tendency to narrate habitual states of affairs gives way to narrating primarily *norm violations* and *emotionally charged experiences*. In such narratives the child is concerned with events that transpired in relation to what should have transpired. Katharina Meng, for example, found that two-thirds of German three-year-olds' spontaneous narratives of personal experience concerned notable, unexpected events, and all of the narratives by four-and-a-half- and six-year-olds focused on such events.[66] Judy Dunn's naturalistic observations of American children and families further indicate that the issues that were most upsetting to children at 18 months were those that they communicated about most effectively at three years.[67]

In summary, young children's narratives of personal experience bring into focus variable, probable, and appropriate orderings of life events, either by reviewing normal, routine activities or by casting an event as unanticipated in light of what would normally be expected. Developmental psychologists Jerome Bruner and Joan Lucariello report that young Emily's narratives display increased linguistic marking of canonical versus noncanonical actions over developmental time.[68] Emily marks canonical actions through adverbs such as "again," "sometimes," "usually"; modal auxiliaries such as "have to," "gotta," and "supposed to"; and the simple present tense depicting normative, habitual states and actions. Noncanonicality is marked through adverbials such as "once," "one time," and "one day"; modals such as "not supposed to"; and contrastive conjunctions such as "but" and "or." In addition, Emily uses rhetorical structures that intensify the significance of events, such as repetition, vowel lengthening, and emphatic stress. With age Emily uses more varied combinations of these grammatical forms, distinguished in boldface in the excerpts below:[69]

Emily 23 months, 6 days: Then Emily got the blanket
and set the dinner
Emmy ate **one time**
and **one time** Emmy sick.
Emmy wanted dinner
Emmy ( )

and Emmy ate the ice
and took dinner.

Emily 28 months, 18 days: **If ever** we **go** to the airport,
we **have to** get some luggage.
If I **have to go** to the airport,
hafta take something for the airport, to the
airport
or you can't go.
Need your own **special** bus (carry me)
And they **z-o-o-m, o-o-m, zoom, zoom, zoom.
Zoom.**

Emily 28 months, 18 days: **One day** Daddy was eating dessert,
He's **not supposed to** have dessert . . .
Dessert, dessert, des-o-kay, dessert.

In addition to these developmental trends, children's narratives become rhetorically richer in part because children are able to articulate longer and more complex propositions. The mean length of intonational units in Emily's narratives, for example, increases from 21–36 months of age.[70] Masahiko Minami also found that Japanese children's personal narratives display greater verbal complexity across developmental time.[71] Complexity was measured in terms of utterance and discourse structures, including intonational units called *verses,* which are thematically grouped into larger units called *stanzas.*[72] The elicited personal narratives of five-year-olds displayed a greater proportion of stanzas containing four or more verses (30.6 percent) than did the narratives of four-year-olds (14.6 percent). As they develop, children also articulate more complex plot structures, a phenomenon that will be discussed in the section below on linearity, along with richer marking of psychological perspective, which will be considered in the section on moral stance.

Over developmental time children initiate personal narratives more often. Peggy Miller and Linda Sperry, for example, used the unit of "narrative episode" to chart development of storytelling competence among young Euro-American working-class children. A narrative episode included one or more child utterances, addressed to an interlocutor, depicting a particular distant past event involving the child or someone in the child's life. At 19 months, the children produced an average of .84 narrative episodes per hour. At 32 months old they produced an average of 2.2 narrative episodes per hour.[73]

Local expectations about how to tell personal narratives also influences the rhetorical shaping of children's renderings of life experience. As noted earlier, communities such as the working-class Euro-American community of Roadville encourage children to "stick to the facts" in recounting events, while communities such as the working-class African-American community of Trackton promote heightened dramatic renderings of children's experiences:

> People in both Trackton and Roadville spend a lot of time telling stories. Yet the form, occasions, content, and function of their stories differ greatly. They structure their stories differently; they hold different scales of features on which stories are recognized as *stories* and judged as good or bad. The patterns of interaction surrounding the actual telling of a story vary considerably from Roadville to Trackton. One community allows only stories which are factual and have little exaggeration; the other uses reality only as the germ of a highly creative fictionalized account. One uses stories to reaffirm group membership and behavioral norms, the other to assert individual strengths and powers. Children in the two communities hear different kinds of stories, they develop competence in telling stories in highly contrasting ways.[74]

Masahiko Minami and Allyssa McCabe also found striking differences in standards of good personal narrative between American and Japanese children.[75] Both Euro-American and African-American children strive to tell lengthy and detailed personal narratives, but the middle-class Japanese children in this study told succinct narratives in which experiences are usually recounted in three utterances. Further, although middle-class Euro-American children elaborately recount a single reportable experience, the middle-class Japanese children briefly recounted a string of three related experiences. In the following excerpt, for example, a seven-year-old child weaves three experiences of injury into a unified personal narrative:[76]

Part 1: Injury in kindergarten
Stanza A: Got hurt in kindergarten
(a) When (I was) in kindergarten
(b) (I) got (my) leg caught in a bicycle,
(c) (I) got a cut here, here.

Stanza B: Aftermath of injury
(a) (I) wore a cast for about a month.
(b) (I) took a rest for about a week.
(c) and (I) went back again.

Part 2: An iron bar
Stanza C: Fell off an iron bar
(a) (I) had a cut here.
(b) (I) fell off an iron bar.
(c) Yeah, (I) had two mouth.

Part 3: Hernia operation
Stanza D: The first operation
(a) Um, um, (I) was born with a hernia, (I) heard.
(b) As for the first hernia,
(c) as a little baby, (I) got an operation.

Stanza E: The second operation
(a) As (I) didn't have an operation for the other one,
(b) as an early first grader, (I) was hospitalized
(c) and (I) got an operation.

The Japanese children's practice reflects a cultural ideology in which verbosity is frowned upon and a haiku-like esthetic of poetic brevity is praised. Observing mother-child interactions, Minami and McCabe found that Japanese mothers socialized their children into this rhetorical format by cutting off the child's recounting of an experience after three utterances. American middle-class mothers in the study, on the other hand, allowed children to hold the floor for longer periods of time and pressed them to supply detailed information about the circumstances, actions, and outcomes of the recounted personal experience.

In summary, the personal narratives of young children display an orientation toward both unusual and usual experiences and toward both rhetoric and sense-making. Developmental milestones such as number of words, episodes, descriptive detail, and sequential complexity, however, need to be considered within local cultural value systems for narration, including ideological preferences for facts, exaggeration, verbosity, and poetic succinctness.

Linearity

The narrative dimension of linearity covers a span of possibilities for linking events that compose an experience. Narratives of personal experience may depict events *linearly,* that is, one event anticipating, causing, or otherwise leading to another in a coherent, progressive, forward-moving time line, or *nonlinearly,* that is, open to the vagaries of possibility, unpredictability, and indeterminacy. Highly linear narratives link events within a plot structure with a beginning that builds to a middle, then resolves into an ending. In linear narratives, protagonists have thoughts and feelings oriented to the future and perform actions seen as future-implicative. Protagonists act in response to an unsettling event to attain goals, with varying degrees of success. Their behavior is cast as a reaction to changes in human and worldly conditions. In nonlinear narratives, the contour, meaning, ordering, and logic of experienced events is cast as irregular or ambiguous. Nonlinearity may reflect a cultural aesthetic, an artful strategy, or the spontaneous, back-and-forth reasoning of personal narrative as a sense-making practice. Narratives of personal experience are generally not completely linear or nonlinear but rather entertain degrees of nonlinearity. Nonlinearity opens narrators to the possibility of restructuring default perspectives on remembered events; however developmental studies of children's personal narrative focus almost exclusively on linearity as the endpoint of narrative. Below we attempt to broaden the concept of narrative competence to comprise both linear and nonlinear aesthetics and formats.

TEMPORAL MARKING

At 21 months, Emily's narratives of routine events depict temporally free-floating sequences of generic events. Emily uses narrative primarily to work out canonical orderings of routine events in her life.[77] Emily casts these events in *simple present* and *progressive* tense and temporally orders them using "when" and "then" (e.g., "when Daddy comes then Daddy come and get Emmy"). According to developmental psycholinguist Julie Gearhart, by 23 months 6 days Emily shifts to predominantly *past* tense verbs to depict specific, interrelated past actions carried out by herself or her father. For Emily, the developmental transition into narratives of specific past experience involved not only the marking of tense but also incorporation of transitivity and agency.

Temporal Sequencing

Emily's monologic narratives about routine events before the age of two display great precocity in narrative sequencing. Gearhart notes, for example, that "86% of the simple present utterances begin with sequencers."[78] This results in a series of several temporally connected utterances such as the following:[79]

Emily 22 months, 17 days: **after** my nap
    then Carl come over my house
    then Emmy go Caldor's in the mall
    when Daddy wake Emmy up
    when Emmy wake up.

Young Emily's personal narratives displayed greater *linearity* as she advanced in age, in that they contained fewer repetitious intonation units and greater chronological flow, one event leading to another.[80]

In conversational environments, however, children's earliest attempts to narrate experience generally take the form of a *single utterance* that requires listeners to fill in precursors or outcomes of events.[81] Emily's dialogic narratives with her parents during this period, for example, do not contain sequencers.[82] In Miller and Sperry's developmental study, only 30 percent of the two-year-old Caucasian-American working-class children's conversational narratives included two or more temporally ordered past acts, and all but one appeared after the children were producing utterances whose mean length was greater than 2.5 morphemes.[83] Similarly, Meng found that German three-year-olds' spontaneous narratives of personal experience consisted largely of one statement or a short statement followed by an adult question and child response.[84] The four-and-a-half-year-old children in the study routinely produced a narrative sequence of events.

Aristotle disdained narratives that were merely chronological sequences of events.[85] Heath categorizes such narratives, consisting of a
string of temporally ordered events, as a distinct genre called a *recast*.[86]
Recasts are logically relatively simple in that they do not center around a
breach of expectations nor do they link events into a plot structure. In
Aristotle's terms, they lack unity. Because they are usually elicited and
prompted by adults rather than volunteered by the child, recasts tend to
be grammatically, lexically, and phonologically relatively flat. The following excerpt is a recast told by members of a Euro-American family at
dinnertime:[87]

Mother: *((turning to Lucy))* I (.) really don't wanna ask you about your
day mouse cuz we all know it was not the best

Father: [Well? (.) (we wanta)

Mother: [You wanna tell Daddy about what (.)
what happened this morning?

Father: mhm? (.) I wanna hear about <u>that</u>

Mother: You woke up (.) and then what

Lucy: Okay we went um to our swimming lessons?
and then we went to see (.) Snow White (.)
<u>Wait!</u> There was a note right there *((pointing to center of table))*

Father: Yes I saw
(0.2 pause)

Lucy: (Three film's playing)

Father: mhm (I do/knew)
(0.6 pause)

Lucy: Then we went to McDonald's <u>for</u> lunch.

Chuck: (and they had Leggos?)
(0.4 pause) *((Dad looks to Chuck, then turns back to Lucy))*
<u>and</u>

Lucy: <u>I</u> got a Big Mac (.) (and um)

Mother: Christopher got the [hamburger

Lucy: [Then we came ho::me (.) [then I

Chuck: [(I know)

Lucy: went to gym and you know what gym's like? . . .

In this recast, Lucy's mother asks that Lucy recount her day to her father. Although her mother prefaces the telling with the comment that

Lucy has not had the best of days, the telling itself does not reveal a problematic event. Rather, Lucy, her younger brother Chuck, and their mother simply delineate a sequence of scheduled activities in which Lucy participated, alone and with Chuck.

PLOT COHERENCE

Beyond temporally sequencing events, competent narrators in many communities articulate how events are causally interrelated within the framework of a *plot*. That is, they detail how a setting gave rise to an unexpected, reportable problematic event, which in turn provoked a protagonist to respond in a certain manner or which altered the condition of a person or object. This more complex genre of personal narrative Heath refers to as an "account," while others call it a "story."[88] In contrast to recasts, which tend to be elicited, these narratives are often launched by the teller who wishes to recount an experience.

Young children have difficulty constructing coherent personal narratives.[89] In Meng's study, for example, four-and-a-half-year-old German children's conversational narratives typically depicted temporal sequences of events, but two-thirds of these sequences were hard to understand. By the age of six, half of the children's narrative sequences were still difficult for others to decipher. Even more dramatically, Carole Peterson and Allyssa McCabe found that elicited personal narratives from four-year-old Euro-American children contain temporally disconnected series of actions.[90] Further, while five-year-olds in the study narrated coherent sequences of events, their narratives ended at the climactic event and failed to articulate its resolution. By six years of age, however, the children produced full narratives from setting to complicating action and its resolution.

The probability that a child will narrate a temporally ordered sequence of events with a beginning, middle, and end dwindles as the child's narrative focus shifts from spontaneous relating of familiar personal experience to researcher-elicited, less familiar thematic content. Ruth Berman and Dan Slobin note the great difficulty that young children display in narrating a wordless picture book (*Frog, Where are You?*).[91] While Emily at 23 months regularly produced temporally and causally organized spontaneous personal narratives and while 30 percent of the two-year-olds' conversational narratives in Miller and Sperry's study contained event sequences, three-year-old speakers of English, German, Spanish, Hebrew, and Turkish telling the frog story generally could not link the pictures frames into a unified account. Rather, they tended to construe each picture as an isolated, local event. This resembles A. N. Applebee's characterization of preschool children's elicited fantasy narratives as "heaps," i.e., depicting disconnected characters or events.[92] Berman and Slobin conclude, "In general, although 3-year-olds have considerable command of the lexico-syntax of their native tongue, they fail to demonstrate knowledge of narrative structure."[93]

Examining the effects of thematic content on narrative complexity, Judith Hudson and Lauren Shapiro compared features of elicited personal and fictional as well as scripted narratives from four- to eight-year-old Euro-American children.[94] Four-year-olds included more structural elements (e.g. setting, evaluation, narrative high point) in personal narratives and scripts than in fictional accounts. The preschool children "included few elements of story grammars into their story narratives. The only element in more than 25% of the narratives was explicit temporal sequencing . . . But inclusion of a setting statement fell below the use of setting markers in preschooler's personal narratives."[95]

These observations are also supported by Aylin Küntay's research comparing Turkish preschoolers' telling of the fictional frog story and their spontaneous conversational narratives of personal experience.[96] Küntay found that the children are more sophisticated in establishing new referents and scenes in relating personal narratives than in the picture-book task:[97] "That is, in personal stories, participants are set up in independent clauses which are followed by narrative-advancing clauses. By setting the character-introductory function aside from the rest of the narrative, children signal their intention to add further information about the character in question. In picture-based stories, presentational clauses can be evidenced, but often carrying the function of listing what 'exists' on a page. Mostly, however, children just plunge into describing the visible activities that each of the mentioned characters are engaged in." The narrative challenge presented to preschoolers by a picture-book task is also reported by Berman and Slobin. Drawing from the dissertation research of Tanya Renner,[98] they note that the three-year-olds tended to personalize the picture-book storytelling, inviting the researcher to digress into related personal experiences, as in the following excerpt:[99]

I see that the boy and the dog look at the frog.
He lies on the small bed.

But I've got a big bed!
Bigger even than my sister.
And I've got a . . .

These observations suggest that children's narrative skills need to be evaluated in terms of genre, topic, interlocutors' participation, and activity setting.

LINEAR TRAJECTORIES

The studies reviewed thus far indicate that, in certain settings and communities, children are encouraged to recount linear narratives, and narrative development is indexed by the child's increasing ability to articulate a relevant and informative temporal and logical progression of events. Linearity, however, can be a challenge to young children. Küntay found, for example, that three- to four-year-old Turkish children tended to produce nonlinear narratives when they initiated a telling on their own. They recounted linear narratives primarily when adults elicited personal experiences and together co-narrated them. Notice in the translated excerpt below how the adult interviewer (IN) guides two-year-old Beril along a linear path back to the temporal and causal origins of his leg injury:[100]

IN: Let me see what happened to your leg, Beril.
    where was it? that place,
    what happened here?
Beril: where?
IN: what happened here?
Beril: I fell down in the countryside
IN: where did you fall down?
    where did you fall down?
Beril: in the meadows
IN: how did you fall down in the countryside?
    what were you doing?
Beril: to my sister . . . I was going
    runningly immediately
    I was killing the insect
    fell down immediately
IN: were you killing the insect?

> what was the insect doing to you?
> Was (it) biting you?
> Beril: no
> was falling down I
> IN: what were (you) doing?
> Beril: I was falling down
> IN: were you falling down?
> but you are saying "I was killing the insect"
> you were running
> then what happened?
> did you fall down?
> Beril: I fell down, of course.

As Küntay notes, it is the interviewer who drives the narrative back in time. The interviewer directs the narrative interaction from the present leg injury ("Let me see what happened to your leg, Beril") to the event that precipitated the injury ("What happened here?") to the event that precipitated this event ("How did you fall down in the countryside?") to the event that precipitated this latter event ("What was the insect doing to you?"). Remarkably, Beril is able to supply all but the initiating event immediately leading up to her fall (Figure 2.1). It is not always adults who drive a narrative linearly forward or backward in time. Children can also push adult co-tellers along a linear progression of events as well. In the excerpt below from a middle-class Euro-American family dinner interaction, it is seven-year-old Oren who urges his mother to help him remember the succession of events that transpired when he accidentally ate a chili pepper in a restaurant when he was two years old:[101]

> Oren: ((to sister)) I ate that chili pepper?
> .h ((imitating action of eating it))
> and Mom thought it was a bean? (.)
> and I ate it?
> and I burned to death
> ((turns to Mother))
> → Oren: What happened. - what
> Mother: You burnt your mouth
> → Oren: (Was) it all over?
> Mother: ((nodding yes)) (It was/I thought)

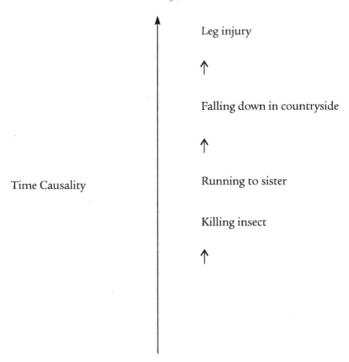

Leg injury

↑

Falling down in countryside

↑

Time Causality   Running to sister

Killing insect

↑

Fig. 2.1. Beril's leg injury narrative

→ Oren: Did I hafta go to the hospital
Mother: *((shakes head, low voice))* (Nah)
→ Oren: What (.) (did they) hafta do?
Mother: We gave you ice
→ Oren: Where
Mother: In your mouth

In this passage, Oren and his mother co-narrate two successive problematic events and their aftermaths: Oren's eating of a chili pepper
(problematic event$_1$) caused a burning sensation in his mouth. This response becomes a problem needing remedying (problematic event$_2$).
Oren asks, "Did I hafta go to the hospital," exploring one possible
means of relieving his problem. But his mother recounts that they instead gave him ice at home (Figure 2.2). In summary, linearity can be a
great comfort to narrators by offering a soothing logic and ordering of
events. Linear narratives of routine life events by very young children
like Emily establish a predictable trajectory of everyday activities. And

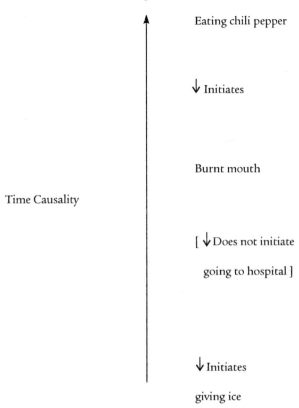

Eating chili pepper

↓ Initiates

Burnt mouth

Time Causality

[↓ Does not initiate

going to hospital]

↓ Initiates

giving ice

Fig. 2.2. Chili pepper narrative

linear narratives that center on a breach of expectations reinforce and reaffirm narrators' sense of the normative and culturally familiar and acceptable paths for redressing the breach. Daniel Siegel notes that determinate narratives of this sort have an adaptive function.[102] They allow children and other interlocutors to learn from patterned ways of approaching life situations. In emphasizing familiarity and predictability, linear narratives promote continuity and stability of self in the world.

NONLINEARITY

Siegel emphasizes that while mental well-being is enhanced by narratives that create a sense of stability and coherence, mental health also requires the flexibility to embrace the unpredictable and emergent, i.e., the nonlinear quality of human experience: "Flexibility . . . involves the capacity for variability, novelty, and uncertainty."[103] Pathological states of mind are associated with imbalances between these dispositions—the assumption of either overly rigid or highly abrupt, unstable, incoherent behaviors and emotions. Ideally we are able to achieve a healthy state of mind and sense of self by regulating the desire for continuity in light of the disruptive fact of worldly discontinuity.

Children's narrative practices display nonlinearity in four important ways: (1) narrating experience may unexpectedly trigger a child's *emotional outburst* in the present time, (2) a child may recount experience *incoherently*, (3) a child may *question or dispute the certainty* of some facet of recounted experience, and (4) a child may reformulate a previously recounted experience or recount a series of similar experiences, creating *parallel discourse structures*.

Emotional Outbursts. Like a bolt of lightning, the remembering of a past life experience through narrative can catapult the teller into intense emotions associated with the experience. Suddenly, the past leaps into the present, sometimes taking interlocutors by surprise. An example of such a radical emotional and temporal shift is found in the ensuing portions of the chili pepper narrative. The chili pepper incident begins with Oren thinking it was very funny that when he was two years old, he ate a chili pepper that his mother thought was a green bean:

  Oren: (Mommy) <u>Wasn't it funny?</u> (when - wh-)
     Wasn't it funny when you (.) thought that thing was a
     pickle? and I ate it?
 Mother: No that <u>wasn't</u> funny. (.)
     I thought it was uh um: *((looks at Father))* (.) a green bean.
  Father: *((nods yes))*
  Oren: And (.) it was really a <u>chili</u>? (.) it was really a <u>chili</u>? (.)
     When I was about *((turns to Mom))* how old?
 Mother: *((looking to Father))*
     How old was he Don? when that happened?
  Father: Two
 Mother: Was he even two?
     (1.0 pause) *((no noticeable affirmation from Dad))*
  Oren: yeah I was two:? (.) and then (.) and then you know what
     happened? (.)
     ((to sister)) I <u>ate</u> that <u>chili</u> pepper? *((imitating action of eating it))*

> and Mom thought it was a <u>bean</u>? (.) and I <u>ate</u> it?
> and I <u>burned</u> to death ((*turns to Mother*))
> What happ<u>en</u>ed. (.) what
> Mother: You burnt your mouth.

At a certain point in the middle of remembering events, Oren determines that his mother not only *was* but now still *is* to blame for his painful eating of a chili pepper and that, as a consequence, he is going to pay her back in kind *now.* Oren retaliates physically and verbally in the present moment:

> Mother: You were <u>hurt</u>ing. (.) your mouth hurt (.) it was burned=
> (it was like (.) I-) We were in a restaurant . . .
> Oren: <u>YOUR FAULT</u> (.) <u>YOUR FAULT</u> ((*pointing at Mom and reaching over
> until he's touching her cheek with index finger*)) . . .
> Mother: It <u>was</u> my fault . . .
> Mother: I thought it was ((*Oren now pinching both of Mom's cheeks*)) a green
> pepp<u>er</u>
> .HHHHH (.) ((*pulling Oren's hands away*))
> <u>OW</u> that really <u>hurts</u> honey?
> Oren: your fault (.) (I get to do whatever I want to do once)
> (that was my fee?) .he he .hh
> Mother: ((*shakes her head no slightly*))
> Oren: ((*lolling back in chair, to Mom, laughingly*))
> just like (it) happened to me . . .
> it happens to you

In this passage, Oren's emotions ignite in the present: He pinches his mother's cheeks, responding to both her culpability and his fury. While his mother reels in pain from his retribution, Oren gleefully states a "just desserts" rationale: "Your fault (.) (I get to do whatever I want to do once) . . . (that was my fee?) . . . just like (it) happened to me . . . it happens to you." This nonlinear outcome of narrating a life experience illustrates how temporally remote events can wreak unexpected consequences for protagonists present at the time of the telling.

Incoherence. While narrative incoherence may be the result of recounting an emotionally charged experience, it may also be the product of a child's cognitive limitations. The developmental studies noted through-out this chapter document young children's difficulties recounting a temporally continuous and logically unified narrative of personal experience. While normally developing children eventually become skilled in culturally configured coherent narration, children who suffer from neuro-psychological disorders such as autism continue to recount personal narratives that skip relevant events or fail to make a logical link between events.[104] In the excerpt below, for example, Erin, a high-functioning autistic child, specifies a setting that is internally incoherent and contains information that seems irrelevant to the central narrative event of her father fracturing his leg.

	Erin:	Oh, and (.) well (.) .hhh
Setting 1:		Dad was born in San Bernardino.
Setting 2:		and about two months ago
Unexpected event:		he broke- fractured his leg on a skateboard.

The setting contains two elements, namely the background information that "Dad was born in San Bernadino" and the point of time in the past "about two months ago." Although the two elements are linked by the conjunction "and," Setting 1 and Setting 2 do not appear related in any obvious manner. Further, Setting 2 is thematically related to Erin's father's skateboard accident, but Setting 1 does not appear related in any obvious way. Looking more closely at the interactional setting of Erin's narrative, however, we realize that Setting 1 is tied to information Erin's mother (Barbara) is providing to the researchers (Elinor and Olga) about Erin's father's family background:

Interview response:	Barbara:	And then (.) his father I believe is born .hmm here (.) in New York I mean
Turn attempt:	Erin:	Oh, and (.)
Interview response:	Barbara:	and then they migrated out here
Turn attempt:	Erin:	Oh, and (.) well (.) .hhh Dad was born in San Bernardino. and about two months ago he broke- fractured his leg on a skateboard.

Erin's utterance "Dad was born in San Bernadino" is thematically continuous with Barbara's narrative about how Erin's father's family migrated to California. The problem is that syntactically and intonationally Erin fuses this information into her own narrative about Dad's recent skateboard accident, creating an incoherent story beginning.

Uncertainty. Nonlinear personal narratives may reflect neither emotional vulnerability nor cognitive immaturity or deficits but rather a child's uncertainty about the nature and direction of life events. At this point, our discussion turns to the key narrative function of making sense out of life events. Many times children and adults are unsure of the thoughts, emotions, and actions of protagonists, or the temporal ordering, logic(s), or resolution of events, if any. The narrators may engage in what Morson calls "sideshadowing," that is, they explore alternative possible versions of experience or construe narratives as rough drafts, without specifying a final explanation or outcome.[105] Children narrate as a means of problem-solving, either by themselves, as in the case of young Emily in her pre-sleep monologues, or together with parents or peers in conversational narratives of personal experience. Carol Feldman's analysis of Emily's narratives from 24–32 months offers insight into the centrality and development of problem-solving narration early in life.[106] At two, Emily's monologues are full of sideshadowing. She alternates between possible realities, as in the following narrative about a broken crib:[107]

Emily 24 months, 4 days: In the bed falling down.
Actually the bed broken.
Huh, huuh, Daddy funny.
The bed broken.
Anybody can put it away.
Emmy go to sleep.
Maybe the baby and the mommy buy different
   crib . . .
The crib did it . . .
the tree did it.
The crib.
But **I don't know** which kind of lady bought the
   crib . . .
But that one fell down.
That crib **must** been,

> that tree must been,
> broke that tree.
> That must fell down.
> **I don't know** what lady bought it.
> But the lady went to get this new crib.
> But then this is one was, bring it back (seat) . . .
> And the you not supposed broke the tree.
> (Broke) up.

The thrust of the narrative is not entirely clear, but Emily weighs alternative accounts of what happened. First, she replaces "the bed fall down" with what she marks to be a more accurate assertion, "Actually the bed broken." She then goes on to alternate between "the crib did it," "the tree did it," "the crib," "that crib must been," "that tree must been," and so on. Either she can't decide whether the crib or the tree fell and broke or whether or not the tree broke the crib. Emily is also unsure who bought the new crib: "I don't know what lady bought it." In entertaining alternative possible versions of experience, Emily draws upon a limited range of linguistic structures that index doubt and degrees of truth, including the mental verb predicate "don't know," the adverb "maybe," and the discursive juxtaposition of oppositional statements. Over developmental time, Emily is able to be clearer about her uncertainty and to voice uncertainty not only about what happened but also why it happened, along with possible reasons for thinking one way or another, as in the excerpt below:[108]

> Emily 32 months, 8 days: Today Daddy went,
> trying to get into the race
> but the people said no
> so he, he has to watch it on television.
> **I don't know** why that is,
> **maybe** cause there's too many people.
> **I think** that's why, why he couldn't go in it . . .
> So he has to watch it on television . . .

Here Emily uses two mental verb predicates ("don't know," "think") to express uncertainty and incorporates the opinions of others through direct reported speech ("the people said no"). But more interesting, she makes three meta-cognitive assertions about the rationale behind the decision to exclude her father from the race. First, she explicitly declares, "I don't know why that is," then provides a possible reason, "maybe cause there's too many people," and comes to possible resolution, "I think that's why, why he couldn't go in it."

Uncertainty about the details and logic of events continues to characterize everyday narrative practices as children grow older. The following exchange involving Turkish preschoolers—six-year-old Gaye and five-year-old Naz—and researcher Aylin Küntay illuminates how peers may not be tolerant of a narrator's uncertainty about events. Küntay has asked the children, "Did any of you do anything interesting in the weekend?" Naz passes the opportunity to narrate, claiming no tellable event transpired:[109]

> Naz: I didn't do anything strange *((interesting))*
> We just stayed at home
> then we went out

But Gaye launches a narrative with a dramatic unexpected event:

> Gaye: ee we had an emergency patient situation on Monday
> sey, my grandfather's eye became all bloody
> all of a sudden, it seems his eye became all bloody
> and also tomorrow *((yesterday))* it became (all bloody)

While this information is cast as factual, at this point the narrative becomes nonlinear, as Gaye dwells upon her own and her parents' knowledge of these events:

> Gaye: we **didn't see** it, **of course**
> I- I- we **didn't see**
> **maybe** my mother and father **might have seen**
> but I **didn't see**
> I **never saw**
> **maybe** also my mother and father **did not see** (it)

Gaye becomes concerned with her own lack of direct perceptual knowledge, that she did not actually see her grandfather's bloody eye, and she wonders if her parents "might have seen" or "maybe . . . did not see" it as well. Rather than continuing this line of narrative inquiry, however, Naz becomes annoyed that Gaye is telling a story full of uncertain information:

> Naz: then why are you seeing- then why are you telling here?
> Gaye: but
> Naz: if you **didn't see** (it) ((*interrupts*))

Gaye attempts to regain her right to tell by claiming that (using the evidential past marker) she did see the bloody eye on a previous occasion:

> Gaye: sa- but I **saw** that it became all bloody
> I- before it became (all bloody) ((*before this last relapse*))
> ya- then it went away,
> [it happened again
> Naz: [it happened again
> Adult: [aaah ohh god!

But these evidential claims are not sufficient for Naz, who insists that if Gaye did not see the bloody eye this time around, she should not be recounting the story:

> Naz: but you say "I **didn't see**"
> If you **didn't see,** why do you [( )
> Gaye: ·[no

Perhaps bullied by Gaye, Naz shifts to a stance of certainty, that she did eventually see the eye:

> Gaye: first- first I **hadn't seen** it
> then I **saw** it
> Naz: hmmh, when it bled again, you **saw,** right
> Gaye: ha ((*yes*))
> Adult: hmmh

In part because Gaye and Naz have different ideas of the degree of certainty needed to tell a personal narrative, the narrative ends without a resolution of the problem of grandfather's bloody eye. After all, Naz had previously relinquished her opportunity to narrate, because she felt it did not meet the criterion of tellability. In this exchange, standards for narrative as problem-solving clash with those for narrative as performance.

Parallelism. In this discussion, we focus on narrative parallelism as a cultural esthetic. Children's renditions of personal experience are influenced by what Dell Hymes calls "ethnopoetics," that is, vernacular, artistic shaping of texts, especially the rhythm and patterning of verbal units.[110] Hymes proposes that recurrence of linguistic forms (lexical, grammatical, phonological, discourse) to mark off narrative segments is associated with fine storytelling performances in American Indian and other communities and mourns the paucity of this aesthetic in modern Euro-American narration:[111] "In terms of storytelling ability we may be in much poorer shape than the traditional American Indian. We may not have as many good storytellers. Good storytelling gets washed out by all the media and events that influence people's experience with the language."

The artful repetition of forms and themes creates nonlinear narratives. The richest material on young children's poetic use of repetition in personal narrative comes from studies of African-American children's narrative practices at home and school. Heath's observations of Trackton children indicate that toddlers' first narratives contain repetitions that function as poetic refrains.[112] Recall two-and-a-half-year-old Lem's narrative excerpted earlier about hearing a church bell. This narrative begins and ends with the refrain "Far now" ("Way/ Far/Now/ It a church bell/ . . . I hear it/Far/Now). By three years Lem is using rhyming as well as alliteration and lexical and phrasal repetition, as in the following narrative about how Lem was scolded for trying to follow his older brother Tony on nearby train tracks:[113]

Lem: Track?
　　　Can't go to de track
　　　dat track
　　　to dat train track:
　　　Big train on de track
　　　Tony down by de track:

Mamma git 'im

Track

Train track:

He come back.

The storyline here is recounted within a web of parallelisms. Like the church bell narrative, this excerpt begins and ends with the refrain of "track," which is also repeated throughout the telling. Lem elaborates "track," using variable, parallel forms, e.g., "de track," "dat track," "dat train track."

When children like Lem enter American public classrooms, they confront a radically different narrative aesthetic, one that prizes linearity. Sarah Michael and James Gee demonstrate that kindergarten teachers favor the linear narratives of Euro-American middle-class children over alternative narrative formats valued by working-class African-American children.[114] The narratives of kindergarten-aged African-American children during "sharing time" and other classroom activities display the elaborate parallelisms that are valued in their communities.[115]

An example of children narrating parallel sequences at school comes from James Gee's discourse analysis of a sharing-time story recounted by a seven-year-old African-American child.[116] Below we reproduce two stanzas of a story about grandmother sneakily eating all the cakes prepared for her birthday party:[117]

Stanza 5	*Stanza 6*
15. last night	19. (she knew we was makin' cakes)
16. my grandmother snuck out	20. an' we was sleepin'
17. an' she ate all the cake	21. an' gobbled em up
18. an' we hadda make more	22. an' we hadda bake a whole.

Integrating Gee's analysis into the present discussion, we see that within each stanza there is a linear structuring of time and logic in which a setting lays the background for the unexpected tellable event, which is followed by the family's attempt to handle the problem created by this event. Across stanzas, however, there is nonlinearity in that the teller reformulates and elaborates the sequence of events recounted in stanza 5.

Setting	Setting
Unexpected event	Unexpected event
Attempt to handle	Attempt to handle

Courtney Cazden, Sarah Michaels, and P. Tabors argue that parallelisms in these sharing-time personal narratives can provide details not supplied in earlier formulations.[118] For example, stanza 6 augments the setting depicted in stanza 5 to inform the listener that her grandmother "knew we was makin' cakes" and that "we was sleepin'." In addition, stanzas can contain both reformulations and new information that pushes the narrative forward. For example, after several more stanzas, the cakes narrative repeats the earlier narrative elements of grandmother eating cakes and the family baking more cakes, then spirals forward:

Stanza 9
31. an' we kept makin' cakes
32. an' she kept eatin' 'em
33. an' we finally got tired of makin' cakes
34. an' so we all ate 'em.

Putting stanza 9 together with stanzas 5 and 6 (and leaving out complex intervening events), we find a parallelism-infused logical unfolding of events in which the grandmother's eating birthday cakes prepared for her led the family to "make more," which grandmother continued to eat, which then made everyone "tired of makin' cakes," which led them all to stop and eat cake.

In addition to parallelism in the development of a single narrative topic, parallel structures may be found across different thematically related narratives told one after another. Parallelism of this sort is characteristic of Japanese personal narratives among both adults and children. In this aesthetic, tellers recount a string of haiku-like thematically linked experiences.[119] When parallelism-infused narratives are told to listeners outside the community, they often sound confusing. Indeed, many Euro-American teachers find such narratives unfocused.[120] Expecting stories to proceed linearly and to relate causal events to their effects as the storytelling proceeds, teachers sanction children whose stories contain parallelisms, criticizing them as pointless ramblings.

In summary, linearity in narrative is neither universally idealized nor necessarily favored across all settings within a community. Within the United States, linearity seems to be prized when narrative is driven by utilitarian ends (wherein informing is primary and time is constrained) more than when it is organized around expressive ends (wherein attention to the aesthetics of form, dramatic revelation, and a tension among elements of text and between text and audience are primary).[121] This same sensibility is shared by writers and performers across many languages, social groups, and nations. *Montage,* the modification of time, and *mise en scene,* the modification of space, are, for example, central to modern narrative, in which achronological cuts back and forth in time and across parallel events capture a multiplicity of perspectives.

Moral Stance

A sine qua non of membership in a community is recognition and respect of moral standards of right and wrong. Every community holds members morally accountable for their actions, thoughts, and feelings. They are treated as moral agents and expected to do what is good for particular situations, roles, relationships, institutions, and society broadly speaking. An abundance of communicative resources are dedicated to maintaining morality, including narratives of personal experience. For adults and children alike, everyday conversational narrative is a medium for determining moral truths, through either consolidation of what members believe or reasoning that calls into question existing moral horizons.

The primary way in which personal narrative conveys morality is through its focus on the unexpected turn of affairs, hence the reinforcement of what is normative and valued. In some cases, the morally correct behavior is made explicit, as in the working-class Euro-American family narrative interaction below:[122]

Mom: Did you wear your glasses today at school?
Linda: Only when um (.) (there) was (something)
        on the chalkboard and then I (go/wore em) (.)(put em on)
Mom: and you left them at schoo:l

Linda: *((very softly))* (mhm)

→ Mom: Honey <u>you</u> can't <u>do</u> that. . . .

Linda: well I- I- I 'm always (.) I'm always for<u>ge</u>ting.

In other cases, the appropriate way of behaving is left implicit, as in the following narrative by a five-year-old Turkish child:

Sami, 5 years, 9 months: I had a car like this

                              I put it into the water when I was little

                              It worked

→   That is, we had taken (it) for repair

→   After that it worked

                              Its motor worked.

In this narrative, Sami's recounting of taking the toy car to be repaired implies that the proper way to take care of toy cars is to keep them out of water. His narrative also articulates how such a problem should be remedied: After taking the car for repair, "its motor worked."

    Even when an unexpected event is not part of a personal narrative, however, the temporal and logical sequencing of events expresses common-sense notions of what should happen in a particular set of circumstances. Consider, for example, Emily's early canonical narratives of personal experience. These narrative efforts brought to conscious awareness the normative order of everyday experience. The use of the simple present tense in these narratives conveys a timeless truthful quality to what happens when. Recall as well that Emily uses modals of disapprobation and approbation like "can't" and "have to" and "supposed to" as well as lexical items like "okay":

→ Emily, 24 months, 4 days: I can't go down the basement with jamas on.

                                I sleep with jamas.

→   Okay sleep with jamas.

Emily 28 months, 18 days: If ever we go to the airport,

→   We have to get some luggage.

→   If I have to go to the airport,

→   hafta take something for the airport, to the

                              airport.

Similarly, when adults elicit, provide, and reformulate what happened in an experience, they instill a moral ideology of the course of life events. Scaffolding of this nature is illustrated in the recast narrative produced by a Turkish mother and her three-year-old son Le:[123]

> Mother: Where did we first get on as were were going to
→   Yalova, dear?
>   Le: ferry boat
→ Mother: then what did we get on?
>   Le: then we got on a taxi
→ Mother: and then what did we get on?
>   Le: and then we got on mini-bus, went to the baths.

Narrative interactions of this sort both review a particular set of events and iterate what is a normal way of participating in an activity or reaching a goal (e.g., going to the baths).

In addition to communicating the normal, expected order of events, personal narratives also convey how children should feel about events, as in the beginning of the following narrative told by two five-year-old middle-class Canadian girls to the mother of one of the girls:[124]

> Kepmen: ((voice excited)) You know what my Mum did?
> Bronwyn: She ran into a tree.
>   Adult: Ooh (0.3 pause) is she hurt?
> Kepmen: Na (0.3 pause) yep.
→ Adult: Oh, poor Mum.

"Narrativization provides a means, early in life, for the child to accomplish one of her first 'developmental tasks': to differentiate and then re-integrate action, affect, and cognition," note Bruner and Lucariello.[125] Emily's narratives at 22–23 months, for example, tend to lack emotional perspective-marking. By 28–33 months, however, the bulk of her narratives display her stance toward events.[126] The narration of emotional stance becomes more linguistically varied over developmental time. Two-year-old Caucasian-American working-class children, for example, first rely upon facial, gestural, and other somatic stance displays, along with lexical and discursive expressions of emotion.[127] Three-year-old German narrators similarly relied primarily upon kinesic and prosodic displays of stance, while older children incorporated a range of lexical, grammatical, and discursive forms to this end.[128]

Personal narrative is largely dedicated to holding people accountable for their conduct. All over the world tellers scrutinize the conduct of protagonists in some eventful situation. Sometimes we are asked to give accounts of ourselves; other times we narrate accounts of others' deeds. As philosopher Alasdair MacIntyre notes, "I am not only accountable, I am one who can always ask others for an account, who can put others to the question. I am part of their story, as they are part of mine. The narrative of any one life is part of an interlocking set of narratives. Moreover this asking for and giving of accounts itself plays an important part in constituting narratives. Asking you what you did and why, what I did and my account of what I did, and vice versa, these are essential constituents of all but the very simplest and barest of narratives."[129] In judging themselves and others as moral creatures, tellers tend to recount either the *virtues* or *vices* of protagonists. Virtue and vice are assessed in relation to a circumstance and to a person's and group's well-being. Both virtue and vice emphasize moral order, virtue as a case of moral excellence and vice as an offense against moral order. In some communities, adults talk freely about children's good deeds; in others, such talk is shunned at all costs, because of fear of the evil eye, because praise is reserved for exalted beings, or for other reasons.[130] In a comparison of middle-class Euro-American and Taiwanese families, Peggy Miller, Angela Wiley, Heidi Fung, and Chung-Hui Liang found that the American parents were more likely to recount incidents that shed praise on their children,[131] as in the following excerpt told to the researcher:[132]

→   Mother: You'll get a big kick out of this one.
                 Friday night, we were just sitting around.
                 Jim took Friday off.
                 I don't know what we did
                 but we were just sitting here at night.
                 Jim and I were sitting on the ground
                 and Jack was ( ).
                 She puts her hand on me and says,
→   "Me happy."
→   And I'm, like, "That's good, Mollie. You happy."
→ Researcher: I love it, it sounds so cute.

→ Mother: I said, "I don't think I ever heard anyone say that,"
→ and Jim says, "I know *I* never heard anyone come up with
( )."
Researcher: Me happy.

Miller also found that working-class Euro-American mothers recounted pride-filled stories of their children. In the following excerpt, a mother tells the researcher a story about how her daughter cleverly rebuffed a prompt to call her mother a creep:[133]

Mother: Johnny told her the other night,
he says to her, "Isn't your mother a creep?"
... And he keeps tellin' her all these things
→ and she says, "Na huh."
→ She says, "You are, Daddy. You're the creep."
Researcher: *((laughs))*
Mother: That's what she told him.
→ He like to come off that chair...

Narratives of personal experience often focus on the moral transgressions of others. Across many settings, families, and communities, adults use narrative didactically to point out the error of children's ways. Basil Bernstein was one of the first to note cultural differences in the socialization of moral values through talk about children's social mistakes. Bernstein contrasted middle-class British parents' focus on getting the child to strengthen interpersonal relationships through appreciating another person's feelings ("You made Sally feel sad") with working-class parents' focus on getting the child to recognize how to behave in particular social roles ("Boys don't cry").[134] Miller and her colleagues found that Taiwanese family narratives centered on the transgressions of children more frequently than Euro-American family narratives. Most of the transgressions involved inappropriate public conduct, as in the following narrative interaction between a Taiwanese toddler, Chung-Chung, and his mother:[135]

Chung: ... In the zoo
I, that slide
I didn't let other kids play

Mother: Yes. It was your fault, wasn't it?

Chung: Yes

Mother: Papa was mad at you.

      . . .

Chung: So many kids were playing on the slide

        Chung-Chung wanted to play on it

        I want I myself, I myself to play on it

        Chung-Chung

        So many kids, I didn't get to play on it

Mother: See how selfish you are?

Here Chung-Chung's mother reinforces Chung-Chung's confession of wrongdoing and overrides his statement of mitigating circumstances, with a sweeping moral indictment. Shaming of this sort is often followed by an explicit statement of a social rule and a promise of compliance:[136]

→ Mother: Saying dirty words is not good.

    Child: Wooooo.

→ Mother: Is it right? Saying dirty words is not good.

Misako Steveron also found that Japanese parents recounted personal experiences about a child's failure to display respect, empathy, or meet social obligations. In the excerpt below, a seven-year-old Japanese child, Shin, recounts an experience that his mother finds morally reprehensible. Shin's narrative is precipitated by his five-year-old brother Kei's relating an event concerning an ice-cream vendor:[137]

     Kei: There was an ice-cream vendor around here yesterday.

Mother: Was he around here. Shi::n.

     Kei: Aro[und here, ( )

   Shin: [To[day with Ruuji I

     Kei: [He was near [Taka's house

Mother: [Was he there

     Kei: Yes.

   Shin: When I went to [play at Ruuji's [house

Mother: [Yes   [Yes

   Shin: I ate an ice cream (from the vendor) with the ring ring bell

Mother: Who bought it for you

   Shin: With Ruuji, Ruuji bought it for me.

Mother: How about money.

   Shin: A: : WHAT. ( )

Mother: Ruuji. From whom did Ruuji get the money.

   Shin: Well, (from) grandpa.

Mother: How much did he get.

→   Kei: A: :n you fool. ( )

→ Mother: What are you doing.

→   When somebody buys something for you

→   or when you have received something from somebody,

→   you have to tell me, OK.

    Kei: He is telling you.

Mother: He is telling me what happened before.

→   You have to tell me the same day (it happen)

→   because I have to say thank you.

While moral positions and strategies are locally organized, socialization of morality through narrative pervades childhood in every household and community. In some communities, children's conduct is the subject of teasing narratives. This practice has been reported as widespread among Kaluli (Papua New Guinea),[138] Samoan,[139] Euro-American working-class,[140] Mexican-American,[141] Inuit,[142] and Athapaskan Indian[143] families, among others. For example, in the following excerpt of Athapaskan Indian children, an older sibling (M) publicly teases a younger sister (A) about being an unreliable baby-sitter:[144]

    M: . . . there was a girl name A

        She was home alone yesterday

        with this baby

        He was

        he he both not even much

        not even

    A: Big liar!

    M: Just little small baby

        and then um

→   A got scared

    A: NO WAY!

```
      B:  Of [course
              [Big, he's just lying. Don't believe him.
              [He's a big liar.
  →   M:  [She got scared
  →       She [went to my house
      A:        [Don't believe him don't believe him.
  →   M:  She ran to my granny's
      A:  Don't be[lieve 'm
  →   M:              [And, and she said, um
              Where's Dave?
              Tell him to come home right now . . .
```

As analyzed by Suzanne Scollon, at least two moral messages are at work in this exchange. While M's narrative contributions position A as a culturally incompetent figure, A vehemently challenges M's authority and right to characterize her comportment. A's challenge is based upon the Athapaskan sensibility that "narratives are told about legendary characters or about one's own personal experience, but not about the affairs of others that one does not witness directly."[145] Thus, M chides A for conduct as a protagonist, but A chides M for conduct as a narrator.

Those who recount a personal narrative often portray themselves as virtuous and others as culpable.[146] Children are prone to this moral disposition from an early age. Psycholinguist Michael Bamberg illuminates fine-grained evaluative stance-marking in elicited narratives by four- to ten-year-old American children.[147] Children's assignment of moral responsibility in narratives about a time when they "made someone real angry" differed from that in narratives about a time when they "were angry." Both preschool and older children diffused their own culpability in making another angry through vagueness markers:[148]

  →   we were fighting maybe
  →   I don't really know

and by making themselves invisible as a responsible party:

      it was a couple of years ago
      when I took the crab away from my brother
      then I stuck my fist out

→   and he ran right into it
→   and got a bloody nose.

In narrating about a time when *they* were angry, however, the younger and older children identified the other party as the agent responsible and themselves as victims of a transitive action:

→   When my sister slapped me across the face
→   just because she didn't let me in her room
        and I wanted to play a game
→   but she wouldn't let me
→   and she slapped me across the face.

These children show themselves to be sophisticated construers of moral order, using narrative to carefully locate themselves as positive moral agents in a world of good and bad behavior.

We conclude this discussion of moral stance with a statement of the obvious, namely that moral framings of good and bad focus on dispositions of import to families and other community institutions. Specific behaviors come under moral scrutiny through the lens of personal narration. In most families, the moral framework of narrative addresses worldviews and comportment that facilitate a child's social, emotional, and physical well-being. In some families, however, judgments of what is a virtue and what is a vice can socialize children into unhealthy relationships with the world. In an effort to examine the role of narrative interaction in socializing distressing psychological dispositions, Lisa Capps and Elinor Ochs carried out a case study of a family in which the mother was diagnosed with agoraphobia—a disorder characterized by a fear of being in a place where it may be difficult to escape or obtain help if a person experiences a panic attack or other distressing symptoms.[149] Sufferers of agoraphobia remain in or close to their homes to avoid panicking in an unsafe location and spend much of their time ruminating, often in narrative form, about actual or imagined anxious experiences. Their children are themselves at risk for developing an anxiety disorder,[150] either as children or adults. Capps and Ochs' case study indicates that collaborative narrative activity apprentices children into envisioning themselves as helpless beings in a world spinning out of control.[151] In recounting disturbing experiences, the children used a grammar of ·

abnormality and helplessness routinely employed by their mother, including adverbs denoting the irrational ("all of a sudden," "out of the blue"), mental verbs that denote heightened awareness ("I would think, Okay there's a hospital and a doctor's office, and if anything should happen to me . . ."), and presenting themselves as non- or diminished agents. Further, when the children narrated themselves as in control in a distressing situation, their mother often remarked that she did not remember the situation, downplayed the seriousness of the situation, or reframed the child's take-charge conduct as embarrassing ("she's always spoken her mind"). These and other narrative practices transcend the moment of the interaction, laying enduring emotional foundations for living.

Summary

Developmental studies suggest, on the one hand, that as children grow older, their inclination to narrate habitual events is subsumed by the tendency to recount norm violations, and single utterances give way to temporally ordered, causally coherent narrative sequences. On the other hand, when children use narrative as a medium for making sense out of events, they are less willing to produce a seamlessly linear account and more prone to doubts, questioning, and weighing alternative possible versions of an incident.

When children are integrated into narrative interactions, they participate in building understandings of what is right and wrong, tasteful and distasteful, preferred and dispreferred, helpful and unhelpful, and continua of assessments within these and other polar attributes. Although the excerpts above display overt moralizing messages, moral positions are usually implicitly encoded, requiring children to link grammatical and discursive displays of moral stance to other elements in a narrated situation. Narration of personal experience provides critical information about what children can expect to experience over the course of a lifetime. Such activity builds understandings of what it means to be a person and a member of a community; that is, a history of being in the world. As such, narrative dynamics impact children's mental and physical well-being. In many families, narrative activity socializes children into productive understandings and expectations. In some families, however, narrative activity can potentially apprentice children into harmful life perspectives. When a parent suffers from a psychological disorder, for example, that disorder may organize how he or she transforms experience into narrative and vice versa. Children as overhearers, addressees, and co-narrators with such family members may be drawn into a similar disabling worldview, setting the groundwork for intergenerational transmission of the disorder.

3

LAUNCHING A NARRATIVE

In Pirandello's *Six Characters in Search of an Author,* the protagonists search for a theater director who can help them realize the story within them. They say, "We really are six characters, sir, very interesting ones at that. But lost. Adrift," and urge the director, "The drama is inside us. It *is* us. And we're impatient to perform it."[1]

All of us resemble Pirandello's characters. We have unrealized narratives within us whose telling awaits the attentive ears and voices of conversational partners. For a variety of reasons, people the world over feel compelled to recount their experiences to others. Recall in Chapter 1, for example, the urgency with which Dad initiates a narrative about an advertisement he saw on his way home from work. Dad has a story that he has "got" to tell, and his family rivets their attention on him:[2]

→ Dad: I got to <u>tell</u> you what they were advertising in Glenview (.)
        on Glenview Boulevard on the way home
  Sean: *((looks at Dad))*
  Beth: *((looks at Dad))*
  Mom: What. *((anxiously))*

Unrealized narratives may concern freshly recalled activities of the day or fragmented memories of remote events; they may be emotionally charged or deemed trivial. The would-be narrator may have a perspective that he or she wants aired and appraised, as is apparent in Dad's gleeful revelation of the nature of the advertisement:

Dad: WE could <u>have</u> a:: <u>pit bull</u> [and <u>shepherd</u> and part <u>rottweiler</u> puppy

Mom: [((*jerks back away from Dad*))

Dad: HA HA HA HA ha ha ha ha ha

Dad designs this narrative in a way that steers family members to visualize themselves as owners of a pit bull–shepherd–rottweiler puppy: He shouts out "WE" and emphatically stresses the predicate "<u>have,</u>" rather than the modal of possibility "could." He also emphasizes each threatening breed in the puppy's makeup. Dad's narrative also builds suspense by prolonging the revelation of the available pet: He draws out the sound of the article "a::" that precedes the description of the puppy. The design of the telling leads Mom to recoil in horror at the thought.

Alternatively, the would-be narrator may seek others' assistance in developing a point of view on events. While even the simplest predication conveys a point of view—through choice of grammatical form, lexical content, prosody, stylistic register, dialect, language, and the like, narratives have the potential to build more elaborate perspectives on events. Narratives may present and evaluate multiple perspectives, cause-effect relations, and implications. Like Pirandello's six characters, we may recognize that we need others' input to adequately comprehend experience. Yet, accomplishing this goal is often quite difficult.

Securing a Listener's Attention

The first and most fundamental step in successfully launching a narrative is to establish shared attention on the story to be told. If others are already attending, an interlocutor may launch directly into recounting the narrative.[3]

Mom: (Oh) this <u>chair</u> broke (.) today.

Dad: I know.

Mom: <u>No::</u> I mean it <u>rea:lly</u> broke today.

Alternatively, when one has not secured the attention of those present, this goal may be pursued through a number of linguistic and interactional devices, including *summoning another by name, kin term, or title* or *posing a question:*[4]

→ Oren: Mommy (.) <u>wasn't it funny?</u> when (.) wh-
              Wasn't it funny when you (.) thought that thing was a pickle?
              and I ate it?
Mother: no that <u>wasn't</u> funny.

directing another to look, listen, remember, or guess:

→ David: *((holding up a battery))* . . . look I find battery.
  Toby: I see: that Jiji's.[5]

→ Chopper: . . . <u>Gu</u>ess what. (0.8 pause) We was comin' home.[6]
→   Marie: Remember that red <u>blazer</u> you got on the other- you had on
              the other day? (3.0 pause)
  Dottie: Me?[7]

repeating and using emphatic stress:[8]

→   Bea: <u>Guess</u> what. <u>Guess</u> what. Uh- We- w- an' we was up finger-
              waving?=and I said, I said, I said I said *((does motion))* like
              that.=I did.

touching the desired addressee, and pointing at an object:[9]

→ Allison: *((crawling into mother's lap and pointing to microphone))* man/
  Mother: The man put the microphone on.

Charles Goodwin has delineated additional, subtler strategies speakers may employ to gain the attention of a wandering listener. Speakers, may cut off and restart an utterance to summon interlocutors to turn toward the speaker:[10]

      We went down t[o- (0.2 pause) When we went back . . .
         [*((recipient gaze at speaker))*

Sometimes speakers pause while delivering an utterance, giving listeners an interval in which to establish eye contact or otherwise demonstrate involvement:[11]

> He pu:t uhm, [( ) Tch! Put *crab*meat on . . .
> [((*recipient gaze at speaker*))

Although securing the attention of others is challenging for all speakers, it is particularly so for children. Attention-getting behaviors are among the earliest, most important acts a normal child learns. Their cries may not necessarily be intentional, but newborns rapidly appreciate their communicative significance as they come to associate such acts with the attention they secure from others.[12] During the first year of life, normal children develop an extensive repertoire of nonverbal and verbal attention-seeking behaviors. Children intentionally use them not only to signal distress, but to initiate pleasurable exchanges and share objects of interest.[13] In many societies, for example, an infant's smiling, cooing, and gesturing while gazing at an object frequently elicit not only the attention of others, but queries such as "What's that?" Toddlers are socialized to use culturally appropriate names or kin terms to summon the attention of others. Sometimes they are prompted to call out to another and then prompted to report particular events.[14] In turn, toddlers often expect full attention and persist until they see and hear that everyone is listening. Two-year-old David, for example, delays his telling until Mom and Dad not only gaze at him but also voice their readiness to hear his story:[15]

	David:	Mommy? (1.5 pause)
		Daddy?
	Mom:	Yeah?
→	David:	<u>Daddy?</u>
→	Mom:	Say "yeah."
→	Dad:	Yes, David?
	David:	Remember when? Remember . . .

In a number of communities, adults and older children do not select toddlers as narrative partners. Rather, they wait for children's attention span and communicative competence to mature.[16] In other places, adults and older children choose youngsters as recipients for their stories. This practice, common to many middle-class American and European households, can be frustrating, however, in that the attention of the designated child recipient may be very difficult to capture. Those trying to capture a small child's attention routinely use directives to "Look!" and "Listen!," repetition, exaggerated intonation, high pitch, amplified volume, facial affect, gestures, and questions.[17]

Story Prefaces

While it may be difficult to capture the attention of others, interject an utterance into the flow of conversation, and procure a response, getting stories off the ground is particularly challenging. Because narratives entail multiple sentences or clauses, would-be tellers need to obtain permission to maintain the floor for extended discourse. To this end, instead of abruptly launching a narrative, speakers often transition into the telling with the cooperation of other interlocutors.

When we see a printed text, a title or other visible feature may initially identify the text as a possible narrative. Narratives told in conversation do not have titles, but they do often have *story prefaces*. Using data from American conversation, Harvey Sacks has illuminated how stories characteristically emerge in everyday social interaction.[18] Conversational narratives often begin with a two-part story preface in which 1) a teller indicates his or her desire to tell a particular story and thus to dominate the floor across a series of turns; and 2) interlocutors then either permit or do not permit the teller to continue. The story preface helps to pique the interest of interlocutors. As Sacks notes, "it is an utterance that asks for the right to produce extended talk, and says that the talk will be interesting, as well as doing other things."[19] Some story prefaces are general, such as "Do you know what?" or "You want to hear a story?," while others relate more specifically to the events to be recounted, such as "Did I tell you what Debbie said about George t'day?"

Alessandro Duranti recorded just such a story preface in the conversation among men in a Western Samoan village.[20] The story preface ("Do you know the funny thing . . . that happens to me") is initiated by Tāvō, who wishes to recount events surrounding the mysterious disappearance of his watch. Tāvō addresses his story preface to Fonotī, who has just entered the dwelling:

Story preface: Tāvō: *Ke iloa le mea malie Fogoki*
                       Do you know the funny thing Fonotī

                       lea e kupu iā a'u?
                       that happens to me?

      Fonotī: *'O le ā?*
                       What is it?

    Story: Tāvō: *I le pō fo'i ga kākou kalagoa kalagoa*
                       In the night (when) we talked and talked

                       (kou-) 'o a'u moe
                       (you) I sleep

                       ga'o a'you
                       only me

                       ae 'ave (e) le kagaka la'u uaki.
                       and ((*advers.*)) someone takes my watch.

Tāvō's story preface is a common one across the world's speech communities. "You know what?" often anticipates news reports or personal narratives. When others respond to "You know what?" by asking "What?" or otherwise attending, they invite the speaker to deliver the news.[21] In the interaction cited above, Fonotī's response, "What is it?," gives Tāvō the go-ahead to reveal what happened.

Launch Failures

Sometimes, however, story prefaces such as "You know what?" or "Guess what" or "I gotta tell you what happened" fail to secure a go-ahead from intended addressees. For a number of reasons, including persistent listener inattentiveness, disinterest, and disapproval, addressees may not provide feedback that allows a would-be narrator to continue.

INATTENTIVENESS

A common basis for the demise of a potential narrative is failure to capture the intended audience's attention. Consider, for example, five-year-old Sean's failed attempt to inject a topically related experience into the following family narrative interaction:[22]

Dad: *((looks at Mom))* Well she told me (.8 pause) she suspected that- she
      knew that there was a <u>cat</u> going in there but she didn't know
      it was Cocoa.

Mom: <u>Oh.</u> *((looking at Dad))*

Sean: Well KNOW WHAT NELSON SAID? *((looks up from plate))*

Dad: Periodically see, Cocoa [goes in there.

Sean's experience lies at the border of a contribution to the ongoing
narrative and is a narrative in its own right. Sean employs the "You
know what?" story preface. Sean enhances the attention-getting impact of his query by speaking loudly (indicated by capital letters) and
emphatically (indicated by underlining). In addition, Sean increases the
likelihood of his capturing attention by displaying that his news is
relevant to the topic at hand. He does so by beginning with the response
token, "Well," which often indicates nonalignment with a previous remark.[23] Mom and Dad have been building a narrative in which a neighbor unwittingly trapped Cocoa the cat in her garage. Sean's "well" precedes an alternative account for why the cat was in the garage. Despite
all of these attention-getting strategies, Sean's bid for the floor is
ignored.

Unsuccessful in garnering the floor, Sean interrupts Dad's comment
with another attempt:

Dad: Periodically see, Cocoa [goes in there.

Sean: [KNOW WHAT NELSON SAID?
                                 [*((looking at Mom))*

Mom: She [probably leaves messes in there.
          [*((looking at Dad))*

This time Sean fixes his eyes on Mom in an effort to secure her as principal addressee. Mom, however, continues to look at Dad and does not respond to Sean's question. Undaunted, Sean tries yet again. His third attempt to gain the floor is successful:

Sean: [<u>MOM?</u> KNOW WHAT NELSON SAID?
       KNOW WHAT NELSON SAID? RAYMOND'S BROTHER?

Mom: Hmm?

Sean's success in obtaining recognition may derive from three enhancements: 1) designating his addressee by name ("<u>MOM?</u>"), 2) repeating his question ("KNOW WHAT NELSON SAID? <u>KNOW WHAT NELSON SAID?</u>"), and 3) identifying the major protagonist, Nelson, as his best friend Raymond's brother ("RAYMOND'S BROTHER?"). Although Mom's "Hmm" acknowledges Sean and implicitly supplies permission to continue, Sean emphatically repeats his attention-getting story preface yet again:

> Sean: <u>KNOW WHAT NELSON SAID?</u>
> NELSON IS RAYMOND'S BROTHER.
> KNOW WHAT NELSON SAID?

It is as if Sean needs more than a mere "Hmm" as evidence that his listener is attending. Sean recounts his narrative only after securing an explicit request for information from Mom and Dad and eye contact from Mom:

> Mom: [What <u>did</u> Nelson say?
> [(((*flashes glance at Dad, looks at Sean*))
> Dad: What did Nelson say, Sean?
> Sean: <u>HE,</u> Um <u>HE SAID THAT</u> um, he said that <u>cats hibernate.</u>

DISINTEREST

Failure to incite listeners' interest in a pending story is yet another impediment to getting a narrative off the ground. Successful story prefaces often pique the listener's interest by identifying a relevant, newsworthy story focus. In the following conversation, an American mother at first fails to garner her five-year-old daughter's interest in an unspecified narrative event:[24]

> Mom: You know what happened?
> (0.8 pause)

A 0.8-second pause is quite a long time in Euro-American conversational interaction. Usually pauses of this length indicate a reluctance to engage.[25] When Mom gets no response to her query, she rephrases her story preface to include the name of the protagonist, who is her daughter's friend.

> Mom: You know what happened to Billy?

Her daughter's interest is apparently piqued; this time she invites Mom to continue the narrative:

Daughter: What
    Mom: He may not be going to Carpenter with you.
Daughter: Why.
    Mom: His family had some problems
Daughter: Why?
    Mom: Because (.) (she didn't get him) into childcare at the Center
        (0.4 pause)
Daughter: Why? (he couldn't)
    Mom: There wasn't enough room.

In this and similar cases, the teller's story preface elicits a go-ahead by establishing the pertinence of the narrative to those present.

There are other reasons as well why a story preface might not pique listeners' interest. If listeners already know the story, for example, they may not want the teller to relate it again.[26] In some cases, the narrative is curtailed completely. In other cases, listeners take over the telling of the prefaced narrative events, silencing the would-be storyteller. This transpires when nine-year-old Dennis previews the focus of his upcoming narrative for his brother Tommy:[27]

> Dennis: You know what my teacher says (.) when somebody hasta go to
>   the bathroom (.) Tommy, somebody hasta go to the
>   bathroom?

Rather than granting Dennis permission to continue the narrative, Tommy takes over the telling and delivers the punchline:

> Tommy: You have a half of a half of a half of a second.

Tommy's response to Dennis's story preface displays his prior knowledge of the pending narrative. In the talk that ensues, Dennis indicates his surprise at Tommy's prior knowledge, asking him how he knew. In his response, Tommy chastises Dennis for not remembering his considerable acquaintance with the story's protagonist:

Dennis: how did you ((laughing)) kno::w?
Tommy: Dennis I was in her class for a whole entire yea::r.

Story prefaces that anticipate old news risk being pre-empted or curtailed by a co-present teller.

DISAPPROVAL

A potentially engaging and newsworthy narrative may also be thwarted on the grounds that a listener disapproves of either the topic or the circumstances of the telling. The following family dinner interaction illustrates a father's attempt to quell a narrative that his eleven-year-old daughter Beth launches, based on his discomfort with the topic. Dad initially cooperates with Beth until it dawns on him that the impending narrative concerns a letter he once wrote to his boss citing the company's lack of appreciation and requesting a minuscule raise. Indeed, Beth seems to employ a strategy of slow disclosure to snare her father's attention and interest along with the rest of the family present. Beth first simply summons and obtains her father's attention:[28]

Beth: DAD?
Dad: Yeah?

Beth then orients his attention to a letter in her hand, whose content is not disclosed. Although she has read the letter (as is apparent in subsequent talk), she poses an indirect question about its contents. Dad's curiosity is aroused, giving Beth license to continue:

Beth: I found this ((holds up letter))
(0.4 pause)
Or Mom and I found this and I'm <u>wondering</u> what it is.
Dad: Oh?

Beth goes on to read the contents of the letter, and Mom fills in the surrounding circumstances:

```
Beth:  It says "Dear   [Chuck I regret to inform you
Mom:                   [((looks at Dad))
       You were resigning at=
Beth:  =to inform you that"
```

At this point, Dad tries to smother the emergent narrative by forcefully asserting his disapproval and gesturing "Halt!" to Beth:

```
Dad:  LET'S NOT   [LET'S DISPENSE WITH THIS BETH!
                  [((raises arms, palms extended toward Beth))
```

Beth then voices her capitulation, and Dad repeats his disapprobation, albeit in a gentler tone:

```
Beth:  O:ka::y
Dad:   Let's just dispense with this right now.
```

But the cat has been let out of the bag. It is too late. Six-year-old Sean's curiosity reignites the narrative before the flames have died down.

```
Sean:  What is it?
```

Mom follows suit by asking Dad another question, to which Dad responds:

```
Mom:  Were you really gonna resign?
Dad:  Yeah I was.
```

In replying, Dad reneges his "dispense-with-this" stance. His response becomes the basis for probing further the circumstances surrounding the letter and the flourishing of a narrative:

```
Mom:   You were?
Sean:  [Wh-
```

Mom: [That was like seventeen years ago
Dad: I know I started to write this letter *((looks at Mom))* . . .

In addition to topic disapproval, would-be narratives can be aborted because it is not the right time or place to tell the narrative. For example, Beth actually tried to launch the narrative about the embarrassing letter earlier in the family dinner conversation. Her attempts to secure her father's attention, however, failed, largely because her parents were in the thick of an ongoing story about pit bulls. In the sequence below, Beth tries to summon Dad from the kitchen, just after Mom has introduced her narrative:[29]

Mom: Joe and Charlotte have a pit bull. *((looking at Dad))*
      (0.4 pause)
Beth: DAD? *((calls from kitchen to dining room))*
Dad: Oh my. *((looks up from plate at Mom))*
Mom: We got on the subject [the other day. I don't know <u>how</u>
                              [*((Beth returns to the table, sits down))*
      it came out, but I was glad I never told him about pet-
      [people who own pit bulls because I might have offended him.

After returning to the dinner table, Beth tries again to launch the letter story, again to no avail:

Beth: [I FOUND THIS
Mom: *((flashes glance at Beth, looks back at Dad))* He said his mother-in-law
      got locked out in the backyard.

While Mom briefly glances at Beth, she does not veer off her storytelling course. This practice socializes children into the importance of narrative timing in getting a narrative off the ground.

Sometimes story launchings go awry even when a designated listener is paying attention, interested and approving, if someone else intervenes and responds instead of the designated listener. Taylor refers to such interference as "pass interception," using the football metaphor to capture how an account aimed at one person is overtaken by another. In the following passage, for example, Dad intercepts a question Mom explicitly directs to eight-year-old Dick:[30]

Mom: Dick do <u>both</u> classes go on the field trips?
Dick: [((*looks at Mom*))
Dad: [Yeah.

In this sequence, although Dick immediately looks up at Mom when she addresses him with a question, Dad pre-empts Dick's reply. Although interceptions of this sort often go unnoticed, they have the effect of temporarily, or sometimes enduringly, stifling the voice of the designated addressee and the conversational relationship that could have emerged between the addressee and the original speaker.

As indicated in the above excerpts and discussion, launching narrative episodes involves artful orchestration of interaction. Would-be storytellers draw upon grammar, intonation, gesture, and a variety of story preface structures to involve those in their midst in the narrative construction of life experience.

Launch Control

Up to this point, our focus has been on how people get conversational narratives off the ground. We now consider the extent to which a person has control over *when* a narrative about his or her experience gets launched and by *whom*. Studies of multiparty conversation indicate that narratives about one person's experiences may be launched by someone else, even when the more knowledgeable experiencer is present.[31]

Charles Goodwin analyzes a conversation in which one of the interlocutors, Phyllis, launches a narrative about a "big fight" that her husband Mike, who is also present, has witnessed but she has not:[32]

Phyl: <u>Mi</u>ke siz there wz a big <u>fi</u>ght down there las' night,
Curt: Oh rilly?
   (0.5 pause)

In initiating this story preface, Phyllis determines *when* the story about the fight is to be recounted. Further, as Goodwin notes, Phyllis's preface creates an emotionally charged *framework* for the upcoming story. Finally, this preface begins to designate *who* will assume the role of primary storyteller, namely Mike, by establishing him as the source of her information, i.e., she heard about the fight from him.

Phyllis continues to craft a story preface that highlights Mike's authority and recruits him as a storyteller. After her preface receives uptake from Curt ("Oh rilly?"), Phyllis asks for confirmation of the name of one of the central protagonists:

Phyl: Wih *Keegan* en, what.
      Paul [de W<u>a::ld</u>?
Mike: [*Paul* de <u>Wa</u>:l d. Guy out of . . .

Given that Mike is the only one present who witnessed the fight, he is the only one who can confirm the name. In requesting confirmation, Phyllis draws Mike into the story preface and positions him to continue as the principal teller.

Although it might seem unlikely that someone would initiate a narrative concerning an experience of a co-present interlocutor, this practice is quite common in some social groups. As noted in Chapter 2 (Table 2.1), Ochs and Taylor's study of American family dinner interactions indicates that nearly half of the stories about fathers' and mothers' experiences and roughly two-thirds of the stories about the children are launched by another family member. This study indicates that spouses are most likely to launch narratives about one another, whereas mothers are most likely to launch narratives that feature the lives of children, as exemplified below:[33]

→ Mom: Chuck did you tell Daddy (.) u:m what happened at karate
          ((speaking extremely fast)) when you came (in in your new)
          uniform? What did (Daisy) do for you?
Chuck: *((to Dad, smiling))* um (.) she (got my belt) an <u>DE:?:N</u> she gave me
          (back/that) new one

Through story prefaces such as "did you tell Daddy . . ." mothers control *when* a narrative is launched, *who* is to be the primary teller ("Chuck"), and *what story details* are to be highlighted ("what happened at karate . . . when you came (in in your new) uniform? What did (Daisy) do for you?").

In the family dinnertime conversations observed by Ochs and colleagues, children rarely launched narratives about themselves or about other family members. Blum-Kulka's observations of Jewish American and Israeli families, in contrast, reveal an exception to this trend, whereby children routinely launch narratives about their daily activities. In the following passage, for example, four-year-old Sandra initiates discussion of her day:[34]

    Child: Mommy, to who will I tell how my day goes?
    Mother: Okay let's hear your day.
    Child: well, I play puzzles and ( ) and ( ) and I made ( ),
    Mother: A what?
    Child: a shoe-print . . .
    Father: So what else did you do today, Sandra?
    Child: um ( ) beads, puzzles, and I played clock.

Children also solicited narratives of the day's events from other family members, as in the following exchange between Andrew (age nine), Ellen (age seven), and their mother:[35]

    Andrew: What happened at work today Mother?
    Mother: Well I bet you, one power trouble at work today.
    Andrew: Oh really. ((laughs))
    Mother: ((laughs)) Oh God.
    Ellen: You should drop your jobbie.

As Blum-Kulka notes, in many of the families she observed, "telling one's day" stories took on a ritualistic tone. This narrative activity involves formulaic stylistic features, clear discourse boundaries concerning acceptable topics and appropriate ways of telling, and demarcated roles that eventually become reversible.

The Travails of Story Launchers

Pirandello's characters search for someone who can help them realize the stories within them. In everyday life we seek out others who might help us to get our narratives off the ground. Pirandello's characters walk into an ongoing play rehearsal and plead their case to the director. In ordinary life we interject bids for a spate of narration time into ongoing conversation. We ask for others' attention and work to incite interest and acceptance. We elicit others' approval to begin unraveling the stories of our lives. In this sense, from their inception, life narratives are joint productions. Pirandello's characters are brimming with stories to air and work to engage a reluctant director and audience. But this is not the only scenario that pervades social life. An alternative scenario involves directors seeking to extract the daily life stories from reticent interlocutors, either for their own information or for the benefit of others present. This dynamic can result in a standoff, whereby the reluctant teller withholds accounts of lived experience altogether. For example, at American dinner tables, children sometimes completely ignore parental solicitations of daily life events, as in the interaction below, when Dad queries nine-year-old Adam:[36]

> Dad: Well why don't you tell me what strokes you've learned (.)
>   you've learned, in swimming

Adam ignores him. Dad then tries again:

> Dad: What strokes, what s-

But his attempt to launch a swimming lesson narrative from Adam gets derailed by an extended dispute between Adam and Mom about his table manners. When the feud subsides, Dad tries yet again:

> Dad: So what happened (.) what happened today in swimming?

At this point, Adam responds to Dad disinterestedly and cryptically:

> Adam: *((under his breath))* Oh well, I don't know (dive)

After several turns of conversation, in a voice barely louder than a whisper, Adam mumbles another bit of information:

> Adam: we, for a while

Encouraged, Dad tries to pursue a specific line of questioning, but Adam stalls, making Dad repeat his query:

> Dad: How are ya doing in (your) diving?
> Adam: In what?

Dad then repeats his question more emphatically. But there is no pay-off, for Adam closes down the narrative probing:

> Dad: How are you doing in <u>div</u>ing?
> Adam: I don't know.

At this point, perhaps in desperation, Dad gives up on trying to co-launch a narrative with Adam and turns to Mom to access the narrative of the swimming lesson.

As mentioned in Chapter 2, the plight of Dad and Adam reverberates in households across America. Children actively and ingeniously obstruct the narrative probing of their daily lives. Sometimes they mumble and profess ignorance ("I don't know"); at other times they provide dismissive, one-word responses (e.g., "nothing," "fine") to open-ended narrative evocations (e.g., "What did you do at . . .," "How was . . . today?"), and on still other occasions they compress the entire day's events into one activity, as in the following:[37]

> Mom: Sharon?
> Sharon: Yes?
> Mom: I wanted to know what you did (._ in kindercamp today . . .
> → Sharon: All I did was take a nap
> Mom: That's all you did all day long?
> Sharon: yeah
> Mom: You took a <u>nap</u> all day long?
> Sharon: yea:h
> Mom: <u>Boy</u> (.) You must not be tired at all?
> (1.6 pause)
> Did you? (.) get up for a few minutes (.) at all (.) to play or
> do anything?
> Sharon: no.

The launching of a narrative manifests the disequilibrium between the desire to share life experience and the desire to shield those experiences from public scrutiny. At different times, each of us is a character seeking out or retreating from an author, and an author seeking out or retreating from a character in the making.

4

THE UNEXPECTED TURN

This chapter examines a central feature of many tellable narratives of personal experience, namely the recounting of an unexpected turn of events. It has been widely noted that tellers are prone to communicate unusual life events. These are the events that people notice and that are of interest to others in one's community. In addition, these events may be puzzling or evoke strong psychological reactions. Throughout this volume, we have emphasized that everyday conversational narrative is dedicated to making sense out of such incidents, evaluating them in terms of the status quo. We focus here on how everyday tellers recount the unexpected turn. Our discussion first considers how tellers establish the setting of the unexpected event then the presentation of the event itself.

Settings

Narratives of personal experience that strive for thematic coherence contain settings that provide circumstances, frames of mind, and background information relevant to making sense of the central narrated incident, i.e., the unexpected event or events. Settings have the potential to go beyond simply contextualizing events—they may explain them as well. They may, for example, introduce certain understandings and values, which turn out to be held by certain protagonists or tellers but not others. The discrepancy in assumptions partly accounts for why a protagonist behaved in an unforeseen way. Similarly, the setting may introduce autobiographical or historical background that could lead to surprising acts, thoughts, or feelings of particular protagonists. In relatively linear personal narratives, the settings may foreshadow the unexpected event, even though in the actual experience it transpired without warning. Such settings thus paradoxically anticipate at the time of the telling what was unanticipated at the time of the experience told. In other narratives, tellers may slowly disclose facets of the setting that shed light on the unexpected event. And in highly indeterminate narratives, they may leave the setting incomplete or unarticulated and the unexpected event unrooted in a definitive narrative logic.

Settings that Foreshadow

In every social group, members learn that certain events are usually anticipated and followed by others. Recall that very young children are preoccupied with narrating the routine order of life events. Certain expectations about what is likely to happen next are shared by a wide range of people. For example, questions anticipate answers; pleasing performances anticipate applause. Others may be limited to a more restricted group, such as a family's knowledge of the idiosyncrasies of their house and yard or players and fans' knowledge of game rules. In baseball, for instance, hitting a pop-up into the infield with runners on first and second base anticipates the batter being declared "out" (infield fly rule). Narratives cohere in part because tellers rely upon interlocutor's background knowledge about typical orderings of events over time. In the following excerpt, the setting of the narrative informs interlocutors about the mechanics of a door leading to a family backyard that houses two pit bulls:[1]

> They have a house? they have a-
> → the door to the backyard locks automatically
> → when it closes behind you?

This information is part of the family's shared knowledge, the teller's knowledge, and now the interlocutors' knowledge. Having this knowledge sets up certain expectations, namely, that anyone going through this backyard door will be trapped in the backyard with the dogs, if they don't disengage the lock beforehand. This setting foreshadows the central narrative drama in the story above, in which the protagonist was ignorant of this state of affairs and unwittingly entered the backyard.

Similarly, the narrative setting below establishes a mother's expectations about pancake-making with her two-year-old daughter:[2]

Mother:	She was cookin for me, you know, not too long ago.
	I was makin pancakes
→	so I figured she wouldn't put nothin in it, you know.
→	I figured she'd do like I say.

Here the teller recounts her schema for making pancakes with her daughter. She expects that her daughter will not tamper with the usual recipe ("I figured she wouldn't put nothin in it") and will follow her instructions ("I figured she'd do like I say"). In laying out these expectations, the teller foreshadows that the opposite of what she "figured" will transpire.

In the narratives of Meg, who suffers from agoraphobia, narrative settings reveal a double set of expectations: those the teller deems *conventional*—expected of and by normal people—and those based on *self-knowledge*—derived from past bouts of emotional fragility. In a narrative about a family vacation to Niagara Falls, for example, the setting juxtaposes Meg's personal fear with the general positive anticipation of all those in her midst. In the initial portion of the setting, Meg delineates her trepidation about taking the elevator down to the base of the falls:[3]

Meg:	We decided to go down into the falls?
	You can take this elevator that goes down this <u>shaft</u>
	through the ro:ck?
→	. . . Well we- I- I when- I (0.4 pause) realized
→	I (0.2 pause) was feeling anxious about the prospect of getting
	And I'd never <u>really</u> been afraid of elevators before
→	but I- I realized I didn't want to do: it.

This portion of the setting already forebodes the possibility of upcoming disaster. Meg then contrasts her personal reservations with everyone else's conviviality:

→ Meg: But I was afraid to (0.2 pause) ruin everybody's good ti:me.
So I put on my little <u>rain</u> jacket that they give ya
and we got on the elevator and went down.

Once at the base of the falls, Meg tries to display the expected *persona* of a marvelling tourist and to conform to conventional expectations of what one should do and feel in this locale. And at first she seems to succeed:

Meg: Hhh we got down and
(0.5 pause)
And and in<u>side</u> the rock is just like a- a ma:ze of tunnels
(0.2 pause)
And you eventually you eme:rge to (0.4 pause)
→ a spot right behind
→ where the actual (0.4 pause) <u>wa</u>ter is <u>fa</u>lling-
→ it's it's <u>beaU:tiful.</u>

Meg recounts her viewing of the falls as an extraordinary opportunity to stand within arms' reach of a natural wonder. She renders herself fortunate to occupy a spot "right behind where the actual (0.4 pause) <u>wa</u>ter is <u>fa</u>lling." With exaggerated intonation, she attests to its aesthetic splendor: "it's <u>beaU:tiful.</u>"

The Unexpected Event

Narratives of personal experience build dramatic tension through narrative settings that establish information about physical entities, social activities, common sense, specialized knowledge, emotional dispositions, and the like. Tension heightens when the routine chain of life events is broken by an unexpected incident. As Heath notes, conversational narratives that recount fairly predictable events are usually elicited.[4] These tend to be ritualized language practices, as when family members recount their daily activities, or narratives that an interlocutor is coached into telling. More eventful narratives of personal experience, on the other hand, are usually unsolicited. When interlocutors have something they want others to hear, they generally bid for the floor to launch a telling. Like screenwriters who establish a compelling dramatic premise (the "setup") in the first pages of their scripts,[5] and then guide the story to its resolution, competent interlocutors in communities everywhere draw their conversational partners into the narrative process by depicting an incident that is out of the ordinary and engaging them in determining its features and significance. But the unexpected incident is not only a ploy for performing a tellable narrative. In recounting the unexpected experience, tellers attempt to reconcile what they *expected* with what was *experienced*.

In the story of the two-year-old cook, for example, the narrator's initial expectations about her daughter's role in pancake-making give way to a surprising turn of events:[6]

Mom:	So I had stirred up.
	She says, "I want to stir it,"
	and I says, "OK, get up here and stir it."
	She's stirrin it.
	When I came in, she's done had pepper, salt.
Unexpected event:	I don't how she got the peanut butter open.
	And I left the butter sittin here,
	and she done had all the butter all in it,
	it was all over the plate and everything.
	She's a cooker alright.
	Everywheres.

The pancake story delineates a rupture between one person's *expectations of conduct* and the *conduct displayed*. In particular, the story relates a break in what the mother expects her daughter to do in assisting with the pancake-making and what her daughter does. The daughter proves to be a more active and independent chef than her mother had anticipated: She adds novel spices, manages to open a jar of peanut butter, and puts in butter along with smearing it "all over the plate and everything."

The unfolding Niagara Falls story also depicts a rupture in expectations, in this case between a normal person's *expected emotions* as a tourist at Niagara Falls and the *emotions displayed* by the suffering protagonist in the course of the narrated events. Even Meg's earlier fears did not prepare her for the crisis she experiences. Meg recounts to researcher Lisa Capps:[7]

	Meg:	Hhh and when such debilitating panic
Unexpected		I became claustro*pho:bic*
event:→	Lisa:	Umhm
	Meg:	And I-I realize of a typical
		tourist seeing Niagara Falls
	Lisa:	That's right hh
	Meg:	And I remember not only
		that she experiences twinges
		"Beth I'm MAmma's really afraid"
		I told William "I gotta get out of here
		I'm not- I'm not feeling good"

The Niagara Falls story depicts a rupture between the emotions expected of a typical tourist seeing Niagara Falls and the emotions Meg reports to have experienced. While sensations of fear and trepidation are common in the face of powerful natural phenomena, Meg's psychological responses are excessive. Furthermore, though aware of her personal vulnerability, Meg did not expect to experience such debilitating panic. Exceeding her own worst fears as well as conventional standards for the Niagara experience, Meg renders herself pathological: it is not only that she experiences twinges of claustrophobia but that she "became claustro<u>pho:bic</u>."

Slowly Disclosed Settings

Out of design or improvisation, tellers may recount the unexpected tellable event before disclosing all of the setting relevant to interpreting the event. Designwise, skilled storytellers may hold back the setting as a rhetorical move to build dramatic tension, as in Algy's narrative excerpted in Chapter 1, which begins with a description of being drunk and riding home in a car driven by a creature with great hairy arms. This technique is referred to as slow disclosure.[8] In everyday conversational narrative, slow disclosure may ensue when a teller first states a tellable event, then once the interlocutor's attention is secured (see Chapter 3) the event is contextualized and given significance through a setting. This narrative practice is illustrated at the outset of the story about $320 paid for daycare, excerpted in Chapter 1:

Unexpected	Marie:	Bev walked up? (and/she) handed me
event: →		three twenty?
	Jon:	mhm
		(0.6 pause)
Setting: →	Marie:	And I <u>thought</u> she only owed me
		Eighty . . .

Here Marie first asserts that a mother handed her \$320, soliciting her husband's attention and signaling that her discourse is incomplete through rising intonation. Only after she secures her husband's attention does Marie contextualize the unusual nature of the \$320 payment, i.e. that it seemed like an overpayment.

Similarly, in the teacher's story excerpted in Chapter 1 about a racial incident in class, the unexpected event is presented first, followed by slowly disclosed crucial details of the setting:

	Teacher:	One >little boy little girl< came up °to me: (0.2
		pause) uh:: yesterday (0.4 pause) you know (0.6 pause)
		and this has been my <u>o</u>nly incident (0.4 pause) ah:: (.)
		Miss Ek is (0.4 pause) sh- (.) little black girl came up,
Unexpected		she said "Would you please tell that boy to stop
event: →		calling me a
		<u>ni</u>gger
		(0.6 pause) [and
	LE:	[Mm hm
	Teacher:	so I said (.)
		a::nd <u>it</u> was <u>some</u>body from my <u>cla:::ss?</u>
		(0.2 pause) so I was like "<u>oh my gosh:::</u>" (1.0 pause)
	LE:	°Mm hm
	Teacher:	Uh:: <u>so</u>:: I asked him
		I said you know (0.2 pause) "Why would you call her
		that.
		So (0.4 pause) d- do you talk about <u>me</u> like <u>that</u>
		when you get home"
		And [this kind of thing
	LE:	[Mm hm
	Teacher:	He said >no=no=no<

		Well I said it to her because she's been saying "f- you" (0.4 pause)
		to me:: [all the time
Setting:	LE:	[Oh::
	Teacher:	So [she had a part in it
	LE:	[Mm hm
	Teacher:	He had a part in it
		He admitted that had (.) done it
		She admitted her part
		And today I saw them playing together

As in the daycare payment story, the teller waits until the interlocutor displays attention and interest before laying out the relevant background that gives meaning to the unexpected event. The child's racial slur is at first bewildering and then partly explained as a response to an earlier insult to the child. The interviewer shows noticeable relief and affirmation throughout the teacher's informative account of the contextualizing circumstances.

Those who regularly interact and tell stories together often have considerable background about protagonists, even if they did not participate in the events being recounted. In many communities, co-telling among friends and family means that bits and pieces of the setting may belatedly emerge, as different interlocutors contribute what they believe to be related background to an already specified unexpected event. These delayed settings may consolidate the storyline that is already in motion or may reroute the explanation of events in a very different direction. Divergent settings produced by different co-tellers can characterize a protagonist's unexpected behavior in morally opposite tones. In one setting, the protagonist looks good; in another, he or she is made to look reprehensible. This dynamic is particularly characteristic when at least one of the co-tellers is also a protagonist of the narratives of personal experience. As noted in Chapter 2, a teller who is also a protagonist often tries to cast himself or herself as virtuous. Elinor Ochs, Ruth Smith, and Carolyn Taylor refer to this phenomenon as the "Looking Good Principle."[9] There are risks, however, when recounting such a narrative to an intimate: the moral glow may be dashed when someone recalls a rather discrediting background detail. Such a disclosure transpires in the story about the girl who lifted up Lucy's friend's dress in front of the boys and received only one day's detention. Recall that Lucy, supported by her mother, at first took a self-righteous stand about the principal's punishment. Then, without warning, Lucy's younger brother Chuck brings up the embarrassing fact that Lucy herself went to one day's detention the year before:

Setting: →	Chuck:	Lucy? (.) you only ever went to it <u>once</u> - right?
	Father:	*((clears throat))*
		(1.0 pause) *((Lucy arches her back, eyes open wide, looks shocked, starts shaking her head no once; Father looking at her))*
	Mother:	<u>You</u> can tell us can't you?
	Father:	I'm <u>list</u>ening
	Lucy:	*((low to Chuck, glaring))* thanks
		(0.4 pause)
Confirmed: →	Lucy:	*((louder))* [<u>yeah</u> that was
	Mother:	[she was in it once?
		(0.6 pause)
Confirmed: →	Lucy:	Once.

Lucy's confirmation of this new piece of the setting revises the meaning of the upsetting event, namely that now the basis of Lucy's indignation is that the girl who perpetrated the appalling dress-lifting incident received the same detention as was meted out to Lucy.

The airing of this skeleton in the closet well into the narrative may have been an innocent act on the part of Lucy's younger brother. In other narratives, however, revelations of the setting have a decidedly combative quality, with co-tellers having a stake in how context renders them as moral protagonists. This is illustrated in a narrative excerpted in Chapter 1 that involves a husband (Jon) and a wife (Marie) disputing the wisdom of their decisions in an incident earlier in the day. For Marie, the troubling unexpected event is that Jon did not tell their daughter Janie where a set of photo negatives were so that Marie could give them to a friend who was there at the time. Marie prefaces her narrative with a question to Jon that elicits an important and incriminating piece of the setting:[10]

Marie: Jon (.) Do you have those negatives from the (pony) pictures?
Jon: Yeah (.) They're a:ll in your cabinet *((pointing))*

Having secured this information, Marie uses it to launch a complaint, which unfolds into a narrative argument:

Unexpected event: → Marie: I wish you woulda told (Janie)
cuz that's why I sent her down
(cuz/and) Susan wanted em (.)
when she came? (.)
(so she could) go
(if) she took my roll of film

When Marie's account portrays Jon as culpable, Jon is quick to defend himself by supplying his own version of the setting of the communicative exchange between his daughter and him:

Jon: *((with slight shrug))* Sorry (.)
I told Janie I didn't have time to come in (.)
⌈ Janie didn't ask me that (.)
│ What Janie asked me was (.)
│ Can I get the negative fo:r Susan's picture (.)
Setting: → │ That meant I had to go through all those
│ negatives
│ and I was- I said "Hey I .h (.) I don't
⌊ tell her I don't have <u>time</u> to do that right now."

In Jon's new statement of the circumstances, his daughter Janie posed a different request, which demanded time and effort he could not expend at that moment ("I don't have <u>time</u> to do that right now"). In other words, the setting that Jon supplies makes the demand unreasonable and exonerates himself. (Jon was repairing the plumbing at the time.) But Marie continues to mine details of the setting that support Jon's culpability until Jon makes explicit her accusatory demeanor:

Marie: Are they all together? (.)
Could I have gone through it?
(0.4 pause)
Jon: Sure *((nodding yes))*
Marie: Did you know Susan [was here?
Setting: → Jon: [(there are thirteen?) . . .
I didn't know anything . . .

Marie: Are they se[parately packaged?

Jon: [(how) are you trying to find blame?

The conflict continues for a number of turns and escalates through the use of defensively and offensively deployed elaborate settings:

Jon: I'm sorry. (.) kay? It's not my fault.=
I did the best I could with the information that I was given . . .

Setting: → ⌈ I did not know . . . that you needed to know the location of the (.) film . . .
('f) Janie had come out and said to me (.) "Dad will you tell M:Mommy where the films are from the pic?tures"
⌊ I would have said "Yes? Janie"

Marie: Well [when she's about=

Setting: → Jon: [Janie came out

Marie: =eight or nine I bet she'll be able to do that . . .

Setting: → Jon: <u>YOU:</u> are over eight or nine are you not?

Setting: → Marie: Ye:s (.)
and that's exactly what I told her to say?

Jon: That's right?

Marie: is to find out where the negatives were . . .
so I could give them to Susan
(0.2 pause)

Jon: (I) see (.)

Setting: → Well she didn't she di-
she didn't give me your message=
. . . in the form you asked it

Setting: → Marie: B[ut (.) did you know Susan was <u>here?</u>

Jon: [(you know)

⌈ <u>No:?</u> (.) I didn't know <u>who</u> was here Marie
Setting: → I didn't know <u>what</u> was going on. (.)
⌊ I was busy with <u>plumb</u>ing
(0.6 pause)
Is it really ex-stremely important to you to prove that I did something wrong?

(0.4 pause)

[Is that (.) Is that

Marie: [not ex<u>trem</u>ely important *((half-laugh))* nho:

Jon: important enough to carry it to this: (.) extre?:me

Here the children intervene, reminding their parents that they are being filmed. As analyzed by Carolyn Taylor, the children seem aware that the divergent, morally loaded framings of past experience fuel present marital tensions.[11]

Splintered Settings

In some narratives of personal experience, the unexpected event is splintered, i.e. cut off, from a setting that could explain it. Tellers sometimes articulate a setting but then abandon it. In so doing, storytellers produce a highly fragmented narrative of personal experience (Figure 4.1). While narrative discontinuity of this order may be a product of a narrator's momentary distraction, forgetfulness, embarrassment, or deception, it is associated with abnormal discontinuities in a person's identity, memory, and consciousness.[12] Those with disorganized attachment experiences in childhood, dissociative personality disorders, posttraumatic stress, and agoraphobia, among other disturbances, may produce highly fragmented narratives of distressing experiences. Daniel Siegel notes that those suffering from these disorders: "have as their hallmark profound impairments in the ability to shift smoothly across states of mind. Abrupt state shifts may be associated with segmented behaviors, thought processes and emotions and may be reflected in divided autobiographical narratives."[13]

Lisa Capps and Elinor Ochs' study of Meg's panic stories indicates that her stories dwell upon the *immediate setting* (the immediate time, place, and event) and not *longer term circumstances* that could explain the

Setting

Unexpected event

Fig. 4.1. Narrative discontinuity, I

Earlier setting

Immediate setting

Unexpected panic attack

Fig. 4.2. Narrative discontinuity, II

onset of panic (Figure 4.2). Meg portrays herself as helpless, abnormal, and unable to understand why she responded so anxiously and fearfully to the immediate situation, e.g., why she panicked at the base of Niagara Falls, on a skiing vacation, sitting on a plane, diving into a swimming pool, during a traffic jam, and reading a book. Meg uses adverbs and adverbial phrases such as "out of the blue," "all of a sudden," and "unaccountedly" to mark the onset of the panic attack:[14]

→ and all of a sudden
   I (0.4 pause) uh became aware of feeling (0.4 pause) just anxious unaccountably.

→ All of a sudden
   I realized I wanted very much to be off the plane.

   I mean I had all these attacks
→ that just seemed to come out of the blue.

These grammatical markers cast the panic episode as irrational and sever it from earlier narrated circumstances and events that could provide a logic for anxiety.

A set of circumstances and events characterize the earlier settings of these stories: 1) Someone (usually a family member or friend) proposes an activity involving Meg's participation; 2) Meg has reservations but does not voice them; 3) instead she agrees to participate.[15] For example, in recounting the biggest panic attack of her life, Meg mentions the following setting: In the middle of baking cookies, wrapping presents, and maneuvering around a house guest in their crowded home, Meg's husband proposes that the family take a visiting cousin to lunch:[16]

Early setting: → So, in th *midst* of this, this long-lost cousin calls us
  and and says," I'm in Lomita staying at the Marriott."
  And my husband says,
  "Oh it would be so good to see you again *Harriet.*
  Let us come and take you to lunch."

Meg feels overwhelmed:

Early setting: → And I remember (0.6 pause) not really wanting to go
  (0.3 pause) that morning . . .

but keeps quiet and accommodates her husband's wishes.

The pattern of silence and accommodation outlined in many of Meg's panic narratives offers a candidate rationale for panic, because it is precisely in the midst of participating in the dispreferred activity that Meg panics and flees as soon as she is able. Yet, instead of a continuous linking of events (along the lines shown in Figure 4.3a), Meg narrates a broken spiral of causality, as indicated in Figure 4.3b. The consequences of splintering explanatory settings from the panic episode may be that sufferers of panic disorders such as agoraphobia are never able to comprehend the roots of their attacks of anxiety. Because they see their panic as "out of the blue," they feel as if they have no control over their emotional states and conduct in public. Because they associate their panic attacks only with the immediate setting, they avoid those situations (e.g., diving in pools, traveling on freeways, going on skiing trips) to the extent that many sufferers confine themselves to the immediate vicinity of their home. A sufferer's recovery may then be grounded in part in therapeutic reflection on narrative severings of settings and construction of a more integrated context that set the stage for disruptive life incidents.

Positive and Negative Unexpected Events

We now turn to the character of the unexpected incident that constitutes the focus of these and other narratives of personal experience. The unexpected turn of events may be cast as *positive,* that is as a welcomed occurrence, as in the narrative openings below:

a.   Early setting

Proposal to participate in undesirable activity
does not lead Meg to communicate reservations

but instead leads Meg to accommodate and
participate in undesirable activity

Leads to panic attack

b.   Early setting

Proposal to participate in undesirable activity
does not lead Meg to communicate reservations

but instead leads Meg to accommodate and
participate in undesirable activity

Immediate setting

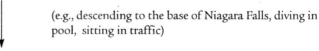

(e.g., descending to the base of Niagara Falls, diving in
pool, sitting in traffic)

Leads to panic attack

Fig. 4.3. (a) *Continuous storyline;* (b) *discontinuous storyline*

Shirley: Ah'm <u>n</u>ot suhpri̱zed. .hh Listen, u-
→ <u>s</u>omething <u>v</u>ery very: <u>c</u>ute happened
las'night et the <u>W</u>arehouse.
Geri: Wha[t.
Shirley: [.hhhhh Yih<u>KNOW</u> Cathy, (.) Larry
Taylor's ex girlfriend[17] . . .

→ Mother: Oh <u>tell</u> them I bet they don't know the good news
Rhoda: <u>I</u>: do.
Sharon: *((pointing to Mom with both hands))* <u>You</u> tell em
(0.4 pause) *((Sharon looks away))*
→ Mother: [Don't you wanta [tell your special news?
Corky: [no
Rhoda: [She <u>go:ts</u> a new <u>mo:</u>lar=[18] . . .

Carl: Well
last night,
my father,
was at work,
he every Thursday night they have this thing,
that everybody has this dollar,
and it makes up to a hundred dollars,
and my
and you've gotta pick this name out,
→   and my father's name got picked
→   so he won a thousand dollars
→   a hundred dollars
Teacher: Tell us what he's gonna do with it.[19]

In these interactions, the narrated incidents are cast as "cute," "good news," or a stroke of good fortune ("my father's name got picked").

In reviewing our own corpora of narratives and a vast array of articles and books containing narrative excerpts from different languages, social groups, and phases of the life span, we have been struck by the dearth of narratives that focus on positive life events from start to finish. Indeed, as Bruner proposes, it may be *trouble* that compels people to narrate: "Trouble is the engine of narrative and the justification for going public with a story. It is the whiff of trouble that leads us to search out the relevant or responsible constituents in the narrative, in order to convert the raw Trouble into a manageable Problem that can be handled with procedural muscle."[20] While people do recount unexpectedly positive events to others, such news is often portrayed as a triumph over adversity or an unexpected relief from a less than desirable state of affairs.

Conversational narratives of personal experience generally depict unexpected events that are unsettling in one way or another. The central narrated events tend to be sources of some combination of fear, frustration, misunderstanding or confusion, irritation, shame or disapproval, malaise, and sympathy.

FEAR

→ Meg: And I'd never <u>really</u> been afraid of elevators before,
but I- I realized I didn't want to do it.
(0.3 pause)
→ But I was afraid to ruin everybody's good time,
so I put on my little <u>rain</u> jacket that they give you
and we got on the elevator and went down.[21]

FRUSTRATION

→Nancy: The m<u>all</u> wz [pa <u>::</u>cked.
Shane: [oh yes?
        (0.5 pause)
Nancy: Because of Valentine's Day?
        (0.5 pause)
Vivian: [Mm<u>hm?</u>
→Nancy: [Oh <u>h</u> : G<u>o:</u>[:d
Michael: [<u>Cra</u>zy
Shane: [<u>Yah</u> it [would.
Vivian: [Oh is <u>that</u> what it was from?
→Nancy: We're driving r<u>ou</u>nd and round parkin' spot and evry°th'ng.°[22]

MISUNDERSTANDING OR CONFUSION

Mother: Ellen opened (up) that bottle that I (bought) her at work?
Sharon:. mhm?

Mother: and it sp-
Rhoda: uh huh:?
Mother: *((chuckling))* sprayed <u>all</u> *((gesturing with her hand over her head))*
over everything (.)
→ and Justin thought it was champagne? (.)
and he said (.) "<u>Why:</u> : *((with half-laugh))* do you have cham<u>pagne?</u> at
the <u>pre</u>school"
(0.2 pause)
Rhoda: (because they like to [drink?)
Sharon: [(<u>WHY:</u> do you have champagne?)
Mother: *((shakes head horizontally))* and I said (.)
→ I had to tell him it's not champagne
so he wouldn't go home and tell his parents
((high-pitched voice)) "<u>Guess</u> what teacher Priscilla had."[23]

IRRITATION

Annette: And <u>Ar</u>thur said that <u>you</u> said
→ that <u>I</u> was showin' off just because
I had that <u>bl:ou</u>se on.[24]

→ Tāvō: *Ke iloa le mea malie Fogoki*
Do you know the funny thing Fonotī

lea e kupu iā a'u?
that happens to me?
Fonotī: *'O le ā?*
What is it?
Tāvō: *I le pō fo'i ga kākou kalagoa kalagoa*
In the night (when) we talked and talked

(kou-) 'o a'u moe
(you) I sleep

ga'o a'u
only me

→ *ae 'ave (e) le kagaka la'u uaki.*
and *((advers.))* someone takes my watch.[25]

SHAME/DISAPPROVAL

Chung: ... In the zoo
       I, that slide
       I didn't let other kids play

→ Mother: Yes. It was your fault, wasn't it?

Chung: Yes

→ Mother: Papa was mad at you. . . .

Chung: So many kids were playing on the slide
       Chung-Chung wanted to play on it
       I want I myself, I myself to play on it
       Chung-Chung
       So many kids, I didn't get to play on it

→ Mother: See how selfish you are?[26]

Ann: Karen has this new hou:se. en it's got all this like (o.2 pause)
      ssilvery:: g-gold wwa:llpaper, .hh (h)en D(h)o(h)n sa(h)ys,
      y'know this's th'firs'time we've seen this house.=Fifty five
      thousan dollars in Cherry Hill.=Right?
      (o.4 pause)

Beth: Uh hu:h?

→ Ann: Do(h)n said. (o.3 pause) dih-did they ma:ke you take this?
      [wa(h)llpa(h)p(h)er? er(h) di[dju pi(h)ck

Beth: [hh!   [Ahh huh huh[27] . . .

MALAISE

→   A: I'm so:: ti:yid. I j's played ba:ske'ball t'day since the firs' time
      since I wz a fresh'n in hi:gh sch[ool.

B: [Ba::sk(h)etb(h)a(h)ll? (h)[28]

SYMPATHY

Mother: Judy Wilson was on the ski trip and she was uh (pause)
      I don't know what they call it- snowboarding?

Dad: Oh [that

Mother: [Or something like that, it's like a surfboard.
      She was standing up on it and she fell and broke her wrist.

Dad: Yeah those are dan-

Mother: And the thing <u>is</u> she's supposed to be in this big <u>piano</u> recital or
contest in a couple of <u>weeks</u> and now she can't play the piano
in the recital.

→ Dad: OH <u>NO!</u> That's too bad.[29]

As is evident in the excerpts above, tellers' and protagonists' fear, frustration, misunderstanding/confusion, irritation, shame/disapproval, malaise, and sympathy, among other types of discontent, form the emotional nucleus of many narratives of personal experience.

In some narratives, the central unexpected incident is viewed from both poles of the affect continuum, that is, as *both* a positive and negative occurrence. In some cases, the *same narrators* cast events in this double light. Such a bipolar perspective pervades the following narrative about finding Nellie, a missing neighborhood cat. At first, the narration dwells upon the happy occasion of locating Nellie:[30]

→Father: I found out where Nellie wa:s
   Sean: [((*looks at Father*))
Mother: [((*looks at Father*))

But when the particulars of this fortunate occurrence are revealed, the narrators shroud the event with more distressing emotions:

  Mother: WHERE? ((*sounding alarmed*))
           (0.4 pause)
           How do you know?
           (0.4 pause)
   Father: Alice told me.
  Mother: Where? ((*looking down at plate*))
→ Father: Locked in her garage [since Sunday
→ Mother: [H:::uh ((*looks up*))
→   Since <u>Sunday.</u>
   Father: Yeah
  Mother: H::uh how do you kno:w?
          that- [I mean how did <u>she</u> know
   Father: [She- she <u>heard</u> her me:<u>ow</u>ing (0.4 pause) this m<u>orn</u>ing
         she had just been <u>gone</u>
         and she opened her garage.

In recounting how and where Nellie was found, Father intimates that there is a culpable party. He identifies Nellie's whereabouts as "locked in her garage," which provokes Mother to respond with mild incredulity ("H:::uh"). The verb "locked" describes a specific, intentional, past action. The mention of "since Sunday" augments the gravity of the action, a judgment that is reinforced by Mother's emphatic echo: "Since Sunday." Father does not yet point a finger at the person responsible for this action; nonetheless, in specifying that Nellie was "locked in her garage," Father sets up the strong probability that the responsible party is Alice, who is the owner of the garage and cat.

At this point, the narrative turns squarely to gruesome particulars of Nellie's plight. First, Mother projects a tragic outcome that could have transpired:

→ Mother: A::::w. You know? she could have ss- she could have DI:ED
        (0.2 pause)
→   I mean how long can you go without water?

When one of the children (Beth) begins to laugh, her brother (Sean) stresses the seriousness of the events:

→ Sean: [It's not funny Beth

While Sean is admonishing Beth, his father and mother further dramatize the dire circumstances of the trapped cat:

→ Father: [I don't [know how long
  Mother: [S- so this morning? she-
→   I mean she had been hearing the cat meowing for two days and
        finally she traced it?
  Father: No she hasn't- she wasn't <u>home</u> Sunday
  Mother: O:h
→ Father: She <u>left.</u>
        (0.4 pause)

Although Mother imagines Alice as desperately searching for her wailing cat, Father revises this sympathetic reading with the grim picture of Alice obliviously leaving home without a thought of Nellie. The next lines of the narrative explicitly lay blame on Alice:

→ Father: She closed her garage and <u>left</u>
            and- and Nellie was <u>in</u> there.

In this manner, the narrative takes on characteristics of a near tragedy
("I don't know how long"), in which the cat almost perishes in the wake
of her owner's negligence ("She <u>left.</u> (0.4 pause) She closed her garage and
<u>left</u> and- and Nellie was <u>in</u> there.") The narrative travels back in time to
reveal the pivotal problematic event of this narrative: Alice unthinkingly
locked her cat in her garage then left her to suffer for days.

   In other cases, *one interlocutor* casts the pivotal event positively, while
another regards it in a negative light. Emanuel Schegloff analyzes a conversational exchange in which the purchase of a desired waterbed is
good news for one interlocutor but a disappointment to another:[31]

      Debbie: hhh m: u- guess what I've-(u-) wuz lookin' in the
   →   paper:. (.) have you got your waterbed yet>
        Nick: Uh huh, it's really nice too, I set it up
   → Debbie: Oh <u>rea</u>:lly? Al<u>rea</u>dy?
        Nick: Mm humm
               (0.5 pause)
   → Debbie: Oh-no but you h- you've got it already?

The purchase and arrival of the waterbed is a happy sequence of events
for its owner, Nick ("it's really nice too"). However, the events turn out
to be problematic for Debbie ("Oh-no"). As Schegloff notes, Nick's news
of the purchase foils Debbie's attempt to announce how she found an
ad in the newspaper for a really discounted waterbed ("guess what I've
. . ."). That he bought a bed and has set it up already is a letdown for
Debbie, as subsequent interaction further reveals:

      Debbie: O::<u>hh:</u> hu[h, I couldn't be[lieve you c-
        Nick: [Oh (°it's just)   [It'll sink in 'n two
                 day[s fr'm now (then) *((laugh))*
   → Debbie: [*((laugh))*
                 Oh now cuz I just got (.) I saw an ad in the paper for a real
                 discount waterbeds' I w'z gonna tell you 'about it.

As noted, divergent evaluations of narrated events can lead to open conflict among interlocutors. In the following narrative confrontation be-

tween spouses at dinnertime, for example, the wife casts the purchase of a dress as a gift from mother to daughter for a special occasion, but her husband brings up a setting that recasts it in a negative light:[32]

> Wife: And then we went to this other um - this dress store?
> →   a:nd (my Mom) bought me a dress for the wedding (.) (for   wedding).
>   (3.8 pause) ((*husband looks at wife, then starts to eat, then looks back at wife*))
> → Husband: (you're kidding)
>   Wife: hun uh ((*shaking head no*))
> Setting: → Husband: (I thought you had a dress.)

Here the husband first expresses incredulity ("you're kidding") and then adds that he was under the impression that his wife had already owned a dress for the occasion ("I thought you had a dress"). Indeed, it turns out that <u>his</u> mother had previously bought his wife the dress in question.

These composites of positively and negatively valenced events illuminate the potential for positively viewed events to take on negative sentiments over the course of the telling. Thus, in recounting a positive event, one is vulnerable to responses that may deflate as well as enhance one's contented disposition. Indeed, while a teller may relate an experience in an effort to secure a particular response, there is no guarantee that the anticipated or desired response will be forthcoming. The turn-by-turn shaping of the unexpected event in conversational narrative yields unanticipated, sometimes conflicting, sometimes undesirable renderings of events. As such, conversational narrative involves risks as well as opportunities for resolving lived experience.

Legitimizing Expectations

The meaning of an unexpected event rests in large part on the legitimacy of the expectations. Legitimacy is grounded in a number of factors, including the authority and influence of the person holding the expectation, the extent to which the expectation is espoused by members of one's community, and its historical and legal validity. Authority and influence are wielded by narrators and protagonists, who appeal to interlocutors' alignment with institutionalized knowledge and values.

In the pancake story, for example, Mom is narrator and thus in a prime position to establish what is normal in the situation. She is also the more mature of the two protagonists. She uses the setting of the story to establish and evoke background knowledge. First, she introduces an activity scenario: "She was cookin for me." Then she adds: "you know." In so doing, she marks the scenario as familiar and predictable and invites confirmation of this shared knowledge. The narrator then spells out her expectations about the scenario:

Mom: I was makin pancakes
　　　so I figured she wouldn't put nothin in it, you know.
　　　I figured she'd do like I say.

These expectations concern the mother-daughter relationship, in particular the mother's knowledge and control over her child. The narrator uses "figured" and "you know" to frame her expectations as commonplace and invite confirmation.

In her role as narrator, Meg too is in a position to legitimize expectations. She could have rendered her own fearful expectations as entirely reasonable and others' enthusiasm as foolhardy. But she does not. In the setting of the story she casts herself as an emotional deviant. Her "feeling anxious" is contrasted negatively with "everybody's good time." Indeed, she couches her fearful anticipation as a toxic threat that can "ruin" the experience for everyone. She surrenders her own authority as protagonist and narrator to that of what she perceives to be the majority perspective.

Meg legitimizes the expectations of *others* over her own, but a narrator may privilege her *own* expectations and challenge the legitimacy of others' expectations. This dynamic is illustrated in the detention story. Despite asymmetry in age and authority, nine-year-old Lucy espouses the moral superiority of her own expectations over those of her principal concerning what is just punishment for a student's transgression. Lucy and the school principal share the expectation that pulling "Vicky's <u>dress</u> up t'here" constitutes a transgression and that transgressions should be punished. They differ, however, in their expectations concerning the magnitude of an appropriate punishment. Whereas Mrs. Andrews felt one day's detention to be adequate, Lucy feels this is an insufficient followup ("all she did was get a <u>day</u> in de<u>ten</u>tion").

When expectations are breached, we are compelled to evaluate them in light of what transpired. The theme of this chapter is that everyday storytelling is the primary vehicle through which human beings engage in this process. In collaboration with their interlocutors, tellers examine their own and others' expectations about what should or could happen in life. Narrative interaction, in other words, facilitates a philosophy of life and a blueprint for living. We interpret and anticipate experience through narrative engagement.

Breaches of expectation spark a variety of responses not only at the time of the narrated event but also at the time of the telling. One outcome of such narrative deliberation is *reaffirmation of personal or group worldviews*. In the detention story, for example, Lucy and her mother formulate a unified mother-daughter stance, in opposition to the school principal.

The occurrence of a breach may also prompt narrators to *reconfigure* previous expectations. In the detention story, Lucy and her mother reconfigure their view of the principal, in light of their expectations of suitable punishment for a grievous transgression. The principal's conduct leads Lucy and her mother to lower their expectations of her ("I don't think Mrs um Andrews is being fair"). Similarly, in the pancake story, the daughter's improvisations prompt the narrator to reconfigure her expectations of her daughter. Mom reassesses her two-year-old daughter's unexpected actions with a combination of pride ("She's a cooker alright") and exasperation ("[Pancake batter] *Every*wheres").

In some cases, the unexpected experience and the repeated recounting of it can have radical, even devastating effects on one's view of oneself in the world. For Meg, the unexpected onset of severe anxiety during events that ordinary people manage (e.g., visiting Niagara Falls, taking an elevator, reading a book, riding in a car or plane, going on a family vacation, jumping in a swimming pool, attending a friend's graduation) drastically reconfigures her assessment of daily life activities. Any activity she contemplates is viewed as a potential site for an anxiety attack. Indeed, this is how the Niagara Falls narrative continues:

→ Meg: After tha:t? I um the rest of the trip? (0.3 pause) I was afrai-
I did take an elevator a couple of times in our <u>hotel:</u>
(0.3 pause)
(But) I remember when we got to the airport to fly <u>home</u>
after the whole end of our trip?

(0.2 pause)

→   I remember I wouldn't take the elevator at the airport.

(0.3 pause)

I don't know <u>why</u> I'd- I had been in the elevator (0.3 pause)
   at the ho<u>tel?</u> with no real <u>prob</u>lem but

(0.4 pause)

→ Meg: I began then to avoid the elevators that was the [first
   Lisa: [Umhm
→ Meg: you know avoidance right there.

Panic becomes an ever-present threat to her well-being, leading her to avoid numerous activities outside the safety of her home.

Telling stories about unexpected events, modifying expectations to include the future possibility of such ruptures, and reconceptualizing persons, relationships, activities, and moral frameworks in relation to these ruptures are all ways of imposing order on life experience. Even panic experiences become orderly when given referential labels, predictive power, and moral weight.

5

EXPERIENTIAL LOGIC

In Chapter 4, we examined the contours of the unexpected event in everyday narratives of personal experience and the pivotal role of settings in explaining the significance of such events. Even when recounted after the unexpected event, settings can contain information that, paradoxically, anticipates a break in life as usual. In this sense, settings potentially establish the foundations of a narrative's experiential logic, although not all narrators achieve or necessarily desire a seamless unity of experience. An abiding theme of this book is that conversational narrators strive to make sense of life events in light of their desire for both coherence and authenticity of experience, and often the two conflict. In this chapter, we continue to probe the role of anticipation in relation to these two narrative proclivities.

On the one hand, anticipation is the human dynamic that leads protagonists, tellers, and audiences alike to move through a sequence of events and understand why they do so. In society in general and in everyday narrative in particular, each recounted event potentially projects one or more possible next event(s). This future-potential is part of the cultural meaning of events and central to the coherence of narrative, in the sense that the occurrence of one event understandably gives rise to another and an intention understandably leads to behavior directed toward a goal, which may or may not be attained. The capacity of anticipation to yield a unifying storyline is realized through a range of discursive strategies, including foreshadowing and backshadowing, wherein a future is not just implicated but also destined (see Chapter 1). As interpreted by Michael Bernstein and by Gary Morson, these techniques suppress alternative possible futures in favor of a highly linear progression of events that evidences an Aristotelian beginning, middle, and end.[1]

On the other hand, anticipation has an untamed, anxious edge, which can prompt those recounting personal experience to disrupt the orderly logic of past events and voice pangs of concern for what the past means for them at present and for their uncharted future. This interpretation of anticipation is based on Martin Heidegger's phenomenological concept of temporality, wherein a primal human "Care" about death, and thus the future, infuses, organizes, and overwhelms how we remember and re-present the past.[2] In this view, past events become less remote and more intimate when people invest them with a sense of engagement and concern for what lies ahead in the life course. The past is then pulled or "stretched" into the realm of present consciousness, including trepidation about the future. In this sense, the apprehended past still endures, still *is*. This face of human time is quintessentially nonlinear, in that past, present, and future are sensed holistically.

In the sections that follow, we examine how anticipation creates and disrupts a narrated logic of events. We relate anticipation to two related narrative structures: the *temporal sequence*, in which events are arranged along a continuous or discontinuous temporal succession; and the *explanatory sequence*, in which a situated event is seen as bringing about one or more actual or possible effects. Temporal sequences are not necessarily recounted in chronological order; indeed, nonchronological ordering enhances the dramatic quality of a narrative and, in any case, is difficult to achieve when a number of interlocutors contribute bits and pieces of the narrative storyline. Explanatory sequences in everyday personal narratives resemble scientific hypotheses when they not only provide explanations of the lived world but also are open to challenge and revision.[3] They also resemble logical explanations when they interweave events in terms of premises, implications, entailments, and consequences. Scientific and logical explanations, however, tend to be cast as universal, ahistorical laws, while narrative storylines tend to be cast as specific, situated *affordances,* wherein some particular property, condition, or behavior facilitates and makes probable the realization of some other property, condition, or behavior.[4] As the horizontal surface and softness of a mattress affords lying down and a cup handle affords grasping, situated events afford the probability that other specific events will ensue. As noted in Chapter 4, these situation-specific affordances are rooted in individual and cultural expectations. Hence, a protagonist's communication of anxiety affords feelings of others' sympathy and assistance; a protagonist's possible overpayment for daycare affords another protagonist's examination of the bookkeeping records; a student protagonist's racial taunt affords telling the teacher, which in turn affords the teacher's investigation of the incident, and so on. These narrative affordances are based on tellers' and listeners' knowledge of autobiographical and historical precedent and immediate situational contingencies that render a course of events more or less probable.

Temporal Sequence

A basic property of narrative is that it arranges events along a time line. Ruth Berman and Dan Slobin's cross-linguistic observations of narrative competence indicate that children as young as five years old routinely "sequentially chain one utterance to the next, and . . . one event to another."[5] The chronological dimension accounts for the appeal and ubiquity of narrative. As captured by Robert Musil in *Man without Qualities,* narrating lends an irresistible orderliness to otherwise cacophonous human experiences, making "terrible things" part of a temporal flow.[6] The story of Meg's panic experience at Niagara Falls, for example, does not make explicit the *cause* of Meg's avoidance of the elevator that descends to the base of the Falls. Indeed, at the end she acknowledges "I don't know <u>why.</u>" What the narrative *does* provide, however, is a step-by-step account of what happened when.

Time lines are articulated through a range of culturally symbolic forms, especially grammar. To achieve a sense of temporal coherence, tellers use a repertoire of linguistic structures available in their speech communities. These forms are extrinsic to the individual in the sense that they are grounded in society and history. At the same time, they divulge how time is experienced and nuanced by protagonists and tellers. The grammar of time creates and reflects human consciousness of temporal distance, boundaries, and duration, among other qualities. In addition to tense/aspect marking, tellers use grammatical forms such as adverbs, adverbial phrases, and numeric adjectives to situate events at a *point in time:*

    Doug: No you haven't met Chips (.)
→   Chips just came back in June (.)
          He used to be on (field) <u>service</u>[7]

Teacher: One>little boy little girl< came up °to me:
→   (0.2 pause) uh:: yesterday . . .
→   It turned out because they were in first grade together
→   and had a problem two years ago[8]

    Mom: *((looking to Dad))* how old was he Dan?
         when that [happened?
→ Dad: [two
→ Mom: Was he even two?
         (1.0 pause)
→ Oren: Yeah I was two:?[9]

    Algy: I was walking back from Newton Abbot to Ashburton
→   And (.) in the wintertime.[10]

   Stacie: This lady, her baby
         She had um - she had a little girl
         She dressed her little girl up
→   Oh, it was Eastertime.[11]

→Police: So *you* can start telling me a bit what happened that evening
         and what the reason was . . . for what you did
Suspect: Mm. (2.0 pause) Yeah.
         We were going to go down . . . and check out.
         We had heard that there was a party going there then . . . on the
          beach in Norrby.

Police: Mm
Suspect: And so we drove out there.
→   I think, but I don't remember whether it was a Thursday or
           what it was (2.0 pause)
→   I have an idea it was a weekday.[12]

or within *a unit of time:*

   Dennis: You know what my teacher says (.)
               when somebody hasta go to the bathroom (.) Tommy,
                  somebody hasta go to the bathroom?
→ Tommy: You have a half of a half of a half of a second."[13]

   Doug: What other exciting things (happened) at <u>work?</u>
              ((*clears throat*)) Well we've gone through: (.)
→   three presentations in two da:ys.[14]

   Byers: He run with a pack good?
   Moore: Oh yes, oh yes.
→   And he'll stand . . . he'll stand three nights out a week.[15]

or, in relation to temporally *prior, concurrent, or subsequent events:*[16]

→ Oren: and then (.) and then you know what happened? (.)
             I <u>ate</u> that <u>chi</u>li pepper? .hh and Mom thought it was a <u>bean?</u>
             (.) and I <u>ate</u> it?
→   and I <u>burned</u> to death.[17]

→ Meg: And you eventually you eme:rge . . .
→   when I got down there I became claustro<u>pho:bic</u> . . .
→   After tha:t? I um the rest of the trip?
             (0.3 pause)
             I was afrai- . . .
→   that was the first (.) avoidance right there.[18]

→ Nadine: When we were youngsters we elo:ped,
               and were marr[ied in Maryland:,

→   Jim: [Went to Elkton.
     Nadine: to Elkton Maryland,
       Jim: hh
→   Then we got [married in Jamaica,
    Nadine: [The- the <u>se:</u> cond time we had
             all s[orts of (0.1 pause) property and everything
→   Jim: [Then we got married in Saint Pa:t's.[19]

Such structures serve as sign posts, locating and bounding events in time, filtered through the teller's perspective and concerns. As such, these forms are fundamental to developing a narrative logic that tethers the present to what has been and what is yet to come.[20]

Sequencing the Past

We tend to think of personal narratives as encapsulating a *past* life experience: "I got to tell you what happened." Narrators prototypically craft scenes, actions and sentiments as anterior to the present time of the telling. As Livia Polanyi notes, "narratives . . . tell about a series of events which took place at specific unique moments in a unique past time world."[21] Similarly, Charlotte Linde proposes, "The skeleton of any narrative is the sequence of past tense main clauses."[22] Indeed, reference to a time anterior to the present is amply evident in the narratives excerpted throughout this book.

These excerpts affirm that narrators recall and bring to present attention experiences that have transpired. Depending upon local linguistic repertoires, narratives orient to the past through the use of the past tense:

   Oren: Mom thought it **was** a <u>bean?</u> (.)
          and I **ate** it?
          and I **burned** to death[23]

Annette: And <u>Arthur</u> **said** that *you* **said**
          that *I* **was showin' off** just because
          I **had** that <u>bl:ouse</u> on.[24]

as well as historical present tense:

> Meg: She was visiting them
>   and they didn't know that (.3 pause) she was back-
>   in the backyard with the pit <u>bull.</u>
>   And all of a sudden she **yells**
>   "CHARLOTTE! CHARLOTTE! Open this door!"[25]

and adverbials:

> Sam: **The week before I went back** I did 2.5 hours every day revising
>   for my exams[26]

> Mom: (Oh) this <u>chair</u> broke (.) **today**
> Dad: I know
> Mom: <u>No::</u> I mean it <u>rea:lly</u> broke **today**[27]

among other temporal constructions in a narrator's language. These forms cast narrated events as completed some time prior to the present moment of narration.

Sequencing the Instantaneous Present

While an orientation to the past prevails in tellings of personal experience, personal narratives may be grounded in other time zones as well. Tellers may relate an experience occurring in the instantaneous present, for example. According to Randolph Quirk and his colleagues, "the instantaneous present occurs where the verb refers to a single action begun and completed approximately at the moment of speech."[28] The action takes place immediately before a speaker encodes it, but is treated as happening at the moment of telling. Shirley Brice Heath refers to such narratives as *eventcasts.*[29] Sports commentators and coaches rely on present-time narration, as in the following excerpts of sports-announcer talk:

> it **is** LeClair **brushing** on to Hull,
> back to LaPointe to Leetch

it **drops** to Kevin Hatcher,
SHOOTS ONE[30]

Greg _Andrwzick_ set to kick it off (1.5 pause)
They **kick** it deep
Going with the hurry up offensive,
the nose of the ball at the eighteen
(0.5 pause)
First an ten,
three ten to play in the quarter
(1.0 pause)
(Complete) to _Skip Hicks_[31]

This kind of on-line reporting also characterizes certain narratives of personal experience in settings outside athletics. Carolyn Taylor describes just such a present-time narrative told during an American family's dinnertime. In the excerpt below, Derek uses present-tense verbs and adopts a sportscaster speaking style in narrating an unfolding encounter between his younger brother Sammy and his parents:[32]

Derek: Sammy**'s attacking** Daddy? mm . . .
The match **is** _on_ Sammy and Daddy . . .
And Sammy (.) **is** _mad_ . . .
Now he**'s hitting** Mohhmmy . . .

This passage exhibits the characteristic features of a personal narrative in that it articulates a sequence of life events located in a specific time and place and told from a personal perspective.

Sequencing the Unrealized

Narratives depicting life experiences can also be situated in the terrain of the _irrealis,_ that is, the not yet realized. Such narratives may be couched as predictions, expectations, suggestions, orders, and hopes that delineate a series of unrealized life events. For example, sportscasters' narratives of game plays project not only what is happening but also what they anticipate. The football commentaries analyzed by applied linguist Lexie Woods are threaded with such projections:[33]

> McNown
> (1.0 pause)
> on the post
> (1.2 pause)
> **catchable**
> (0.7 pause)
> but incomplete to McE.

In this passage, the broadcaster uses "catchable" to create drama and establish expectations about what could happen in the upcoming play of the game. He then narrates what actually takes place "but incomplete to McE," resolving the dramatic tension of this episode.

Similarly, in the excerpt below, for example, Sally uses the verb "unna" ("going to") and a series of present-tense verbs to suggest a possible scenario for her upcoming birthday party:[34]

Sally: <u>Mommy!</u> I know what **I'm unna do** for my birthday? (.)
    Could we paint our face for our birthday?
Mom: If you want . . .
Sally: *((counting on her fingers as she speaks))*
    Mommy, **paint** our face, number one (.)
    Okay, now. **go** to the park, number two,
    Daddy **has to play** monster, number three,
    U:m: (.) number !FOU:?:r! **go** to miniature <u>golf</u>
    And number five **go** to UCLA pool (.)
    And number <u>SIX?</u> (.) **kiss** Mommy,
    Ha-ha I'm just kidding.

Narratives of unrealized events may cast generic persons in hypothetical scenarios. In the following excerpt, for example, Jon posits a plausible scenario in support of a prior claim that today's world rewards cheating another person:[35]

Jon: **If the lady at the grocery market over<u>pays</u> you** . . .
    <u>you're</u> supposed to think "<u>Hey:</u> that's <u>great</u>"

and walk out the *((laughing))* sto:re
'n "She gave me back (.) .h <u>twenty</u> dollars too <u>much?</u> cuz she
must've thought I gave her a fifty."

In this sequence, Jon establishes a hypothetical scenario ("If"), which specifies a familiar cultural figure ("the lady at the grocery market"), a plausible action ("over<u>pays</u>") and a generic person ("you") who engages in duplicitous actions, deemed consistent with current cultural values.

Similarly, in the following excerpt presented by Shoshana Blum-Kulka, nine-year-old Jordan and his father offer competing versions of what is expected of a halfback on a soccer team in the generic case of a forward aiming to score a goal:[36]

Jordan: Okay (.) **a forward comes down the field.**
He really has to think "I AM ABOUT TO SCORE!
He's really happy
He's going at top speed. You, you know what **you're**
supposed **to do?**
Father: What?
Jordan: **You're supposed to plant a detour for him.**
Father: What do you mean plant a detour?
Jordan: Well **you're supposed to throw yourself in front**
of him and try to knock his, and try to knock the ball away.
Father: **You don't throw yourself, you just try to kick and get**
the ball away from him.
Jordan: **You have to run in front of him and charge at him.**

Drawing on the indefinite article "a" and simple present tense, Jordan first presents a routine hypothetical situation in soccer ("a forward comes down the field"), which he elaborates. Using the indefinite pronoun "you" and the modal "supposed to," Jordan then poses and responds to a rhetorical question concerning what is required of a halfback. When his father presents an alternative account, Jordan becomes more wedded to his hypothetical chain of events: A halfback is not only "supposed to" but "has to" charge at the forward.

It is important to note that a teller may sequence an experience in an *unrealized past* as well as unrealized present and future realms. That is, a teller orders events that could have or should have happened at a time prior to the telling. Such passages often convey a moral stance or heighten the point of the personal narrative.[37] In the following excerpt, Beth recalls how roughly she used to treat her doll, after which her mother proffers a more troubling scenario that might have happened:[38]

> Beth: I'd just get <u>mad</u> at her
> I'd go SHUT UP! BE QUIET!
> And I'd <u>shake</u> her.
> I'd just go BE QUIET! BE QUIET!
> I'd get annoyed with her when company left.
> And I'd just go OOH!
> Mom: I didn't know you had these sadistic tendencies
> . . . I think it was a good thing you had <u>her.</u>
> (0.3 pause)
> **If you had a baby <u>sister</u> or something,**
> **you might have beaten up on <u>her</u> instead.**

Positing hypothetical past scenarios is characteristic of narrative interactions in Euro-American speech communities. Interlocutors often react to accounts of what happened by presenting feared or desired alternatives.

Heath notes that American coaches constantly generate hypothetical past scenarios as preferred alternatives to a player's unsuccessful moves. For example, in the passage below, a baseball coach advises young Randy, who has just missed a fly ball, on how he could have successfully caught the ball and tagged out another baseman:[39]

> Coach: Here again, Randy, the most important thing.
> **If you backed up two steps and**
> **got off the bag,**
> **(then) you could have grabbed that ball**
> **and made the play.**

Irrealis narratives from family dinner conversations resemble hypothetical narratives that transpire in scientific laboratories. Scientific laboratories are not usually perceived as locales for narratives of personal experience. Yet in informal problem-solving deliberations of physicists recorded by Ochs, Gonzales, and Jacoby, the scientists routinely produced hypothetical personal narratives that articulated hypothetical scientific procedures they might undertake and possible outcomes they might expect.[40] For example, in the excerpt below, Miguel, an experimental physicist, portrays for Ron, the lab director, a hypothetical procedure ("if you waited at the temperature (.) T nought minus T D for half a second") and its consequence ("then you're raising also the temperature to T nought"):[41]

Miguel: **What would happen if you waited at the temperature (.) T nought minus T D for half a second.**
Well first of all **you can't**
but **if you were able to** (.) eh:m-
you're waiting for half a second
but then **you're raising also the temperature (.) to T nought and that takes a certain amount of time** (.) almost half a second maybe

Much like the personal narratives presented earlier, Miguel's narrative posits a possible scenario: "What would happen if you waited at the temperature (.) T nought minus T D for half a second." Before unpacking this scenario, he emphasizes that such a scenario can never actually occur: "Well first of all you can't." Again, like the family narratives, Miguel posits an expected or predictable sequence of actions and responses: "you're waiting for half a second but then you're raising also the temperature (.) to T nought and that takes a certain amount of time (.) almost half a second maybe." Throughout this narrative, the protagonist is the generic "you," meaning anyone who engages in the posited activity.

Sequential Meaning

The meaning of a narrated event derives in part from its position in a particular temporal sequence. Event at $time_n$ takes on meaning when it is understood as a precursor of $event_{n+1}$; similarly, $event_{n+1}$ takes on meaning as a follow-up to $event_n$.

$$Event_n \longleftrightarrow Event_{n+1}$$

In Meg's Niagara Falls narrative, for example, the experiences of taking an elevator to the base of the falls and navigating a maze of tunnels accrue meaning when followed by an attack of anxiety. The descent would mean something quite different if followed by a romantic marriage proposal. Similarly, Meg's anxiety accrues meaning in relation to the antecedent experiences of the elevator ride and maze of tunnels. In particular, the anxiety is rendered as a claustrophobic reaction.

$$\text{Event}_n \longleftrightarrow \text{Event}_{n+1} \longleftrightarrow \text{Event}_{n+2}$$

| Elevator | Maze at | Claustrophobic |
| descent | base of falls | attack |

This claustrophobic attack also accrues meaning when the teller foreshadows that it was "first" in a long line of phobic behaviors. The teller arranges specific events to formulate an account of the development of her psychopathology. Specifically, she represents her decision not to take the elevator at the airport as the "first . . . avoidance," foreshadowing a key symptom of agoraphobia:

$$\text{Event}_n \longleftrightarrow \text{Event}_{n+1} \longleftrightarrow \text{Event}_{n+2} \longleftrightarrow \text{Event}_{n+n}$$

| Elevator | Maze at | Claustrophobic | Avoidance |
| descent | base of falls | attack | behaviors |

Like a sound in a melodic phrase and a phrase in a musical score, a narrated event—e.g., not taking an elevator at the airport—is constantly transformed by anticipation. Telling a narrative brings the present and the future to bear on the past.

Tellers do not typically recount a past experience in lock step with the chronological order in which it unfolded. Rather, they tend to shift in nonlinear fashion back and forth in time, recounting a consequent event prior to mentioning its precursors. In some cases, tellers strategically delay disclosure of particular details for dramatic effect. As Erving Goffman noted, a narrative "falls flat if some sort of suspense cannot be maintained."[42] In other cases, the recounting of an event may spontaneously spark a co-teller to mention an earlier event. For example, in the following narrative exchange between Patricia and her husband Dan, Patricia recounts a chronological sequence of events in which she goes shopping with her Mom:[43]

$Event_n$: Patricia: =and then we went to this other um (.)
$Event_{n+1}$:   this dress store? (.)
$Event_{n+1}$:   a:nd my Mom bought me a dress
$Event_{n+2}$:   for the wedding (.) for Pam's wedding.

In this passage, Patricia recounts a temporal progression in which she and her mom "went to this other . . . dress store" ($event_n$), then her mom bought her a dress for Pam's wedding ($event_{n+1}$). At this point, however, Dan expresses his incredulity and refers back to an earlier shopping expedition with his mother for the very same occasion ($event_{n-2}$), after which Patricia notes that her "mother didn't like it" ($event_{n-1}$):

          Dan: you (had) a dress right?
$Event_{n-2}$: Patricia: [your <u>mo</u>ther bought me it.
                   [((slightly nodding yes once))
$Event_{n-1}$:   My mother didn't like it.

Here, as in many interactions, an interlocutor moves the narrative further back in time to incorporate prior relevant information into the current discussion.

Episodes

Putting events in a temporal sequence not only orders them with respect to each other; it creates an overarching interpretive frame. Just as a succession of notes does not necessarily constitute a melodic phrase, so events that are randomly recounted do not make a story. Like notes, the narrated events need to be cast as members of an ordered set. Like a melodic phrase, such a set constitutes a coherent narrative unit called an *episode*.

Episode

$$\ldots \text{Event}_n, \text{Event}_{n+1}, \text{Event}_{n+2} \ldots$$

Episodes have generally been treated as textual units consisting of an articulated chain of events that cohere around a focal character, topic, or goal.[44] More recently, episodes have also been identified in terms of sustained organization of participants in the verbal interaction.[45] In this perspective, episodes are jointly constructed by those involved in the communicative situation. According to Natascha Korlija's useful dissertation on this topic, three dimensions mark the transition from one episode to another in all discourse contexts:[46]

(a) A sequence, i.e. the prior episode, seems to have faded out and . . . the actors start to talk on a different prosodic level . . .,

(b) New referents in new constellations and situations are being introduced, which may mean that episode-internal devices such as pronouns (anaphoric expressions) are not carried on

(c) A new participation structure is developing, i.e. . . . . the actors involved change roles (e.g. initiator, main speaker, main addressee, story protagonist etc.) from the prior chunk of talk to the new one.

Telling and interpreting narrative entails apprehending events as components of a larger episode, rather than as juxtaposed happenings.[47] Consider, for example, the Niagara Falls narrative. Narrative competence—on the part of tellers and listeners alike—requires configuring the recounted events, both actions and feelings, as components of an episode of anxiety that transpired at the base of the falls. As Harvey Sacks puts it, an interlocutor listening to a story "is continually engaged in figuring out what each sentence means, using the prior-so-far and what it looks like it's developing into to do that work."[48]

In this way, organizing events into a narrative episode is a sense-making activity. With fellow interlocutors, we knit actions, thoughts, and feelings into an episode, and weave episodes together into the narrative of our lives. This narrative practice undergirds psychological well-being.

A hallmark feature of debilitating psychological disorders is precisely an inability to make narrative sense out of events, i.e. to piece them together into coherent episodes. As will be discussed in Chapter 6, survivors of trauma often lack narrative access to experience. Mired in a quandary between the desire to organize emotionally significant events and the inability or fear of doing so, they may suffer profound narrative fragmentation.[49] Plagued by flashes of remembered sights, sounds, smells, and other sensations, sufferers struggle to articulate distressing events. As noted by Laub and Auerhahn:[50] "Trauma overwhelms and defeats our capacity to organize it . . . We can only relate to such events as if they had not happened. Knowing them, making sense of them, putting them in the order of things, seems like an insurmountable (yet unavoidable) task." Survivors of trauma, then, have difficulty conceptualizing the traumatic event, much less integrating it with others to form a coherent narrative episode and linking episodes to form an extended narrative sequence.

Narrative sequences may be composed of a single episode or multiple episodes. The Niagara story excerpt, for example, contains:

an episode in which Meg has the jitters prior to taking the elevator
to the base of the falls,
an episode at the base of the falls, in which she "became
claustrophobic," and
an episode in the aftermath of the Niagara experience, in which she
avoids the elevator at the airport and thereafter.

When tellers knit together events into episodes and episodes into larger multiepisodic tales, they are guided by local norms and preferences for constructing narratives. Certain American Indian communities, for example, organize their storytellings around units of two and four. Anthropologists Ron and Suzanne Scollon describe Athapaskan story organization as follows: "The story had two main episodes, plus an initial and final making four sections. Each of the main two episodes was subdivided again in units of two and four."[51] Alternatively, Euro- and Anglo-American written and spoken narratives are typically organized around episodic units of three, as in *Goldilocks and the Three Bears*.[52] Interesting, the Scollons note that when an Athabaskan speaker relates a story in Athabaskan, he renders it in twos and fours, whereas when he relates the story to them in English, he renders it in units of three. The Scollons analyze the shift as the teller's accommodation to Anglo-American listeners, whose feedback parses the story into three segments.

In contrast to the infinite trajectories of mathematical sequences, narratives of personal experience contain a finite number of events and episodes. Yet they have the potential for ongoing augmentation of events and episodes with each telling, with the passage of time, and with the collaborative contributions of other interlocutors who fill in and extend the narrated stream of events.

Explanatory Sequence

Although many scholars consider temporal sequencing to be an important property of narratives of personal experience, some argue that this property is not sufficient to distinguish personal narrative as a genre. In this perspective, personal narratives, especially those that center around an unexpected, problematic event, articulate storylines that *explain* events. In Chapter 4, we considered how narrative settings lay the groundwork for explaining unexpected events. The present discussion examines how linear storylines are constructed when the unexpected event itself is cast as explaining ensuing events and how they may yield to nonlinearity in light of interlocutors' emergent doubts and concerns.

As noted earlier, the explanatory power of the unexpected, problematic event often rests on its potential to bring about, i.e., to *afford*, changes in protagonists' actions and states or in the state of the world. Narrated affordances are not inevitable consequences of problematic events, and as such, contrast with categorical laws, formulae and principles. In personal narratives, the occurrence of an unexpected event sets in motion the *probability* that a subsequent state or action will occur. Affordances infuse the chronic nature of narrated events with a sense of anticipation. As the problematic event is recounted in an unfolding narrative, interlocutors draw upon common sense, personal background knowledge, and the narrative thus far to anticipate the intentions, emotions, physiological states, and/or actions that the event is likely to afford. In so doing, tellers and listeners construct and revise, utterance by utterance, an evolving logic of events.[53]

To illustrate explanation through affordance, we consider non-goal-based and goal-based responses to unexpected, problematic events.[54] In the present discussion, we consider the possibility that a single narrative may manifest both or only one of these responses. As proposed by Jean Mandler and Nancy Johnson, *non-goal-based* responses include changes in a person's psychological or physiological state, unplanned actions, and/or changes in an object's physical state (see Figure 5.1a). *Goal-based* affordances include initiation of a person's *efforts to attain a goal*.[55] As analyzed by Nancy Stein and her colleagues, the story protagonist conceptualizes and executes a *plan* in response to some unexpected, problematic turn of events.[56] Tellers often cast the problematic event as provoking a protagonist's *attempt* to resolve it (see Figure 5.1b). Both kinds of narrative sequence can be extended through the process of recursion, in which a non-goal-based response or a goal-directed attempt itself becomes a problematic event, which then gives rise to further non-goal-based responses or goal-directed attempts and so on (see Figure 5.1c). Integrating non-goal-based and goal-based narrative sequences, we find the following components useful to understanding the logic of events in everyday narratives of personal experience:

Setting: time, location, physical, psychological, and socio-historic conditions, bodies of knowledge and other relevant background information

Unexpected event: unanticipated, usually problematic, incident

Psychological/physiological response: change in person's thoughts, emotions, or somatic state, provoked by unexpected event, unplanned action, attempt, physical response, and/or another psychological/physiological response

Object state change: alteration of the state of an entity in the physical world

Unplanned action: unintended behavior (non-goal-directed)

Attempt: behavior initiated to attain a goal and resolve a problematic unexpected event

Consequence: Repercussion of psychological or physiological response, object state change, unplanned action, or attempt

These narrative components do not exhaust the character of personal narratives, but rather constitute the major building blocks that tellers use to compose storylines. The recounting of temporal-spatial, psychological, or socio-historical settings lays the groundwork for understand-

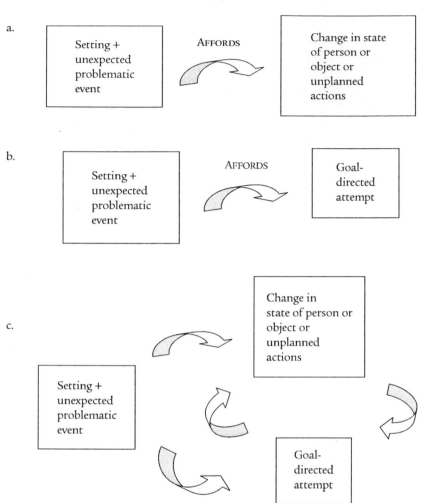

Fig. 5.1. (a) *Non-goal-based affordances;* (b) *goal-based affordances;* (c) *narrative recursion*

ing the unexpected event, which affords a range of responses, including one or more psychological or physiological responses, a change in the state of a physical object, a random action and/or the initiation of one or more planned attempts to handle the event by pursuing a goal. Tellers weave together these narrative components to form more or less coherent logics of experience.[57]

In conversational narratives of personal experience, a logic of events is built collaboratively by a range of interlocutors. In some cases, interlocutors collaboratively *supply* a narrative component, as in the following excerpt in which Jon completes his wife's depiction of the unexpected event:[58]

	Marie: you know what thou:gh (.)
	I started questioning was (.)
Supplies psychological response:	the fact she gave me (.) <u>no no</u>tice. (.)
Supplies unexpected event:	she just called up after the
	accident and said.
Supplies unexpected event:	Jon: Yeah "I'm not coming anymore"

In other cases, co-tellers try to shape the direction of the narrative explanation by eliciting a particular narrative component from conversational partners, as illustrated below:

Elicits setting: Jon: <u>YOU:</u> are over eight or nine are you not? . . .
Elicits setting: Marie: But (.) did you know Susan was <u>here</u>?[59]

Elicits unexpected event:	Tāvō:	*Ke iloa le mea malie Fogoki*
		Do you know the funny thing Fonotī
		lea e kupu iā a'u?
		that happens to me?[60]
	Mom:	Judy Wilson broke her wrist on the
		ski trip
	Dad:	Oh <u>no::</u> ((*leans back in chair, looks at Mom*))
	Mom:	Hm hm hm
Elicits unexpected event:	Dad:	What was she doing?[61]
Elicits psychological response:	Julia:	[But was I actin stupid w[ith them
	Bea:	[Nope, no[62] . . .

These narrative components play a double role: They predicate or evoke thoughts, feelings, and actions of *protagonists* at the time of the recounted incident; yet *tellers* as well insert what *they* think and feel at the present time of the telling, how *they* would have responded in the recounted situation, and/or how they will respond to such situations should they arise in the future. Tellers, for example, commonly recount the past psychological responses of protagonists:

Meg: And we got halfway back to the church and
then I started when I started having

(0.6 pause)

those weird just ph- pure physical anxiety.

Psychological response: I began to feel shaky inside, like a (0.6 pause)
like a (0.5 pause) like a motor was vibrating
inside me.[63]

Psychological response: Male informant: I remember us arguing . . .
I got very upset.[64]

Alternatively, tellers can communicate their *own* current psychological reaction, even when they had no protagonist role in the past recounted incident. A teller's psychological response is depicted in the excerpt below when the interviewer (LE) reacts to the narrative incident (see Chapter 1) recounted by a teacher about a racial incident in her class:[65]

Psychological response (teller): LE: Yeah:: (0.6 pause)
[that's scary (0.4 pause)

Psychological response (protagonist-teller): Teacher: [(((coughing with laughter))

Psychological response (teller): LE: It's scary because then
what do you do?

Psychological response (protagonist-teller): Teacher: Right

It is especially common for co-tellers to contribute psychological responses that show sympathy and otherwise align with one another's point of view on the recounted events, as does the interviewer toward the teacher in this exchange. In this and other ways, tellers interweave their own psychological responses with those assigned to the protagonists.

Given that narrative accounts can embrace tellers' behavior, the logical progression and outcomes of unexpected events can be extended beyond the past to encompass what transpires at the *present* time of the telling, a point that we expand upon in a later section. Here we point out only that events that transpired in the past can afford the onset of present time responses by those participating in the narrative interaction.

We now consider how tellers use narrative components to build a narrative logic in which the initiation of particular actions or changes in a protagonist's or teller's psychological or physiological state or an object's physical state are cast as anticipated responses to an unexpected event. These actions and states make sense, because tellers and listeners understand them in light of the unexpected, problematic event, which renders them reasonable reactions or next moves. We examine first sequential progressions from unexpected, problematic events to *non-goal-based* responses. In the opening portion of the narrative of Judy Wilson's snowboarding accident, cited in Chapter 1, the co-tellers recount a non-goal-based sequence in which an unexpected event gives rise to a protagonist's *physiological response:*[66]

Setting:	Mom:	Judy Wilson was on the ski trip
		and she was uh (0.3 pause)
		I don't know what they call it-
		snowboarding?
	Dad:	Oh [that
Setting:	Mom:	[Or something like that, it's like a surfboard.
		She was standing up on it
Unexpected event:		and she <u>fell</u>
Physiological response (protagonist):		and broke her <u>wrist.</u>

In this passage, Mom draws her interlocutor into depicting the setting, then recounts the central problematic event of this narrative: Judy Wilson fell down while snowboarding. This event primes the listener for the physiological response that follows—that Judy Wilson broke her wrist—in that falls while snowboarding afford the possibility of breaking a bone. The narrative does not evolve into a goal-directed sequence—it does not reveal how the broken wrist was medically handled or other actions taken—but goes on to portray the *co-tellers' psychological response* to the accident:

Psychological response (teller):	Dad:	Yeah those are dan-
Psychological response (teller):	Mom:	And the thing <u>is</u>
		she's supposed to be in this big

Setting:	<u>piano</u> recital or contest in a couple of <u>weeks</u>
Consequence:	and now she can't play the piano in the recital.
Psychological response (teller):	Dad: OH <u>NO!</u> That's too bad.

Non-goal-based sequences may also depict a logical progression of how an unexpectedly problematic event gave rise to a *change in the physical state of an object.* In the excerpt below, for example, Molly recounts to her husband Patrick that a chair split and broke and tries to determine if he was responsible for precipitating the chair's state:[67]

Object state change:	Molly:	(Oh) this <u>chair</u> broke (.) today
Psychological response:	Patrick:	<u>I</u> know
Object state change:	Molly:	<u>No::</u> I mean it <u>rea:</u> [lly broke today
Psychological response:	Patrick:	[I know I know?
Elicits psychological response:	Molly:	Oh you knew that it was split?
Psychological response:	Patrick:	yeah?,
Object state change:	Molly:	The whole wood('s) split?
Object state change (confirmation):	Patrick:	yeah,
Elicits unexpected problematic event:	Molly:	Oh did <u>you</u> do it? (0.4 pause)
Psychological response:	Patrick:	I don't know if I <u>did</u> it [but I saw that it <u>wa:</u> s
Psychological response:	Molly:	[oh
Unexpected problematic event:		yeah I sat <u>down in it</u>
Object state change:		and the whole <u>thing</u> split

The broken chair narrative moves backward in time by first presenting a change in the condition of the chair, then investigating the event that precipitated this state of affairs (see Figure 5.2). The unfolding of the narrative logic behind the broken chair proceeds nonlinearly. The narra-

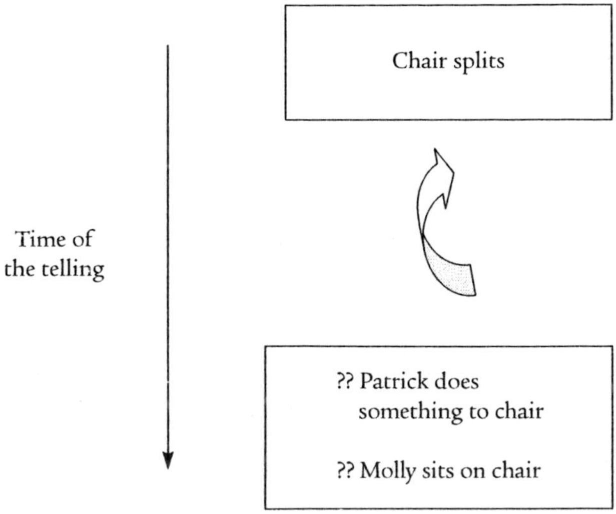

Chair splits

Time of
the telling

?? Patrick does
something to chair

?? Molly sits on chair

Fig. 5.2. Broken chair narrative I

tive takes on characteristics of slow disclosure or what Elinor Ochs, Ruth Smith, and Carolyn Taylor call a "detective story."[68] Slow disclosure is related to both Molly's and husband Patrick's unwillingness to assume ultimate responsibility for breaking the chair. The narrative begins with Molly's announcement that "this chair broke (.) today." When her husband Patrick notes that he is already aware of this fact, Molly upgrades her news to "it rea: [lly broke today." When Patrick again responds that he is aware of this condition, Molly examines the implications of this state of affairs: Effectively, she blames her husband for his knowledge.[69] Once Patrick responds affirmatively to both "Oh you knew that it was split?" and "The whole wood('s) split?," Molly tries to accuse him: "Oh did you do it?"

But Patrick is not willing to take responsibility. Pausing briefly, he replies, "I don't know if I did it [but I saw that it wa: s." Patrick does not actually deny the accusation; instead, he denies knowledge that he "did it." Molly then finally reveals that "I sat down in it and the whole thing split." Like Patrick, she too is not taking responsibility for affording the change of state. In contrast to an utterance such as "I sat down in it and split the whole thing," Molly simply juxtaposes her action and the present condition of the chair but does not cast herself as the agent. The

Unexpected problematic event
+ attempt:

Molly: and the whole <u>thing</u> split
so I—I ti[e:d ((bending over as if to
indicate where on chair))

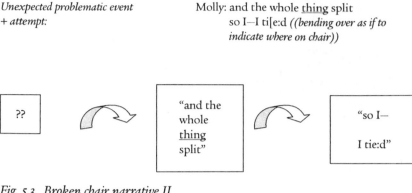

Fig. 5.3. Broken chair narrative II

Attempt:

Patrick: ((somewhat bratty intonation))
That's (a) <u>rea:l</u> <u>si:gn</u>
that you need to go on a <u>di:</u>et.

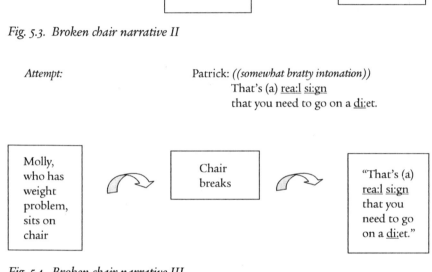

Fig. 5.4. Broken chair narrative III

logic of the narrative is left dangling as to who and what actually broke
the chair.

Eventually, the sequence progresses to recount husband and wife's
goal-directed attempts to resolve the problem of the split chair. That is, the
splitting apart of the chair becomes itself an unexpected problematic
event. Molly's proposal leaves dangling who caused the chair to break
and focuses instead on the split chair as a problem that she capably attempted to repair (Figure 5.3). The attempt to resolve the problem proposed by her husband, however, focuses on Molly, whose weight is cast
as bringing about the chair's condition (Figure 5.4). Patrick's narrative
logic links the broken chair to Molly's weight problem. Ribbing her,
"That's (a) <u>rea:l</u> <u>si:gn</u> that you need to go on a <u>di:</u>et," he indirectly blames

her. In a manner akin to a "whodunnit?" narrative in which each teller points the finger at the other, the story builds dramatic tension through spousal arbitration of what constitutes the event that afforded the chair's splitting apart. Unlike highly linear narratives, however, the narrative concludes with no clear resolution .

The mother-in-law meets pit bull narrative (see Chapter 4) also illustrates how tellers use narrative components to build a goal-oriented progression of events:[70]

Setting:	Meg Joe and Charlotte have a pit bull . . . We got on the subject the other day. I don't know h<u>ow</u> it came out but I was glad I never told him about pet- people who own pit bulls because I might have offended him
Unexpected event:	but he said his mother-in-law got locked out.
Setting:	They have a house? they have a- the door to the backyard locks automatically when it closes behind you?
Psychological response + *unexpected event:*	And and *((laughingly))* she went out in the backyard
Setting:	she was visiting them and they didn't know that (0.3 pause) she was back- in the backyard with the pit<u>bull.</u>
Attempt (that implies *psychological response):*	And all of a sudden she yells "CHARLOTTE! CHARLOTTE! <u>Open this</u> <u>door!</u>"
Psychological response:	*((laughs, covering mouth with hand))*

After providing *setting* details on Joe and Charlotte's pit bull, automatic locking gate, and visiting mother-in-law as well as her own attitude toward pit bulls as pets, the teller presents the *unexpected problem-*

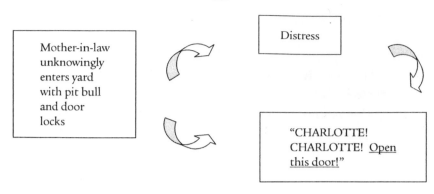

Fig. 5.5. Pit bull narrative

atic event driving the narrative: Ignorant of the pit bull and the gate, the mother-in-law went into the yard and "got locked out." This problematic situation gives rise to the mother-in-law's distress—indexed through her loud, emphatic voice—and her goal-oriented *attempt* to escape the problematic situation by yelling for help in opening the backyard door (Figure 5.5). Meg's own psychological responses infuse her account of the pit bull incident: In recounting the setting, Meg verbalizes her disapproval of pet pit bulls, and her nervous laughter conveys her stance toward the mother-in-law's encounter with Joe and Charlotte's pit bull. In this manner, the process of narrating interweaves present and past consciousness of teller and protagonist.

A Logic for Present and Future

Relatively linear narratives depict a setting that anticipates an unexpected, problematic past event, which in turn anticipates one or more non-goal-directed past responses or goal-directed attempts to resolve the problem. In this manner, tellers establish a set of expectations as to how the narrative will proceed, which in turn establishes a coherent framework for interpreting a past experience. As Meg's side comments and nervous laughter in recounting the pit bull narrative indicate, however, narrative logic can transcend the succession of past events to embrace present and as yet unrealized emotions, thoughts, and actions of protagonists, tellers, and listeners.

Heidegger's philosophy emphasizes that the past is humanized and

authenticated when a person feels the concerns borne in an historical incident.[71] An involved and preoccupied being-in-the-world (*Dasein*)
is the bedrock of human knowledge:[72] "As concerned preoccupation
with the world Dasein lets itself *encounter* its world. Concern as the basic
mode of Dasein permits encounter. In thus letting the world be en-
countered, Dasein *discloses* the world. All knowing, which as a mode of
being of concern is built upon concern, merely *lays out, interprets* the disclosed world and happens on the basis of concern." One way of inhabiting the consciousness of the past is to fathom its implications for current and future life worlds. A past experience, for example, may *reinforce*
a sense of continuity, as, for example, when the Niagara Falls and other
panic narratives foreshadow and establish the teller, Meg, as a veteran
sufferer of agoraphobia. In a narrative about her experience being pregnant, Meg's present condition is a riveting concern that infuses her account:[73]

> Meg: At the time I had anxieties
>   but I hadn't become agoraphobic yet.
>   I had, you, like I said the glimmerings of what was to come, but
>   it wasn't full blown yet.

Alternatively, past incidents may lead tellers and listeners to *rethink* their
perspectives, as when students in a beauty school revise how they will
handle future customers in light of their teacher's (Mrs. Collins) account (see Chapter 1) of the ruined reputation of a hair care professional:[74]

> Mrs. Collins: And she gave me a french twist and she didn't do this
>   and girl you know I ain't going back and I got to sit in
>   the salon so hour . . . ((*narrative continues*))
> Tina: Word of mouth can either make you or break you
> Mrs. Collins: Make you or break you that's way that's right so you
>   need to if don't have but one client
> Lynn: You need to give a:::LL you *got* to that one client . . .

Such narrative exchanges alter what Ricoeur calls one's present "hori-
zon of expectations."[75]

In these temporal meanderings, the past is often cast as a logical warrant for tellers' current and future states and actions. Tellers use past experience, for example, to launch and justify present time practices such as:

Narrating past experience		Present requests

Past   *Present*   *Future*

Osman:

Emre was playing
with the motorcycle
not at all (.) he didn't
give the motorcycle
to us one (.)
he played a lot
with the motorcycle

Request →   **when I wake up early
                                                        today, we will play**

                        is that OK?[76]

Narrating past experience		Present advice

Past, past time   *Present, present time*   *Future, unrealized time*

Mom:

Miss (Graw) said
you cried and cried
at nap time?

Laurie:

[((*nods her head
yes several times*))

Annie:

[she did (.) she
wanted (her) Mama

Mom:
She said that was
because (.) this was
your first day to be at
school? without me:?
(0.6 pause)

        but honey? (.)
        I only work (.)

this (.) it was only this
week that I worked
there all week?
because it was the
first week of school
[but
Annie:
[she cried at three
o'clock too
(0.2 pause)

        Mom:
        but after this? (.)
        It- I only work one
        day a week? there
        and that's Tuesday

Mom:
Laurie? (.) you
didn't take yer
((shaking head no))
blanket to school
either did you.
Laurie:
No I (for)got it
(0.4 pause)
Jimmie:
(you forgot it
at a school)
Laurie:
((nods yes once))

Jimmie:
(you left it at
school?)
Laurie:
((nods yes))
Mom:
No (.) she left it
at <u>home</u>
(1.0 pause)
Roger:
She left it (.) here
today
Advice →

Mom:
We'll hafta get it
out of the closet (.)
and put it over
there with the
<u>lunch</u> stuff
(2.0 pause)
Jimmie:
Yes (.) so you could
bring it [( ) school
Mom:
    [(in the
morning) (.) mhm?
Jimmie:
<u>yeah</u> and you'd
<u>BETTER</u> (.) take care of your (.)
your (.) your (.) <u>blankie</u>

Past	*Present*	*Future*

Bron:
Yesterday I
almost died.
Heather:
No you didn't.

Bron:
Heather, that's
true!
Mom:
Well, tell her

what happened

tell her

what happened, Bron
Bron:
I was choking and
I couldn't br-eathe,
and I hadded to (.)
I hadded to try all the
things to breathe with it,
that was why we got
the jellybean outta
my throat.
Mom:
We were really
worried there,
because she got really (,)
ah, boy, scary
Advice →

Mom:
**You gotta be
careful when you
eat candy, love,
or anything**

Bron got it stuck right
in her windpipe . . .
Bron:
Yes, Yah! I was crying[77]

| Narrating past experience | | Present teasing |

Past   *Present*   *Future*

Dad:

I got to <u>tell</u> you

what they were
advertising in Glenview
(.) on Glenview Boulevard
on the way home

Sean:

((looks at Dad))

Beth:

((looks at Dad))

Mom:

What. *((anxiously))*

Teasing →

                                      Dad:

                                        WE could <u>have</u>
a:: <u>pit</u> <u>bull</u> [and
<u>shepherd</u> and
part <u>rottweiler</u>
puppy

Mom:

*((jerks back away
from Dad))*

                                        Dad:

HA HA HA HA
ha ha ha ha ha

Mom:

Oh yeah[78]

| Narrating past experience | | Present threat |

Past · *Present* · *Future*

Bea:
And Ro*chele* called her
<u>Bald</u>headed right-in-
fronta-her face. She said
"You <u>bald</u>headed
<u>thing.</u>"
because she was messin'
with Rochele . . .

Threat →

Barb:
I better not see
Kerry to<u>day.</u> I'm a
say "Kerry I heard
you was talkin'
'bout me"
Bea:
I a s[ay
Barb:
     [Then she
gonna say

"I ain't- <u>What</u> I say
about you."

I say "Ain't none
yer <u>bu</u>siness

<u>**what you said.**</u> **=**

You come say it in
front of my <u>fa</u>ce

what=you been tell
every-body else."
(0.4 pause)

((*falsetto*)) OO:, and
I can put more and
I'm a put some °bad
words in to<u>day</u>[79]

| Narrating past experience | | Present accusation |

| Past | Present | Future |

Oren:

Did I love it the
ice in?

Mother:

You were <u>cry</u>ing

(0.8 pause)

Oren:

I didn't like it (in there)

Mother:

((*shakes head no*))

you were <u>hurt</u>ing (.)

your mouth hurt (.)

it was burned . . .

Oren:

(I know) . . .

| **YOUR FAULT** | **YOUR FAULT** |
| | ((*pointing at Mom and reaching over until he's touching her cheek with index finger*)) |

Mother:

It <u>was</u> my fault

I thought it was a

um (.) green pep<u>per</u>

Retribution →	((*Oren now pinching both of Mom's cheeks*))
	Mom:
	HHHHH (.)
	((*pulling Oren's hands away*))
	<u>OW</u> that really <u>hurts</u> honey?

Oren:

your fault(.) (I get to do whatever

I want to do once). (that was

my fee?) . . . he he .hh

Mom:

((shakes her head no slightly))

Oren:

hh *((laugh))*

((lolling back in chair to Mom

laughingly))

Just like (it) happened

to me . . . it happens to you'[80]

As some of these excerpts indicate, accounts of the past can unsettle interlocutors' emotional equilibrium at the time of their telling, evoking
anxieties, anger, and *other intense emotions* that otherwise simmer under
the surface of decorum and public presentation of self (Figure 5.6). Co-
narrating the experience of mistakenly eating a chili pepper when a toddler, for example, triggers seven-year-old Oren's anger and aggression
toward his mother for allowing this to have transpired. Similarly, narrating her pregnancy experience of several years past leads Meg to imagine
being pregnant in her present agoraphobic condition:[81]

> Meg: When I think about pregnancy <u>now.</u>
>
> I have a lot more anxieties.
>
> Pregnancy <u>itself</u> is kind of a form of confinement.
>
> You're in it for the *long haul* once you start.
>
> It's <u>irrevocable.</u>?
>
> You can't (.) shouldn't take drugs.
>
> What if?
>
> What if you get high anxiety?
>
> You can't be popping Xanax, you know?
>
> . . . But what if I need some intervention?
>
> My gosh if I were pregnant I'd (.) you know?
>
> You can't (.)

Capps and Ochs suggest that Meg's agoraphobic condition is perpe-
tuated through her tendency to narrate life incidents as actually or po-

Fig. 5.6. *Past as warrant for intense emotions*

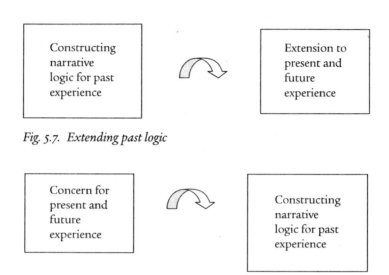

Fig. 5.7. *Extending past logic*

Fig. 5.8. *Concern organizes narrative*

tentially menacing at some past, present, or yet to be defined future time.

The concept of affordance applies in a complex manner to these and other present and future effects of past experience. On the one hand, constructing a narrative logic for some past experience affords co-tellers' extension of that logic to current and future experience (Figure 5.7). As noted, the narrative logic constructed for past events can precipitate present-time thoughts, emotions, and actions. In addition, the ways in which past events are temporally and causally connected through narrative afford the expectation that such events will be similarly connected in the future. That is, the past provides a blueprint for the time to come.

On the other hand, following Heidegger, co-tellers' abiding and overwhelming concern with present and future experience affords how they remember, compose, interpret, and otherwise construct a narrative logic for past experience (Figure 5.8). That is, how co-tellers forge connections among past events is rooted in their preoccupation with their lives at the moment and to come. In some narratives of personal experience, a present concern triggers a return to past experiences. The broken chair narrative, for example, is initiated when Molly examines the kitchen chairs as she sets the table. Similarly, the chili pepper narrative is triggered by the family's preoccupation with a spicy guacamole dip that Mom has prepared for dinner. The following interaction precipitates Oren's initiation of the narrative:[82]

Father: whadid you put in (here/it) (.) chili peppers?

?: heh

Mother: no: ((shaking head no))

Father: what

Mother: uh yeah chili peppers (.) is it very spicy?

Father: no (.) it's not that spicy= . . .

(It's spicy)

Mother: (not a) lot though

Father: (huh)

Mother: (not a lot of it/it had a lot of em)

(2.0 pause)

you wanta know what I put in it?

Father: ((slight raise of head))

Mother: guacamo- I mean avocado. tomatoes. lemon juice. garlic powder?

some hot salsa and chili pepper

Oren: ((as if gasping for breath, facing Mom))

I ate hot salsa and chili?

((Oren pretends to die in his chair))

Mother: ((leaning over to Oren, smiling, as if taking his protest as a joke))

ye:s

(1.0 pause) ((Oren flops back on chair, gasping as if expiring))

uh (.) we lost Oren

(0.4 pause)

[well: he was a great kid.

Narrative of past experience starts here.

Oren: [(Mommy) (.) wasn't it funny? (when (.) wh-)

Wasn't it funny when you (.) thought that thing was a pickle?

and I ate it?

As in the chili pepper incident that transpired when he was a toddler, Oren again does not realize that the guacamole is spicy. When his mother eventually reveals that she used hot salsa and chili peppers, Oren gasps for breath and pretends to die in his chair. It is at this very moment that Oren launches the chili pepper narrative. When Oren twists his mother's cheeks at the end of recounting his earlier chili pepper experience, he may be reacting to multiple sources of distress, spanning multiple time zones. Present experience infuses both the remembered past and the subsequent "j'accuse!" dramatic sequence. Situated in its immediate context, the chili pepper narrative dramatically illuminates how narrative activity brings the present to bear on the past, and uses the past to organize how one thinks, feels, and acts in the present and future.

In the African-American cosmetology school studied by L. Jacobs-Huey, one of the teachers (Ms. Smith) strongly advises her pupils to keep quiet and not spread rumors or gossip when they become hair stylists in the future. Her admonitions lead one of the students (Kayla) to initiate a personal narrative about a past incident that illustrates the point:[83]

Past	Present	Future
		Ms. Smith:
		Okay let's say for
		instance if you
		working in a salon
		and they have things
		that are not so good
		in the salon, it's not
		your point to go tell
		your cousin or your
		clients or point it out
		to certain people
		because most of the
		time, they'll never
		notice it if you don't
		say anything about it.
	You you know it's there	
	because you see it all the	
	time.	

If you have to tell
some-body, you tell it to the
owner, or you
tell it to somebody in charge. But
it's not a good thing to go
spreading rumors about it or to
talk about it to people who ain't
got nothing
to do with it, because
they're (not in it?)

Kayla:
. . . and a lot of
things that I've
learned through
the years from w-

a lots get salons in
trouble is too much
gossip
Ms. Smith:
that's what
I'm talking about.
Things that you . . .

Narrative of past experience starts here:

Kayla:
I mean some people,
this particular lady
where I'm from, they
had to close down
their shop, because
people they had spread
so much different things
about hh the that everybody
stopped coming. And
telling and people got to
telling beauticians they
been (.)

Advice →

Kayla:

**if somebody tell you
something, you don't go
tell everybody and the
next person**
Shayla:
**soon as that person leave,
they** ((*caricatured voice*))
"yap yap yap yap yap"

Kayla:
And they out of business
Right they ain't never got
back in business. The
daughter starts drinking
and the mom, she just
"I don't know."
And they used to have
one of the best, I mean
they used to do a lo::::t
of hair. I mean, you go
in there, you had to
wait for like two or
three hours!

Advice →

Ms. Smith:
**and that's a
sad way to go out
of business too**
((*low volume*))
Kayla:
yep
Ms. Smith:
cause it's going
to make it just that
much harder to come
back.

In this interaction, the present and future are not separate from narratives of past personal experience; rather, they are primary forces shaping how the past is constructed. Like Meg when she recounts her panic experiences mindful of her present diagnosis of agoraphobia and like Mrs. Collins when she tries to alter the future habits of her students through horror stories of past professional blunders, Kayla, with help from Shayla, recounts a past-time narrative about a beauty shop that closed down with an eye to supporting her teacher's present advice. For these co-tellers and others, the practice of narrating life events affords the intertwining of memory and anticipation, yielding a blend of past, present, and future human involvement with the world.

Prototypical narratives of personal experience articulate events in the past that are relevant to both the present and the future. Yet, as many of the above examples illustrate, co-tellers' attention to present and future experience itself can have a narrative logic, wherein ongoing and unrealized events are temporally and/or causally ordered. In these narrative interactions, a past experience is treated not as self-contained and complete but rather as unfinished business that kindles a (re)thinking of possible and anticipated experience in terms of a series of steps or moves. Young Laurie's crying at school, for example, is narrated as a continuing problem that affords a future sequential logic: The family formulates a plan in which Laurie is to bring her blanket to school for solace, and they will put the blanket in a place to ensure they will bring it to school. In this and other narratives, the logical orderliness of future events resembles that imposed upon past time events. In both temporal domains, a problematic event affords one or more non-goal-directed or goal-directed responses. Laurie's mother's absence from school earlier that day, for example, afforded Laurie's crying, which may have been both a psychological response and Laurie's attempt to handle this loss; her crying in turn affords her family's present attempts to alleviate her sense of loss in the coming days (Figure 5.9).

A more specific parallel between past and present experience characterizes the chili pepper narrative. In this case, the link is one of just desserts or "an eye for an eye": Oren's mother caused Oren to experience pain in the past; this in turn provokes Oren to cause (via pinching her cheeks) his mother to experience pain at the present time (see Figure 5.10). A similar parallelism characterizes the narrative of personal experience excerpted below, which is embedded within a toast. Toasts are interesting in that they make explicit the human preoccupation with the future by voicing a desire to control destiny. Many toasts contain sequences of events that are temporally and/or causally ordered to yield a beneficial future for the recipient.[84] The passage that follows is taken

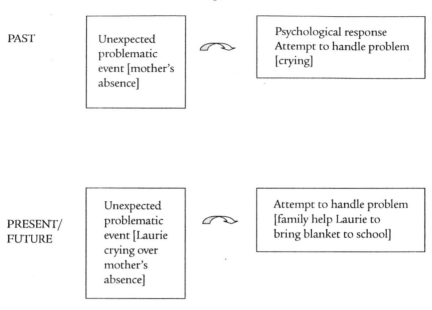

Fig. 5.9. Analysis of Laurie's blanket narrative

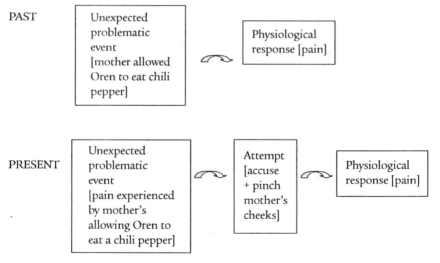

Fig. 5.10. Analysis of chili pepper narrative

from a series of toasts at a Russian family's celebration of the New Year. In toasting her newborn Russian-American grandson Joshua, Tanya first recounts that his mother (her daughter Olga) let her parents sleep when she was a baby:[85]

Tanya: *Ya by Hotela, Djoshik, po russki*
  I would like, Joshua, in Russian

  skazat´ tebe chto tvoya mama
  to tell you that your mommy at

  vtvoyaom vozraste uzhe davala roditelyam pospat´
  your age could already let your parents sleep
Olga: *Djoshik, ona ne pomnit*
  Joshua, she does not remember *((negative headshake))*

After Olga's dismissive interruption, Tanya goes on to posit a parallel future for Joshua:

Tanya: *Da, i poetomu, mozhet byt ti budesh takoy zhe kak tvoya mama*
  Yes, and this is why may you be like your mommy

  I kogda mama budet hotet´ spat´ ti budesh igrat´ tiho I dash´
   ey pospat', da?
  and when she wants to sleep you will play quietly and let her
   sleep, yes?

The parallel structure that links past to present and future can be represented as in Figure 5.11. In these and other ways, narratives of personal experience reckon with the vicissitudes of life and the need for continuity by stretching the implications of life experience across time past, present, and unrealized. Narrative memory is shaped by the ever-present concern for and anticipation of the future. Further, every telling of what transpired before provides a more or less coherent logic that affords an unsettling moment (as in the chili pepper narrative) or affirmation (as in the beauty salon narratives) of one's consciousness of life now and anticipated.

  In this chapter we have proposed that everyday personal narrative is characterized by free-flowing temporal border crossings, in which tellers alternatively reflect back and project forward to build experiential logics. A shift to another temporal dimension can occur at any point in narrating an experience as a nonlinear flashforward or flashback. At its extreme, the shift may occur right at the start of a narrative ("I got to <u>tell</u> you what they were advertising in Glenview (.) on Glenview Boulevard on the way home. WE could <u>have</u> a:: <u>pit</u> <u>bull</u> [and <u>shepherd</u> and

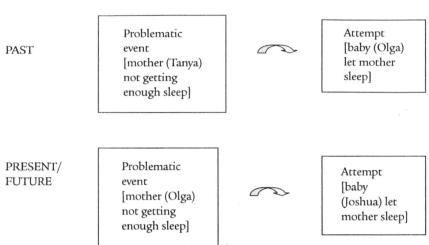

Fig. 5.11. Analysis of Russian toast

part <u>rottweiler</u> puppy"). Such abrupt temporal shifts indicate that tellers may be so eager to communicate the future relevance of a past experience that they may skip recounting that experience and instead leave it to interlocutors to reconstruct from the future-oriented predication. Further, the domains of past, present, and yet-to-be-realized time are not neatly segmented in narratives of personal experience. The analyst can not always delineate a boundary point where, for example, a recounting of previous events terminates and a projection of unrealized events begins. Rather, narratives ebb back and forth across different time zones, as narrators mine the significance of life events. Such temporal elasticity lies at the very heart of personal narrative, in that narrative time is human time, and human time flows back and forth from moments remembered, to the unfolding present, to moments imagined. The implications of an experience may remain unarticulated, out of reach of the analyst's perception, yet pervasively, these temporal extensions are voiced, forming part of the emergent narrative logic.

6

BEYOND FACE VALUE

Chapters 4 and 5 examined how the quest for coherence and authenticity of experience organizes the storylines of personal narratives. Each telling reverberates across past, present, and unrealized time, yielding a more or less integrated logic of personal experience. In this chapter, we examine how particular storylines are influenced by stereotypes and conventional plot configurations of human experience.[1] In an effort to make sense out of what transpired, tellers often view protagonists as tokens of a type and incidents as instances of scenarios that have cultural and historical resonance. This proclivity renders us like Pirandello's characters, who wander in search of an author who can locate them in a plot.

Typically, tellers indirectly invoke a more generic plot structure by drawing an analogy between a narrated experience and similar life incidents. In so doing, tellers cast the particular experience as part of a larger set of familiar circumstances. Prevailing plots and typifications lend coherence and stability to lives-in-the-making, but also jeopardize the authenticity of the unique experience.

The practice of stepping out and above the details of a particular experience and viewing it in light of generic forms and themes is akin to the theory-building activity of working scientists.[2] Consider, for example, the following exchange that takes place in a university physics laboratory. Miguel, a graduate student, has just finished rehearsing a conference presentation, which ran overtime. Ron, his mentor and co-author, advises Miguel on what to omit and what to include:[3]

Ron: And then (.) I don't think it makes any sense to define Hamming
distance. Just don't bother with it.

Cut it out. 'Cause you never use it anyway. . . .

You can't DO it. I mean at twelve minutes.

Miguel: That's what I claimed.

(That)/(And) there was no way I could pack all this material

[( )

→ Ron: [Well I I am trying to cut this down right now so that you ca:n
say something,

'Cause I think not to say something (0.2 pause) means that you
measured d delta dT. Big deal.

Ron's assessment, "Big deal," is one of many that attempt to socialize
Miguel into the rhetoric of science. As a theoretician, Ron prefers the co-
authored presentation to be more than a report of a procedure ("you
measured d delta dT"). The presentation needs to "say something"; an
account of what was measured does not constitute "saying something"
in the world of theoretical physics.

To "say something" in this context is to distill the *significance* of measured changes in atomic spins. A concern with significance—how particular observations relate to general dynamics and models of the world—
pervades the everyday discussions of working scientists. They spend
hours trying to articulate the upshot of ongoing research activity, i.e.,
whether or not their findings support, contradict, or revise other scientific findings and assumptions. Discourse analyst Patrick Gonzales has
analyzed how enthusiasm ebbs and flows in relation to how scientists
perceive the meaning of their research efforts. When they think they
have made a genuine discovery, the interaction looks like this:[4]

→ Ron: This is terribly exciting.

(1.2 pause)

Miguel: (I mean)

Ron: The fact that you get a time ( ) which is not ten day

(0.2 pause)

or ten to the minus fifth seconds

(0.5 pause)

but a time comparable to the crossover time from power law to
stretch exponential

(1.0 pause)

→   I mean that's a <u>very</u> exciting (.) prospect. . . .
        It's in<u>cre</u>dible. This thing gets more and more interesting. . . .
        IN<u>CRE</u>DIBLE that you could pick that ou:t. . . .
        I want to phone up NSF (.) Gary,
        (0.2 pause)
        and tell them that (.) just because you have a theory doesn't
          mean it's right.

Alternatively, when discoveries dissolve into mere *artifacts* of their experimental procedures, the laboratory scientists' bubble of optimism pops.[5] Indeed, Ron is driven nearly to distraction when he realizes two weeks before the conference presentation that what he had thought to be an "INCREDIBLE" discovery in spin glass dynamics now appears to be only the effect of a half-second waiting time before the equipment attains a particular temperature:[6]

  Miguel: I am tending more and more to think
→   that this b over a is purely uhm: (.) experimental artifact.
         (0.2 pause)
         And there's nothing (.) we cannot measurements: <u>C</u>ool faster
           than half a second. (That's: : impossible)
         (4.5 pause)
    Ron: I see
         (0.2 pause)
         What you're saying is that b over a:
         (0.2 pause)
→   oh: dear. That's horrible.

Ron explicitly reformulates the disappointing upshot of what Miguel is saying in terms of "significance":[7]

→   Ron: So this half second then doesn't seem to have any significance.
→ Miguel: Tha<u>:</u>t's the point.

Fathoming the underlying importance of occurrences is crucial to problem-solving in nearly every avenue of human experience—occupational, legal, political, artistic, and recreational. Drawing inferences from texts is also an important *literacy* skill and is central to informal and formal education around the world. According to Shirley Brice Heath, literacy involves not only attending to a text but also interpreting the text in relation to relevant experience or knowledge and, ultimately, using the text or the text and relevant experience or knowledge to create broader understandings.[8]

Heath and other scholars emphasize that literacy is essentially a set of culturally organized practices that are closely linked to oral discourse practices.[9] The dialogue excerpted from physics laboratory meetings, for example, matches the criteria for a literacy event. The physicists are looking at texts that are both spoken (e.g., a conference presentation and informal progress reports) and written (graphs of results printed on overheads or drawn on the blackboard). They juxtapose these texts with what is known in the field and strive to forge a new, general understanding of some phenomenon. In a similar manner, Heath describes how in the African-American working-class community of Trackton, adults read aloud newspapers, instructions, and other documents, which in turn frequently motivates others to recount related experiences and analogies and to eventually construct generalizations concerning the topic at hand.

A good illustration of how text and talk are interwoven comes from Jill Kushner's study of Sephardic Jews' efforts to revitalize Judeo-Spanish language.[10] Language instruction revolves around story texts, which are mined for moral implications and relevance to life. The discussion below is provoked by the story of a poor man who had no food at home, but nonetheless invites a stranger to share a Sabbath meal and returns home to find the kitchen miraculously full of food. Prompted by a question from one of the students, the teacher distills larger meanings of the text:[11]

→ Teacher: It was a sto:ry o::f (1.5 pause) . . . a miracle,
             Because this man went to synagogue,
             He was a good Jew,=
Student 1: =Kon el ayudo del Dio,
             With G-d's help
Teacher: He had no money,
             He had no food in his house,
             But still he went to the right thing. (.)
             He went to the synagogue to pray on Shabbabat.
             Which is, the- the greatest mitzvah that you can do.

Student: Yeah.

Teacher: Shabbat [supersedes <u>all</u> <u>ho</u>lidays.

Student 2:   [It is?

Teacher: Shabbat is (.) the <u>ho</u>liest day of the week.

           [<u>A</u>:ways.

Student 1: [Yeah.

Teacher: And so this man went with a [good <u>heart,</u>

Student 2:   [Better than (.) giving to the

           poor?

Teacher: Yeah Shabbat is the most important day.

           We're suppose [to keep the Sabbath.

Student 2:   [Well I'm cursed.

Teacher: That's right. We all are.

In this prelude to a lengthy discussion, the teacher dwells upon the general principle of observing the Sabbath above all else. Despite challenges from one of the students, this principle is cast as relevant both to the time of story text and to current life ways. ("Shabbat is (.) the <u>ho</u>liest day of the week. <u>A</u>:ways.") Links between text and personal experience are subsequently elaborated in the form of related personal narratives. At one point in the discussion, the teacher inserts:

Teacher: M-my father used to bring home everybody.

And later she recounts a lengthy story that begins:

Teacher: Well (.) don't laugh. (.) . . .

           That happened to one of my <u>aun</u>ties.

           She-she had empty kettles on the <u>stove</u>

           And one of my uncles went by the house,

           It was Friday.

           They had no money.

The teller goes on to depict how the uncle solicited offerings of food from family members and filled the empty pots before the auntie returned home. As Kushner aptly notes, these interpretive forays cast the teacher as moral authority and transform the language lesson into cultural apprenticeship.

A key property of the literacy and scientific practices described above is interpretation that goes beyond the face value of a text. This property also characterizes everyday narrative practice when co-tellers faced with perplexing life events articulate generic templates for understanding them. Like working scientists, everyday tellers apply vernacular models of situations to the particulars of the experience under narration. Similar to interpreters of written texts, they treat the narrated account as a discourse to be mined. Broader implications of the narrated experience are linked, for example, to culture or human nature. This practice is central to narrative, and, in turn, this narrative practice is central to participation in society, lifelong learning, and invention of cultural coding systems.[12]

Plot Structures

In Chapter 5, we examined ways in which *particular* narrative storylines are constructed, but we delayed elucidation of the notion of "plot," because it is linked to *generic* forms of story organization. Plot lies at the heart of Aristotle's concept of narrative as interpretive poetics. A plot links events into a familiar trajectory, including a beginning that sets up the complicating action or dramatic conflict, which unfolds in the middle, and is resolved at the end:[13]

> Clearly, then, the first principle and, as it were, the soul of tragedy is the plot, and second in importance is character . . . Now a thing is a whole if it has a beginning, a middle, and an end. A beginning is that which does not come necessarily after something else, but after which it is natural for another thing to exist or come to be. An end, on the contrary, is that which naturally comes after something else, either as its necessary sequel or as its usual [and hence probable] sequel, but itself has nothing after it. A middle is that which both comes after something else and has another thing following it. A well-constructed plot, therefore, will neither begin at some chance point nor end at some chance point, but will observe the principles here stated.

Similarly, Paul Ricoeur identifies the plot as the thematic connective tissue that binds events into a coherent narrative:[14] "The narrative structure that I have chosen as the most relevant for an investigation of the temporal implications of narrativity is that of the 'plot.' By plot I mean the intelligible whole that governs a succession of events in any story. This provisionary definition immediately shows the plot's connecting function between an event or events and the story. A story is *made out of* events to the extent that plot *makes* events *into* a story." For Aristotle and Ricoeur, plot carries a universalizing message, e.g., the tragic human condition. The power of everyday and literary narrative is rooted in its capacity to rise above the details of specific events to address their philosophical and higher meanings. That is, tellers are not bound to report what happened, but can venture into more general realms by situating what happened in relation to probable and possible plot scenarios.

These scenarios are culturally constituted and serve as guides to understanding what transpired. In the framework of Pierre Bourdieu, plots are part of a community's *habitus*. That is, they are "strategy-generating principles . . . [that] enable agents to cope with unforeseen and ever-changing situations."[15] Historian Hayden White sees plots as *explanations* in that they make events intelligible through familiar schemata.[16] Similarly, Carol Feldman considers plots as *cultural models* that afford communally recognizable interpretations of experience.[17] Medical anthropologists note the healing value of cultural plot lines, which encourage tellers to fashion unfamiliar, sometimes disturbing experiences into prevailing narrative frameworks. As Cheryl Mattingly notes, this process may be assisted by a healer who "tries to connect a person's individual experience to an ideal or preferred narrative, and healing itself is equated with the rhetorical task of persuading the patient to see herself in a certain way."[18] Yet the plotting of psychic interiors on to comforting narrative frames is full of obstacles, not the least of which is the nagging sensation that one's life is more fragmented than the experiential world depicted in cultural stories. In Mattingly's words, "On the one hand, narrative is elevated to the very thing which guarantees us the ability to have a self, at least in the sense of something we perceive as unified and whole. On the other, it turns out to be a kind of trickster, a rhetorical ploy by which we disguise the genuine nature of ourselves—as splintered and discontinuous."[19] In this chapter, we view emplotment as a collaborative, sense-making practice that attempts to reconcile socio-cultural and personal realities.

A number of studies analyze personal narrative in terms of generic plots. Jerome Bruner, for example, extracts from particular autobiographical accounts overarching plot structures: "The larger overall narratives were told in easily recognizable genres—the tale of a victim, a *Bildungsroman*, antihero forms, and *Wanderung* stories, black comedy, and so on."[20] In *Minding the Law*, Anthony Amsterdam and Bruner detail why and how individual incidents are mapped on to legal categories and genres: "For all that we speak disparagingly of consensual categories as 'stereotypes' the familiarity of these stereotypes provides a basis for people's sense of identity as a community, the grounding of their culture . . . They obey the rules laid down by precedent in the law, by the institutionalization of customs, by tradition, or entrenched protocol or immemorial convention—all rooted in some recognizable theory or narrative of government, guild, community, folk, or *who We are*."[21]

In everyday personal narrative, tellers move from the particular to the general when they characterize experiential details in relation to typifications of moral conduct, character traits, life stages, physical conditions, and the like. The typifications often apply to *society as a whole* ("We're living in a culture where . . .") or to a *social group* ("You see what happens, with- specially with New Yorkers," "I guess I do sort of define myself as an agoraphobic"). These stereotypes may be codified in a noun phrase, an assertion, or a longer stretch of discourse, such as a second story. Below we discuss these manifestations.

Consider first how tellers infuse accounts of personal experience with generalizations about society as a whole. In the narrative exchange between Jon and Marie about the meaning of a parent's daycare payment, Marie goes on to tell Jon that this parent (Bev) falsified insurance claims to get cash. As Marie wraps up the story, Jon extracts its more general moral underpinnings in the form of a *summary statement*:[22]

> Marie: and she felt all proud of that (.)
> she was talking about how this secretary had saved the[m
> Jon: [yeah
> Marie: so much mo[ney and ma:de hundreds of dul- dollars? (on it)
> → Jon: [We're living in a culture *((quiet, professorial tone, gesturing with hand))* We're living in a culture whe:re it seems appropri<u>ate</u> (.) a:nd even gr<u>at</u>ifying. (.) to do something and to get something that you weren't supposed to.

Here Jon posits a general trend toward moral decay. The generality is evident in Jon's use of the inclusive "we," impersonal "you," habitual present progressive "(are) living," and durative present tense "seems." In so doing, Jon makes explicit a theoretical framework for understanding and explaining the insurance fraud incident.

Jon does not let the matter rest; rather, he goes on to support his general conclusions with a *hypothetical second story*. Second stories, as noted by Harvey Sacks, are linked by interaction and theme to the telling of prior stories in conversation. They are dialogic in that they extend attention to a previously narrated character or experience. Often the second story confirms that a narrated experience is part of a larger pattern:

> So that though I start with a possible sense of uniqueness I can solve that uniqueness problem by just telling somebody else the story . . . and they will simply come up with one if they have one. And not only will they come up with one if they have one, they will often know one that somebody else has come up with. The consequence of that is the familiar phenomenon of "Until I had this trouble I didn't think anybody had it. When I had it it turned out that lots of people have it." One finds, when something happens to one, that ranges of things you never knew existed exist, and that lots of people turn out to be in exactly the same situation.[23]

The use of second stories in everyday conversational interaction is similar to the use of precedent in legal decision-making. Legal scholar Ronald Dworkin notes that "the doctrine of precedent . . . means the doctrine that decisions of earlier cases sufficiently like a new case should be repeated in the new case."[24] Like judges, co-tellers of personal experience review each account for familiar characteristics and analogies with previous situations that have come into public light and often pass judgment accordingly. Second stories highlight criteria of a first story that lay foundations for categorizing experience. The second story provided by Jon elaborates the overarching moral gloss he has imposed on Marie's account of the fraudulent insurance claim, i.e., a prevailing trend toward moral decay:[25]

> Jon: I mean (.) it's like if the <u>la</u>dy at the grocery market gives <u>you</u> . . .
>   if the lady at the grocery market over<u>pays</u> you . . .
>   something . . . <u>you're</u> supposed to think "<u>Hey:</u> that's <u>great</u>" and
>   walk out the *((laughing))* <u>sto:</u>re
>   'n "She gave me back (.) .h <u>twen</u>ty dollars <u>too much</u>

    cuz she must've thought I gave her a fifty"
Marie: mhm ·
 Jon: you know .h
    and you're not supposed to conside[r yer-
Marie: [mm *((looking away and down*
    toward table))
 Jon: consider whether or not that comes out of her <u>pay</u>
    i[f the drawer doesn't balance at the end of the night .h
Marie: [(I know)
 Jon: or whether it's the ethic (.) <u>right</u> thing to do
    is to say "Hey lady you (.) you: (.) gave [me too much money"

This second story likens cheating insurance companies with cheating "the lady at the grocery market." That is, he implies that both cases involve someone consciously and gleefully obtaining money undeservedly, with total disregard for potential negative impact on innocent others. The second story together with Jon's assertion of rampant moral decline provide a template for interpreting the first story: Both incidents exemplify a pattern of behavior that is undermining the moral fiber of society.

 The tendency to use a second story to interpret a particular experience against a canvas of broad social trends is further exemplified in a sequence of two narratives examined in Chapter 1 that focus on blasphemy. The first depicts a specific incident in which young Beth's math teacher uses the expression, "Oh my God":[26]

 Beth: My math teacher? I don't <u>like</u> her.
    She's always- she'll go
    "I know you're (.) when you look at this math problem,
    you're probably thinking 'Oh my G-O-<u>D</u>' *((brassy tone))*
    (0.4 pause)
 Lisa: Your math teacher [says that?
 Beth: [Yeah, she says it a lot.
    (0.4 pause)
    Or- or when she's upset or something
    she'll go "OH *((grunts))* uh"
 Mom: "Oh God?" *((soft, tentative tone))*
 Beth: She'll go "Oh Go:d" *((scornfully))*
 Mom: Yeah, that's not very (0.6 pause) good.

This prompts Beth's Mom to relate the incident to a more general code of conduct:

Mom: I remember once-
   I don't know where it was, somewhere in my church-going
      experience
   I- (0.2 pause) was told that you should never take-
   to say "Oh my God" unless you're really <u>talking</u> to God.

While the first narrative ends with Mom's assessment, "That's not very (0.6 pause) good," the second provides a more enduring moral template for evaluating the math teacher incident, validating Beth's appraisal, and guiding her future perspective on life: Mom invokes the Church as an authoritative source ("somewhere in my church-going experience I- (0.2 pause) was told . . .") and uses the normative modal "should" and the temporal absolute "never" to articulate a generic moral coding of the math teacher's transgression.

In addition to relating a life incident to patterned ways of thinking, feeling, and acting in society in general, tellers may reach beyond the particulars first by identifying the protagonists as *members of a social group*, then stereotyping the behavior patterns of that group. In a set of radio talk show stories in New York analyzed by Sacks, for example, a blind caller (B) first recounts how people do not give her the right of way, ending with the lament:[27]

   B: . . . In other words, if they see me wih the ca:ne, trav'ling the city
      essetra, hh why do they not give me, the so called right of way.
      Etcetera.

After some repartee, the talk show host (A) responds:

→   A: You see what happens, with- specially with New Yorkers,
      i:s thet they get a::ll precoccupie::d with their own problem::s
   B: [Yes
→   A: [with the::- fallout an' the pollution, en the [b-en the landlord,
   B: [Yeah mm hm.
      Yeah.
→   A: [And they don't-
   B: [( )
   A: Nuh <u>wait</u>aminnit. Lemme finish,

B: Guh 'head

→ A: And they don't <u>no</u>tice (pause)

In this exchange, the talk show host (A) constructs those who ignore the blind caller as typical New Yorkers and then goes on to typify their existential condition. In articulating a set of problematic scenarios that plague New Yorkers, A offers an exculpatory explanation for why New Yorkers act the way they do: their preoccupations blind them to noticing the caller's white cane.

A similar explanatory move is seen in the narratives told by Anaishinaabeg Indians to medical anthropologist Linda Garro. Some tellers attributed their diabetic condition to a categorical difference between the eating habits of one social group, namely "the white man," and those of the Anaishinaabeg community prior to the white man's influence:[28]

> I'll say where **somebody** gets sugar diabetes is the food we eat.
> **Nobody** ate canned food before.
> (pause)
> It's **the white man's** fault.
> **White people** put too much chemicals in the food.
> **Anaishinaabeg** never had sugar diabetes.
> **Nobody** ate canned meat before.
> What **someone** used to eat was salt pork, dried beans and eggs.
> Other things were also eaten.
> **People** would plant their own gardens for the winter.
> Corn was planted for **they** would eat it during the winter
> along with other foods.
> For example, soup was made.
> In the past, **Anaishinaabeg** used to eat cow hocks,
> like the pork hocks **they** have today.
> That's how **someone** used to eat in the past.

The explanatory contrast between the teller's community and that of the white man is sustained in this narrative excerpt through generic pronouns such as "somebody," "nobody," "someone," and "they" as well as categorical terms such as "white man," "white people," "people," and "Anaishinaabeg."

In some narrative interactions, tellers refer to a group stereotype to explain how a protagonist appears as well as acts. In the Italian family narrative interaction below, Rita and her husband Italo have been telling relatives about Rita's first encounter with her future mother-in-law. Rita, who grew up in Rome, accompanied Italo to the village where his parents live. The demeanor of Italo's mother is explained as typical of a village woman of a certain age:[29]

Rita: *sta signora, (pause) la madre, mia suocera.*
This lady, (pause) The mother, my mother-in-law.

(pause) *piccola piccola. secca secca.*
(pause) Little little. Withered withered . . .

→ Italo: *(mbe´) quando l´ha conosciuta c´avra´*
cinquant´ anni
(well) when she met her, she must have been fifty years old

→ *viveva al paese.*
She was living in the village.

Rita: *tutti i capelli stra:ni proprio da de paese*
all stra::nge hair, really village-like *((smirking))*

vestit-
dress-

→ Daria: *da paese proprio*
really village-like

Rita: *si´ vestitino::*
yes little dress::

→ Italo: *c´aveva cinquantaquattr´anni gia´.*
She was fifty-four years old already.

Rita: *m:b- e::: fiorellini co´ ´n collettino*
well- and::: little flowers (on the dress) with a little collar

ma (´na persona) (dico)
but (a person) (I tell you)

→ Italo: *era una donna ormai da parecchi anni viveva al paese*
She was a woman at this point who for many years was living in
the village

Rita: *ma possibile che questa donna ce l´ha con me?*
But is it possible that this woman has something against me?

Daria: *eh infatti,*

yeah exactly,

→ Rita: *proprio la classica donna che vive al paese:*

Really the classic woman who lives in the village:

senza pretese senza niente.

without ambitions, without anything.

Daria: *pero´ pel figlio ce l´aveva,*

However for the son she did have (ambitions),

Rita: *eh.*

yep. *((raising her chin))*

In this narrative excerpt, Rita's mother-in-law is configured in terms of two stereotypes: one related to age (e.g., "She was fifty-four years old already") and the other, more prominent, related to locale (e.g., "Really the classic woman who lives in the village"). These two categorizations provide the organizing principle for the mother-in-law's appearance (e.g., little and withered, wearing a conservative and unstylish dress with a little flower print and a little collar) and mindset ("without ambitions, without anything"). More important, the stereotypes help to explain the future mother-in-law's antipathy toward young Rita by juxtaposing the latter's youth and urbanity with the former's age and village mentality.[30] The typifications also project a framework for interpreting the future mother-in-law's preference that her son marry a local girl whose family makes prosciutto:

Daria: *pero´ pel figlio ce l´aveva,*

However for the son she did have (ambitions),

Rita: *eh.*

yep. *((raising her chin))*

Paula: *pero´ voleva i prosciutti (zi´) eh,*

However she wanted the hams (aunt) huh

Rita: *eh.*

yep. *((nodding))*

→ Paula: *tu cittadina, he: he.*

You city girl. *((laughs))*

In the excerpt above, tellers used two distinctions—*where one lives* and *stage of life*—both to portray protagonists as social personae and to account for their behavior. Cultural scenarios for stages of life, e.g., the "terrible twos," motherhood, retirement, and so on, are often used in everyday personal narratives as explanatory principles for why a particular protagonist thought, felt, or acted in a certain way. A stage-of-life stereotype is invoked in the following narrative interaction among members of an African-American family. In this exchange, analyzed by Marcyliena Morgan, a younger family member (MM) asks three older female relatives to reminisce about their teenage years:[31]

```
    MM:  What (.) what (.) what (.) I MEAN (.) what was teena- being a
         teenager like I mean what was::
    JM:  O:h I was: gor[geous
    BR:                [OH well by that time HO:NEY? her hea:d was SO:
         big
     R:                [O:H my GO:D O:H my GO:D
         (.)
→   MM:                This is the Coca-Cola pha:se?
→   BR:                O::H BABY the whole works
         (.)
         She was the only one
         (.)
→        She ran in the Miss black WHAT ((high pitch)) EV:ER thing they
         was RUNNING in those da:ys
     R:  Sure di:d
```

Here JM's teen years are typified by MM as "the Coca-Cola pha:se." This descriptor casts JM's physique and attitude as emblematic of the curvaceous, sexy Coca-Cola bottle type. In so doing, MM offers a more general rationale for JM's vanity ("her hea:d was SO: big"). MM uses the typification to step out of the narrative, identifying JM's situation as a life "pha:se," a move elaborated in BR's subsequent schematization of JM's beauty pageant competitions "in those da:ys."

Many autobiographical narratives display a plot structure organized around a *turning point* at which a central character undergoes a transformation of identity.[32] Autobiographical narratives of members of the organization Alcohclics Anonymous, for example, conventionally portray a heightened awareness of and change in how they see themselves. The following narrative was recorded by Illkka Arminen in an Alcoholics Anonymous meeting in Finland:[33]

Old self:	.mth I recall some: y- some years ago hh when I got here, to this AA-community and, (1.5 pause) my- I was feeling very stro- uh strongly inferior and (1.0 pause) and er:m uh:h (1.0 pause) I belittled myself and (0.8 pause) I was ashamed of my past and (1.0 pause) my deeds and (1.0 pause) <all these things and> (0.8 pause) I was on that trip
Turning point/ new self:	and (1.6 pause) I noticed that (0.8 pause) .mth these kind- (.) these kind of thought (.) have vanished from my mind (.) quite largely and (2.0 pause) u::h I noticed that maybe I can = that I've become a bit healthier in this respect. (0.5 pause).
New self assessing old self:	hhh I (.hh) n(.hhh)oticed that(,hh)t I've <completely> in vain belittled myself, (1.0 pause) when I was watching the group around, that I've completely <fully> in vain, (1.0 pause) >so< u:h-I-I: >this doesn't mean that I would criticize,<
Turning point/ new self:	>but I believe that I've like < uu:h- in some way myself e:rm (1.0 pause) begun to change, = my wife said today that, (0.3 pause) .mth she agrees with you, (0.3 pause) the-er:m you don't quite trust yourself.

Betsy Rymes examined the turning point plot structure of narratives of urban U.S. adolescents attending a school for former high-school dropouts. In the following excerpt, Gracie recounts to Betsy why she dropped out and why she now attends the present school:[34]

Old self:	Gracie:	Yer: : I was a gang member.
	Betsy:	Uh huh.
	Gracie:	A long time. yer friends, your Surroundings. If you wanna belong to a group you have to show 'em you can prove it.
	Betsy:	Ye[a: : h
	Gracie:	[Peer pressure.
		(0.6 pause)
Turning point/ new self:	Gracie:	And no:w that I c- I regret it?

Betsy: Uh huh,

Gracie: cause now I have to- I wanted to come
back to school because of my son, so,
(0.2 pause)
.hhh if I wanna be a good mom and a
good example. I have to show it to my
son.

This narrative exemplifies a genre Rymes calls the "success story" or alternatively the "dropping in story", i.e., the narrative of the teenage dropout who sees the light, returns to school, and commits to an exemplary life. Rymes contrasts the characteristics of the success genre with those of the genre of dropout narratives:[35]

> While tellers . . . distance themselves from their previous reprehensible actions, they do so by identifying a former self as the perpetrator of those actions . . . In the dropping out narratives, protagonists often portray their actions as perpetrated on behalf of a gang or neighborhood, or to protect younger siblings . . . In the dropping in stories, however, authors describe the abandonment of such loyalties, but . . . typically invoke the voice of children or friends whom tellers say they can best help not by being fellow gang members, but by being responsible to their own future, and, most importantly, by getting an education.

As such, cultural genres support the rejection and formation of identities across the life span.

Tellers may construct coherence across life transformations by portraying the change as *inevitable or anticipated* in some way. Harold Garfinkel describes a person called Agnes who, until adolescence, was considered to be a boy but who reports that she had felt like a girl. She narrates the self in gender categories as follows:[36]

→Agnes: I've always wanted to be a girl;

→ I have always felt like a girl;

→ and I have always been a girl
but a mistaken environment forced the other thing on me.

The transgendered narrator configures the past self as comprising an inner female identity that conflicted with an externally imposed male identity. Eventually this person leaves home and assumes a public female identity (Agnes), undergoing an operation to facilitate this transformation. Garfinkel notes the complexities of distinguishing between what one reports to have felt and believed in the past from what one feels and believes in the present. Was Agnes truly just passing as a boy in her youth? Did she experience any male identity at all? And is her narrated gender identity currently realized?

Sometimes the genre that one uses to portray changes in life experience is drawn from the world of medicine or psychotherapy. Tellers can cast themselves or others, for example, as sufferers of a psychological disorder, and prevailing assumptions about the disorder are recruited to explain a protagonist's behavior.[37] The disorder can define phases of one's life, such that a biography or autobiography is cast as a diagnostic profile. The clinical genre of agoraphobia, for example, permeates the autobiographical narratives of Meg excerpted throughout this volume. Meg charts a trajectory of time-related selves from normality to abnormality. Across a series of narratives, she makes explicit an autobiographical transformation from a past "pre-agoraphobic" to a current "agoraphobic" self. In narrating her first pregnancy, for example, Meg recounts:[38]

> Meg: I didn't worry,
>   and it never <u>occurred</u> to me to be <u>afraid</u>
>   because I was without my car.
>   I mean it was-
> →   <u>I</u> was all very (pause) pre-agoraphobic still.

In this passage, Meg compartmentalizes her past and present modes of being in the world. Narrative accounts of her self in the height of her anxiety are flooded with the label "agoraphobic":

> → Meg: I guess I do sort of define myself as an agoraphobic
>   and I don't ( )
>   uh I look at other people as normal
>   I just feel bad ( ) of what I'm depriving them of
> →   because of my agoraphobia

Many of Meg's narratives about the past foreshadow her current debili-
tated self. For example, Meg wraps up a narrative about an anxiety-rid-
den family ski trip with the insight:

→ Meg: That was the first glimmerings of the agoraphobia
        that I was going to have later down the road.

Capps and Ochs' longitudinal study of this agoraphobic woman and
her family spans several years. In a more recent conversation with Lisa,
Meg recounted her progress in overcoming her agoraphobic symptoms
and identity:[39]

→ Meg: I can't say that I'm (0.3 pause) <u>phobia</u> free,
        but one good thing is that lately I um (0.2 pause) find
        that I don't dwell on, (0.4 pause)
        I don't think of myself, (0.3 pause) first and foremost as an
→   agoraphobic and and . . . when I was really in (0.2 pause) the worst
            throes of this (0.3 pause) disorder,
→   that was really my <u>identity.</u>

In a subsequent narrative, Meg continues to cast the specific events of
her life in terms of her status as an agoraphobic, both in her own and
others' eyes. In her account of the aftermath of a successful trip to see
her dying father, for example, Meg steps outside the particulars to provide her acquaintances' diagnostic appraisals of this experience:[40]

Meg: Anoth- an interesting thing too that's been going on since I got
        <u>ba:ck</u> um (0.2 pause) um you know I've h- had a lot of
        congratulations from people [who knew what a big deal it was
Lisa: [I be:t
Meg: for me to get on a plane and fly home
        and <u>now</u> of course (.) well wishing friends are telling me
        ((enthusiastic voice)) "This is <u>great</u> now you can go on the women's
            retreat out in (0.2 pause) Marriot Springs with us"
→   or "Now (0.2 pause) you should be able to do anything"
        and my sister is saying "<u>Great</u> now you can fly up to Oakland
            and visit me"

Meg then provides her own contrasting diagnostic gloss of the situation:

Meg: and (0.2 pause) they don't realize that yes I <u>did</u> this thing
→ but it doesn't mean that I'm totally over [all my ph<u>o</u>bias
Lisa: [°Mhm mhm
Meg: and (.) and
(0.3 pause)
Lisa: that's tough=
→ Meg: It was almost like a flu:ke (.) or really a (.) act of GOD in my eyes
that I was able to do thi:s in the midst of all that I'm going
through
with my phobias:

Such metacommentary casts experiences within a pathological auto-biographical paradigm. In this paradigm, most ventures remain out of reach of the helpless protagonist, and even successful ones are cast as "flukes" and "acts of God" rather than as goal attainment. Paradoxically, the continual positing of such diagnostic attributions itself is a criterial symptom of agoraphobia. That is, the diagnostic meta-commentary that positions the self as a passive object both reflects and perpetuates the predicament.

These excerpts illustrate how a teller can cast life events as segments in a plot in which different facets of a self prevail: The novice member of Alcoholics Anonymous at first "belittled" himself, then became a psychologically "healthier" person through continued membership in the group. Gracie, the self-described former gang member now casts herself as a student who strives to be a "good mom." And in Meg's narratives, the agoraphobic self at first has the status of a mere "glimmer," then is cast "first and foremost" as a feature of her identity, then becomes less prominent, as Meg begins to overcome the power of this distressing self. Unlike Gracie's self-categorization as successful student and good mom, however, Meg does not articulate a positive identity that is a counterpoint to her psychological disorder. Because its symptoms are so pervasive and lingering, agoraphobia, like chronic depression and many other psychological disorders, undermines the cultivation of alternative potential selves.

Personalizing Cultural Templates

The discussion thus far emphasizes the potentially comforting nature of culturally generated narrative templates. Such templates offer a structure for imbuing personal experiences with conventional meaning and coherence. Yet tellers' attempts to interpret individual experiences in terms of the panoply of available cultural templates yield markedly variable outcomes. Tellers may *hyperpersonalize* a cultural template (a genre or plot structure). That is, the teller may fully absorb a cultural model in rendering individual experience—the "we" becomes "I." Consider, for example, the political aftermath of the autobiography of Nobel Laureate Rigoberta Menchu. Her testimonial of the horrific suffering inflicted on her family and community by the Guatemalan army in *I, Rigoberta Menchu: An Indian Woman in Guatemala*[41] has been contested by anthropologist David Stoll, who pointed out inaccuracies in her story. He claimed that certain atrocities happened, but they did not involve members of Menchu's family.[42] In an interview with a reporter from *El Pais* newspaper, Menchu responded to this challenge:[43]

Reporter: You have been reproached for having taken others' experiences as your own.
 Menchu: ... I can not force you to understand.
→   To me, all that has been the history of my community is my own history.

Menchu's appropriation of other Guatemalans' experiences as her own represents an extreme example of the personalization of collective experience and cultural stories. Rather than losing her individuality through identification with common experience, she makes it her own, as is apparent in the title of her testimony.

Tellers may also *hypopersonalize* a cultural template. They may feel uncomfortable identifying with a social group or its worldview. Unable or unwilling to identify with a cultural model in rendering individual experience, the "I" lacks a communal voice. In contrast to Menchu's seamless alignment with recognized genres of experience, these tellers struggle with existing cultural templates for articulating their life stories. A case in point is the autobiographical account of Adelaide/Abel Barbin's gender transformation that took place in mid-nineteenth-century France.[44] According to Vincent Crapanzano's analysis of Barbin's memoir, Barbin was deemed female at birth and grew up comfortable with the identity of Adelaide. As an adult, Adelaide was medically determined to be anatomically male and forced to assume a new identity as Abel. This gender transformation was inextricably tied to a shift in Barbin's appropriation of cultural genres of narration. In Barbin's memoirs, the life experiences of Adelaide Barbin are narrated in a distinctly conventional feminine genre, but the life experiences of Abel Barbin exist only as narrative shards—disconnected incidents written on slips of paper in no identifiable or orderly style, which appear in the memoirs largely due to the editor's labors. The smooth conventionality of the female life narrative wraps the early lived self in a comforting and unquestioning normative language and worldview. In contrast, the fragments of the written male life reveal the tortuous efforts of a person unable to adopt the gender-specific genre expected of him.[45]

An unwillingness and inability to embrace and personalize the storylines of a specific social group also characterize the relation of some tellers to genres of racial experience. Though born to two Black parents, the well-known journalist Anatole Broyard, for example, "wanted to be a writer, not a black writer."[46] According to Henry Louis Gates, Jr., Broyard endeavored to ignore his Black self to the detriment of his writing career. Indeed, the highly respected Broyard was never able to complete the novel about his father and childhood that he so longed to write, despite a long-standing commission for the work. The authenticity of the novel that would establish him as a truly great writer hinged on his willingness to identify himself as a Black child and a Black man. That is, as a writer Broyard tried to shed his Blackness only to suffer irreversible writer's block.

The predicaments of Barbin and Broyard demonstrate that tellers are faced with a tension between a need to authentically render personal experiences and a need to apprehend them in a manner that aligns with what is familiar and acceptable to others. Eliminating what is unique about a person's experience in favor of wholesale adoption of cultural plotlines is incompatible with what it means to be a vital, questioning human being, as is utter failure to acknowledge established interpretive frames. For the most part, tellers try to reckon lived experience in the balance between these extremes.

One way in which these tensions are played out is through lifelong revision of prevailing interpretive templates. For the most part, tellers are not restricted to a single cultural frame of reference or even to a given set of interpretive frames. Rather, each telling of life events provides an opportunity to revisit and reformulate the status quo. These interpretive options are captured by Arthur Frank in *The Wounded Storyteller.*[47] "Those who try to make sense out of their serious illnesses through narrative can adopt a received medical gloss for their condition, e.g., a 'restitution story' that renders the illness transitory and medicine triumphant. Alternatively, their narrative may take the form of a 'quest story' that: recognizes that the old intactness must be stripped away to prepare for something new."[48] Moreover, Frank notes: "The quest story faces a dual task. The narrative attempts to restore an order that the interruption fragmented, but it must also tell the truth that interruptions will continue. Part of this truth is that the tidy ends are no longer appropriate to the story. A different kind of end—a different purpose—has to be discovered."[49]

The ability to reflect upon the fit between specific life experiences and normative understandings is a hallmark of cognitive maturity. In Chapter 2, we delineated how the development of narrative competence in childhood entails a transition from narrating only scripted routine events to narrating experiences that deviate from these social expectations. Even two-year-old children use personal narrative as a vehicle for calling into question and refining canonical templates that structure daily life.[50] Narrative competence requires the redrafting of stereotypes and other categorizations for apprehending experience. In cases of autism, children have great difficulty differentiating cultural scripts from their own or others' unique experiences, relative to normally developing children. Their personal narratives tend not to provide details of the situated events, and discrepancies between a lived experience and cultural expectations are rarely articulated and used as a basis for reflecting upon and modifying canonical models.

For the majority of tellers, narrative activity both reinforces expected and preferred situational frameworks and makes salient enigmatic events that elude readily accessible interpretive frames.[51] Not only children but also adults as they traverse their life course are confronted with an ever-changing environment, rife with opportunities and demands for distilling new templates for thinking, feeling, and acting in the world. Personal narrative provides a mechanism for grappling with and organizing such experiences. Like scientists discerning whether an observation is an experimental artifact or a true discovery, tellers consider whether a set of events is ephemeral, a mere blip on the experiential record, or whether it represents, like the fall of the Berlin Wall, a sea change. Personal narrative is ubiquitous because of its interpretive elasticity: With the help of conversational partners, tellers can configure the point of an experience on several planes, from relating it to analogous situations, to reiterating familiar interpretations, to generating novel hypotheses and conclusions.

We conclude this discussion with the notion that going beyond face value in everyday narratives requires acts of imagination—the transformation of experience into images.[52] Telling a narrative entails envisioning, to some degree, the interpretive grids that listeners will apply to the narrated experience. As the narrative unfolds, interlocutors' contributions fuel and revise the imagined construals of events. This dialectic process is akin to that depicted by the protagonist in Italo Calvino's novel *If on a Winter's Night a Traveler,* who concludes, "The mirror walls reflect on my image an infinite number of times."[53] Applied to conversational narrative, participants' imaginings reflect and refract each other's visions of life experience.

It is through acts of imagination that tellers cast particular sensations, thoughts, actions, and circumstances in terms of cultural categorizations ready at hand. Thus, in the Italian city-girl story, when co-tellers portray the future mother-in-law, they reflect on her image as the stereotypical "classic woman who lives in the village." Similarly, when a co-teller portrays the math teacher who swears, she configures her image in terms of the blasphemous sinner. Likewise, Meg imagines herself as an agoraphobic and her actions as diagnostic of this condition. Tellers who recount turning-point experiences cast themselves in transition from one cultural image to another, e.g., the high school dropout to the good mom, the despairing alcoholic to the recovering member of Alcoholics Anonymous. These imaginings stand in stark contrast to the more fragmented forays of tellers such as Barbin and Broyard, who can not fully imagine themselves in a designated cultural frame of reference. For yet other tellers, the act of imagining is driven by the belief that new interpretive frames that resonate with experience will emerge from the narrative quest. In these varied ways, acts of imagination laminate the particular and the general, transporting the telling and the tellers beyond the information given.

7

Narrative as Theology

An enduring theme of this volume is that everyday narrative activity offers a forum for grappling with the meaning of unexpected, often problematic life events. Narrating allows co-tellers to distill the details and logic of a particular experience and to reflect upon the implications of the experience for the future. As such, a narrative of personal experience does much more than codify a remembered past; it anticipates life's continuing dramas. The present chapter explores the notion that narrative activity draws interlocutors into probing moral dimensions of human experience. In shaping their accounts, co-tellers not only give temporal and causal order to events, they also evaluate events from a moral perspective. Once a person's comportment is incorporated into narrative, it is portrayed in relation to standards of right and wrong and is vulnerable to public moral accountability. As philosopher Alasdair MacIntyre notes:[1] "Asking you what you did and why, saying what I did and why, pondering the differences between your account of what I did and my account of what I did, and vice versa, these are essential constituents of all but the very simplest and barest of narratives." For some, the search for moral meaning involves matching personal experience to traditional ethical canons. For others, narrative activity depicts moral dilemmas whose contours are obscure and whose solutions are not readily at hand. In both contexts, the moral shaping of a particular lived experience helps co-tellers to understand how they should conduct themselves in similar circumstances in the future. In this manner, everyday narrative activity offers moral guidelines for overcoming obstacles and achieving goodness for oneself and one's community.[2]

These properties lend a spiritual quality to everyday narrative activity. In this chapter, we relate narrative interactions that lead co-tellers to weigh the moral goodness of acts, thoughts, and feelings to the activity of praying. We first suggest that prayer has properties of personal narrative in that personal narratives may appear in a prayer that seeks divine assistance with some baffling, distressing, or otherwise unusual life experience. In these cases, the genres of prayer and narrative organize each other. We then propose that ordinary narratives of personal experience have prayer-like properties, in that tellers often solicit the support of others in coping with uncertain life events and discerning standards of goodness to pursue.

Narrative in Prayer

At Sunday school five-year-old Susan tries to wrest a ceramic crucifix away from her classmate Dana:[3]

    Susan: I was playing with it before you came.
    Dana: It's my turn.
    Susan: Just a minute.
    Dana: ((begins to cry))

Their teacher, Terry, walks over to where the girls are squabbling and places a hand on Dana's shoulder:

    Terry: Dana is sad.
    Susan: But it's still my turn.
    Terry: Do you want to say why you're sad?
    Susan: [WHY?
    Dana: [No. ((soft, almost inaudible voice))

Following Dana's unwillingness to articulate the source of her sadness, Terry invites the girls to join her in a prayer:

    Terry: Let's say a prayer.
            Dear, sweet Jesus,

We miss Dana's Nanna.
She was a strong and wonderful woman,
and she is very special to us.
We know that you are taking good care of her,
and we're thankful that she is in Heaven with You. Amen.
Dana: Amen.

Terry's prayer serves both to soothe Dana and to inform Susan of the recent death of Dana's grandmother (Nanna). Terry's prayer provides an account of past and present circumstances, including expected emotions surrounding them. In this sense, the prayer is a form of narrative.

Terry's prayer manifests central properties of narrative activity: (1) securing attention of (co-present and godly) recipients through prefaces and summons, (2) providing a setting, (3) introducing a reportable, often problematic, event, (4) articulating consequent events/circumstances and psychological responses, and (5) closing with a coda. These properties are delineated below:

Preface: Let's say a prayer.
Summons: Dear, sweet Jesus,
Psychological
response
(problem) to
implied past
event: We miss Dana's Nanna
Setting: She was a strong and wonderful woman, and she is very special to us.
Psychological
responses plus
present events/
circumstances: We know that you are taking good care of her
(Solution): and we're thankful that she is in Heaven with You.
Coda: Amen. Amen.

The parallels between narrating and praying become more explicit in the subsequent exchange between Susan and Terry. Following the prayer about Dana's Nanna, Susan first recounts a conversational narrative about her own relatives' deaths and then reformulates it as a prayer narrative:

Psychological responses (problem) to implied/stated past events:	Susan:	I'm sad because I miss my great-grandmother, and my great-grandfather, and my great-great-grandmother and my great-great-grandfather. They died before I was even born,
Psychological response (problem):		and I really miss them
Proposal for future event (solution)/preface:		Let's say a prayer.
Response to preface:	Terry:	Would you like to?
Summons:	Susan:	Dear Heavenly Father,
Psychological response (problem) to implied/stated past events:		I miss my great-grandmother and my great-grandfather, and my great-great-grandmother and my great-great-grandfather
Psychological responses to past events:		I'm sad because they died before I was even born, and I really miss them. It's really sad when people die before I was born. The saddest.
Coda:		Amen

As codified above, Susan's prayer reproduces the structural features of her conversational narrative. Positioned as it is, however, the prayer narrative is more than an echo; it is initiated in an attempt to resolve the distressing emotions detailed in her conversational narrative. As such, the entire sequence constitutes a narrative plan. Susan's prayerful solution ("Let's say a prayer") emulates her teacher's response to Dana's sadness ("Let's say a prayer").

Both Terry's and Susan's prayers recount personal experiences of loss. Terry's rendering presupposes the event of death, while Susan states it explicitly ("they died before I was even born"). Both link a present problematic emotional event—missing a loved one, feeling sad—with an antecedent event. Susan goes on to extrapolate a more general emotional principle from her experience ("It's really sad when people die before I was born. The saddest.") For both Terry and Susan, praying itself is a mode of handling distressing events.[4] Terry, in addition, constructs a prayer that contains an antidote to distress. She responds to the problematic event of mourning a death by predicating a consequent circumstance in which Jesus is protecting Dana's Nanna in Heaven. Terry's prayer narrative locates the departed loved one in a desirable place and assuages loss and sadness with certainty ("We know that . . ."), security ("you are taking good care of her"), and thankfulness.

Participation in Prayer

Prayer is a form of communication in which there is a conscious and active attempt to enter into dialogue with a higher power.[5] As described by William James, in its ideal form:[6] "Prayer is religion in act . . . no vain exercise of words, no mere repetition of certain sacred formulae, but the very movement itself of the soul, putting itself in a personal relation of contact with the mysterious power." James illustrates this ideal with the following excerpt from a Christian's diary:[7] "God is more real to me than any thought or thing or person . . . I talk to him as to a companion in prayer and praise, and our communion is delightful." In praying, one attempts to reach beyond oneself to enter into the presence of the divine—whether it be nature or a deity. Many experience a profound sense of unification:[8] "I felt that I prayed as I had never prayed before and knew now what prayer really is: to return from the solitude of individuation into the consciousness of unity with all that is." Prayer helps to bring about a sense that one is not alone, that one has accessed a higher power, and that one's voice is being heard.

This model of prayer presumes a dialogic relation between the individual who prays and the higher power to whom the prayer is directed (see Figure 7.1a). However, this model does not account for the social nature of many prayers. As we have seen, people often pray in the company of others. In these situations, the interaction is multiparty rather than strictly dyadic (see Figure 7.1b). Most prayers communicate some kind of problem. Praying allows the problem to be aired and shared with those present as well as with the divine. When praying is communal, as in church and family gatherings, participants provide support for each other through their presence and their prayerful contributions. Terry's prayer, for example, is directed at both Jesus and Dana. Terry conveys

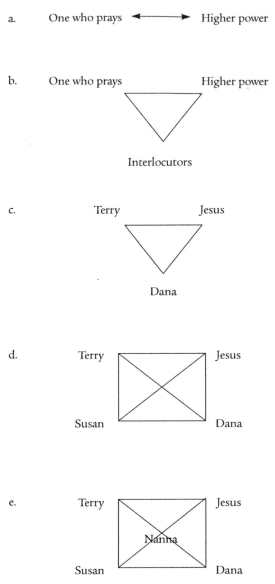

Fig. 7.1. *Dyadic and multiparty frameworks of prayer*

her compassion for Dana by inviting and affirming Jesus's active involvement in Dana's and her Nanna's lives (Figure 7.1c). But the arena of participation is broader still, for Terry's prayer also attempts to draw Susan into a similar supportive stance and worldview about the meaning of death (Figure 7.1d). We might also consider Dana's Nanna to be a participant in this prayerful union, as an object of concern and an evoked presence (Figure 7.1e). Through prayer, those present, prayed for, and prayed to are brought together. In the case here, it serves to remediate the distance between Dana and her beloved Nanna as well as between Dana and her peers. As such, the activity of praying itself is restorative.

Forms of Prayer

While giving voice to personal problems, prayers usually request divine assistance. Petition is one form of prayer.[9] When the petition concerns oneself, the prayer may take the form of a *direct petition,* as in the following prayer initiated by five-year-old Jesse in the presence of his Sunday school teacher:[10]

Jesse: Dear God,
           Please help my Mommy to come live with us.
           She doesn't live with us any more and I want her to.
Terry: That's hard, isn't it.
Jesse: I want her to come back and live with us
           because she should live with Daddy and me.
Terry: Do you want to talk to God some more, Jesse?
Jesse: Oh yeah.
           Amen.

Once again prayer and narrative blend into one another. Jesse's petition to God ("Dear God, Please help . . .") narrates a desired future event (". . . my Mommy to come live with us") and an antecedent problematic circumstance ("She doesn't live with us any more and I want her to"). Terry responds to this plea to God, offering her own consolation about the recounted predicament ("That's hard, isn't it"). In this move, she brings the sequence of problematic past and desired future events from an interchange with God into the realm of ordinary conversational narrative. Through her commentary and request for affirmation, she becomes a co-author of the narrative. In response to her query, Jesse reformulates the prayed-for future event ("I want her to come back and live with us") and provides a moral justification ("because she should live with Daddy and me"). Rather than continuing the narrative at this profane level, however, Terry invites Jesse to redirect his thoughts and concerns to God ("Do you want to talk to God some more, Jesse?"). Jesse seems to interpret this invitation as an admonition that he has left his prayer unfinished ("Oh yeah") and hastily provides the appropriate closing ("Amen").

In addition to petitioning directly for oneself, people petition on behalf of others. Terry's prayer can be seen as an *intercession* on behalf of both Dana and her Nanna. Similarly, the following excerpt from a dinner grace articulates an intercession on behalf of a family friend:[11]

> Beth: And Lord
> We pray for Rick Hansen.
> And we pray that you be with him
> and help him to heal quickly in the hospital.
> Help him to get over his condition.

Like direct petitions, intercessions often weave together implied or stated past, present, and future events, imbuing them with positive sentiments.

Prayers can also express *praise and thanksgiving*, as in the following family dinner graces:

GRACE #1 [12]

> Father: In the name of the Father and of the Son
> and of the Holy Spirit
> (0.6 pause)
> Thank you Lord for the gifts
> that we are about to receive from Thy heavenly bounty. (.) May
> they not bring us condemnation Lord
> but help us to eternal life.
> We ask this in Jesus' name.
> and we ask that this food be blessed. in the name of the Father
> the Son and the Holy Spirit
> Amen
>
> Mother: Amen
> (0.2 pause)
>
> Dick: Amen

GRACE #2 [13]

> Mother: Dear Jehovah our father (.)
> We thank you for this food (.)

Thank you for the nice day we had today
We went to the park with all of our friends (.)
We thank you for the beautiful creations
that we have to enjoy (.)
Please help us to (.) show love to one another . . .
This we pray in Jesus name
Amen

GRACE #3[14]

Laurie: I wanna pray *((clasps hands))* . . .
Jesus?

Mother: [Wait a minute Laurie
[((irritated, throwing arms up in semi-despair))
I'm not sitting down *((sits down))*

Laurie: 'kay (.) Jesus? (.) please (.) um (.) help us to love and .hh um
(.) Thank you for letting it be a n:ice day and for taking a fun
nap? hh (.) a:nd (.) for (letting) Mommy go bye and I'm glad
that I cwied to[day? cuz I [like cwying .hh and

Annie: [((snicker))

Roger: [((snicker))

Laurie: I'm glad (that anything/everything) happened today
in Jesus name *((claps hands))* A:-MEN!

Roger: [amen *((clapping lightly))*

Mother: [amen

Jimmy: [A:MEN

Like other forms, these three mealtime prayers flow across time, linking
present events and feelings (e.g., "We thank you for this food") to past
(e.g., "we went to the park with all of our friends," "for letting it be a
n:ice day and for taking a fun nap? hh (.) a:nd (.) for (letting) Mommy go
bye") and/or projected imminent ("that we are about to receive from
Thy heavenly bounty") and distal ("May they not bring us condemna-
tion Lord but help us to eternal life") scenarios.

People often combine various forms of prayer. For example, Terry's
prayer is both an intercession and an expression of thanksgiving.
Similarly, Grace #1 combines a petition with thanksgiving. All three of
these forms are combined in the following prayer activity during a
Sunday school class. Four-year-old Rosie and her twin brother Adam

dash into the classroom breathless. Rosie quickly kneels, clasps her hands in prayer position, bows her head, closes her eyes and begins:[15]

> Rosie: Jesus,
>   help me <u>not</u> to be like my brother Adam
>   and take other people's turn in the front of the car.
>   Thank you that <u>I'm</u> not mean like him.
>   Amen.

Rosie's prayer combines petition and thanksgiving. Further, although directed to "Jesus," it is designed to be overheard by her teacher and classmates, as well as her brother.

Rosie's prayer provokes an immediate retort from Adam, followed by a similarly spirited counter-prayer of thanksgiving for one and all to hear:

> Adam: No fair! Take it back!
>   Jesus
>   thank you for not believing <u>anything</u> Rosie says
>   because she's a big liar.

At this point, the teacher, Terry, intervenes. She instructs Rosie and Adam and the other children to display appropriate prayer decorum, reminding them to use reverent voices when addressing God in the Atrium (their classroom):

> Terry: When we talk to God in the Atrium,
>   we use our quiet, Atrium voices
>   (0.8 pause)

Terry then models the appropriate voice and content of prayer:

> Terry: Dear Lord,
>   Please help us all get along, together.
>   We are sorry when we fight.
>   And thank you for our brothers and sisters.
>   Amen.

Terry's prayer combines intercession ("Please help us all get along, together"), confession ("We are sorry when we fight"), and thanksgiving ("thank you for our brothers and sisters") to convert sibling rivalry into mutual appreciation.

The combining of different prayer forms produces complex narratives that portray the unfolding of events over time. Petitions and intercessions project desired future outcomes of troubling past and current events. Praise and thanksgiving can feature past, current, or unrealized events. And while confessions focus on past transgressions, they imply a change of state underway.

Inflecting Narrative for Prayer

When narratives are expressed in the form of prayer, they are inflected with the register features that distinguish praying from other activities. These features include kinesic and linguistic markers that vary across communities, situations, and persons. For example, the prayer narratives cited in this chapter involve bodily postures such as kneeling, folding hands, bowing heads, and closing eyes. Linguistic features of these prayers include:

> reverent voice quality (e.g., "We use our quiet Atrium voices");
> honorific titles for deities (e.g., "Sweet Jesus," "Heavenly Father," "Lord," "Jehovah our father");
> archaic/formal lexicon (e.g., "Thy," "bounty") and syntax (e.g., "May they not bring us condemnation Lord");
> formulaic expressions (e.g., "In the name of the Father and the Son and the Holy Spirit," "in Jesus name," "Amen"), and
> appropriate predicates for petitioning, interceding, praising, giving thanks, and confessing sins among other acts.

Children's prayers often violate expectations concerning appropriate demeanor, delivery, and content. For example, in Grace #3 above, five-year-old Laurie violates expectations concerning the *positioning* of family members and the *timing* of grace.[16] She starts to say the grace before her mother sits down at the dinner table, for which she is reprimanded ("Wait a minute Laurie. I'm not sitting down"). Similarly, in Sunday school class, Rosie and Adam are chided for using inappropriate *voice quality* in praying ("When we talk to God in the Atrium, we use our quiet, Atrium voices"). Rosie and Adam are also admonished for their *dispositions,* in particular for using the discourse of humble petition and thanksgiving to condemn and shame their sibling.

Children have difficulty maintaining the genre requirements of prayer. In the midst of praying they may, for example, shift into conversational narrative. In the excerpt below, David, who is two years, nine months old, intertwines the two genres in the course of constructing a bedtime prayer with his father:[17]

Prayer:	Father:	Should we say our prayers?
	David:	Ummm: <u>Okay.</u>
	Father:	De::ar God.
		Bless Mo::mmy,
	David:	and Daddy,
	Father:	and <u>David.</u>
	David:	and Gra::nny, and <u>Veronica,</u>
		and Kira, and Sonya,
		(0.4 pause) and <u>O::H</u> <u>don't</u> forget <u>RUBY</u>
		(0.3 pause) and <u>Raymond,</u>
		and Ellie::, and Sandro
		and <u>crazy</u> Ma::rco
		and my <u>BIG truck</u>
		and my little trucks and (0.2 pause)
Conversational narrative:		<u>OH</u> do you? Do you? Do you
		remember when Sandro said
		when Sandro said,
		"Hello David?
		You bring my <u>little</u> trucks over <u>there</u>"
		And I DID
		Can we play <u>that</u> game?
		<u>Can</u> we?
Prayer:	Father:	and God Bless Bop and Nanna,
	David:	and Uncle Todd,
Conversational narrative:	Father:	and Aunty Molly and Uncle Pete,
	David:	and do you know what Uncle Pete's
		other name is?
		"MY FRIEND UNCLE PETE!"

'Member when Uncle Pete
came to my <u>home?</u>
But I don't think Spike and Nate
((N.B. Uncle Pete's dogs)) are coming, <u>no.</u>
No I don't <u>think</u> so.

Prayer: Father: God bless Spike and Nate.

Conversational narrative: David: But I play <u>basketball</u>
and I say "Spike and Nate
YOU <u>DON'T</u> PLAY!
YOU STAY <u>THERE.</u>"
How about we put
Spike and Nate in the basement.

Father: Yea::h, I remember that.
Spike and Nate are <u>big</u> dogs
aren't they.

David: But I <u>think,</u> they're not <u>coming.</u>

Father: When Uncle Pete comes on Saturday?
Yeah he probably won't bring Spike
and Nate.
Yeah.

David: Yeah.
Daddy can you tell a story about
what David did today?

Father: Okay,

Prayer: are we done with our prayer?

David: AMEN! AMEN! AMEN!

As David itemizes persons and objects to bless, he bursts into mini-narratives that he associates with them. Each of the blessed entities holds for him a store of memories and emotions, which he wants to share. His petition to bless "Sandro and <u>crazy</u> Ma::rco and my <u>BIG truck</u> and my little trucks" touches off an invitation to "remember . . . when Sandro said, 'Hello David? You bring my <u>little</u> trucks over <u>there.</u>' And I DID." These pride-infused remembered events in turn touch off a desired continuation of these events in the future: "Can we play <u>that</u> game? <u>Can</u> we?" Similarly, David's father's petition to bless "Aunty Molly and Uncle Pete" inspires David's recollection that "Uncle Pete's other name is . . . 'MY FRIEND UNCLE PETE'" and the events that transpired "when Uncle Pete came to my <u>home</u>" with his dogs Spike and Nate. In David's account, happy and worrisome past events intermingle with projected events ("But I don't think Spike and Nate are coming," "How about we put Spike and Nate in the basement"). David seems to use prayer to sort out what the past holds for his future.

In this bedtime interaction, David's father scaffolds extensively the activity of saying the bedtime prayer: He launches the activity by inviting David to "say our prayers," provides the opening prayer frame ("De::ar God. Bless Mo::mmy"), supplements the list of persons to bless ("and <u>David</u>," "and Aunty Molly and Uncle Pete,"), models intonation and voice quality, and redirects David's forays into conversational narrative back to prayer-inflected discourse ("and God bless Bop and Nanna," "God bless Spike and Nate," "are we done with our prayer?"). In these ways, David's father socializes David into the discourse of praying.

Children's prayers also display discrepancies between the explicit performative function of a prayer and its message content. As noted above, there are a number of functional varieties of prayer; for example, petitions, intercessions, praise and thanksgiving, and confessions. These functions are often codified through predicates such as "Help me/us," "I/We pray for . . .," "Thank you," and "Forgive me/us." Among adults, the content of prayer is typically consonant with these functions. Thus, petitions and intercessions solicit support for a future desired circumstance (e.g., "help us to eternal life"; prayers of praise and thanksgiving acknowledge the source of a desirable circumstance ("We thank you for the beautiful creations"); and confessions reveal transgressions. Young children have difficulty meeting these felicity conditions when their prayers stray from highly formulaic discourse to recount particular, personal situations.

Such inconsistency between ostensible function and content characterizes young Laurie's prayer in Grace #3 above. At first, Laurie adheres to conventional expectations concerning grace:[18]

Laurie: 'kay (.) Jesus? (.) please (.) um (.) help us to love and .hh um
(.) Thank you for letting it be a <u>n:ice</u> day and for taking a fun
nap?

This portion of the grace displays generic features of prayer: invocation of God ("Jesus?"), petition for assistance ("please (.) um (.) help us to love") and thanksgiving ("Thank you for letting it be a n:ice day and for taking a fun nap?). Folded into the prayer is a compressed narrative about Laurie's day at kindergarten, cast as a positive experience ("ni:ce day" "fun nap") resulting from God's munificence ("Thank you"). As in other cases, the prayer and narrative interpenetrate: Narrative emerges through and is inflected for prayer, and prayer takes on the features of personal narrative.

Laurie's prayer then takes a subtle turn:

Laurie: hh (.) a:nd (.) for (letting) Mommy go bye and I'm glad
              that I cwied to[day? cuz I [like cwying .hh and

Annie: [((snicker))

Roger: [((snicker))

Laurie: I'm glad (that anything/everything) happened today
              in Jesus name ((claps hands)) A:-MEN!

Roger: [amen ((clapping lightly))

Mother: [amen

Jimmy: [A:MEN

Although Laurie continues to frame her experience as positive ("I'm glad"), the recounted events themselves ("Mommy go bye," "I cwied today") appear at odds with these feelings. Indeed, the utterances "I'm glad that I cwied today" and "I like cwying" seem emotional oxymorons, in that crying following departure of a loved one usually signals distress.[19] Whereas Laurie's earlier narration of happy events fits well with the design features of thanksgiving, the evolving problem-centered narrative clashes. The unburdening of troubles is tucked into the discourse of gratitude, rather than linked to Laurie's earlier, truncated petition to "please . . . help us to love." Perhaps it is this misfit that provokes her older siblings, Annie and Roger, to snicker while Laurie says grace.

Beyond these structural inconsistencies, there is more to fathom in Laurie's grace. Laurie seems to use the moment in which the family gathers for grace to articulate and cope with a significant experience in her life that day—Laurie's mother did not stay with her at kindergarten, then Laurie cried. Grace assists Laurie in several ways. First, in electing to say grace ("I wanna pray"), Laurie gains an opportunity to garner the attention of not only Jesus but also family members seated around the table. Among families who eat together, dinner is usually the first opportunity of the day to communicate with one another for a sustained period of time. For these families, dinnertime provides a setting for recounting the day's events, making plans, and problem-solving more generally.[20] Produced in the opening portion of the meal, grace offers a privileged spot for introducing events of concern. When Laurie couches her account of what transpired at kindergarten in the grace, she manages to get these events aired before other family members recount their narratives. Further, grace offers the added caché of pre-empting all other bids to take over the floor, an advantage of particular import in Laurie's family, where four children compete for parental and each other's attention. Family members saying grace silence others. A short time after grace is over, the family turns to Laurie's kindergarten experience. They talk about her crying ("Miss (Graw) said you cried and cried at nap time?"), the reason why she cried ("She said it was because - this was your first day to be at school without me"), and how she can comfort herself in the days to come ("We'll have to get [your blanket] out of the closet - and put it over there with the lunch stuff").

Yet another advantage of grace is that it provides a conventional moral framework for Laurie to formulate her understanding of the day's events and herself. Through grace, Laurie projects a model self, one who is loving and grateful despite adverse circumstances. She is putting her best face forward, giving a happy gloss ("Thank you for letting it be a ni:ce day") to a time of woe. Grace in this sense offers a moral code for living. In adopting this code, Laurie tries to create a positive public self-image.[21] As Vincent Crapanzano aptly notes, however, code-use brings disadvantages as well as advantages:[22] "Dialogue . . . is never dyadic; for even when only two are conversing, they are always making reference to—struggling with—a third, that authority-giving function that governs the conventions of dialogue . . . And though we, coming from as individualistic a society as we do, condemn that conformity . . . we must, I think, recognize the sometimes desperate desire to succumb to an already warranted narrative of the self."

The awkward discrepancy between the genre of grace and Laurie's experience lays bare the potential pain of forcing one's self to conform to a genre. Laurie's unpolished pairings of a conventional grace frame "Thank you for" with "letting Mommy go bye," and its associated sentiment "I'm glad that" with "I cwied today" captures the potential absurdities of cultural practices that transpose personally upsetting experiences into positive ones. Like a traditional war memorial that attempts to substitute feelings of pride for the pain of loss, the genre is an emotionally valenced collective representation of the past.[23]

A more practiced grace sayer would likely select an unambiguously desirable circumstance for which to give thanks. In this way, the requirements of the genre filter which experiences are put into words. Alternatively, a practiced grace sayer would articulate the positive aspect of the painful experience, e.g., "Thank for helping me to be strong and letting me say goodbye to Mommy" or "I'm glad that I cried today, because afterwards I felt better." Such paraphrases are more semantically cogent and contextually appropriate than Laurie's prayer but may undercut emotional authenticity. In this sense, the conventions of genre can distance the interlocutor from the experience he or she is trying to communicate.

Narrative as Prayer

What can we learn from how children pray? When children fail to use prayerful voices, display irreverent demeanor, shift fluidly between prayer and conversation, and utter situationally inappropriate prayer discourse, they indicate that the line between the sacred and the secular is difficult to maintain. Prayer is a home for narrative just as conversation is. Both are venues for relating and sorting out the significance of experience. Narrative can be inflected for sacred or secular settings, but the genres intermingle when one oscillates between the more formulaic language of prayer and ordinary discourse. The rituals of prayer often give way as generic messages transition into more detailed tellings of lived experience and as the emotional impact of talking about life experiences overwhelms adherence to conventions of genre.

The sacred and the secular also come together at the level of social interaction. As exemplified throughout this chapter, praying can be a communal activity. The prayers at mealtime, bedtime, and church events examined here are directed at not only higher powers but also those congregated. The prayers we have examined in this chapter are not produced in a foreign language or "in tongues" but in a code that is accessible to others in the surround. Those praying also monitor their voice quality and other aspects of their demeanor to conform to social norms. Others present are sometimes referenced through body posture, gaze, and words (as when a daughter turns to her father to remind him of the family obligation to intercede on behalf of a church member); and sometimes others present contribute components of the prayer underway (as when father and son construct a bedtime prayer.)

We have emphasized how aspects of conversational narrative characterize the activity of praying. But the inverse is also worth contemplating: How might aspects of prayer characterize the activity of narrating experience in conversation? Erving Goffman wrote extensively on the sacred quality of everyday social interactions.[24] For Goffman, social encounters are rituals in which participants display varying degrees and kinds of deference to the self-image each puts forth: "It is therefore important to see that the self is in part a ceremonial thing, a sacred object which must be treated with proper ritual care and in turn must be presented in a proper light to others."[25] From our perspective, the prayer-like character of everyday narrative typifies the sacred in the commonplace. To pray is to enter into dialogue with a higher power and strive for communion, in an effort to align with what is right and good and to understand one's position in the universe. We have seen throughout this chapter how prayer and conversation flow into each other: One begins to pray and ends up recounting a personal narrative, or one recounts personal events then is moved to reformulate them as prayer.

We take this relation one step further by envisioning conversational narrative as an extension of prayer. A key commonality between praying and narrating with others is that both activities involve a quest for moral clarity and legitimacy. Conversational narratives are never simply informative; they are always imbued with moral meanings. Through conversational interaction, co-narrators build a moral perspective on life events. As Charles Taylor notes, narratives orient people to standards of what is good and right: "Thus making sense of my present action, when we are not dealing with . . . the issue of my place relative to the good, requires a narrative understanding of my life, a sense of what I have become which can only be given in a story. And as I project my life forward and endorse the existing direction or give it a new one, I project a future story, not just a state of the momentary future but a bent for my whole life to come."[26] What constitutes the moral high ground may be treated as pre-determined, or this terrain may be worked out as part of the narrative process.

We are not suggesting that when people initiate a conversational narrative, they enter directly into dialogue with the divine. Rather, we propose that narrative activity—whether in prayer or conversation—always invokes a higher good, and in so doing, engages with a cosmic point of reference (Figure 7.2). The moral perspective arrived at is part of a larger paradigm revisited each time a narrative is told. This ongoing engagement with a higher good is captured in the following diary entry, cited in William James' *Varieties of Religious Experience.*[27] In this passage, the writer treats this moral force as a conversational partner:

> [F]or although I had ceased my childish prayers to God, and never prayed to *It* in a formal manner, my more recent experience shows me to have been in a relation to *It* which practically was the same thing as prayer. Whenever I had any trouble, especially when I had conflict with other people, either domestically or in the way of business, or when I was depressed in spirits or anxious about affairs, I now recognize that I used to fall back for support upon this curious relation I felt myself to be in to this fundamental cosmical *It*. *It* was on my side, or I was on *Its* side, however you please to term it, in the particular trouble, and it always strengthened me and seemed to give me endless vitality to feel its underlying and supporting presence.

The diarist portrays *It* as a companion and point of reference amid his "domestic" and "business" interactions with other people. The *It* is an unseen ally, as he navigates challenging relationships and events.

Just as prayer has the potential to restore a sense of moral equilibrium, so too does conversational narrative, which is also value-laden. Like prayer, conversational narrative can be a solace, an opportunity to unburden oneself. For better or for worse, narrative provides a conventional, albeit looser frame for sorting out personal experience. Just as a Sunday school teacher uses prayer to configure events of import to children, interlocutors rely upon narrative to configure daily life experience. In praying, people appeal to an omniscient divinity and to those assembled; in collaborative storytelling, people appeal to one another and attempt to align with a greater good.

These prayer-like properties of ordinary narrative are evident in the interaction between David and his father as their bedtime prayer winds down. Recall that just before his prayer ends, David asks his father to recount the events of David's day:[28]

Higher good

Co-narrator   Co-narrator

Fig. 7.2. Higher good in narrative

David: Daddy can you tell a story about
        what David did today?
Father: Okay,
        are we done with our prayer?
David: AMEN! AMEN! AMEN!

That David solicits this telling in the context of an unfinished bedtime prayer signals a close affiliation between praying and storytelling. David himself has been chafing under the confines of the "God bless . . ." format of bedtime prayer to elaborate on his past and projected experiences. Throughout the prayer, he initiates animated recollections:

RECOLLECTION #1[29]

David: OH do you? Do you? Do you
        remember when Sandro said
        when Sandro said,
        "Hello David?
        You bring my little trucks over there"
        And I DID
        Can we play that game?
        Can we?

RECOLLECTION #2[30]

David: 'Member when Uncle Pete
        came to my home?
        But I don't think Spike and Nate
        ((N.B. Uncle Pete's dogs)) are coming, no.
        No I don't think so. . . .

> But I play <u>basketball</u>
> and I say "Spike and Nate
> YOU <u>DON'T</u> PLAY!
> YOU STAY <u>THERE.</u>"
> How about we put
> Spike and Nate in the basement.

David imbues these accounts with moral weight and invites his father's validation. In asking his father to remember these events with him, David seeks affirmation that they occurred and that his past, present, and future comportment is morally correct. In this way, David positions not only God but also his father as adjudicators of his thoughts and actions (Figure 7.3).[31] In a similar spirit, David asks his father to recount David's day. It is as if David wishes to hear a coherent version of himself—the life of David on this day—before he shuts his eyes for the night. This request is in keeping with other ritual practices designed to ease the passage from wakefulness to sleep and from being with loved ones to separation.[32] Initiated in the closing moments of prayer, David may also expect the story to be overheard by God, who has been called to bless loved ones.

David's request is striking in that his father has not been with him during most of the day. More commonly, people forward the right to tell a narrative about themselves to someone who is knowledgeable about the narrated events.[33] Designating his father as primary narrator of David's day allows David to relive it with him under his protective wing. Protection comes both in the form of fatherhood and in the narrative schema David's father provides for assembling and evaluating the disparate elements of David's day. In particular, the emergent narrative 1) configures David's day as a sequence of largely predictable events and 2) positions the family protagonists in a spatial constellation that predictably shifts over time during David's day. This map of the day and David's spatial relation to loved ones is highlighted in boldface in the narrative below:

Waking up: Father: Today **David** slept in **his bed,**
                            until the <u>sun,</u> came up!
                            <u>Just</u> (0.2 pause) like (0.2 pause)
                            you're going to do <u>tonight.</u>

God

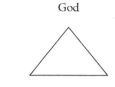

David   David's father

Fig. 7.3. Secular and sacred voices in prayer

Cuddling with Mommy:		And when the sun was up
		He went ***down stairs***
		and he cuddled **with Mommy.**
	David:	Umhm. But **where's Mommy?**
	Father:	She's **downstairs.** And **where was Daddy** when you were cuddling With Mommy?
	David:	**Daddy** was at **work!**
Getting treats at Fat Apples:	Father:	and then **David and Mommy** went *to?*
	David:	**FAT APPLES!** . . .
Throwing rocks and sticks in the rose garden:	Father:	
		And then what did **David and Mommy** do?
	David:	Go to the **roses** and throw rocks and sticks, and one went <u>ALL</u> the way <u>under</u> the bridge. . . .
Playing with Veronica (babysitter):		
	Father:	And then who came?
	David:	GRANNY!
	Father:	No:::,
	David:	VERONICA!
	Father:	Veronica loves David. And then **Veronica and David** played and played. **Where** did Veronica and David play?
	David:	**At my home and at Veronica's**

house. . . .

Mommy and Daddy come	
home:	Father: And <u>then</u> what?
	David: And then **Mommy came back,**
	and then **Daddy came back.**
	And Daddy said,
	"**<u>Where's</u> <u>my</u> David?**"
Mommy and Daddy and	
David eat and play:	Father: And then **Mommy and David and**
	Daddy ate our supper and played
	with Thomas *((a toy train))*
David goes to bed:	and <u>now</u> **David's** going to **bed!**

The collaboratively produced narrative functions much like some of the prayers we have previously examined. It resembles the Sunday school teacher's prayer on behalf of Dana's departed Nanna in that both identify loved ones and chart the paths their lives have taken and will continue to follow in the future. The Sunday school teacher plots a comforting path in which Dana's Nanna joins Jesus in Heaven (Figure 7.4a). Similarly, David and his father plot a circular path in which David experiences a series of separations and reunions, beginning and ending with David in bed (Figure 7.4b).

That David is anxious about this calendar of separations and re-unions is indicated throughout the narrative interaction. When his father recounts how "when the sun was up he went downstairs and he cuddled with Mommy," David immediately asks about the present whereabouts of his mother:

→David: Umhm. But where's Mommy?
Father: She's downstairs.

In addition, even though David recounts that "Daddy was at <u>work!</u>," and even though he and his father recount that David and his mother went to Fat Apples for their morning treat, David goes on to include his father in the Fat Apples episode:

→Father: and then David and Mommy went *to?*

a.

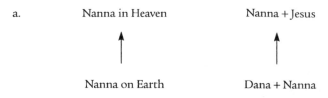

b.

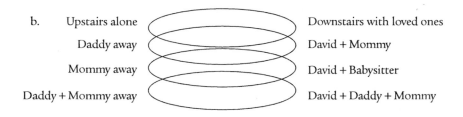

Fig. 7.4. Charting life paths through (a) prayer, and (b) everyday narrative.

→David: FAT APPLES!
  Father: And what did David have?
  David: a dog cookie because I don't <u>like</u> the flower cookie, no.
      And I say, "Can I have a <u>sticker?</u>"
      And the lady said "yeah,"
      But she didn't give me a <u>big</u> sticker.
  Father: She gave you a little sticker?
  David: Umhm.
  Father: And what did <u>Mommy</u> have?
→David: And Mommy had a <u>cranberry</u> scone, <u>two</u> <u>cranberry</u> scones and
      <u>Daddy</u> had a bl<u>ue</u>berry.
  Father: Those are my favorite.

When the narrative reaches the point when the babysitter Veronica arrives, David tries to narrate that "Granny" came, holding on to family ties. And when he recounts the return home of his parents, David narrates his father as searching for him:

  Father: And <u>then</u> what?
  David: And then Mommy came back,

and then Daddy came back.

→ And Daddy said,

"Where's my David?"

Father: And then Mommy and David and
Daddy ate our supper and played
with Thomas.

At each point David's father offers a reassuring response: He (1) locates the current whereabouts of Mommy; (2) affirms David's knowledge that blueberry scones are Daddy's "favorite," while at the same time maintaining David and Mommy as the two narrative protagonists of morning activities; (3) affirms that the babysitter "loves David" in response to David's wanting Granny's if not his parents' affection; (4) responds to the need to rejoin "my David" by reuniting "Mommy and David and Daddy" for the duration of the day up to this point.

David is not the only child to lapse into narrative before falling asleep at night as a means of sorting out remembered and anticipated experiences. In Katherine Nelson's *Narratives from the Crib*, she analyzes a 15-month span of bedtime narratives of a toddler named Emily, beginning at 21 months of age.[34] Emily recounted these narratives after her parents conversed with her and put her to bed. Sometimes Emily would go over events that happened, paraphrasing earlier co-narration with her family about these events. She would then use her remembered understandings of the past to figure out what to expect in the future.

Nelson emphasizes bedtime narrative problem-solving as a vehicle for Emily to build generic understandings of how events proceed. Ordinary narration helps children to construct schemata of life experiences:[35] "Thus by this age [28 months] she is taking her parents' talk as the basis for constructing a picture of future events, but building into that picture logical inferences based on her own prior knowledge of how things are . . . This passage also suggests that she finds it satisfying to construct and elaborate a coherent account of how things are, based on various sources of information—her own experience, parental input, and logical inference." These bedtime narratives allowed Emily to work through anxieties, especially concerns about separation from her loved ones. As noted by Carol Feldman:[36] "In these narratives, Emily's principal purpose is to formulate more clearly a disturbingly unclear idea. They pose a puzzle at the beginning (often as a statement beginning 'I don't know,' or as a contradiction.) Often, then, there is a series of statements beginning with *but, maybe, because* that have the pattern of logical reasoning. They often end with Emily's resolving the disturbing puzzle for herself." Emily and David's narrative activity suggests that the struggle to create a coherent life story begins early in life, before two years of age. Almost as soon as language emerges, children use symbolic representation to recount and cope with unsettling events and build a moral framework for living. Their early narrations alone and with others are laced with views and anxieties about what is right and good.

In this manner, vernacular narrative, like prayer, responds to uncertainties and offers guidance about what one should expect in the course of life with others. While they do not usually make explicit their petitions for help and blessing in times of trouble or articulate thanksgiving for positive experiences, interlocutors engaged in conversational narrative seek similar ends as those who pray. Both prayer and ordinary narrative provide a more or less generic format for distilling meaning out of chaotic events and for reconciling the conflict between conventional expectations and idiosyncratic experience. We can think of ordinary narrative as secularized prayer, that is, as an opportunity for even the nonreligious to actively work out a *situational theology*. This theology applies to the particular recounted experience and builds an existential paradigm that is vulnerable to modification over time.

The paths that prayer and everyday narrative chart are strewn with notations of cultural sanctions and virtues: The Sunday school teacher conveys that being in Heaven with Jesus is good through giving thanks for this outcome; Emily invokes a soothing moral correctness when she recounts "and Emmy and Daddy and Mommy have go sleep,"[37] and David's father conveys approval when narrating "Today David slept in his bed, until the <u>sun</u>, came up" and optimistically forecasting that this event will be repeated this very night: "<u>just</u> (0.2 pause) like (0.2 pause) you're going to do <u>tonight.</u>" These evaluations define protagonists and narrators as persons whose actions have moral weight. As such, conversational narrative joins prayer in offering an opportunity to assess and build moral character and position the self in a cosmic order.

8

UNTOLD STORIES

Writing home from the frontlines of World War II, Nick Martin withheld details of the risks he faced. A letter to his mother, dated 2 May 1945, recounts:[1] "I think I told you we have been flying supplies to the front in Germany. A couple weeks ago we were flying back from Germany, and as we crossed the Rhine our wing hit a barrage balloon cable. It took a hunk out of our wing, but we landed safely in Holland." Intended to soothe, this account glosses over crucial details of Martin's brush with death. Twenty-four years later Martin retells the episode:[2]

I didn't tell her that the balloon had a dynamite charge that slid down the cable, exploded and sent shrapnel tearing through the plane, some of it just a couple feet from my head. Nor did I tell her the "supplies" we had been carrying were hundreds of gallons of gasoline, and how lucky we were it had already been offloaded.

I also didn't tell her that after the 4-foot stretch of the trailing edge of our left wing had been blown off, the ship began shaking violently. As radio operator, I took time to message the base to tell what had happened. When I left my compartment, I found crew members wearing parachutes standing at the now-removed back door waiting for the captain's order to jump. I quickly looked around for a chute of my own. There were none. Through error, the ground crew had put one too few on board. I lurched back to the men hanging on at the open door, shouting above the din, "Say you guys didn't see an extra parachute anywhere, did you?"

No, they said. Then one of them added, "We'd do anything in the world for you, Martin, but, uh . . ."

I stumbled to the front of the plane, where the captain was fighting his quivering wheel, and told him my predicament. He ordered everyone to hang tight; he would try to set it down.

The Germans still held the northern Netherlands, but the Allies controlled the south. We made a bumpy landing at a British Royal Air Force base near Eindhoven.

Putting the pieces of one's life experiences together in narrative is one way in which a human being can bring a sense of coherence and authenticity to his or her life. The narrative that Martin recounts in 1945 focuses on the *objective* events of the plane hitting a cable, damaging the wing, and landing. The narrative minimizes danger, emphasizing instead the safe return to land. Alternatively, the narrative recounted in 1999 provides a more *subjective* re-living of events. In this anxiety-packed account, Martin becomes a central protagonist whose life is preserved largely because of his actions, thoughts, and emotions. Like Nick Martin, all of us depend upon telling a narrative to remember our experiences. Yet, circumstances organize how our memories are codified in narrative form or even whether they are narrated at all. A life episode may be too painful or too distant to put into words; or tellers may perceive a rendering of events to be inappropriate or politically unfeasible for the interlocutors who populate one's surroundings. In these and other circumstances, certain narratives remain untold.

The present chapter integrates generalizations posited in earlier sections of the book to discern the conditions that obstruct narration of significant life experiences. In particular, we return to four narrative dimensions—*tellability, tellership, linearity,* and *moral stance*—to illuminate how the past becomes invisible. In the realm of tellability, a sequence of events may not be reportable, because the would-be teller cannot access his or her memory of the events (e.g., early childhood or traumatic life incidents). Further, both high and low participation in tellership may divert certain events from narrative expression. In addition, certain stories may not be related, because a preference for linearity privileges a culturally and autobiographically coherent, recognizable organization of events over plunging into still inchoate details of what happened and why. Alternatively, the pursuit of narrative authenticity may yield a swirl of unrelated memories that do not constitute a storied sequence. That is, untold stories may result from both overdetermined and underdetermined structuring of personal narratives. Moral stance also deflects narratives, in that tellers find it difficult to confront community and institutional ideologies and sensibilities about what should not be told. A leitmotif of the chapter is that, in the face of a past that eludes them, tellers nonetheless shroud their narratives with credibility.

Tellability

SCHEMATA AND MEMORY

In Chapter 1 we noted that personal narratives concern life events that are more or less tellable. That is, personal narratives across speech communities generally concern unexpected rather than predictable experiences. Although tellers can transform just about anything that happened into a tellable account, events that violate the status quo are prototypically the basis of everyday narration. The inclination to narrate the unusual and leave life routines unnarrated emerges in the course of human development. As reported in Chapter 2, very young children initially narrate both habitual and unexpected events in their lives, but as they grow older, they are drawn more to recounting narratives that center around a specific, unexpected incident.

This developmental progression is partially linked to narrative as a problem-solving activity. While both children and adults use personal narratives to reconcile disparities between their worldview and an unexpected experience, young children are also absorbed with sorting out their daily routines and use narrative to work out a coherent structuring of quotidian events in their lives. As Katherine Nelson notes: "the basic general function of memory for any organism is to provide guidance for action . . . for predicting what will happen . . . The most useful type of evidence comes from events that are frequently repeated."[3] This perspective suggests that young children recall routine events in order to anticipate them.

The developmental trend away from recounting canonical events may be only apparent, however. Frederick Bartlett was among the first to point out that recollection is mediated by modeling and stereotyping:

"Remembering appears to be far more decisively an affair of construction rather than one of mere reproduction . . . In remembering a man constructs on the basis of one 'schema.'"[4] Experimental research on memory supports the notion that schemata for repeated events organize how people recall a specific episode and "are a major source of errors in recollective memory, just as they are in other forms of memory."[5] As a result, schema-based memories promote narration of certain facets and orderings of events and filter out others from the narrative record.

As noted in Chapter 6, schemata are applied to a wide range of events, activities, paradigms, and objects in the world, including the self. The "self schema," as Bruner and Feldman refer to it, shapes the narrated self, in that each telling of life experience privileges, i.e., accommodates to, one's current autobiographical perspective.[6] This notion resonates with philosophical approaches to memory. Ricoeur's comprehensive treatment of time and narrative, for example, emphasizes Husserl's notion that memory is always tainted by the present time, in that the present is a realization (or failed realization) of past expectations.[7] Moreover, Heidegger posits that our representation of the past is influenced by our preoccupations with our present and future life world.[8]

In the realm of everyday narrative encounters with family and acquaintances, tellers favor certain experiential components over others to portray an enduring picture of their lives. The tendency to narrate their thoughts, feelings, and deeds in a positive light, for example, is characteristic of many tellers talking about their role as protagonists in a past incident (see Chapters 1 and 4). Alternatively, sufferers of a psychological disorder such as agoraphobia often narrate the self as helpless, fearful, and abnormal (see Chapter 5).

Autobiographical memories influence not only how we tell but also how we interpret narratives. Like the Heisenberg effect of the observer upon the observed, interlocutors map their lived and imagined involvements in the world onto renderings of experience such that even the most silent of listeners is an author of an emergent narrative.[9] This process resonates with how listeners contribute to the creation of music. As Bernard Holland notes: "When a musician does not give us everything we expect to hear, we supply the missing elements in our minds . . . Music played feeds music heard . . . [In] Beethoven's C-minor Piano Sonata . . . by the time the A natural actually arrives, the resonating B flat has long since evaporated from the vibrating piano strings. But we want to hear it, and so our imaginations, aided by surrounding harmonic events, keep it alive. We in our small way have become composers, too."[10]

In psychoanalysis a similar disposition prevails. The analyst uses a client's present symptomatic behavior to reconstruct a story of the client's past life experience and reject other possibilities. Roy Schafer summarizes this proclivity:[11]

> Reconstructions of the infantile past and the transferential present are interdependent. This is so because, upon reviewing what is at any moment taken to be true of the past, one raises questions and suggests answers concerning features of the transferential present. Similarly, in reviewing what is at any moment taken to be true of the transferential present, one raises questions and suggests answers concerning the infantile past. For example, present feelings of inadequacy direct the inquiry toward life-historical prototypes, and accounts of a never-satisfied father direct the inquiry toward transference fantasies of a never-satisfied analyst.

Heidegger supports the idea that each representation of the past (what he calls "repetition") opens new possibilities for conceptualizing one's present and future existence. Similarly, audiences bring the remembered past to co-author theatrical performances. As delineated by Vaclav Havel:[12] "We may not identify with a certain way of seeing and thinking, a certain kind of fantasy and humor . . . at all, but simply experience it suddenly, know it and feel it as something possible, as something we can enter into, understand, follow. Our enjoyment comes from a new understanding of ourselves: we consciously experience something that had hitherto existed in us only as a potential."

Bruner and Feldman also point out that the self schema not only shapes autobiographical narrative but is also shaped by it and in that sense is reflexive. Although memory influences how we co-narrate and co-author experiences, narrative practices in turn influence how experiences are subsequently encoded, retained, and revised in memory. To phrase it another way, our identities are malleable and are altered as we narratively reflect on life events. In this way, autobiographical memory both guides and is guided by narrative. Both are in flux, ever subject to reformulation.[13]

CHILDHOOD AMNESIA

In addition to the effects of mental schemata upon the selective recall of past experience, events may remain unnarrated because they transpired early in childhood, at a point when the experiencer had not developed requisite memory skills. Adults' explicit memories of their experiences before three years of age are generally absent or severely limited, a phenomenon known as *childhood amnesia*.[14] While Mary Mullen observes that "the average age of earliest memory is consistently found to be in the vicinity of 3½ years,"[15] Katherine Nelson notes that some adults have difficulty accessing childhood memories through the first eight years of life.[16]

Sigmund Freud was the first psychologist to document the paucity of adult memories of early childhood.[17] Attributing childhood amnesia to repression of emotional traumatic childhood events, specifically the upset surrounding early sexual identification, Freud emphasized the profound and persistent influence of narratively inaccessible experiences. Although the reasons for childhood amnesia have not been determined, considerable evidence of the phenomenon has accrued since Freud's initial observations.[18] This evidence suggests that while very early childhood memories generally do not attain narrative expression because of cognitive and neurological immaturity, young children display limited ability to symbolically represent past experience from the second year of life.[19]

More or less unconsciously encoded, early experiences of the world are recalled predominantly as sensations, emotions, and behavioral responses.[20] The capacity to narrate personal experience is tied to children's acquisition of the ability to recognize persons and objects as permanent entities, discern relations between objects, and symbolically represent objects and relations, especially in the form of language.[21] Not coincidentally, these developmental achievements also undergird the capacity for explicit memory; that is, the ability to consciously reflect on and verbalize past events. Explicit memory includes semantic memory (e.g., facts, routines, ideas) as well as episodic memory (e.g., specific life episodes), the latter central to narrating personal experience. It requires cognitive and neural processes that allow memories to be accessed and articulated.[22] Among other variables, the development of explicit memory is facilitated by the acquisition of language and the development of certain areas of the brain. As noted by Siegel: "Autobiographical or episodic memory requires a capacity termed 'autonoesis' (self-knowing) and appears to be dependent upon the development of frontal cortical regions of the brain. These regions undergo rapid experience-dependent development during the first few years of life . . . and are postulated to mediate autonoetic consciousness."[23]

Although current understandings of childhood amnesia have relied largely on adults' recollections of their preschool years, Robyn Fivush has proposed re-conceptualizing the phenomenon in light of research on *what children themselves are recalling during the critical period between two and four years of age.*[24] This is particularly important in identifying possible discontinuities in the content, organization, and duration of memory early in development, and discerning processes underlying such shifts. Although not yet able to symbolically represent these experiences through language, the considerable learning young children display attests to their ability to remember certain events. Infants who are 9 months old, for example, are able to reproduce a single act through delayed kinesic imitation.[25] By 16 months, children correctly reproduce the temporal ordering of familiar multi-act sequences in immediate and delayed recall and can immediately recall novel sequences of actions that display a logical causal order.[26] Delayed recall of other, more arbitrarily ordered sequences of actions, however, seems out of the reach of 16- and 20-month-old children.[27] Further, Karen Sheingold and Yvette Tenney found that in contrast to four-year-old children, three-year-olds recall almost nothing about the birth of a younger sibling.[28]

These findings suggest that repeated experiences are central to autobiographical memory. This notion is supported by attachment researchers, who have documented enduring effects of children's attachments to caregivers during infancy on their relationship to caregivers in the years that follow, as well as on their intimate relationships as adults.[29] This continuity suggests that even early interpersonal experiences that are not made into narrative are encoded in memory and provide a template for subsequent life experience.

TRAUMA

Besides the effects of schema-based memory and childhood amnesia, events may remain inaccessible for narration because they are too painful. As noted throughout this volume, many personal narratives that adults recount revolve around violations of norms and otherwise troubling events.[30] Although not always supported by their interlocutors, narrators of personal experience use this discursive activity to understand unsettling emotions and events through conversational narrative.

Beginning with Pierre Janet, Joseph Breuer, and Sigmund Freud, many physicians and psychologists have argued that traumatic stress interferes with the integration of traumatic events within the sufferer's ongoing conscious experience, thought, and action.[31] Even though emotionally significant events are transformed into narrative, overwhelmingly traumatic events may be blocked from explicit memory and narration. As summarized by Dan Siegel: "The degree of stress will have a direct effect on memory: Small amounts have a neutral effect on memory; moderate amounts facilitate memory; and large amounts impair memory."[32] Memories of trauma are encoded by processes such as repression and dissociation that make them difficult to retrieve as coherent, verbal narratives. Conceptualizations of the underlying mechanisms (i.e., repression, dissociation) differ, but this view of trauma and memory prevails, grounded in the notion that when consciously reflecting on an experience poses too great a risk to one's psychological security, the emotions and events are isolated in memory, detached from the identities they threaten.[33]

But not completely. In the words of van der Kolk, "the body keeps the score," albeit unconsciously, concerning an individual's traumatic history. Traumatic symptoms include "hypervigilance, psychological containment or 'numbing,' and intrusive ideation and images that signify the loss or inaccessibility of affective and psychological strengths."[34] As dramatically exemplified in the symptoms of post-traumatic stress disorder (PTSD), traumatic memories invade conscious experience in the form of static, unarticulated, but vivid sensations and images. A combat veteran with PTSD, for example, may not be able to recall a helicopter crash in which he witnessed the death of his best friend. Yet his nightmares, reflexive aversion to the sound of planes, and avoidance of airports suggest that he has an implicit memory of combat trauma.

Sometimes implicit memories are manifested through behavioral reenactment. Lenore Terr, an expert on memory and trauma, describes a case in which an eight-year-old girl, Eileen Franklin, witnessed her father rape and murder her best friend by pummeling her over the head with a shovel.[35] By the time Eileen's teacher spoke to the fourth grade about their classmate's disappearance, Eileen could no longer consciously remember what happened. However, she became withdrawn at school, and began pulling out the hair on one side of her head. Most likely, Eileen unconsciously set out to duplicate the horrible wound she had seen her father inflict on her best friend.

Fragmented, debilitating recollections of this kind remain as such until they are voiced within an adequately supportive environment, and co-narrated into a coherent sequence of events and reactions.[36] Psychotherapy with victims of post-traumatic stress, for example, involves assembling and integrating experiences that have been split off in memory within a safe, secure environment. When memories are re-experienced and expressed in this supportive social context, a web of associations emerges. These associations are the basis for an autobiographical narrative that is coherent and inclusive. Indeed, generating a coherent narrative may be more central to healing than reviewing every aspect of a traumatic event in search of what really happened.[37]

Tellership

As the last paragraph suggests, whether or not and how an experience gets narratively aired depends on the conditions of tellership. Who is present and who participates in the narrative interaction? Is the tellership highly active, with multiple interlocutors shaping the unfolding tale? Are tellers reluctant to reveal certain experiences to particular interlocutors? Do interlocutors facilitate a teller's narrative representation of the past? Or do they cut off, revise, ignore, or otherwise resist a narrator's formulation of life experience?

HIGH CO-TELLERSHIP

Narrative interactions in which interlocutors actively contribute to the co-telling of personal experience would seem the ideal condition for flushing out details and perspectives. Indeed, adults who encourage their children to co-narrate with them promote the development of sophisticated narrative skills in childhood. Yet, as noted in Chapter 2, active conversational partners may drown out one or another version of what happened by reformulating or contradicting the casting of past events. Below, we examine the Janus-faced character of active co-tellership.

On the positive side, studies of recollections of personal experiences point to the role that others play in facilitating the retrieving, elaborating, and interpreting of life events. Across the life span, adults and children alike are dependent upon conversational partners in remembering and reconstructing past events through narrative.[38] Memories of experiences are often (re)invoked by others who participated or are otherwise familiar with these experiences. As often happens when familiars look together at baby pictures or photo albums, family members, older acquaintances, or even friends and clinicians may reconstruct childhood experiences through co-narration.

As noted in Chapter 2, the collective unearthing of past experiences may involve young children in certain families and communities. Like Husserl and Heidegger, psychologist Jean Mandler emphasizes the importance of verbally reinstating memories for long-term retention.[39] Similarly, Nelson posits that it is young children's increasingly competent and willing involvement in memory talk that facilitates the preservation of autobiographical memories.[40] Focusing on Caucasian Americans, developmental research suggests that families vary greatly in the extent to which and how they co-tell narratives of personal experience and that these differences impact how elaborately children in these families recount the past.[41] Robyn Fivush and Elaine Reese observed that children in some families learn to "exhibit an elaborative or reminiscent narrative style" in which they "integrate events, people, and relationships into a larger life story" and "provide richly detailed and progressive accounts of events."[42] An example of such interaction follows:[43]

Father: You did fall down, didn't you?
    You got your foot caught in one [a root] and went plop fell right
        down in the sand.
    Did it hurt?
Child: No
Father: Yes, I don't remember,
    but I think you cried a little bit, didn't you?
Child: Hum
Father: Well, let's see, what else did we do?
    I think we just went for a walk
    and then we sat down when we got back in the woods
    and we looked around.

It was really pretty up there as I recall.
It's all green, trees are all green,
and there were the birds, chirping, and singing.
I think it was pretty nice.
That was fun.
Now I think we just went back and got in the car,
and drove back to Pete and Pauli's.
Remember that?

Child: Ha

Father: That was our vacation to Michigan, wasn't it?

Children in other families, in contrast, learn "sparse forms" of narrative
that emphasize "repetitive or practical remembering" in brief conversational interactions, as in the sequence below:[44]

Mother: Do you remember last Easter?

Child: Yeah

Mother: What did we do at Easter?

Child: What

Mother: What did we do at Easter?

Child: Yeah

Mother: Can't remember?

Child: Yeah

Mother: We dyed Easter eggs

Child: Yeah

Mother: Who helped us dye Easter eggs?

Child: What

Mother: Do you remember who helped us dye Easter eggs?

Child: Yeah

Mother: Who?

Child: (no response)

Mother: Grandma Shirley

Fivush and her colleagues note that as children develop, they continue
to collaborate in the co-remembering of past life events, but the collaboration is less lopsided and more equally fueled by the participation of
children and adults alike. The image for this transformation is that of a
"spiral": "For reminiscing, the more appropriate model may be a collab-

orative 'spiral' rather than a scaffold. According to this model, it is still the adult who carries much of the task early on when the child is just learning to participate, but as the child becomes more and more competent in recounting past experiences, the adult and child begin to tell more and more elaborately detailed stories, embellishing and enriching each other's contributions to the recount."[45] In summary, these studies suggest that families who draw children into elaborate, affect-laden co-narration make their past experience vivid and memorable. Family co-narration as a whole gains complexity and symmetry, as children participate more actively.

On the negative side, active co-tellership that consists of constant questioning or supplying extensive information about past events for others highlights only certain facets of experience and deflects other facets from narrative expression. The following interaction recorded by Fivush and Nina Hamond illustrates a narrative interaction in which a Mother tries to jog the memory of her 30-month-old daughter:[46]

Mother: Last year, remember it was Halloween. Remember that? Who did
we go trick-or-treating with?
Child: ( )
Mother: Didn't we go with some friends? Who did we go with? Do you
remember who came trick-or-treating with us?
Child: With who?
Mother: With who? You tell me. You had two friends come over. Which
ones went trick-or-treating?
Child: Stacy.
Mother: Not Stacy. Who? Come on.

In this interaction, it is the Mother who decides what becomes a topic for collective remembering and what constitutes accuracy of recall. She appears to grow frustrated by her daughter's unsuccessful attempts to remember the prior event Mother has in mind. A similar form of narrative direction is seen in the following exchange, in which Mom reminds five-year-old Joshua of a game he used to play in preschool:[47]

Mom: Josh remember we played that at preschool? -
someone (.) Cathy blindfolded ... someone
and then then she would pick someone in the circle (.)

and they would stand up
and they would have to say something
to the blindfolded kid? (.)
and then the one who was blindfolded had to guess?
who was talking?
Do you remember that game?

Josh: *((nods yes))* m:m

Mom: That was fun at preschool remember?

Josh: *((nods yes again))*

Here, it is difficult to tell whether or not Joshua remembers the invoked experience. Rather than soliciting details from Joshua, Mom tells him <u>what</u> to remember and <u>how</u> to remember it ("That was fun at preschool remember?"), thus shaping his early memory. In the following exchange, recorded by Fivush, a mother supplies a <u>causal framework</u> for her 32-month-old child's memory of a distressing event.[48]

Mother: Remember when Jason bit you, did it make you angry?

Child: *((nods yes))*

Mother: Did you hit him back?

Child: *((shakes head no))*

Mother: Did you bite him back?

Child: No

Mother: No, 'cause you're a sweet little girl.

As in previous examples, Mother's contributions imbue her daughter's memory with emotional meaning (anger) and autobiographical significance ("'cause you're a sweet little girl").

In some narrative interactions, children may find their memory of events explicitly contested by active adult co-tellers. A child may remember fragments of an early experience that don't mesh with his parent's recollection. In the following exchange, Mom informs four-year-old Jill that she has a dentist appointment the following day. Jill tells Mom she doesn't want to go to the dentist tomorrow, whereupon Mom engages her in collaboratively remembering her last dentist visit:[49]

Jill: *((whiny))* but I don't wa::nt to!

(0.4 pause)

Mom: You said it didn't hurt last time (.) remember?

Jill: *((whiny))* cu- I don't wa:n to: (.) I don't wanta get a pinch

Mom: But it didn't even hurt you last time - remember?

Jill: uh hu:h!

Mom: *((shaking head no))* You told me it didn't hurt you remember? the
dentist said you were a very good patient? *((nodding yes))*
remember?

Jill: I: don't wanta (do my throat)

Here Jill's and Mom's recollections of the dentist visit clash: Mom renders the autobiographical memory in positive terms, and Jill insists it was a negative experience.

Similarly, in the following exchange, three-year-old Evan has a hard time legitimizing his memory of what his father had said to him before dinner. Although Evan's recollection that Dad promised Evan ice cream for dessert if he ate a good dinner is supported by his Mother and his older brother Dick, it is repeatedly contested by Dad. Evan's attempt at establishing the past begins as the dinner winds to a close. Toward the end of dinner, Evan attempts to remind Dad about the promise:[50]

Evan: YOU 'MEMBER I COULD HAVE A

But Dad is occupied, and Evan has to repeat his reminder to Dad and then to Mom:

Evan: DADDY? YOU ('MEMBER) IF I EAT A GOOD DINNER I-
. . . *((Evan is tapping Dad's arm for attention))*
MO:MMY Mommy. (.) you-you 'member (.) (um) if I eat a good
. . . dinner I could have a ice cream

At this point Dad contests Evan's memory, while the rest of the family side with Evan:

Dad: An ice cream? (.) Who said that

Evan: You

Dick: You

(0.4 pause)

Mom: Ooooooo *((laughing))* hehe

→ Dad: I didn't say that

 Dick: Remember? (.) he (.) you said "Daddy (.) could I have a
 i:cecrea:m?" . . .

 Dad: Where was I? . . .

→ Dad: I don't even remember telling you that-
 What was I doing when?

 Dick: Daddy I'll tell you the exact words you said.

 Dad: Tell m- What was I doing (.) where was I first of all?

 Dick: You were sitting right in that chair where you are now.
 (0.4 pause)

 Mom: *((laughing))* hehehaha (.) It's on film (.) they have you.

In this passage, it is not enough for Evan to have remembered Dad's promise or for Evan to have the supported recall of his older brother. Dad denies the remembered event and demands the exact details as positive proof. In the face of Dad's challenge, the children supply further evidence of the remembered event. Dick tells him he can quote his "exact words" and cites the precise locale of the promise: "You were sitting right in that chair where you are now." Mom, who first signals Dad's sinking position with her incriminating "Ooooooooo" and snickering, provides the clinching source of evidence, namely, that the researchers have captured this entire episode on film. Her comment "They have you" may be interpreted to mean both that the researchers "have" Dad on tape and that the children "have" Dad boxed into a corner.

In this family interaction, a child's memory prevails, but often children's memory gives way to that of an adult interlocutor, especially when children are unable to garner support from more mature persons. In dyadic adult-child encounters, children's memories are frequently reformulated, backed by their authoritative status in the family and their appeal to objective facts.[51] In the following excerpt, collected by Fivush, a mother discredits her child's memory by rendering it implausible, given the setting in question:[52]

 Mother: Remember what toy you played with
 that you liked a real lot?

 Child: The sandbox.

→ Mother: She didn't have a sandbox.
 Remember in that playroom,

> she had lots of toys.
> What was your favorite toy
> that you kept wanting to play with.
> Do you remember?
> Child: The airplane.
> → Mother: No, not the airplane. Do you remember?
> Child: What?

In this exchange, the child does not contest her mother's recollection. Rather, she solicits her mother's input regarding her favorite preschool pastime, thus authenticating her mother's version of the truth.

Narrative interactions in which "what actually happened" is contested socialize children into the notion that there is a correct representation of real-world events and that accounts of past experience that are not credible are to be discarded. The rub is that standards of credibility are typically controlled by more powerful interlocutors. Accountability for the accuracy of narratives and asymmetric control over what is accurate is elaborately illustrated in the following dinnertime exchange between members of a middle-class Jewish-American family.[53] In this passage, a mother and father challenge their sons' assertion that they saw a three-foot-long turtle on the lake near their house:

> Sam: um, Jacob ( ) then they tipped over
> and there was this, ya know, a giant turtle,
> ti was coming right at 'em.
> Mother: Where? On the lake?
> Sam: On the lake.
> Mother: They have giant turtles on that lake?
> Sam: Yeah.
> Father: ( ) in the lake they got a giant turtle
> that's only six inches across.
> → Mother: Have you seen it?
> Sam: Oh yeah.
> Mother: How giant is giant?
> Sam: HOW giant is giant?
> About three feet.
> Mother: Show me with your hands how big it is.
> Sam: I can't fit it.

My arms aren't that big.

→ Mother: You really saw a giant turtle? On the lake?

Jacob: About this big? This big?

Mother: Were they like, friendly?

Sam: Its claws were like that long.

Jacob: ( ) and its claws ( )

I'm sure it's fins are that big.

→ Mother: Did you see it, or Jacob?

Sam: Jacob saw it and I did too.

→ Mother: You saw a three foot turtle ((*said as challenge*))

Sam: I didn't say it was exactly three foot,

but approximately three feet.

Mother: Was it like this?

Sam: No, is that three feet?

Father: Was it bigger than the plate you're eating?

Jacob: BIgger than a house?

Mother: I hope not.

I wouldn't want to meet that turtle.

Jacob: Me either.

Yuk. a ( )!

→ Mother: If Jacob says he saw it, it doesn't surprise me.

Sam: He didn't say it was three feet.

→ Mother: But you said it was three feet.

Sam: By the look of its head.

→ Father: By the look of its head,

or did you see its body?

Sam: I saw part of his body.

→ Father: But you didn't see its whole body.

Sam: No.

→ Father: Now we have more of an understanding.

→ Mother: That's called an unconfirmed assumption.

You know what that's worth?

Sam: What?

→ Mother: Nothin.

Although insistence on factuality is most overt in Mother's concluding remarks ("That's called an unconfirmed assumption. You know what that's worth? . . . Nothin."), it is apparent throughout the interaction in the content and manner of the parents' narrative contributions.[54] They contest the veracity of Sam's claim, and reinforce the importance of accurate reporting, by challenging the nature and source of his evidence (e.g., "Have you seen it?," "Did you see it, or Jacob . . . if Jacob saw it, it doesn't surprise me," "By the look of its head, or did you see its body?," "But you didn't see its whole body"), through repeated questioning in a disbelieving tone ("You really saw a giant turtle on the lake?," "You saw a three foot turtle"), and by undermining the precision of his measurement of the turtle ("Show me with your hands how big it is," "Was it like this?," "Was it bigger than the plate you're eating?"). The interrogation continues until Sam qualifies both the source ("By the look of its head," "I saw part of his body") and strength ("I didn't say it was exactly three foot, but approximately three feet") of his claim, and in so doing admits that he was speculating rather than reporting objective facts.

Emphasis on the factuality of narrative accounts is by no means situationally or societally universal. We saw in Chapter 1, for example, that Texan dog traders take pride in stretching the truth and duping other dog traders. Blum-Kulka and colleagues' observations of American and Israeli middle- and lower-class families at dinnertime suggest that while all groups valued accurate representation of what actually occurred, American middle-class parents were most concerned about issues of fidelity.[55] Similarly, Peggy Miller and her colleagues found that caregivers from Chinese and low-income African-American families were "relatively tolerant of fictional embellishments of experience, whereas families in white working-class communities demanded a fairly strict adherence to the literal truth."[56] Shirley Brice Heath's ethnography also reveals cultural differences in the value placed on verifiability: narrative interactions among Euro-American working-class people of Roadville and among middle-class Euro-American and African-American "townspeople" typically placed a high premium on factuality, but this was not the case in the rural African-American community of Trackton.[57] Heath's analysis suggests that absence of a need for verifiability is more common in communities with strong oral traditions, in which relating entertaining stories is as important as, if not more important than, establishing facts.

Disputes over memories of events—particularly those with emotional weight—is the focus in family therapy, in which parental accounts of collective experience frequently prevail over those of children.[58] In their study of Swedish family therapy, Karin Aronsson and Ann-Christin Cederborg articulate the linguistic and interactional resources that family members routinely bring to their talk to display authoritative stance, including *evidential adverbs* like "actually" and "absolutely" and recruitment of *authoritative support*, as in the following narrative dispute between adolescent Sam and his father:[59]

> Father: Your clothing allowance was suspended for five months because
>   you consistently spent it on things other than clothes, and
>   then went and asked your Mother to buy you clothes.
> Sam: That's not actually <u>true.</u>
> Father: <u>That's</u> ABSOLUTELY true, ask your Mother.

Reminiscent of the giant turtle discussion, another consistent marker of high certainty is reference to *exact numbers*. For instance, Sam and his father conflict in their accounts of the amount of time that Sam devoted to studying. Sam supports his position that he has indeed studied hard by specifying the exact time he spent on this task:

> Sam: The week before I went back I did 2.5 hours every day revising for
>   my exams.

Not only does Sam use numbers, he formulates the number as a statistic—2.5—as if he had calculated the average time per day across the number of days studied. But Sam's father is not to be outdone by such displays. He himself gets into the numbers game, claiming:

> Father: Three days you didn't do anything AT ALL.
>   You were watching television all day
>   and went off to Tom's in the afternoon.

Sam and his father continue to clash over the truth:

> Sam: That just ISN'T true
> Father: It IS true,
> Sam: No.

At this point, father not only appeals to other authorities, he specifies the exact number who he believes will back him up:

Father: Well three people will tell you it is.

Displays of relative certainty and displays of positive and negative affect are the building blocks of identities. Each display of high certainty in the dispute between Sam and his father may be seen as an attempt for each to establish himself as an authority, and at the same time establish the addressee as a liar or culprit. Sam and his father become grid-locked in their unwillingness to accept the identities each has attempted to assign the other. Therapists work to establish a more balanced dialogue between parental and child perspectives on past events. This process involves helping family members relinquish their sense of absolute certainty about what they remember, in part through the therapist's modeling of less absolute stances and in part through making explicit the subjectivity and malleability of memory.

The potential for more powerful parties to authenticate certain memories and eliminate others from the autobiographical record has been a concern of psychologists examining children's testimony in legal proceedings. Preschoolers, in particular, are often swayed by leading questions, especially when repeated.[60] Three-year-old children, for example, adopt the assumptions underlying deceptive questions posed by experimenters twice as often as six-year-olds.[61] Although they tend to be less influenced about negative actions against their bodies, they are highly vulnerable to being led to believe false autobiographical experiences.[62]

Recent studies of adult eye-witness testimonies in court attest to the impact of co-telling on a person's narrative recollection of past experience. Adult memory of eye-witnessed events is affected by both prior life experiences and biases and by post-event experiences, reflections, and conversations, including the testimony of others and the displayed dispositions of lawyers.[63] Elizabeth Loftus and her colleagues have conducted "misinformation" experiments, in which participants (generally college students) are shown videos of simulated accidents and crimes. Drawing on evidence that the form of a question influences the content of a response, and that linguistic resources influence memory of events, Loftus demonstrates that witnesses are highly suggestible and can be led to modify their perceptions through questions that contain presuppositions or evoke particular interpretations (e.g., "Did you see <u>the</u> dent in the car?," rather than "Did you see <u>a</u> dent?"; "Did you see a car <u>crash</u> <u>into</u> the bus" vs. "Did you see a car <u>collide with</u> a bus").[64]

In summary, co-telling personal experiences with active conversational partners may suppress explicit memory of past experience when partners contend that certain unremembered events transpired, divert a narrative from the storyline a teller had been pursuing, or reformulate or refuse to validate a narrative detail or perspective.

Low Co-tellership

Like highly active co-tellership, reluctance to co-tell also derails certain renderings of personal experience from narrative expression. Diminished participation in narrative activity may be due to a reluctance to recount a narrative of personal experience. In addition, conversational partners may withdraw as active listeners of an unfolding narrative. We consider the abortive impact of each of these situations on narrative expression.

Reluctance to Recount. Narratives may remain untold due to a would-be teller's failure to recount them in the company of others. Reluctance may be a matter of unwillingness, but in other cases it may be the outcome of a disability. We have seen throughout this volume how essential narrative interaction is to understanding self and society, yet certain disorders inhibit would-be tellers from recounting a meaningful personal experience. This is strikingly apparent in the narrative attempts of children with autism. Even high-functioning children with autism—those whose cognitive abilities are in the average to superior range—display considerable difficulty narrating emotional experiences. They frequently hesitate a great deal, require numerous prompts, and ultimately tend to provide a general gloss of what transpired or recount fragmentary events that are only partly related to an overarching story logic.[65]

The following narrative interaction illustrates the lengths to which the parents of Karl, a young high-functioning autistic boy, go to get him to recount his day:[66]

Father: Karly? (.) Could you tell us about <u>your</u> day?
       (2.0 pause)
Karl: °I had fu:n°

Father: [Say it again?
Mother: [Ha ha ha I want to have [Karly's day!
Karl: [I had fun.
Mother: [I want to be like Karl
Father: [You had fun?
Mother: I want to have fun!
(2.0 pause)
Father: Karly tell us what you did (.) at summer camp today!
(2.0 pause)
Mother: *((bending over closely to Karl's face, giving a vitamin and whispering something to him))* Yep!
(2.0 pause)
Karl: °I went swimming°
Mother: Goo::d
Father: Tell us about it
Karl: ( ) (3.0 pause) *((Karl drinks milk))*
Father: Huh?
(3.0 pause)
Tell us about the <u>fun</u> things you did
(.)
What did you do when you went swimming with summer camp?
(1.0 pause)
Karl: We just played in the wa:ter
((Karl gets up and leaves))
Father: Did you play with anybody? Like Amanda?
Karly come back here please!
Karl: *((from another room))* No:! <u>not</u> with A<u>man</u>da! No!
Father: Karl, come back and talk to us please
You <u>can't</u> do your game right now
. . .
Father: So you (.) jump off the diving board when you are with the summer camp too?
Karl: Never! I never do it!
Father: No?
Mother: Too scary [huh?
Father: [Do you swim across the pool?
(1.0 pause)

Karl: *((in high pitched voice))* I don't wanna talk about <u>it</u>

You're asking questions too much

\>I'm going to press this button to turn the volume off!<

mm<u>m</u> mm<u>m</u> *((pretends to press a button on his head))*

Father: Okay!

Mother: I guess he doesn't want to talk about it Dad!

The first thing to notice is the frequent and lengthy pauses between parental elicitations about Karl's day and his responses. Typically, conversational turns transition with either no or only a brief pause.[67] Longer pauses are more unusual and signal some sort of interactional difficulty, such as lack of attention or disagreement. The pauses that thread the interaction between Karl and his parents signal the difficulty that Karl experiences in sustaining communication, particularly communication about past events. Karl's parents reformulate their queries and look closely in Karl's face to draw him into the narrative world they are attempting to co-construct. In addition, Karl's narrative efforts are minimal; he provides a simple gloss for his day, providing general summaries ("I had fun," "I went swimming," "We just played in the water") or negations of parental formulations of his day (e.g., "No:! <u>not</u> with A<u>man</u>da! No!").[68] These practices leave untold the specifics of Karl's eventful day. His discomfort with engaging in the narrative interaction eventually takes the form of physical withdrawal from the room where his parents are seated. Finally, Karl tells his parents explicitly, "I don't wanna talk about <u>it</u>" and "You're asking questions too much." To stop the interaction from proceeding, he pushes an imaginary button on his head to "turn the volume off." From Karl's point of view, his parents' narrative efforts overwhelm him; the volume of co-tellership is turned too high. From his parents' point of view, however, Karl's reluctance means a life apart.[69]

In the case of autism, the reluctance to recount past experience is rooted in social, cognitive, and communicative *impairments*. Yet family interactions involving typical, competent children can resemble what transpires in Karl's family. In these moments, reluctance to tell others about a past experience is rooted in an *unwillingness* to do so. As noted in Chapter 2, a parent or older sibling may be eager to involve a child in narrative activity, but the child may resist. In the following excerpt, recorded by Robyn Fivush and Janet Kuebli, a six-year-old girl initially opposes her mother's attempt to engage her in recounting the death of her teacher, Karen Butler:[70]

Mother: Remember Karen Butler's wake?
   Child: I don't want to talk about sad parts.
Mother: Well don't talk about the sad parts,
           talk about the happy parts.
           Were there any happy parts to that?
           Was it good s-, to see Molly?
           ((14 conversational turns about who was at the wake))
   Child: I don't want to talk about this anymore.
Mother: You don't want to remember Karen's wake?
           That is a sad time.

In this interaction the child remembers, but does not want to discuss the tragic death of her beloved teacher nor does she want to recount "the happy parts" as per her Mother's suggestion. Like Karl the child may perceive the parental narrative elicitations as emotionally overwhelming.

Caucasian-American parents may go to great lengths to eke out a narrative from their children about the day's events. Like Karl's parents they ask repeatedly, "What happened at [school, camp, etc.] today?," only to be ignored or given a curtailed response.[71] A child's reluctance to narrate may stem from a history of family narrative interaction in which the child's actions and feelings as protagonist and narrator have been the frequent object of parental criticism. Indeed, in the American families recorded by Elinor Ochs, Carolyn Taylor, and their colleagues, parents routinely seized upon the information children provided about their day to advise them about what they should have done in that circumstance or should do in similar situations in the future.[72] The following narrative excerpt of eight-year-old Dick's activities at summer school is, for example, flooded with Mom's and Dad's plans for Dick:[73]

   Mom: Are you working on times tables?
   Dick: Hm ((shakes head horizontally slightly))
           (0.4 pause)
   Mom: Good!
           . . .

cuz I worked you up a nice <u>times</u> tables sheet
that I want you to finish before you go to be::d=

. . .

Dick (.) no joke (.) there's a paper in there

Dick: Okay=

Mom: =you've got one every day (.)
and that'll take you back to school (.) kay?

. . .

Mom: You can look up the answers (.) for three weeks

Dad: No just let him (.) complete 'n mark his own papers
That's all (.) but don't let him [look at the answers

Mom: [But at the end?

Dad: That isn't going to help him any

Mom: Sure it does (.) and at the end of three weeks then no book
Then you're gonna hafta rely on (.) your memory okay?

Dick: Can I do em at school?

Mom: No you're gonna do this tonight before you go to bed.

Given such parental intrusions, it is understandable why some would-be child co-tellers might interpret parental queries about the day's events as setups for the issuance of parental directives and why some children are guarded or silent about their personal experiences.[74]

While the impact of psychological disorders such as autism on co-tellership is fairly consistent across conversational partners and settings, the vast majority of conditions that impede the collaborative telling are less easy to detect. Social-emotional distance that obtains among family members, for example, may be a source and outcome of family narrative practices. Mary Main has found that American children who engage in secure patterns of attachment with their parents (i.e., responsiveness to parental departure and pleasure at reunion) have parents who readily narrate numerous, elaborate, coherent childhood experiences with their own parents; children who engage in avoidance patterns of attachment with their parents (i.e., limited responsiveness to parental departure and avoidance at reunion) generally have parents who insist that they are unable to recall their own childhood experiences.[75] These adults tend to describe their relationships with their parents in extremely favorable terms but have great difficulty supporting these characterizations with detailed autobiographical memories of particular experiences. It is possible that skeletal, dismissive narrative styles are attributable in part to a childhood history of minimal social engagement with family members (i.e., avoidance) and an associated deficit in opportunities for co-narration.[76]

Emotional security thus appears tied not to constant co-narration, but to familiars' *disposition* to co-narrate. Further, their emotional security does not appear to depend on the child's being the principal narrator or central protagonist of a narrated incident. Narrative engagement with others takes many forms: co-tellers can be initiators, contributors, addressees, or those who overhear conversational narratives of their own or others' personal experience.[77] Moreover, child co-tellers need not rely solely upon parents for narrative engagement. In many communities, young children are cared for by older siblings and are expected to converse primarily with them and with their peers.[78]

Reluctance to Listen. Certain storylines do not come to fruition, because tellers perceive their audience to be unable or unwilling to take in an account of what happened. Nick Martin felt that his mother would become too anxious hearing about his brush with death during the war. Others who have had emotionally or physically intense experiences report a similar sensation of listener resistance. Holocaust survivors, as Lawrence Langer reports, repeatedly find themselves in a narrative bind: Their stories cannot be told in a language that listeners understand, because the experiences they recount are outside human comprehension.[79] The urge to tell meets resistance from the certainty that one's audience will not understand. The anxiety of futility lurks beneath the surface of many of these narratives, erupting occasionally and rousing us to an appraisal of our own stance that we can not afford to ignore.

Magda F recalls:
And I looked at them and I said: "I'm gonna tell you something. I'm gonna tell you something now. If somebody would tell *me* this story, I would say 'She's lying, or he's lying' because this can't be true. And maybe you're gonna feel the same way. That your sister's lying here, because this could not happen. Because to understand us, somebody has to go through with it. Because nobody, but nobody fully understands us. You can't. No matter how much sympathy you give me when I'm talking here, or you understand [. . .] you are *trying* to

understand me I know, but I don't think you could." And I said this to them. Hoping that they should never be able to understand, because to understand, you have to go through with it, and I hope nobody in the world comes to this again so they *should* understand us. And this was the honest truth, because nobody, nobody, nobody . . .

Survivors attempting to recount their Holocaust experience sometimes find interlocutors, even their own spouses, walking away or telling them not to go on because it is too upsetting for the survivor.

Those who suffer from chronic or debilitating physical conditions also find active listenership difficult to attain. Listeners, whether professionals in the field of medicine or friends and family members, resist narratives that deviate from the canonical plot that illness is only transitory.[80] Physicians often halt a story that comes uncomfortably close to disclosing the chaos and terror accompanying illness. Friends and family express the fear that the teller will become a narrative wreck, i.e., disintegrate in the course of relating events that have no clear logic or resolution.[81] Not only those who have a chronic condition but also those who care for them may find their stories diverted by interlocutors. Arthur Frank presents the account of a mother of an adult child with a mental disability who feels she cannot recount the realities of her life, even to a parent support group:[82] "'We do not tell our own truth,' she said to me, describing the group. These parents . . . were unwilling to tell their disappointments and frustrations. The raw anguish of such talk was rendered unacceptable by unspoken group norms."

When listeners withdraw their attention, a teller may transform the narrative they are relating. Charles Goodwin's analysis of the lengths to which tellers go to secure a listener indicates that tellers may shift thematic direction in mid-sentence.[83] Goodwin found that tellers who fail to attain a listener often seek out other interlocutors as a recipient of what they wish to communicate. Similarly, Capps and Ochs observed that the agoraphobic woman in their study (Meg) often failed to interest her spouse as an active listener during family dinnertime, whereupon she would turn to her children to assume this role.[84] The withdrawal of the spouse had consequences on the unfolding narratives and beyond. Most immediately, Meg would escalate the dramatic nature of an incident or otherwise heighten its significance. In recounting a near encounter with a pit bull in her in-laws' backyard, for example, Meg repeatedly tries to secure her husband's gaze and involvement, but he looks only fleetingly at her. Eventually Meg shifts from recounting the threat posed by the specific pit bulls to the threat of pit bulls everywhere:[85]

> Meg: And they look so barBARic the way they're tied up with these big
> chains.
> I got to thinking
> these aren't PETS
> (0.3 pause)
> Nobody would treat a pet like that.
> They're strictly there to chew up anybody who might come into
> their yard

Meg's husband William responds to this generalization with one terse comment, "Sure they are," but his gaze is fixed toward his son and not Meg, indexing divided attention at best. William's reticence may be an effort to curb Meg's panicky emotions, especially in front of the children. But his disposition appears to have the opposite effect. As noted by Goodwin, tellers respond to lack of attention by repeating, rephrasing, increasing loudness, emphatic stress, exaggerated intonation, and the like.[86] Meg responds by widening the scope of her fears. Moreover, she shifts the direction of her gaze and her narrative from her spouse to her children as primary listeners. And it is with the children that panic narratives actively proceed. Capps and Ochs propose that this co-telling dynamic may account for why children of an agoraphobic parent often suffer from anxiety disorders as they mature.

These scenarios indicate that resistance to actively listening to certain narratives may reflect a listener's discomfort and sense of instability in the face of the experience recounted. Certain narratives have no easy gloss, and listeners whose autobiographies do not include analogous experiences may feel unprepared to interpret and respond to the narrative account.

Linearity

Human beings are caught between the desire for coherence and the desire for authenticity of life experience. Although both of these proclivities propel and organize everyday narrative activity, coherence dominates authenticity as an existential narrative solution to understanding the past and coping with the future. The construction of seamless linearity through culturally and historically ordained genres of narrative and logics of experience disadvantages and often occludes certain versions of life incidents. Yet, as elaborated by literary scholar Gary Morson, flights into authenticity of past events, characterized by sideshadowing in which details of experiences are dwelled upon, uncertainties aired, potentialities hypothesized, and fragmentation tolerated, also may divert tellers from developing a storyline.[87] As Morson notes, probing into the microcosm of an event can leave how the event fits into a temporal and causal trajectory of events to the vagaries of imagination.

We consider a hallmark of narrative competence to be the ability to strike a balance between coherence and authenticity. As noted in Chapter 2, though young children both probe and impose order on existential uncertainties, their narratives of specific personal experiences often do not maintain thematic and logical continuity. Narratives recounted by children with autism often fall at the extremes of the proclivities for coherence and authenticity. While varying greatly in their abilities, children with autism often recount either highly linear temporal sequences of past events or a single past event with little reckoning of relation to antecedents and consequents.[88] Psychologist Helen Tager-Flusberg reports: "Overall, the findings from this study suggest that autistic children produce quite impoverished narratives, especially when compared to normal children matched for verbal mental age. Thus, their stories were significantly shorter and included fewer propositions; they were less likely to include a resolution, to introduce new characters in an unambiguous way, or to include causal statements."[89] With the help of conversational partners, autistic children with normal to above-average intelligence, however, sometimes engage in more elaborate narrative probings of their experiences that balance coherence with open-ended exploration. In the narrative excerpt that follows, the Chinese-American parents of twelve-year-old Jason prod him (in Chinese and English) to delve into an incident involving a boy who annoys him at school. At first Jason, like Karl (see above), is reluctant to tell this narrative:[90]

Mother: Jeremy Murray jin tian you mei you ni jian hua.
   Did Jeremy Murray talk to you today?
   (1.0 pause)

Jason: Huh?

    (2.0 pause)

Mother: Jeremy Murray

    (1.0 pause)

    Zai shue shao you mei you gen ni jian hua?

    Did he talk to you at school today?

    (2.0 pause)

Jason: He talked to me but

    Mei you yi yi de hua

    It was nothing worth mentioning

    (1.0 pause)

Mother: *Mei you yi yi de hua*

    It was nothing worth mentioning

Father: [( )

    ( )

Mother: [*She me jiao mei you yi yi de hua*

    What does "not worth mentioning" mean?

    (1.0 pause)

    ( )

Jason: I don't know

    (4.0 pause)

Mother: *Ta ge ni jian shen me?*

    What did he say to you?

    "I don't know"

But, unlike Karl, Jason changes his disposition and begins to explore the troublesome incident. Jason signals that he *does* have a story to tell by introducing it with "actually":

Jason: I: (.) actually (6.0 pause) actually (2.0 pause) he pick on me- he picked on me today.

When his Mother asks him to consider the circumstances that provoked Jeremy Murray to pick on him, however, Jason is unable to articulate them:

Mother: Really? °Why°?
Jason: I don't know . . .
Mother: Ta zhen me
          How did he
          (2.0 pause)

          How did he pick on you, what did you do ↓
          (3.0 pause)
Jason: [I didn't do anything.
Mother: [(Why he pick on you?)
Jason: He just bothers me a lot.
Mother: He bother you a lot?
Jason: ((nods his head))
Mother: °Oh°
          [Like what?

Jason cannot satisfy his Mother's queries into antecedents and motives, largely because of impairments associated with autism, particularly deficits in discerning the psychological states of other people.[91] The thematic and logical path that Jason's narrative takes is thus limited by his social and cognitive deficits. Jason's parents attempt to elicit details concerning the strategy that Jason used to handle Jeremy Murray's bullying. Jason is given the opportunity to narrate his own strategy, but instead, he cites details concerning his adversary's taunting:

Mother: [Like what?
Father: [So how you handled it?
Mother: Like what Jason?
Father: How do you handle it?
          (1.0 pause)
Jason: I say "hello"-
          ((animated)) When I say "hello" to him
          He says "AAAAH"
          He gets scared.
Father: Pretend
Mother: [uh hmm
Father: [uh hmm
          (2.0 pause)

Mother: [It's OK, it's alright Jason
Jason: [But I
Then he walked away,
So I <u>wanted</u> to <u>do</u> that
But it wo- (.) it worked in the first place but now it didn't,

In this passage, Jason flushes out a double problem: Not only is there the problem that Jeremy Murray bothers him, there is also the problem that the strategy for handling Jeremy Murray (i.e., saying "hello"), which had "worked in the first place," did not work this time. In response to his frustration, Jason's parents provide further suggestions for handling Jeremy Murray in the future:

Mother: But Jason it's not worth it to-
(2.0 pause)
to get ups- upset
or pay attention on him
Jason: °uh hmm°
Mother: Just ignore him OK?
Jason: I just pretend that Jeremy Murray wasn't here.
Mother: Uh hmm.
(1.0 pause)
That's a smart way
Jason: [OK
Father: [°hmm°

The proposed remedies, however, do not completely soothe Jason. The rationale for Jeremy Murray's taunts continues to elude him:

Jason: I wonder why Jeremy Murray <u>do</u> this to me
Mother: °I don't know°

In summary, this narrative interaction structures a resolute future for Jason (i.e., new tactics for handling his tormentor) but leaves the meaning of past actions unresolved. Jason's parents guide him in building a coherent logic for handling life challenges; at the same time they recognize that coherence of past, present, and future experience is unattainable.

Striking a balance between coherence and authenticity is a hallmark of dynamic co-tellings of experience. Between the highly determined temporal and causal ordering of events and the rejection of conventional plot lines lies a narrative zone that is at once structured and open-ended. This zone provides a conventional but flexible textual space in which co-tellers can co-author life event narratives. Wolfgang Iser makes this point in his reader response analysis of what constitutes good literary prose: "In this way, every literary text invites some form of participation on the part of the reader ... Texts with ... minimal indeterminacy tend to be tedious, for it is only when the reader is given the chance to participate actively that he will regard the texts, whose intention he himself has helped to compose, as real."[92]

Iser's view that literary works gain vitality by leaving some facets of the storyline untold is applicable to narrative more broadly. It matches Havel's view that great theatre and great dialogue engage tellers and audience alike in a "ceaseless process of searching, demystification, and penetration beneath the surface of phenomena in ways that do not depend on allegiance to given, ready-made methodology."[93] In yet another context, Edward Schieffelin captures how fragmented ceremonial narratives among the Kaluli of Papua New Guinea inspire audience members to remember their own past: "Framed in sentiments of loneliness or abandonment, the mention of particular trees, hills, and other details of the locality evoke for the listeners particular times and circumstances."[94] Certain listeners become so emotionally aroused that they rise up and sear the skin of the narrators with sticks burning in the hearth.

Narration and narrative are thus distinct; narration provides the symbolic fuel for interlocutors to author only partially overlapping narratives. Though some lean more toward coherence and others more toward authenticity, all personal narratives are fragmented intimations of experience. Telling surely assists the construction of a tale, but the tale necessarily lies beyond the telling.[95]

Moral Stance Barriers

We have related untold stories to barriers rooted in memory for life events (tellability), interaction (tellership), and genre (linearity). We now consider barriers to expressing life experience grounded in morality. More specifically, we reflect on remembering as a moral practice. Each telling positions not only protagonists but also tellers as more or less moral persons.

We have already noted how tellers strive to represent themselves as decent, ethical persons who pursue the moral high road in contrast to certain other protagonists in their narratives. Central to the virtuous teller is his or her credibility. Even though remembering is imperfect and malleable, tellers of personal experience work to authenticate their memories and, in so doing, to make their narrative accounts sound credible. As William Labov notes: "Reportable events are almost by definition unusual. They are therefore inherently less credible than non-reportable events. In fact, we might say that the more reportable an event is, the less credible it is. Yet credibility is as essential as reportability for the success of a narrative."[96]

Credibility depends in part upon the plausibility of a chain of objective events that can be corroborated. Narrators, however, strategically couch these events within subjective events that cannot be contradicted. The narrators studied by Labov threaded their narratives with subjective events such as thinking ("I thought he was gonna <u>hit</u> me"), knowing ("I didn't know what it was"), talking to oneself ("I said to myself. 'There'll be times I can't put up with this . . .'"), intending ("I was about to hit him"), and feeling ("boy that was an <u>eery</u> night for me comin' home . . .").[97] As Richard Baumann aptly explains: "Narratives are seen as verbal icons of the events they recount, and the problem is one of determining the nature and extent of the isomorphism between them and the means by which this formal relationship is narratively achieved."[98]

Remembering is a subjective and unobservable, and therefore unverifiable, mental state. Nonetheless, tellers who cast events as what they or another "remember" presuppose that the events truly occurred. "Remember" is what linguists call a factual mental verb.[99] Factual verbs presuppose the certainty of a proposition. Thus, when young Evan tells his parents "you-you 'member (.) (um) if I eat a good <u>dinner</u> I could have a <u>ice</u> cream," he poses the promise as a fact about which he is eliciting confirmation. Remembering, then, is an authenticating act: Rememberers publicly claim to have brought to conscious awareness a state, event, or condition that is real in their eyes; they believe it to be true. In this sense, acts of remembering are attempts to seize authority with respect to a topic of concern. For the presupposed truths to become recognized as such, however, these acts require validation by others. Indeed, Derek Edwards and Jonathan Potter comment, "Everyday conversational remembering often has this as its primary concern: the attempt to construct an acceptable, agreed, or communicatively successful version of what really happened."[100] When such validation is not forthcoming, the authenticity of the remembered experience and by implication the reliability of the rememberer is called into question.[101]

Considerable discussion has been devoted to credibility in personal narrative compared to historical accounts. Three decades ago anthropologists Jack Goody and Ian Watt proposed that nonliterate societies have a past, while literate societies have a history.[102] In this perspective, nonliterate societies reconstruct the past through oral narratives, which in turn are continually reconfigured to justify the present. Literate groups, in contrast, can rely as well on histories based upon written records of prior events. The view that historical texts are credible reconstructions of the past runs counter to Hayden White's perception that history is fundamentally a form of narrative. In this approach, historians' concepts of the true past are shaped by the ideological persuasions of the historian or political sponsors or both.[103]

Despite White's claims to the contrary, the distinction between narrative and history lives on in the work of clinical psychologist Donald Spence. Spence contrasts "narrative truth" with "historical truth":

> Narrative truth can be defined as the criterion we use to decide
> when a certain experience has been captured to our satisfaction; it
> depends on continuity and closure and the extent to which the fit
> of the pieces takes on an aesthetic finality. Narrative truth is what
> we have in mind when we say that such and such is a good story,
> that a given explanation carries conviction, that *one* solution to a
> mystery must be true . . . Historical truth is time-bound and is dedicated to the strict observance of correspondence rules; our aim is to
> come as close as possible to what "really" happened. Historical
> truth is not satisfied with coherence for its own sake; we must have
> some assurance that the pieces being fitted into the puzzle also belong to a certain place and that this belonging can be corroborated
> in some systematic manner.[104]

From this point of view, those narrating past life experiences differ from historians in their sense of authenticity. While narrators are concerned with external validation, their sense of authenticity is primarily internal. Narrators strive to build not just any coherent storyline but one that resonates with their sense of who they are in the world. This concept of authenticity is close to Heidegger's point that an authentic capturing of the past takes into consideration a person's concerns.[105] In this perspective, existential preoccupations do not veil reality; instead, they reveal it. Reconstructions of past life events are authentic when tellers direct their attention to and psychically inhabit those events, allowing them to be uncovered. Authentic apprehension of past worlds is facilitated by a person's ongoing concerns with present and potential ways of being in the world.

The distinction between narrative truth and historical truth is a moral issue that extends beyond the academy to international politics. Recall, for example, the discussion in Chapter 6 of the public controversy over the truth of atrocities recounted by Nobel Prize–winner Rigoberta Menchu in her published autobiography.[106] Those who challenged her authenticity abide by the parameters of historical truth, whereas her defenders and Menchu herself adhere to the principle of narrative truth. Menchu's story draws from her sensibilities as an insider, as participant, witness, and one who overhears a multitude of similar incidents. Her story holds emotional resonance for her and for others in the Guatemalan indigenous community. A parallel case involves Benjamin Wilkomirski's memoir of childhood in a concentration camp.[107] Critics, who managed to curtail its publication, established lack of authenticity based on historical records that undermined Wilkomirski's claims. Wilkomirski himself, however, insists that such records are easily falsifiable, whereas the vivid, albeit fragmented, quality of his childhood memories lends authenticity to his story.

Journalist Jane Kramer presents a detailed analysis of political controversies over how collective memories of World War II should be recorded in Germany today.[108] With the fiftieth anniversary of the war approaching, there is a political movement to put individuals' particular memories of the Holocaust to rest in the form of a monument in honor of the victims. Kramer's commentary on the conflict surrounding the German government's efforts to manage the past airs the fundamental tensions between the need for resolution, the importance of active remembering, and the problematic nature of traditional memorialization.

Traditional memorials transform individual memories to collective memory, distilling particular experiences into a common symbol.[109] The traditional memorial is a metaphor that emanates the meaning of an experience. Viewers—including those who are still grieving and those whose knowledge of the war is less direct—come to the memorial and are infused with an unambiguous representation of the experience. Paradoxically, and of concern to those who have suffered, encountering traditional memorials may not compel or even support remembering. Rather, traditional memorials harness individuals' memories and responses within a politically sanctioned narrative account. On the one hand, traditional memorials can have a healing effect by providing a coherent, seemingly collective narrative in the face of the pain of lives lost. On the other hand, these memorials stifle further public narrative explication and questioning of the meaning of what transpired. One risk is that those whose memories are too complex, chaotic, or penetrating to be soothed through symbolic substitution will continue to suffer. Their memories never were politically convenient; now they lose narrative justification. Another risk is that those who do not know about the memorialized events will unwittingly accept the simplified memory and not truly access their meaning through probing co-narration.

Although the risk of forgetting is inherent in any form of memorialization, it is perhaps greater in relation to memorials that articulate a single collective memory through classic iconography, such as a proud soldier with a flag, or through a quote that definitively deems the event "a noble cause well served." As writer and Vietnam veteran Tim O'Brien reflects:

> In a true war story, if there's a moral at all, it's like the thread that makes the cloth. You can't tease it out. You can't extract the meaning without unraveling the deeper meaning. And in the end, really, there's nothing much to say about a true war story, except maybe "Oh."
>
> True war stories do not generalize. They do not indulge in abstraction or analysis. For example: War is hell. As a moral declaration the old truism seems perfectly true, and yet because it abstracts, because it generalizes, I can't believe it with my stomach. Nothing turns inside. It comes down to gut instinct. A true war story, if truly told, makes the stomach believe.[110]

Alternatively, other memorials endeavor to evoke and sustain a multiplicity of personalized memories. The Vietnam Veterans' Memorial in

Washington, D.C., for example, contains elements that trigger individual reckoning with the Vietnam experience.[111] Visitors can read and trace with their fingers the names of the 58,000 soldiers who died. The polished black granite makes visible the reflection of visitors' bodies, including those of the many veterans who journey to the wall, often dressed in battle fatigues. The reflected living images are juxtaposed with the names of the dead and with one another. This intermingling is a form of dialogue, which was slow in coming. The Vietnam War did not end in glory, and the prevailing collective sentiment was a desire to forget and be silent. The memorial has become a matrix for narrative interaction, as veterans collect by the Wall to reminisce with the living and dead.

The aftermath of experiences such as the Holocaust and the Vietnam War teaches us how memories may be politically inconvenient to have and to acknowledge. Milan Kundera recounts that in 1948 the Czech leader Gottwald was photographed with his comrade Clementis; five years later, authorities charged him with treason, hanged him, and airbrushed him out of the picture and out of history,[112] or so they thought. Memories of persons, deeds, and misdeeds are not easily expunged. In the words of Vaclav Havel: "Nothing that has once happened can unhappen . . . Not only will it not cease to exist when its 'owner' goes into another room, or is imprisoned, or when everyone else has forgotten about him, but it will not cease to exist even when he dies, nor even when the last man who ever knew him or knew that someone like him ever existed, forgets about him, or dies. Nothing can ever erase from the history of Being a human personality that once was; it exists in that history forever."[113]

Coda

Debate about the authenticity of narrated memories reverberates through the halls of governments, clinicians' offices, and media venues—profoundly affecting and sometimes dividing members of society in the process. Questions about the extent to which memory is malleable are grounded in fundamental philosophical questions: If we cannot vouch for the reality of the past, can we truly know ourselves in the present?[114] Kundera airs a despairing response to this issue: "Try to reconstruct a dialogue from your own life, the dialogue of a quarrel or a dialogue of love. The most precious, the most important situations are utterly gone. Their abstract sense remains . . . perhaps a detail or two, but the acoustico-visual concreteness of the situation in all its continuity is lost . . . And not only is it lost but we do not even wonder at this loss. We are resigned to losing the concreteness of the present . . . Remembering is not the negative of forgetting. Remembering is a form of forgetting . . . We die without knowing what we have lived."[115] For those who are more optimistic about the recoverability of memory, a driving question is how we can ascertain the accuracy of a memory. Is resistance to suggestion and refusal to modify one's account indicative of truth? The resistance displayed by co-tellers suggests that being impervious is no assurance of accurate recall. Does implicit memory in the form of, for example, somatic sensations, fragmented flashbacks, or dreams index the true occurrence of a past event? Are there differences in the qualities of false and veridical memories? Unanswered, these questions remain hotly contested and fervently pursued.[116] As discussed earlier, although some believe that therapists or clients themselves can induce implicit memories (creating false memories), or that behavioral manifestations can be feigned, others insist on their unequivocal authenticity. The issue has profound emotional and legal consequences for the lives of would-be victims and perpetrators. What are the consequences for one's sense of reality and self-identity when one's memory of even seemingly insignificant events is repeatedly overruled? Or when one becomes convinced that an emotionally significant event did not happen or happened in a radically different manner than one's memory? The risks can include social isolation, persecution, and excruciating self-doubt—plights generally associated with significant psychological distress.

The tension among different concepts of authenticity may be an inherent property of selfhood.[117] As Henri Bergson noted in 1911[118] and others like Kundera[119] and Ricoeur[120] later concurred, we can't credibly reflect upon ourselves in the present, as we experience the moment. Rather, the nonpresent—the past and the possible—is the context for self-making, and the genre most suited for this endeavor is personal narrative. "We seem to have no other way of describing 'lived time' save in the form of a narrative," notes Jerome Bruner.[121] Narration of past and potential selves, in turn, is grounded in our current beliefs and concerns about the past and the possible and in our conviction that our beliefs are true and our concerns central to our self-understanding.

The activity of self-reflection through narrative co-telling, however, also engenders the awareness that beliefs vary in certainty, can be contested, and are vulnerable to change. As such, the process of grounding ourselves is infused with doubt and motion. We come to define ourselves as we narratively grapple with our own and others' ambiguous emotions and events. As a result, narrative constructions of uncertainty as well as certainty play an important role in configuring selves. Paradoxically, we are perhaps most intensely cognizant of ourselves when we are unsure of ourselves, including our memories. The tension between certainty and doubt drives narrative activity in pursuit of an authentic remembered self.

NOTES

REFERENCES

INDEX

NOTES

1. A Dimensional Approach to Narrative

1. Kermode (1967).
2. Bakhtin (1986, p. 106).
3. Mandelbaum (1987b).
4. Toth (1987, p. 117).
5. Bakhtin (1986).
6. Bernstein (1994), Morson (1994).
7. Langer (1991, p. 17).
8. White (1980, p. 23).
9. Morson (1994, p. 6).
10. Bernstein (1994, p. 2).
11. Ibid., p. 16.
12. Morson (1994, p. 7).
13. Bernstein (1994, p. 3).
14. Sacks, Schegloff, and Jefferson (1974), Sacks (1992), Schegloff (1986, 1995, 1997b).
15. Schegloff (1986).
16. Bakhtin (1986).
17. Ochs, Taylor, Rudolph, and Smith (1992).
18. Ochs, Smith, and Taylor (1989).
19. Ochs, Taylor, Rudolph, and Smith (1992).
20. Duranti (1994, p. 152).
21. Goodwin (1989), Goodwin (1990).
22. Schafer (1983, p. 219).
23. Havel (1989, p. 301).
24. Ibid., p. 306.

25. Leitch (1986, p. 130).

26. Labov and Waletsky (1967).

27. Ek, interview corpus on multiculturalism and primary education, Ek and Alvarez (1998).

28. Young (1984, pp. 240-241).

29. Goffman (1974).

30. Holmes (1998).

31. Duranti and Brenneis (1986), Duranti and Goodwin (1992), Ochs and Jacoby (1995).

32. Schafer (1992), Gergen and Kaye (1992).

33. Linguistic anthropologist Charles Goodwin (1981) has illuminated the process of co-authorship by delineating how speakers finely tune their language to capture and maintain the attention of their addressee. For example, when speakers pause momentarily, repeat, rephrase, intensify, or embellish a narrative, it is often in response to an addressee's displayed inattention or disinterest. Sometimes speakers accommodate to their intended addressees to no avail, opting either to drop their narrative or to seek out yet another addressee. Switching addressees is no small feat, as the speaker must then redesign the narrative to meet the interests, knowledge, and social position of the new recipient. Goodwin illustrates this process through analysis of a conversation in which a speaker tries to tell his friends that that he has stopped smoking. Noticing that his friends are not paying attention, he shifts his gaze to his attentive wife. Because his wife knows that he has quit smoking, however, he redesigns his utterance and therefore the gist of the story to highlight points that are new to her: he stopped smoking exactly one week ago.

34. Bakhtin (1981, 1986), Volosinov (1971, 1973).

35. Goodwin (1989).

36. See Capps and Ochs (1995, p. 129).

37. Bakhtin claims: "A word (or in general any sign) is interindividual. Everything that is said, expressed, is located outside the 'soul' of the speaker and does not belong only to him [or her]. The word cannot be assigned to a single speaker. The author (speaker) has his own inalienable right to the word, but the listener has his rights, and those whose voices are heard in the word before the author comes upon it also have their rights (after all, there are no words that belong to no one)" (Bakhtin, 1986, pp. 121-122).

38. Mandelbaum (1987b).

39. Goodwin (1984).

40. Kendon (1990).

41. Schegloff (1982).
42. Lerner (1987, 1991).
43. A related strategy for drawing interlocutors into the co-telling of a narrative is to mention what Mandelbaum (1987b) calls a "mystery item," a comment that piques another's curiosity.
44. Schegloff, Jefferson, and Sacks (1977).
45. Capps, unpublished family dinner corpus.
46. Besnier (1989), Keenan (1976).
47. Goodwin (1979).
48. Ochs (1994, p. 111).
49. Capps, unpublished panic corpus.
50. Capps and Ochs (1995a, pp. 130-131).
51. Ochs, Taylor, Rudolph, and Smith (1992, p. 50).
52. Ibid., p. 53.
53. Goodwin (1986), Mandelbaum (1987a).
54. Taylor (1995a, pp. 149-150).
55. Goodwin (1990), Mandelbaum (1987a, b), Taylor (1995a, b).
56. Goodwin (1984), Goodwin (1991), Jefferson (1978), Sacks (1992), Schegloff (1997a).
57. Sacks (1992, p. 249).
58. Capps, unpublished panic corpus.
59. See, for example, Capps and Ochs (1995a), Goodwin (1990, 1991, 1997).
60. Goodwin (1986, pp. 309-310).
61. Pratt (1977, p. 148).
62. Labov and Waletsky (1967).
63. Shuman (1986, pp. 69-70).
64. Heath (1985, 1986).
65. Capps, unpublished family dinner corpus.
66. Ochs, Taylor, Rudolph, and Smith (1992, p. 43).
67. Capps, unpublished family dinner corpus.
68. Ochs, Taylor, Rudolph, and Smith (1992, p. 64).
69. Labov (1966).
70. Abrahams (1964, 1976), Ben-Amos (1975), Gossen (1976), Haviland (1977), Rosenberg (1970), Sherzer (1983), Tannen (1987).
71. Pratt (1977).
72. Goodwin (1986), Jefferson (1978), Sacks (1992).
73. Jefferson (1978), Sacks (1992).
74. Tannen (1990, p. 80).
75. Jönsson and Linell (1991, p. 426).
76. Goodwin (1981, pp. 156-157).
77. Jefferson (1978).

78. James (1982 [1902]).
79. Ochs (1994).
80. Shuman (1986, pp. 26-27).
81. Langer (1991, p. 164).
82. Hyden and McCarthy (1994, p. 555).
83. Capps and Ochs (1995a, b).
84. Capps and Ochs (1995a, p. 34).
85. Bernstein (1994, pp. 70-71).
86. Musil (1995, pp. 708-709).
87. Havel (1989).
88. Burke (1962).
89. Barnes (1984), MacIntyre (1984).
90. Bruner (1987, 1990, 1991, 1995).
91. Jacobs-Huey (1999, p. 131).
92. Ochs, Smith, and Taylor (1989).
93. Bauman (1986, p. 15).
94. Terasaki (1976), Sacks (1992).
95. Capps and Ochs (1995a, b), Rymes (1997).
96. Ochs, Taylor, Rudolph, and Smith (1992).
97. Ochs, Smith, and Taylor (1989).
98. Bauman (1988, p. 3).
99. MacIntyre (1984, p. 219).
100. Ibid., p. 219.
101. Taylor (1989, p. 48).
102. Rymes (1997, p. 155).
103. Ochs, Smith, and Taylor (1989, p. 244).
104. Goodwin (1990), Ochs, Smith, and Taylor (1989).
105. Bakhtin (1981, 1986), Berman and Slobin (1994).
106. Burke (1962), Fish (1980a, b), Iser (1993), Ricoeur (1981, 1984, 1985, 1988).
107. Abrahams (1964), Young (1987).
108. Labov and Waletsky (1967, 1968).
109. Mandler (1979), Mandler and Johnson (1977), Stein (1982), Stein and Glenn (1979), Stein and Policastro (1984), Stein and Salgo (1984).

2. Becoming a Narrator

1. Sugiyama (1996).
2. Gould and Gould (1988), von Frisch (1967).
3. Deacon (1997).
4. The evidence for non-human primate and early hominid capacity to intentionally represent the past or project a future for others remains

inconclusive and is hotly disputed. Kummer's detailed observations of baboons, for example, suggest that they proceed toward a future destination through trial and error rather than planning of any sort (Kummer, 1995). Moreover, Marshack's proposal (1989, 1991) that cave-dwelling *Homo Erectus* had narrative competence has been questioned (Aiello, 1996; Byers, 1994; Noble and Davidson, 1996).

5. Bauman (1986, p. 4).

6. Ochs (1997), Ochs and Capps (1996).

7. See, for example, Berman and Slobin (1994), Mandler and Johnson (1977), Stein (1982), Stein and Albro (1997), Stein and Glenn (1979), Stein and Goldman (1981), Stein and Policastro (1984), Stein and Salgo (1984), Trabasso, Secco, and Van Den Broek (1984).

8. Pratt (1977).

9. Morson (1994).

10. Nelson (1989).

11. Feldman (1989).

12. Berman and Slobin (1994).

13. Heath (1983).

14. Notable studies include Peggy Miller and Linda Sperry's pioneering study of young, Euro-American working-class children's emerging capacity for everyday personal narrative (1982); Robyn Fivush and her colleagues' examination of the role of co-narration in building children's autobiographical memory, see Fivush (1991, 1994), Fivush, Hamond, Harsch, Singer, and Wolf (1991); Peggy Miller, Heidi Fung, and Judith Mintz's comparison of personal narrative among young Taiwanese and American children (1996); Shoshana Blum-Kulka and Catherine Snow's research on Israeli and American middle-class and working-class family co-narration (1992); Mary Mullen and Soonhyung Yi's study of Korean and American mother-child dyadic narration (1993); Ann Eisenberg's study of conversational narrative skills among Mexican-American children (1985, 1986); Katharina Meng's study of German (1992) and Aylin Küntay's study of Turkish (1997) preschool children's spontaneous narrative activity; and research on development of personal narrative among young Japanese children by Masahiko Minami (1996), Minami and McCabe (1991, 1995), and Kaye Nakamura (1993).

15. Heath (1985).

16. Ibid., p. 18.

17. Rogoff (1990).

18. Ochs (1988), Ochs and Schieffelin (1984, 1995).

19. Meng (1992, p. 241).

20. Preece (1985, 1992).
21. Preece (1992, p. 285).
22. Ibid.
23. Ibid., p. 284.
24. Ibid., p. 280.
25. Ibid., p. 286.
26. Miller et al. (1990).
27. Blum-Kulka and Snow (1992), Heath (1983).
28. John-Steiner (1984), John-Steiner and Panofsky (1992).
29. Scollon (1982).
30. McCabe (1997), Nelson (1990a, b), Snow (1990).
31. Miller (1996, p. 1), Miller, Potts, Fung, Hoogstra, and Mintz (1990). Findings are based on cross-sectional and longitudinal studies of two-and-a-half–five-year-old middle-class children in Chicago and Taipei, Taiwan. The Chicago families were of Euro-American ethnicity. The specific corpus for this study consists of 36 hours of recorded observations of nine children aged two-and-a-half years.
32. Mullen and Yi (1993).
33. Findings are based on audio-recordings of eight Korean and eight Euro-American middle-class mother-child dyads, in which the child ranged from 37 to 44 months. Recordings were made in the home over a one-day period. Recordings were transcribed and coded for number of turns, utterances per turn, and narrative reference to child.
34. Blum-Kulka and Snow (1992).
35. Ibid., p. 195.
36. Ibid., p. 196.
37. Heath (1983, p. 158).
38. McCabe (1997).
39. Demuth (1983, pp. 107–108). This study focused on routines as a context of language acquisition and is based on longitudinal recordings over 12 months of four Sesotho-speaking children ranging in age from approximately two to three-and-a-half years at the onset of data collection.
40. Bloom (1973, p. 207).
41. Heath (1982).
42. Ibid., p. 107.
43. Schieffelin (1990, p. 88).
44. Crago (1988), Eisenberg (1986), Miller (1982), Ochs (1988), Peters and Boggs (1986), Scollon (1982), Watson-Gegeo and Gegeo (1986).

45. Scollon (1982, p. 76).
46. Ibid., p. 89.
47. Brown (1997). These data are drawn from a three-year longitudinal study of children in five Tzeltal Mayan households in which focal children ranging from 1 year 6 months to 4 years of age were videotaped every six weeks.
48. Brown (1997, p. 4).
49. Miller and Sperry (1982, p. 300). These data are drawn from a cross-sectional and longitudinal study of five working-class Euro-American children ranging in age from 1 year 7 months to 2 years 8 months. The data were both naturalistic and elicited. Mothers were asked to encourage their child to "tell about an event that happened in the recent past" (1988, p. 296).
50. Hudson (1990).
51. Ibid., p. 177.
52. Feldman (1989, p. 104). These observations are based on a longitudinal audio recording of one child, Emily, from 21 months 7 days to 36 months 9 days of age, while she lay in her crib at night before falling asleep.
53. Fivush, Hamond, Harsch, Singer, and Wolf (1991).
54. See, for example, Mullen (1994), Mullen and Yi (1993), Han, Leichtman, and Wang (1998).
55. Fivush et al. (1991, p. 381).
56. Ochs and Taylor (1992).
57. Capps, unpublished diary notes on the verbal behavior of her son David during the first two-and-a-half years of his life.
58. Heath (1983, p. 170).
59. See Bauer and Mandler (1989), Nelson (1989), Nelson and Gruendel (1981, 1986), and Schank and Abelson (1977) on scripts.
60. Nelson (1989).
61. Bruner and Lucariello (1989, p. 84).
62. Nelson (1989, p. 67).
63. Hudson (1990), Hudson and Shapiro (1991), Miller and Sperry (1982).
64. Nelson (1989).
65. Eisenberg (1985), Nelson (1989).
66. Meng (1992).
67. Dunn (1988). Moreover, highly routine, familiar events become fused into generalized event representations and are less accessible as distinct narrative episodes.
68. Bruner and Lucariello (1989).

69. Ibid., pp. 87-88.
70. Chafe (1993), Nelson (1989).
71. Minami (1996). This analysis is based upon elicited narratives from ten five-year-old and ten four-year-old middle-class Japanese pre-school children. Each child was asked one or more questions that elicited a narrative about an injury he or she had suffered. The same questions were directed to mothers to elicit similar narratives for comparative purposes.
72. See Chafe (1993) and Hymes (1981) for elaboration of the notions of verse and stanza.
73. Miller and Sperry (1982).
74. Heath (1983, p. 184).
75. Minami and McCabe (1991, 1995). The 1991 study is based upon per-sonal narratives elicited by researchers from seventeen Japanese chil-dren between five and nine years old who had been living in the United States for less than two years. The 1995 analysis is based pri-marily upon personal narratives elicited by eight middle-class Japa-nese mothers and eight middle-class American mothers from their four- or five-year-old children in the course of conversation.
76. Minami and McCabe (1991, pp. 585-586).
77. Gerhardt (1989). This analysis is based upon Emily's speech from 22 months 16 days to 24 months 2 days.
78. Ibid., p. 180.
79. Ibid.
80. Nelson (1989).
81. McCabe (1997).
82. Gerhardt (1989) notes that sequencers seem to go hand in hand with the ordering of routine events, which are not the focus of Emily's dialogic narratives. Monologic narratives that are about specific events also are not prefaced by sequencers, but rather adverbials like "one time."
83. Miller and Sperry (1982). The analysis is based upon longitudinal home observations of five working-class Euro-American children and their mothers from two to two-and-a-half years of age.
84. Meng (1992).
85. Aristotle (1982 [4th century B.C.E.]).
86. Heath (1985). Alternatively, Ochs, Taylor et al. (1992) call temporally linked sequences of past time events "reports," distinct from "sto-ries," which center around a problematic event that provokes psycho-logical responses, outcomes, and/or attempts to handle the problem-atic event.

87. Ochs, unpublished family dinner corpus.
88. Heath (1985), Ochs, Taylor et al. (1992), Stein (1982).
89. McCabe (1997), Quasthoff (1997).
90. Peterson and McCabe (1983, 1991). These studies are based upon elicited personal narratives told by 96 working-class Euro-American children between three-and-a-half and nine-and-a-half years old. Researcher prompts "were about pet adventures, visits to the doctor and hospital, accidents, parties, vacations, and so on" (1991, p. 32).
91. Berman and Slobin (1994). This analysis is based upon a large, cross-linguistic database of elicited accounts of a picture book called *Frog, Where are You?* Data are from preschool, school-age, and adult narrators in five languages: English, German, Spanish, Hebrew, and Turkish.
92. Applebee (1978).
93. Berman and Slobin (1994, p. 58).
94. Hudson and Shapiro (1991). The analysis is based upon researcher-elicited personal narratives, scripts, and stories from 37 preschool (mean age 4 years 8 months), 38 first-grade (mean age 6 years 7 months), and 34 third-grade (mean age 8 years 7 months) lower-middle-class American children.
95. Hudson and Shapiro (1991, p. 118).
96. Küntay (1997, pp. 47–48).
97. Ibid., p. 146. The analysis was based on primarily audio-recorded spontaneous and elicited storybook and personal narratives from 46 Turkish preschool children from three to six years of age.
98. Renner (1988).
99. Berman and Slobin (1994, p. 60).
100. Küntay (1997).
101. Ochs (1994, p. 114).
102. Siegel (1999).
103. Ibid., p. 219.
104. Loveland and Tunali (1991), Sigman and Capps (1997), Tager-Flusberg (1995).
105. Morson (1994).
106. Feldman (1989).
107. Ibid., pp. 109–110.
108. Ibid., p. 112.
109. Küntay (1997, p. 164).
110. Hymes (1996).
111. Ibid., p. 138.

112. Heath (1983).

113. Ibid., p. 173.

114. Gee (1996), Michaels (1981, 1991).

115. Heath (1983).

116. Gee draws upon Chafe (1979, 1993) and Hymes (1981) in analyzing narrative in terms of lines, verses, and stanzas.

117. Gee (1996, pp. 106–107).

118. Cazden, Michaels, and Tabors (1985).

119. Minami (1991).

120. Cazden (1997), Cazden, Michaels, and Tabors (1985), Gee (1986, 1996), Gutierrez, Stone, and Larson (in press), Heath (1983, 1985, 1986).

121. Monaco (1981).

122. Taylor (1995a, p. 273).

123. Küntay (1997, p. 73).

124. Preece (1985, p. 199).

125. Bruner and Lucariello (1989, pp. 94–95), Bruner (1990, 1991), Labov (1972).

126. Bruner and Lucariello (1989).

127. Miller and Sperry (1988).

128. Meng (1992).

129. MacIntyre (1984, p. 218).

130. For discussion of this matter, see Miller, Wiley, Fung, and Liang (1997), Keenan (1974), Ochs (1988).

131. Miller, Wiley, Fung, and Liang (1997). This analysis is based upon two years of ethnographic field recordings of six Taiwanese and six Euro-American middle-class families, each with a two-and-a-half-year-old child and at least one sibling.

132. Miller (1996, p. 192).

133. Miller et al. (1990, p. 296).

134. Bernstein (1972).

135. Miller et al. (1990, p. 301).

136. Miller et al. (1997, p. 564).

137. Steveron (1995, pp. 44–45).

138. Schieffelin (1990).

139. Ochs (1988).

140. Miller (1986).

141. Eisenberg (1986).

142. Crago (1988).

143. Scollon (1982).

144. Ibid., pp. 98–99.

145. Ibid., p. 101.

146. Ochs, Smith, and Taylor (1989).

147. Bamberg (1996, 1997).

148. Bamberg (1996, p. 33).

149. Capps and Ochs (1995a).

150. Capps, Sigman, Sena, Henker, and Whalen (1996), Casat (1988), Silverman, Cerny, Nelles, and Burke (1988).

151. Capps (1996), Capps and Ochs (1995a).

3. Launching a Narrative

1. Pirandello (1929, p. 217).

2. Capps and Ochs (1995a, p. 129).

3. Ochs and Taylor (1992, p. 315).

4. Ochs (1994).

5. Keenan and Schieffelin (1976b, pp. 363–364).

6. Goodwin (1990, p. 245).

7. Corpus transcribed by Francoise Brun-Cottian, cited in Keenan and Schieffelin (1976a, p. 373).

8. Goodwin (1990, p. 304).

9. Bloom (1973).

10. Goodwin (1981, p. 52).

11. Ibid., p. 66.

12. Acebo and Thoman (1995), Lock (1981), Ochs and Schieffelin (1979), Shotter (1995), Zeskind and Collins (1987).

13. Rogoff (1990), Stern (1977), Trevarthen (1979).

14. Ochs (1988), Schieffelin (1990).

15. Capps, unpublished family dinner corpus.

16. Crago (1988), Ochs (1988), Pye (1992), Schieffelin (1990).

17. Fernald (1989, 1992), Fernald and Mazzie (1991), Keenan (1978), Keenan and Schieffelin (1976a, b).

18. Sacks (1972, 1974, 1978, 1992). See also M. H. Goodwin (1990), Jefferson (1978).

19. Sacks (1992, p. 226).

20. Duranti, unpublished transcript. Recorded in 1979, last revision May 21, 1988.

21. Button and Casey (1985), M. H. Goodwin (1981), Sacks (1992), Terasaki (1976).

22. Capps, unpublished family dinner corpus.

23. C. Goodwin (1984), M. H. Goodwin (1990), Pomerantz (1984), Sacks (1992).

24. Ochs, unpublished family dinner corpus.
25. Sacks, Schegloff, and Jefferson (1974).
26. Sacks (1992), Terasaki (1976).
27. Ochs, unpublished family dinner corpus.
28. Capps, unpublished family dinner corpus.
29. Ibid.
30. Taylor (1995a, p. 246).
31. C. Goodwin (1986), Mandelbaum (1987).
32. C. Goodwin (1986, p. 298).
33. Ochs and Taylor (1992, p. 310).
34. Blum-Kulka (1997, p. 115).
35. Ibid., pp. 113-114.
36. Ochs and Taylor (1992, pp. 333-334).
37. Ochs, unpublished family dinner corpus.

4. The Unexpected Turn

1. Capps and Ochs (1995a, p. 130).
2. Miller and Moore (1989, p. 435).
3. Capps, unpublished panic corpus.
4. Heath (1985).
5. Field (1979).
6. Miller and Moore (1989, p. 435).
7. Capps, unpublished panic corpus.
8. Sharff (1982).
9. Ochs, Smith, and Taylor (1989).
10. Ochs, Taylor, Rudolph, and Smith (1992, p. 53).
11. Taylor (1995b).
12. Capps and Ochs (1995a, b), Putnam (1985), Radden (1996), Siegel (1996a, b), Terr (1994).
13. Siegel (1996b, p. 199).
14. Capps and Ochs (1995a, p. 57).
15. Ibid., p. 84.
16. Ibid., p. 89.
17. Mandelbaum (1987b, p. 197).
18. Ochs, unpublished family dinner corpus.
19. Michaels (1991, p. 310).
20. Bruner (1996, p. 99).
21. Capps and Ochs (1995a, p. 48).
22. Mandelbaum (1987b, p. 165).
23. Ochs, unpublished family dinner corpus.

24. M. H. Goodwin (1990, p. 195).
25. Duranti (1992).
26. Miller et al. (1990, p. 301).
27. C. Goodwin (1984, p. 225).
28. Mandelbaum (1987b, p. 24).
29. Capps, unpublished family dinner corpus.
30. Ibid.
31. Schegloff (1995, p. 188).
32. Ochs (1994, p. 120).

5. Experiential Logic

1. Bernstein (1994), Morson (1994).
2. Heidegger (1962, 1992), Ricoeur (1981, 1984, 1985, 1988).
3. Ochs, Taylor, Rudolph, and Smith (1992).
4. Gibson (1979), Norman (1988).
5. Berman and Slobin (1994, p. 66).
6. Musil (1995, pp. 708-709).
7. Ochs, unpublished family dinner corpus.
8. Ek, unpublished interview corpus on multiculturalism and primary education, Ek and Alvarez (1998).
9. Ochs et al. (1992, p. 43).
10. Young (1984, pp. 240-241).
11. Shuman (1986, pp. 69-70).
12. Jönsson and Linell (1991, p. 426).
13. Capps, unpublished panic corpus.
14. Ochs, unpublished family dinner corpus.
15. Bauman (1986, p. 15).
16. Quirk, Greenbaum, Leech, and Svartvik (1985, pp. 1451-1457).
17. Ochs et al. (1992, p. 43).
18. Capps and Ochs (1995a, p. 41).
19. C. Goodwin (1981, pp. 156-157).
20. Heidegger (1962).
21. Polanyi (1985, p. 17).
22. Linde (1993, p. 4).
23. Ochs, Taylor, Rudolph, and Smith (1992, p. 43).
24. M. H. Goodwin (1990, p. 195).
25. Capps and Ochs (1995a, p. 130).
26. Cederborg (1994, p. 126).
27. Ochs and Taylor (1992, p. 315).
28. Quirk, Greenbaum, Leech, and Svarvik (1985, p. 180).

29. Heath (1985).
30. Deby (1997, p. 2).
31. Woods (1997, p. 5).
32. Taylor (1995a, p. 78).
33. Woods (1997, p. 9).
34. Ochs, unpublished family dinner corpus.
35. Ochs, Smith, and Taylor (1989, p. 249).
36. Blum-Kulka (1997, pp. 72–73).
37. Labov and Waletsky (1967).
38. Capps (1995; 1996, p. 13).
39. Heath (1991, p. 109).
40. Ochs, Gonzales, and Jacoby (1996).
41. Ochs, unpublished physics corpus.
42. Goffman (1974, p. 506).
43. Ochs (1994, p. 120).
44. For definitions of episode, see Chafe (1979), van Dijk (1976), van Dijk and Kintsch (1983).
45. Korolija and Linell (1996).
46. Korolija (1998, pp. 42–43).
47. Stein and Glenn (1979).
48. Sacks (1978, pp. 257–258).
49. Janet ([1892]1977), Kihlstrom and Hoyt (1990), Laub and Auerhahn (1993), Reviere (1996), Terr (1994).
50. Laub and Auerhahn (1993, p. 299).
51. Scollon and Scollon (1981, p. 34).
52. Propp (1968).
53. Iser (1993).
54. Mandler and Johnson (1977).
55. Ibid.
56. Stein (1982), Stein and Glenn (1979), Stein and Goldman (1981), Stein and Policastro (1984), Stein and Salgo (1984).
57. Trabasso, Secco, and Van Den Broek (1984). See also Stein and Glenn (1979).
58. Ochs, Taylor, Rudolph, and Smith (1992, p. 62).
59. Ibid.
60. Duranti (1994, p. 152).
61. Capps, unpublished panic corpus.
62. Goodwin and Goodwin (1992, p. 174).
63. Capps and Ochs (1995, p. 34).
64. Hyden and McCarthy (1994, p. 555).

65. Ek. Interview corpus on multiculturalism and primary education
66. Capps, unpublished panic corpus.
67. Ochs and Taylor (1992, pp. 315-316).
68. Ochs, Smith, and Taylor (1989).
69. Ochs and Taylor (1992).
70. Capps and Ochs (1995a, p. 128).
71. Heidegger (1962).
72. Heidegger (1992, p. 168).
73. Capps and Ochs (1995a, p. 32).
74. Jacobs-Huey (1999, p. 131).
75. Ricoeur (1984, 1985, 1988).
76. Küntay (1997, p. 59).
77. Preece (1985, p. 146); previous example Ochs (1994, pp. 128-130).
78. Capps and Ochs (1995a, p. 129).
79. M. H. Goodwin (1990, p. 303).
80. Ochs (1994, p. 114).
81. Capps and Ochs (1995, p. 32).
82. Ochs et al. (1992, p. 43).
83. Jacobs-Huey (1999, pp. 51-52).
84. Solomon (1999).
85. Solomon, unpublished Russian toast corpus.

6. Beyond Face Value

1. Aristotle (1982), Cohn (1987), Morrison (1994), Ricoeur (1985), Swearington (1990).
2. Ochs, Taylor et al. (1992).
3. See Ochs and Jacoby (1997) for a discussion of how timing shapes the rhetoric of scientific discourse and Jacoby (1998) for analysis of conference talk rehearsals as sites of indigenous assessment and socialization into science.
4. Gonzales (1996, p. 135).
5. Lynch (1985).
6. Gonzales (1996, p. 90). See Ochs and Jacoby (1997) for extended analysis of laboratory deliberations prior to delivering a conference paper.
7. Gonzales (1996, p. 92).
8. Heath (1988, p. 366).
9. See Besnier (1995), Biber (1988), Collins (1995), Scribner and Cole (1981), Street (1984).
10. Kushner (1998).
11. Ibid.

12. Bruner (1974, p. 234).
13. Aristotle (1982, pp. 51–52).
14. Ricoeur (1981, p. 167).
15. Bourdieu (1977).
16. White (1980).
17. Feldman (1999).
18. Mattingly (1998, p. 14).
19. Ibid., p. 105. See also Garro (in press), Garro and Mattingly (in press), Good and Good (1994), Mischler (1995).
20. Amsterdam and Bruner (2000, p. 7).
21. Bruner (1990, p. 120).
22. Ochs, Smith, and Taylor (1989, p. 249).
23. Sacks (1992, p. 258).
24. Dworkin (1986, p. 24).
25. Ochs, Taylor, Rudolph, and Smith, (1992, p. 62).
26. Capps, unpublished panic corpus.
27. Sacks (1992, p. 263).
28. Garro (in press, p. 126).
29. Duranti, unpublished Italian transcript corpus.
30. Indeed, a central element of this narrative is the future mother-in-law's decision to lock herself in the bathroom, refusing to interact with Rita.
31. Morgan (1996, p. 418).
32. Bruner (1987, 1990, 1991).
33. Arminen (1996, p. 455).
34. Rymes (1997, p. 192).
35. Ibid., pp. 183–184.
36. Garfinkel (1967, p. 130).
37. Mishler (1995), Spence (1982).
38. Capps, unpublished panic corpus.
39. Capps and Ochs (1995a), Capps, unpublished panic corpus.
40. Capps, unpublished panic corpus.
41. Menchu (1984).
42. Stoll (1998).
43. Aznarez (1999, p. 7).
44. Crapanzano (1996).
45. Although later in life Abel tries to bury his past identity as Adelaide, the perpetuation of past female sensibilities into Abel's present self is implied in the narrator's account of Abel's inability or unwillingness to identify with the coarse values of men. Harold Garfinkel (1967) re-

flects that the resolution between gendered selves is muddled by society's insistence that one has to be either male or female, whereas people like Abel are more complexly gendered. Indeed, a number of scholars across disciplines promote a continuum of genders and have argued that all human beings have male and female identities.

46. Gates (1996, p. 66).
47. Frank (1995).
48. Ibid., p. 115.
49. Frank (1995, p. 59).
50. Nelson (1989).
51. Feldman (1999).
52. *New Encyclopedia Britannica* (1982, p. 307).
53. Calvino (1981, p. 167).

7. Narrative as Theology

1. MacIntyre (1984, p. 218).
2. Crites (1997), Hauerwas and Jones (1997), Taylor (1989).
3. Capps, unpublished prayer corpus.
4. We recognize that much more transpires in this interaction. The prayers also function as justifications for privileged access to the ceramic crucifix under contention between the two girls. Terry's prayer prioritizes Dana's plight over Susan's desires, while Susan's prayer can be read as prioritizing her own plight. Indeed, Susan renders her own problem as more serious than that of Dana when she enumerates several relatives whose deaths occurred before her birth and claims this situation to be "the saddest."
5. *New Encyclopedia Britannica* (1982, p. 948).
6. James (1982, p. 361).
7. Ibid., p. 70.
8. Ibid., p. 395.
9. Hendry (1972).
10. Capps, unpublished prayer corpus.
11. Capps, unpublished family dinner corpus.
12. Ochs, unpublished family dinner corpus.
13. Ibid.
14. Ochs (1997, p. 188).
15. Capps, unpublished prayer corpus.
16. See Duranti (1991) for a detailed account of this phenomenon in Samoan family dinner grace activity.
17. Capps, unpublished prayer corpus.

18. Ochs (1997, p. 188).
19. As noted in Chapter 6, Laurie's teacher and her siblings witnessed Laurie's crying; she was inconsolable throughout the day.
20. Ochs, Taylor, Smith, and Rudolph (1992).
21. Goffman (1959).
22. Crapanzano (1996, p. 125).
23. Capps (1992), Capps, Bjork, and Siegel (1993), Kramer (1996), Linenthal (1995).
24. Goffman (1959, 1967).
25. Goffman (1967, p. 91).
26. Taylor (1989, p. 48).
27. James (1982, p. 67).
28. Capps, unpublished prayer corpus.
29. Ibid.
30. Ibid.
31. See Ochs and Taylor (1992, 1994) for discussion of fathers as panopticons in family narrative activity.
32. Albert, Amgott, Crakow, and Marcus (1979).
33. C. Goodwin (1984), Mandelbaum (1987, 1993), Taylor (1995).
34. Nelson (1989).
35. Ibid., p. 37.
36. Feldman (1989, pp. 98–99).
37. Watson (1989).

8. Untold Stories

1. Martin (1999, p. 18).
2. Ibid., pp. 18–19.
3. Nelson (1990b, p. 308).
4. Bartlett (1932, p. 205).
5. Brewer (1995, p. 45). See also Amsterdam and Bruner (2000), Ceci and Leichtman (1992), Ceci et al. (1994), Conway (1995), Neisser and Fivush (1994), Neisser and Harsch (1992), Rubin (1995), White et al. (1997).
6. Bruner and Feldman (1995, p. 292).
7. Ricoeur (1988, p. 35).
8. Heidegger (1962), Ricoeur (1988, p. 37).
9. Bakhtin (1981), Duranti and Brenneis (1986), C. Goodwin (1984).
10. Holland (1995, p. 25).
11. Schafer (1983, p. 196).
12. Havel (1989, p. 253).

13. See for example Bruner (1990, 1991, 1994, 1995), Capps and Ochs (1995a), Fivush (1994), Fivush, Haden, and Reese (1996), Frank (2000), Haden, Haine, and Fivush (1995), Neisser (1988), Polkinghorne (1988), Schafer (1992), and Spence (1982).

14. Fivush (1991), Fivush and Hammond (1990), Nelson (1990b).

15. Mullen (1994, p. 56).

16. Nelson (1990b).

17. Freud (1953 [1924]).

18. See White and Pillemer (1979) for review; Spear (1979) for a neurological perspective; and Neisser (1962) and Schachtel (1982) for information processing perspectives.

19. Fivush (1991), Fivush and Hamond (1990), Fivush et al. (1991, 1996), Fivush and Reese (1992), Nelson (1990a), Siegel (1999).

20. Goldman-Rakic (1992), Roediger and Craik (1989), Squire (1987), Terr (1994).

21. Bauer and Mandler (1989), Berman and Slobin (1994).

22. Mullen (1994).

23. Siegel (1999, p. 34).

24. Fivush and Hamond (1990); see also Nelson (1990a, b).

25. Meltzoff (1988).

26. Bauer and Shore (1987), Bauer and Mandler (1990).

27. Bauer and Mandler (1990), O'Connell and Gerard (1985).

28. Sheingold and Tenney (1982).

29. Main (1991, 1996).

30. This is noted by Jerome Bruner (1990), by Ochs and Taylor (1992), who found that the American families they studied during dinner tended to recount complaint-narratives, and by Miller and Sperry (1987). See also Polanyi (1985) on violation of cultural roles as a warrant for narration.

31. Breuer and Freud ([1893-1895]1955), Janet ([1892] 1977).

32. Siegel (1999, p. 50).

33. Freyd (1996), Herman (1992), Putnam (1989, 1997), Siegel (1996), Terr (1994), van der Kolk (1994), Whitfield (1995). See Kihlstrom (1996) and Shobe and Kihlstrom (1997), who challenge the assumption that there is something "special" about traumatic memories, and that special techniques are required to recover them. They contend that 1) changes in recollections following traumatic events can be accounted for by normal memory processes, and cite evidence that memory is more likely to be enhanced than impaired by high levels of emotion and stress (e.g., Eich, 1995); and 2) that there is extensive variability in

individuals' memories of traumatic events (e.g., Goodman and Quas, 1997).

34. Barclay (1995).
35. Terr (1994).
36. Freyd (1996), Herman (1992), Putnam (1997), Shay (1994), Siegel (1996), Terr (1994), van der Kolk (1994), Whitfield (1995).
37. Bonanno (1995), Bonanno and Keuler (in press), Capps (1991).
38. Middleton and Edwards (1990), Middleton (1997).
39. Mandler (1984).
40. Nelson (1990a, b).
41. Fivush and Hamond (1990), Fivush (1991), Fivush, Haden, and Reese (1996), Fivush and Kuebli (1997), Rogoff and Mistry (1990), Peterson and McCabe (1992), Snow (1990), Trabasso (1997). See also Johnson (1997) on use of family photos to elicit children's narratives concerning past and hypothetical family interactions.
42. Fivush and Reese (1992, p. 5).
43. Ibid., p. 6.
44. Ibid., p. 7.
45. Fivush et al. (1995, p. 343).
46. Fivush and Hamond (1990, p. 231).
47. Ochs, unpublished family dinner corpus.
48. Fivush (1997, p. 4).
49. Ochs, unpublished family dinner corpus.
50. Ochs (1994, p. 116).
51. Taylor (1995a, b).
52. Fivush (1997, p. 2).
53. Blum-Kulka and Snow (1992, pp. 208–209).
54. As Blum-Kulka and Snow (1992) note, the confrontational parental style adopted here is reminiscent of the rejecting style described by Nelson (1973) and the style McCabe and Peterson (1991) found least conducive to growth in children's narrative production.
55. Blum-Kulka (1997). As Blum-Kulka and Snow (1992, p. 209) comment, "this was also apparent in parents' metapragmatic comments to children: Sixty percent of the Jewish American parents' metapragmatic comments related to fidelity, a much higher percentage than that found in the other groups."
56. Miller, Potts, Fung, Hoogstra, and Mintz (1990, p. 310).
57. Heath (1983).
58. Aronsson and Cederborg (1997), Cederborg (1994), Goldenberg and Goldenberg (1996), Minuchin and Fishman (1981).

59. Cederborg (1994, p. 126).

60. Ceci et al. (1992, 1994), White et al. (1997).

61. Ornstein et al. (1992).

62. Ceci et al. (1994).

63. Loftus (1979).

64. Ibid., Loftus (1980), Loftus and Ketcham (1991). See also Slobin's (1998) analysis of the ways in which linguistic resources influence memory of events. Slobin examines differences in thinking about one type of event—human motion—among speakers of two broad types of languages: those he refers to as "satellite," in which motion verbs depict *manner* of movement (i.e., fly, pop, jump, crawl) and those he refers to as "verb," in which motion verbs depict the *path* of movement (i.e., enter, exit, cross).

65. Capps, Yirmiya, and Sigman (1992).

66. Capps and Ochs, unpublished autism corpus.

67. Sacks, Schegloff, and Jefferson (1974).

68. Frith (1989), Happe (1994), Sigman and Capps (1997).

69. Loveland and Tunali (1991).

70. Fivush and Kuebli (1997, p. 258).

71. Ochs and Taylor (1992), Taylor (1995a, b).

72. Ochs, Taylor, Rudolph, and Smith (1992).

73. Taylor (1995a, p. 140).

74. Ochs and Taylor (1992), Taylor (1995a, b).

75. Main (1991, 1993, 1995a, b, 1996).

76. Main (1993, 1995a, b, 1996).

77. Miller et al. (1990).

78. Heath (1983), Ochs and Schieffelin (1984), Preece (1985), Weisner and Gallimore (1977).

79. Langer (1991, p. xiii).

80. Frank (1995).

81. Dworkin (1993), Frank (1995).

82. Frank (1995, p. 63).

83. C. Goodwin (1979).

84. Capps and Ochs (1995a).

85. Ibid., p. 126).

86. C. Goodwin (1981).

87. Morson (1994).

88. Baron-Cohen et al. (1986), Bruner and Feldman (1993), Hentges et al. (1999), Loveland et al. (1990), Loveland and Tunali (1993), Tager-Flusberg (1995), Tager-Flusberg and Sullivan (1995), Solomon (2000), Capps et al. (in press a, b).

89. Tager-Flusberg (1995, pp. 52-53).

90. Capps and Ochs unpublished autism corpus.

91. Happe (1994).

92. Iser (1993, p. 10).

93. Havel (1989, p. 190).

94. Schieffelin (1976, p. 181).

95. Young (1987).

96. Labov (1982, p. 228). See also Fisher (1987, p. 55), who asserts that all narratives in human life are judged by a "fidelity criterion," against which listeners assess "whether or not stories they experience ring true with the stories they know to be true."

97. Labov (1982, 1986).

98. Bauman (1986).

99. Chafe and Nichols (1986).

100. Edwards and Potter (1992, p. 204).

101. Capps and Ochs (1995a), Fivush (1997), Ochs and Taylor (1992), Taylor (1995). For discussion of a link between validity of memory and attributes of the rememberer, see also Ross (1997).

102. Goody and Watt (1968).

103. White (1980).

104. Spence (1982, pp. 31-32).

105. Heidegger (1962).

106. Aznarez (1999), Stoll (1998).

107. Gourevitch (1999).

108. Kramer (1996).

109. Capps (1991), Capps, Bjork, and Siegel (1993), Kramer (1996), Linenthal (1995).

110. O'Brien (1990, p. 84).

111. Capps (1991), Capps, Bjork, and Siegel (1993).

112. Kundera (1981).

113. Havel (1989, p. 139).

114. See special issue of *Psychological Science,* edited by S. J. Lynn and D. G. Payne (1997). See also Spence (1982).

115. Kundera (1995, pp. 128-129).

116. Mather, Henkel, and Johnson (in press), Payne, Neuschatz, Lampinen, and Lynn (1997), Roediger and McDermott (1993), Sarbin (1995).

117. Neisser (1990), Lifton (1993), Morrison (1994), Rosaldo (1984), Proust (1989/1913), Sampson (1982), Spence (1982), Ochs and Capps (1996), Mishler (1999).

118. Bergson (1911).
119. Kundera (1995).
120. Ricoeur (1988).
121. Bruner (1987, p. 15). See also Neisser (1988, 1990a, b), on narrative as "*a* basis, but not *the* basis of identity."

References

Abrahams, R. D. 1964. *Deep Down in the Jungle: Negro Narrative Folklore from the Streets of Philadelphia.* Hatboro: Pennsylvania Folklore Associates.

—— 1976. *Talking Black.* Rowley, MA: Newbury House.

Acebo, C., and Thoman, E. B. 1995. Role of Infant Crying in the Early Mother-Infant Dialogue. *Physiology and Behavior, 57,* 541–547.

Aiello, L. C. 1996. Terrestriality, Bipedalism and the Origin of Language. In W. G. Runciman, J. M. Smith, et al., eds., *Evolution of Social Behaviour Patterns in Primates and Man.* Oxford: Oxford University Press, pp. 269–289.

Ainsworth, M. D. S., Belhar, M., Walters, E., and Wall, S. 1978. *Patterns of Attachment.* Hillsdale: Erlbaum.

Albert, S., Amgott, T., Crakow, M., and Marcus, H. 1979. Children's Bedtime Rituals as a Prototype Rite of Safe Passage. *Journal of Psychological Anthropology, 2,* 85–105.

Amsterdam, A. G., and Bruner, J. S. 2000. *Minding the Law.* Cambridge, MA: Harvard University Press.

Applebee, A. N. 1978. *The Child's Concept of a Story: Ages Two to Seventeen.* Chicago: University of Chicago Press.

Aristotle. 1982 [4th century B.C.E.]. *Poetics.* Trans. J. Hutton. New York: Norton.

Arminen, I. 1996. On the Moral and Interactional Relevancy of Self-Repairs for Life Stories of Members of Alcoholics Anonymous. *Text, 16(4),* 449–480.

Aronsson, K., and Cederborg, A. C. 1994. Co-narration and Voice Family Therapy: Voicing, Devoicing, and Orchestration. *Text, 14(3),* 345–370.

—— 1996. Coming of Age in Family Therapy Talk: Perspective Setting in Mulitparty Problem Formulations. *Discourse Processes, 21,* 191–212.

—— 1997. A Love Story Retold. Moral Order and Intergenerational Negotiations. *Semiotica, 114,* 83–110.

Aznarez, J. J. 1999. Los Que Me Atacan Humillan a las Victimas. *El Pais,* 24 January.

Bakhtin, M. 1981. *The Dialogic Imagination: Four Essays.* Trans. Caryl Emerson and Michael Holquist. Austin: University of Texas Press.

—— 1986. *Speech Genres and Other Late Essays.* Trans. Vern W. McGee. Austin: University of Texas Press.

Bamberg, M. 1996. Perspective and Agency in the Construal of Narrative Events. In D. Stringfellow, E. Cahana-Amitay, E. Hughes, and A. Zukowski, eds., *Proceedings of the 20th Annual Boston Conference on Language Development,* vol. 1. Somerville, MA: Cascadilla, pp. 30–39.

—— 1997. A Constructivist Approach to Narrative Development. In M. Bamberg, ed., *Narrative Development: Six Approaches.* Mahwah, NJ : Erlbaum, pp. 89–132.

Barclay, C. R. 1995. Autobiographical Remembering: Narrative Constraints on Objectified Selves. In Rubin, 1995, pp. 94–125.

Barnes, J. 1984. *The Complete Works of Aristotle.* Princeton: Princeton University Press.

Baron-Cohen, S., Leslie, A., and Frith, U. 1986. Mechanical, Behavioral and Intentional Understanding of Picture Stories in Autistic Children. *British Journal of Developmental Psychology, 4,* 13–125.

Bartlett, F. C. 1932. *Remember: A Study in Experimental and Social Psychology.* Cambridge: Cambridge University Press.

Bauer, P., and Shore, C. 1987. Making a Memorable Event: Effects of Familiarity and Organization on Young Children's Recall of Action Sequences. *Cognitive Development, 2,* 327–328.

Bauer, P. J., and Mandler, J. M. 1989. One Thing Follows Another: Effects of Temporal Structure on 1- to 2-year olds' Recall of Events. *Developmental Psychology, 25,* 197–206.

—— 1990. Remembering What Happened Next: Very Young Children's Recall of Event Sequences. In R. Fivush and J. A. Hudson, eds., *Knowing and Remembering in Young Children.* Cambridge: Cambridge University Press, pp. 9–29.

Bauman, R. 1977. *Verbal Art as Performance.* Rowley, MA: Newbury House.

—— 1986. *Story, Performance, and Event.* Cambridge: Cambridge University Press.

Bauman, Z. 1988. *Life in Fragments.* Oxford: Blackwell.

Ben-Amos, D. 1975. *Sweet Words: Storytelling Events in Benin*. Philadelphia: ISHI.

Bergson, H. 1911. *Creative Evolution*. Boston: University Press of America.

Berman, R. 1995. Narrative Competence and Storytelling Performance: How Children Tell Stories in Different Contexts. *Journal of Narrative and Life History, 5(4)*, 285–314.

Berman, R. A., and Slobin, D. I. 1994. Narrative Structure. In R. A. Berman and D. I. Slobin, eds., *Relating Events in Narrative: A Crosslinguistic Developmental Study*. Hillsdale, NJ: Erlbaum, pp. 39–84.

Bernstein, B. 1972. Social Class, Language and Socialization. In P. P. Giglioli, ed., *Language and Social Context*. New York: Penguin, pp. 157–179.

Bernstein, M. A. 1994. *Foregone Conclusions: Against Apocalyptic History*. Berkeley: University of California Press.

Besnier, N. 1989. Information Withholding as a Manipulative and Collusive Strategy in Nukulaelae Gossip. *Language in Society, 18*, 315–341.

—— 1995. *Literacy, Emotion, and Authority: Reading and Writing on a Polynesian Atoll*. Cambridge: Cambridge University Press.

Biber, D. 1988. *Variation Across Speech and Writing*. Cambridge: Cambridge University Press.

Bloom, L. 1973. *One Word at a Time*. The Hague: Mouton.

Blum-Kulka, S. 1997. *Dinner Talk: Cultural Patterns of Sociability and Socialization in Family Discourse*. Mahwah, NJ: Erlbaum.

Blum-Kulka, S., and Snow, C. E. 1992. Developing Autonomy for Tellers, Tales, and Telling in Family Narrative Events. *Journal of Narrative and Life History, 2*, 187–217.

Bonanno, G. A. 1995. Accessibility, Reconstruction and the Treatment of Functional Memory Problems. In A. Baddeley, B. A. Wilson, and F. Watts, eds., *Handbook of Memory Disorders*. Sussex, England: Wiley, pp. 616–637.

Bonanno, G. A., and Keuler, D. J. 1998. Psychotherapy without Repressed Memory: A Parsimonious Alternative Based on Contemporary Memory Research. In S. J. Lynn, and K. M. McConkey, eds., *Truth in Memory*. New York: Guilford Press, pp. 437–463.

Bourdieu, P. 1977. *Outline of a Theory of Practice*. Trans. Richard Nice. Cambridge: Cambridge University Press.

Bowlby, J. 1973. *Attachment and Loss*. Vol. 2: *Separation: Anxiety and Anger*. New York: Basic Books.

Breuer, J., and Freud, S. 1955. Studies on Hysteria. In J. Strachey, ed., *The Standard Edition of the Complete Psychological Works of Sigmund Freud,* vol 2. London: Oxford University Press. (Original work published in 1893–1895.)

Brewer, W. 1995. What is Recollective Memory. In Rubin, 1995, pp. 19–66.

Brown, P. 1997. Conversational Structure and Language Acquisition: The Role of Repetition in Tzeltal Adult and Child Speech. Handout at talk presented at the 96th American Anthropological Association Meetings, Washington, DC.

Brown, P., and Levinson, S. C. 1987. *Politeness: Some Universals in Language Usage.* Cambridge: Cambridge University Press.

Brown, R. 1973. *A First Language: The Early Stages.* Cambridge, MA: Harvard University Press.

Browne, M. D. 1993. Failure. In K. Brown, ed., *The True Subject: Writers on Life.* Saint Paul: Graywolf Press, pp. 40–51.

Bruner, J. 1974. *Beyond the Information Given: Studies in the Psychology of Knowing.* London: George Allen and Unwin.

—— 1986. *Actual Minds, Possible Worlds.* Cambridge, MA: Harvard University Press.

—— 1987. Life as Narrative. *Social Research, 54(1),* 11–32.

—— 1990. *Acts of Meaning.* Cambridge, MA: Harvard University Press.

—— 1991. The Narrative Construction of Reality. *Critical Inquiry, 18,* 1–21.

—— 1994. The "Remembered" Self. In Neisser and Fivush, 1994, pp. 41–54.

—— 1995. A Narrative Model of Self Construction. Paper presented at the New York Academy of Sciences, New York.

—— 1996. *The Culture of Education.* Cambridge, MA: Harvard University Press.

Bruner, J., and Feldman, C. 1993. Theories of Mind and the Problem of Autism. In S. Baron-Cohen, H. Tager-Flusberg, and D. J. Cohen, eds., *Understanding Other Minds: Perspectives from Autism.* Oxford: Oxford University Press, pp. 267–291.

—— 1995. Group Narrative as a Cultural Context of Autobiography. In Rubin, 1995, pp. 291–317.

Bruner, J., and Lucariello, J. 1989. Monologue as Narrative Recreation of the World. In Nelson, 1989a, pp. 73–98.

Budwig, N. 1990. A Functional Approach to the Acquisition of Personal Pronouns. In G. Conti-Ramsden and C. Snow, eds., *Children's Language,* vol. 7. Hillsdale, NJ: Erlbaum, pp. 121–145.

Burke, K. 1962. *A Grammar of Motives and a Rhetoric of Motives.* Cleveland and New York: Meridian Books.

—— 1973. *The Philosophy of Literary Form.* Berkeley: University of California Press.

Button, G., and Casey, N. 1985. Topic Nomination and Topic Pursuit. *Human Studies 8*, 3–55.

Byers, M. A. 1994. Symboling and Middle-Upper Palaeolithic Transition. *Current Anthropology, 35(4)*, 369–399.

Calvino, I. 1981. *If on a Winter's Night a Traveler.* New York: Harcourt Brace.

Capps, L. 1991. The Memorial as a Symbol and Agent of Healing. In W. H. Capps, ed., *The Vietnam Reader.* New York: Routledge, pp. 272–289.

—— 1995. Agoraphobia, Gender, and Identity. Paper presented at the Annual Meeting of the American Association of Applied Linguistics, March, Chicago, IL.

—— 1996. Socializing Anxiety through Narrative: A Case Study. *Issues in Applied Linguistics, 7*, 7–18.

Capps, L., Bjork, R., and Siegel, D. 1993. The Meaning of Memories. *UCLA Magazine, 4*, 8–10.

Capps, L., Kehres, J., and Sigman, M. 1998. Conversational Abilities among Children with Autism and Children with Developmental Delays. *Autism, 2(4)*, 325–344.

Capps, L., Losh, M., and Thurber, C. 2000. "The Frog Ate the Bug and Made His Mouth Sad": Narrative Competence in Children with Autism. *Journal of Abnormal Child Psychology, 2*, 193–204.

Capps, L., and Ochs, E. 1995a. *Constructing Panic: The Discourse of Agoraphobia.* Cambridge, MA: Harvard University Press.

—— 1995b. Out of Place: Narrative Insights into Agoraphobia. *Discourse Processes, 19(3)*, 407–440.

Capps, L., Sigman, M., Sena, R., Henker, B., and Whalen, C. 1996. Fear, Anxiety, and Perceived Control in Children of Agoraphobic Parents. *Journal of Child Psychology and Psychiatry, 37*, 445–452.

Capps, L., Yirmiya, N., and Sigman, M. 1992. Understanding of Simple and Complex Emotion in Non-Retarded Children with Autism. *Journal of Child Psychology and Psychiatry, 33(7)*, 1169–1182.

Casat, C. D. 1988. Childhood Anxiety Disorders: A Review of the Possible Relationship to Adult Panic Disorder and Agoraphobia. *Journal of Anxiety Disorders, 2*, 51–60.

Cazden, C. 1997. Speakers, Listeners, and Speech Events in Issues of Universality. *Journal of Narrative and Life History, 7*, 185–188.

Cazden, C., Michaels, S., and Tabors, P. 1985. Spontaneous Repairs in Sharing Time Narratives: The Intersection of Metalinguistic Awareness, Speech Event, and Narrative Style. In S. W. Freedman, ed., *The Acquisition of Written Language.* Norwood, NJ: Ablex, pp. 51–64.

Ceci, S. J., and Leichtman, M. D. 1992. Memory, Cognition and Learning: Developmental and Ecological Considerations. In S. J. Segalowitz and I. Rapin, eds., *Handbook of Neuropsychology,* vol. 7, Amsterdam: Elsevier, pp. 223–239.

Ceci, S., Loftus, E., Leichtman, M. D., and Bruck, M. 1994. The Possible Role of Source Misattributions in the Creation of False Beliefs among Preschoolers. *International Journal of Clinical and Experimental Hypnosis, XLII(4),* 304–320.

Cederborg, A. C. 1994. Family Therapy as Collaborative Work. Ph.D. diss., Linkoping University.

Chafe, W. 1979. The Flow of Thought and the Flow of Language. In T. Givon, ed., *Discourse and Syntax. Syntax and Semantics,* vol. 12. New York: Academic Press, pp. 159–181.

—— 1993. Discourse Research: Prosodic and Functional Units of Language. In J. A. Edwards and M. D. Lampert, eds., *Talking Data: Transcription and Coding in Discourse Research.* Hillsdale, NJ: Lawrence Erlbaum, pp. 33–44.

Chafe, W., and Nichols, J., ed. 1986. *Evidentiality: The Linguistic Coding of Epistemology.* Norwood, NJ: Ablex.

Cohn, C. 1987. Sex and Death in the Rational World of Defense Intellectuals. *Signs, 12(4),* 687–718.

Cole, M., and Cole, S. 1989. *The Development of Children.* New York: Scientific American Books.

Collins, J. 1995. Literacy and Literacies. In W. H. Durham, E. V. Daniel, and B. Schieffelin, eds., *Annual Review of Anthropology.* Palo Alto: Annual Reviews Inc., pp. 75–93.

Conway, M. A. 1995. Autobiographical Knowledge and Autobiographical Memories. In Rubin, 1995, pp. 66–93.

Cowan, G. M. 1964. Mazateco Whistle Speech. In D. Hymes, ed., *Language in Culture and Society: A Reader in Linguistics and Anthropology.* New York: Harper and Row, pp. 305–311.

Crago, M. B. 1988. *Cultural Context in Communicative Interaction of Inuit Children.* Montreal: McGill University Press.

Crapanzano, V. 1996. Self-Centering Narratives. In M. Silverstein and G. Urban, eds., *Natural Histories of Discourse.* Chicago: University of Chicago Press, pp. 106–127.

Crites, S. 1997. The Narrative Quality of Experience. In Hauerwas and Jones, 1997, pp. 26–50.

Daiute, C., and Nelson, K. 1997. Making Sense of the Sense Making Function of Narrative. *Journal of Narrative and Life History, 7,* 207–216.

Deacon, T. W. 1997. *The Symbolic Species: The Co-evolution of Language and the Brain.* New York: Norton.

Deby, J. 1997. The Multifunctionality of HL*H Intonation Contours in

Televised Ice-Hockey Commentary. Paper presented at SALSA V, Austin, Texas, January.

Demuth, K. 1983. The Role of Question Routines in the Socialization of Sesotho Children. In K. Demuth, ed., *Aspects of Sesotho Language Acquisition.* Bloomington: Indiana University Linguistics Club, pp. 57–88.

Descartes, R. 1969. *The Essential Descartes.* New York: Meridian Books.

Dunn, J. 1988. *The Beginnings of Social Understanding.* Oxford: Blackwell.

Duranti, A. 1991. On the Organization of Collective Activities: Saying Grace in a Samoan Village. Manuscript, UCLA.

—— 1992. Intentions, Self, and Responsibility: An Essay in Samoan Ethnopragmatics. In J. H. Hill and J. T. Irvine, eds., *Responsibility and Evidence in Oral Discourse.* Cambridge: Cambridge University Press, pp. 24–27.

—— 1993. Intentionality and Truth: An Ethnographic Critique. *Cultural Anthropology, 8,* 214–245.

—— 1994. *From Grammar to Politics: Linguistic Anthropology in a Western Samoan Village.* Berkeley and Los Angeles: University of California Press.

Duranti, A., and Brenneis, D. 1986. The Audiences as Co-author. Special issue of *Text, 6(3),* 239–347.

Duranti, A., and Goodwin, C. 1992. *Rethinking Context: Language as an Interactive Phenomenon.* Cambridge: Cambridge University Press.

Duranti, A., and Ochs, E. 1986. Literacy Instruction in a Samoan Village. In B. B. Schieffelin and P. Gillmore, eds., *Acquisition of Literacy: Ethnographic Perspectives.* Norwood, NJ: Ablex, pp. 213–232.

Dworkin, R. 1986. *Law's Empire.* Cambridge, MA: Belknap Press of Harvard University Press.

—— 1993. *Life's Dominion: An Argument about Abortion, Euthanasia, and Individual Freedom.* New York: Knopf.

Edwards, D., and Potter, J. 1992. *Discursive Psychology.* London: Sage.

Eich, E. 1995. Searching for Mood Dependent Memory. *Psychological Science, 6,* 67–75.

Eisenberg, A. 1985. Learning to Describe Past Experience in Conversation. *Discourse Processes, 8,* 177–204.

—— 1986. Teasing: Verbal Play in Two Mexican Homes. In B. B. Schieffelin and E. Ochs, eds., *Language Socialization across Cultures.* Cambridge: Cambridge University Press, pp. 182–198.

Encyclopedia Britannica. 1982. Prayer. 15th edition.

Ek, L., and Alvarez, H. 1998. A Multicultural Pedagogy. Presentation in seminar on Social Foundations of Language, UCLA.

Engel, S. 1995. *The Stories Children Tell: Making Sense of the Narratives of Child-hood.* New York: Freeman.

Fader, A. 1996. Wenner Gren Foundation Predoctoral Research Proposal.

Falconer, E. 1994. *The House that Jack Built.* Nashville: Ideals Children's Books.

Feher, M., Naddaff, R., and Tazi, N. 1989. *Fragments for a History of the Human Body.* New York: Zone Books.

Feldman, C. 1989. Monologues as Problem-solving Narrative. In Nelson, 1989a, pp. 98–119.

—— 1999. The Construction of Mind and Self in an Interpretive Community. Paper presented at the University of Southern California Conference on "The Engaged Self," Los Angeles, September.

Fernald, A. 1989. Intonation and Communicative Intent in Mothers' Speech to Infants: Is the Melody the Message? *Child Development, 60,* 1497–1510.

—— 1992. Meaningful Melodies in Mothers' Speech to Infants. In H. Papousek, U. Jurgens, and M. Papousek, eds., *Nonverbal Vocal Communication: Comparative and Developmental Approaches.* Studies in emotion and social interaction. New York: Cambridge University Press, pp. 262–282.

Fernald, A., and Mazzie, C. 1991. Prosody and Focus in Speech to Infants and Adults. *Developmental Psychology, 27,* 209–221.

Field, S. 1979. *Screenplay: The Foundations of Screenwriting.* New York: Dell.

Frith, U. 1989. *Autism: Explaining the Enigma.* Oxford: Blackwell.

Fish, S. E. 1980a. Literature in the Reader: Affective Stylistics. In J. P. Tompkins, ed., *Reader-Response Criticism: From Formalism to Post-Structuralism.* Baltimore: Johns Hopkins University Press, pp. 70–100.

—— 1980b. Interpreting the Variorum. In J. P. Tompkins, ed., *Reader-Response Criticism: From Formalism to Post-Structuralism.* Baltimore: Johns Hopkins University Press, pp. 164–184.

Fisher, W. R. 1987. *Human Communication as Narration : Toward a Philosophy of Reason, Value, and Action.* Columbia: University of South Carolina Press.

Fivush, R. 1991. The Social Construction of Personal Narratives. *Merrill-Palmer Quarterly, 37(1),* 59–81.

—— 1994. Constructing Narrative, Emotion, and Self in Parent-Child Conversations about the Past. In Neisser and Fivush, 1994, pp. 136–157.

—— 1995. Language, Narrative, and Autobiography. *Consciousness and Cognition: An International Journal, 4,* 100–103.

—— 1997. A Self in Time. Paper presented at the meeting of the Society for Research in Child Development, Washington, DC, April.

Fivush, R., Haden, C., and Reese, E. 1995. Remembering, Recounting, and Reminiscing: The Development of Autobiographical Memory in Social Context. In Rubin, 1995, pp. 341–359.

Fivush, R., and Hamond, N. R. 1990. Autobiographical Memory across the Preschool Years: Toward Reconceptualizing Childhood Amnesia. In R. Fivush and J. A. Hudson, eds., *Knowing and Remembering in Young Children,* Emory Symposia on Cognition. New York: Cambridge University Press, pp. 223–248.

Fivush, R., Hamond, N. R., Harsch, N., Singer, N., and Wolf, A. 1991. Content and Consistency in Young Children's Autobiographical Recall. *Discourse Processes, 14(3),* 373–388.

Fivush, R., and Keubli, J. 1997. Making Everyday Events Emotional: The Construal of Emotion in Parent-Child Conversations about the Past. In N. L. Stein, P. A. Ornstein, B. Tversky, and C. Brainerd, eds., *Memory for Everyday and Emotional Events.* Mahwah, NJ: Erlbaum, pp. 239–266.

Fivush, R., and Reese, E. 1992. The Social Construction of Autobiographical Memory. In M. A. Conway, H. Spinnler, D. C. Rubin, and W. Wagenar, eds., *Theoretical Perspectives on Autobiographical Memory.* Netherlands: Kluwer Academic Publishers, pp. 1–28.

Frank, A. W. 1995. *The Wounded Storyteller: Body, Illness, and Ethics.* Chicago: University of Chicago Press.

Frank, G. 2000. *Venus on Wheels: Two Decades of Dialogue on Disability, Biography, and Being Female in America.* Berkeley: University of California Press.

Freyd, J. 1996. *Betrayal Trauma: The Logic of Forgetting Childhood Abuse.* Cambridge, MA: Harvard University Press.

Freud, S. 1953 [1924]. *A General Introduction to Psychoanalysis.* New York: Pocket Books.

Frith, U. 1989. *Autism: Understanding the Enigma.* Oxford: Blackwell.

Fung, H. 1994. The Socialization of Shame in Young Chinese Children. Ph.D. diss., University of Chicago.

Gadamer, H. G. 1976. *Philosophical Hermeneutics.* Berkeley: University of California Press.

Garfinkel, H. 1967. *Studies in Ethnomethodology.* Englewood Cliffs, NJ: Prentice-Hall.

Garro, L. C. In press. The Remembered Past in a Culturally Meaningful

Life: Remembering as Cultural, Social and Cognitive Process. In H. Matthews and C. Moore, eds., *The Psychology of Cultural Experience.* Cambridge: Cambridge University Press.

Garro, L. C., and Mattingly, C. In press. Narrative as Construct and as Construction. In C. Mattingly and L. C. Garro, eds., *Narrative and the Cultural Construction of Illness and Healing.* Berkeley: University of California Press.

Gates, H. L. 1988. *The Signifying Monkey: A Theory of African-American Literary Criticism.* Oxford: Oxford University Press.

—— 1996. White Like Me. *The New Yorker,* 17 June, 66-81.

Gee, J. P. 1986. Units in the Production of Narrative Discourse. *Discourse Processes, 9,* 391-422.

Gee, J. 1996. *Social Linguistics and Literacies: Ideology in Discourses.* London: Taylor and Francis.

Gergen, K. J., and Gergen, M. M. 1997. Narratives of the Self. In L. P. Hinchman and S. K. Hinchman, eds., *Memory, Identity, Community: The Idea of Narrative in the Human Sciences,* SUNY series in the philosophy of the social sciences. Albany: State University of New York Press, pp. 161-184.

Gergen, K., and Kaye, J. 1992. Beyond Narrative in the Negotiation of Therapeutic Meaning. In S. McNamee and K. J. Gergen, eds., *Therapy as Social Construction.* London: Sage, pp. 166-185.

Gerhardt, J. 1989. Monologue as a Speech Genre. In Nelson, 1989a, pp. 171-230.

Gibson, J. J. 1979. *The Ecological Approach to Visual Perception.* Boston: Houghton Mifflin.

Ginsberg, F. 1987. Procreation Stories: Reproduction, Nurturance, and Procreating in Life Narratives of Abortion Activists. *American Ethnologist, 14,* 623-636.

Goffman, E. 1959. *The Presentation of Self in Everyday Life.* Garden City, NY: Doubleday.

—— 1963. *Behavior in Public Places: Notes on the Social Organization of Gathering.* New York: Free Press.

—— 1967. *Interaction Ritual: Essays on Face-to-Face Behavior.* Garden City, NY: Doubleday.

—— 1974. *Frame Analysis: An Essay on the Organization of Experience.* New York: Harper and Row.

Goldenberg, I., and Goldenberg, H. 1996. *Family Therapy: An Overview.* Pacific Grove, CA: Brooks/Cole Publishing.

Goleman, D. 1995. *Emotional Intelligence.* New York: Bantam.

Goldman-Rakic, P. 1992. Working Memory and the Mind. *Scientific American, 267,* 110–117.

Gonzales, P. 1996. The Talk and Social Organization of Problem-Solving Activities among Physicists. Ph.D. diss., UCLA.

Good, B. J., and Good, M.-J. D. 1994. In the Subjunctive Mode: Epilepsy Narratives in Turkey. *Social Science and Medicine, 38,* 835–842.

Goodman, G. S., and Quas, J. A. 1997. Trauma and Memory: Individual Differences in Children's Recounting of a Stressful Experience. In N. L. Stein, P. A. Ornstein, B. Tversky, and C. Brainerd, eds., *Memory for Everyday and Emotional Events.* Mahwah, NJ: Erlbaum, pp. 267–294.

Goodwin, C. 1979. The Interactive Construction of a Sentence in Natural Conversation. In G. Psathas, ed., *Everyday Language: Studies in Ethnomethodology.* New York: Irvington, pp. 97–121.

—— 1981. *Conversational Organization: Interaction between Speakers and Hearers.* New York: Academic Press.

—— 1984. Notes on Story Structure and the Social Organization of Participation. In M. Atkinson and J. Heritage, eds., *Structures of Social Action.* Cambridge: Cambridge University Press, pp. 225–246.

—— 1986. Audience Diversity, Participation and Interpretation. *Text, 6(3),* 283–316.

—— 2000. Gesture, Aphasia, and Interaction. In D. McNeill, ed., *Language and Gesture: Window into Thought and Action.* Cambridge: Cambridge University Press.

Goodwin, C., and Goodwin, M. H. 1992. Assessments and the Construction of Context. In Duranti and Goodwin, 1992, pp. 151–189.

Goodwin, M. H. 1989. Tactical Uses of Stories: Participation Frameworks Within Girls' and Boys' Disputes. In S. Berentzen, ed., *Ethnographic Approaches to Children's Worlds and Peer Cultures.* Trondheim, Norway: The Norwegian Center for Child Research (Report no. 15), pp. 110–143.

—— 1990. *He-Said-She-Said: Talk as Social Organization among Black Children.* Bloomington: Indiana University Press.

—— 1991. Retellings, Pretellings and Hypothetical Stories. In L. Laitinen, P. Nuolijarvi, and M. Saari, eds., *Leikkauspiste.* Helsinki: Suomalaisen Kirjallisuuden Seura, pp. 43–58.

—— 1997. Toward Families of Stories in Context. *Journal of Narrative and Life History, 7,* 107–112.

Goody, J., and Watt, I. 1968. The Consequences of Literacy. In J. Goody, ed., *Literacy in Traditional Society.* Cambridge: Cambridge University Press, pp. 27–68.

Gossen, G. 1976. Verbal Dueling in Chamula. In B. Kirshenblatt-Gimblett, ed., *Speech Play: Research and Resources for the Study of Linguistic Creativity*. Philadelphia: University of Pennsylvania Press, pp. 121-148.

Gottman, J. M., and Katz, L. F. 1989. The Effects of Marital Discord on Young Children's Peer Interaction and Health. *Developmental Psychology, 25,* 373-381.

Gottman, J. M., Katz, L. F., and Hooven, C. 1997. *Meta-Emotion: How Families Communicate Emotionally.* Mahwah, NJ: Erlbaum.

Gould, J. L., and Gould, C. G. 1988. *The Honey Bee.* New York: Freeman.

Gourevitch, P. 1999. The Memory Thief. *The New Yorker,* 14 June, 48-68

Gross, A. G. 1990. *The Rhetoric of Science.* Cambridge, MA: Harvard University Press.

Gutierrez, K. D., Stone, L., and Larson, J. In press. Hypermediating in the Urban Classroom: When Scaffolding Becomes Sabotage in Narrative Activity. In C. D. Baker, J. Cook-Gumperz, and A. Luke, eds., *Literacy in Power.* Oxford: Blackwell.

Haden, C. A., Haine, R. A., and Fivush, R. 1995. Developing Narrative Structure in Parent-Child Reminiscing across the Preschool Years. *Developmental Psychology, 33,* 295-307.

Hall, K. and Bucholtz, M. 1995. *Gender Articulated: Language and the Socially Constructed Self.* New York: Routledge.

Han, J. J., Leichtman, M., and Wang, Q. 1998. Autobiographical Memory in Korean, Chinese, and American Children. *Developmental Psychology, 34(4),* 701-713.

Happe, F. 1994. *Autism: An Introduction to Psychological Theory.* Cambridge, MA: Harvard University Press.

Haraway, D. 1988. Situated Knowledges: The Science Question in Feminism and the Privilege of Partial Perspective. *Feminist Studies, 14(3),* 575-599.

Hauerwas, S., and Jones, L. G. 1997. *Why Narrative: Readings in Narrative Theology.* Eugene, OR: Wipf and Stock.

Havel, V. 1989. *Letters to Olga.* Trans. Paul Wilson. New York: Henry Holt.

Haviland, J. B. 1977. *Gossip, Reputation, and Knowledge in Zinacantan.* Chicago: University of Chicago Press.

Heath, S. B. 1982. Questioning at Home and at School: A Comparative Study. In G. Spindler, ed., *Doing the Ethnography of Schooling.* New York: Holt, Rinehart and Winston, pp. 102-131.

—— 1983. *Ways with Words: Language, Life, and Work in Communities and Classrooms.* Cambridge: Cambridge University Press.

Heath, S. 1985. The Cross-Cultural Study of Language Acquisition. *Papers and Reports on Child Language Development, 24,* 1-21.

—— 1986. Taking a Cross-Cultural Look at Narratives. *Topics of Language Disorders, 7(1)*, 84–94.

—— 1988. Protean Shapes in Literacy Event: Ever-Shifting Oral and Literate Traditions. In E. Kintgen, B. M. Kroll, and M. Rose, eds., *Perspectives on Literacy*. Carbondale and Edwarsville: Southern Illinois University Press, pp. 348–370.

—— 1991. It's about Winning! The Language of Knowledge in Baseball. In L. Resnick, J. Levine, and S. Teasley, eds., *Perspectives on Socially Shared Cognition*. Washington, DC: American Psychological Association, pp. 101–124.

Heelas, P., and Lock, A. 1981. *Indigenous Psychologies: The Anthropology of the Self*. London: Academic Press.

Heidegger, M. 1962. *Being and Time*. Trans. Jon Macquirre and Edward Robinson. New York: Harper and Row.

—— 1992. *The Concept of Time*. Trans. William McNeill. Oxford: Blackwell.

Hendry, G. S. 1972. The Lifeline of Theology. *Princeton Seminary Bulletin, 65*, 22–30.

Hentges, B. B., Gibbs, C., Loveland, K. A., and Pearson, D. A. 1999. Verbal and Non-Verbal Story-Telling in Autism. Paper presented at the Bi-Annual Conference of Society for Research in Child Development, Albuquerque, New Mexico, April.

Herdt, G. 1994. *Third Sex, Third Gender: Beyond Sexual Dimorphism in Culture and History*. New York: Zone Books.

Heritage, J. 1990/91. Intention, Meaning and Strategy: Observations on Constraints on Interaction Analysis. *Research on Language and Social Interaction, 24*, 311–332.

Herman, J. L. 1992. *Trauma and Recovery*. New York: Basic Books.

Herzog, G. 1964. Drum-signaling in a West African tribe. In D. Hymes, ed., *Language in Culture and Society: A Reader in Linguistics and Anthropology*. New York: Harper and Row, pp. 305–311.

Holland, B. 1995. The Sounds of Silence are Many and Varied, *New York Times*, 21 May 1995, 25.

Holmes, J. 1998. Narrative Structure: Some Contrasts between Maori and Pkeha Story-Telling. *Multilingua, 17(1)*, 25–58.

Hudson, J. A. 1990. The Emergence of Autobiographical Memory in Mother-Child Conversation. In R. Fivush and J. A. Hudson, eds., *Knowing and Remembering in Young Children*. Emory Symposia in Cognition. New York: Cambridge University Press, pp. 166–196.

Hudson, J. A., Fivush, R., and Kuebli, J. 1992. Scripts and Episodes: The Development of Event Memory. Special Issue: Memory in Everyday Settings. *Applied Cognitive Psychology, 6*, 483–505.

Hudson, J. A., and Shapiro, L. R. 1991. From Knowing to Telling: The Development of Children's Scripts, Stories, and Personal Narratives. In McCabe and Peterson, 1991, pp. 89–136.

Hyden, M., and McCarthy, I. C. 1994. Woman Battering and Father-Daughter Incest Disclosure: Discourses of Denial and Acknowledgment. *Discourse and Society, 5(4),* 543–565.

Hymes, D. 1981. *"In Vain I Tried to Tell You": Essays in Native American Ethnopoetics.* Philadelphia: University of Pennsylvania Press.

—— 1996. *Ethnography, Linguistics, Narrative Inequality.* London: Taylor and Francis.

Iser, W. 1993. *Prospecting: From Reader Response to Literary Anthropology.* Baltimore: Johns Hopkins University Press.

Jacobs-Huey, L. 1999. Becoming Cosmetologists: Language Socialization in an African American Beauty College. Ph.D. diss., UCLA.

Jacoby, S. 1998. Science as Performance: Socializing Scientific Discourse through the Conference Talk Rehearsal. Ph.D. diss., UCLA.

Jakobson, R. 1960. Closing Statement: Linguistics and Poetics. In T. A. Sebeok, ed., *Style in Language.* Cambridge, MA: MIT Press.

James, W. 1982 [1902]. *The Varieties of Religious Experience.* New York: Penguin.

Janet, P. 1977 [1892]. *The Mental State of Hystericals.* Trans. C. R. Corson. Washington, DC: University Press of America.

Jefferson, G. 1978. Sequential Aspects of Storytelling in Conversation. In J. Schenkein, ed., *Studies in the Organization of Conversational Interaction.* New York: Academic Press, pp. 219–248.

John-Steiner, V. 1984. Learning Styles among Pueblo Children. *Quarterly Newsletter of the Laboratory of Comparative Human Cognition, 6(3),* 57–62.

John-Steiner, V., and Panofsky, C. 1992. Narrative Competence: Cross-Cultural Comparisons. *Journal of Narrative and Life History, 2(3),* 219–234.

Johnson, D. 1997. Understanding and Assessing Attachment Security in Middle Childhood: Implications for Social Competence. Poster presented at the Biennial Meeting of the Society for Research in Child Development, Washington, DC, April.

Jönsson, L., and Linell, P. 1991. Story Generations: From Dialogical Interviews to Written Reports in Police Interrogations. *Text, 11(3),* 419–440.

Katz, L. F., and Gottman, J. M. 1993. Patterns of Marital Conflict Predict Children's Internalizing and Externalizing Behaviors. *Developmental Psychology, 29,* 940–950.

Keenan, E. O. 1974. *Conversation and Oratory in Vakinankaratra, Madagascar.* Ph.D. diss., University of Pennsylvania.

—— 1976. The Universality of Conversational Postulates. *Language in Society, 5,* 67–80.

—— 1978. Questions of Immediate Concern. In E. N. Goody, ed., *Questions and Politeness.* Cambridge: Cambridge University Press, pp. 44–55.

Keenan, E. O., and Schieffelin, B. B. 1976a. *Foregrounding Referents: A Reconsideration of Left-Dislocation in Discourse.* Berkeley: Berkeley Linguistic Society.

—— 1976b. Topic as a Discourse Notion: A Study of Topic in the Conversation of Children and Adults. In C. N. Li, ed., *Subject and Topic.* New York: Academic Press, pp. 335–384.

Kendon, A. 1990. *Conducting Interaction: Patterns of Behavior in Focused Encounters.* Cambridge: Cambridge University Press.

Kermode, F. 1967. *The Sense of an Ending.* New York: Oxford University Press.

Kihlstrom, J. F. 1996. The Trauma-Memory Argument and Recovered Memory Therapy. In K. Pezdek and W. P. Banks, eds., *The Recovered Memory/False Memory Debate.* San Diego: Academic Press, pp. 297–311.

Kihlstrom, J. F., and Hoyt, I. P. 1990. Repression, Dissociation, and Hypnosis. In J. L. Singer, ed., *Repression and Dissociation: Implications for Personality Theory, Psychopathy, and Health.* Chicago: University of Chicago Press, pp. 181–208.

Kitayama, S., and Markus, H. R. 1994. *Emotion and Culture: Empirical Studies of Mutual Influence.* Washington, DC: American Psychological Association.

Kitayama, S., Markus, H. R., Matsumoto, H., and Norasakkunkit, V. 1997. Individual and Collective Processes in the Construction of the Self: Self-Enhancement in the United States and Self-Criticism in Japan. *Journal of Personality and Social Psychology, 72,* 1245–1267.

Kittredge, W. 1993. Doing Good Work Together. In K. Brown, ed., *The True Subject: Writers on Life.* Saint Paul: Graywolf Press, pp. 52–63.

Klein, J. 1996. Klein/Not Klein, *The New Yorker,* 29 July, p. 24.

Kluft, R. 1984. Multiple Personality in Childhood. *Psychiatric Clinics of North America, 7,* 121–134.

Kochman, T. 1981. *Black and White: Styles in Conflict.* Chicago: University of Chicago Press.

Korolija, N. 1998. Episodes in Talk: Constructing Coherence in Multiparty Conversation. Linkoping, Sweden: Ph.D. diss., Linkoping University.

Korolija, N., and Linell, P. 1996. Episodes: Coding and Analyzing Coherence in Multiparty Conversation. *Linguistics, 34,* 799–831.

Kramer, J. 1996. *The Politics of Memory.* New York: Random House.

Kuebli, J., Butler, S., and Fivush, R. 1995. Mother-Child Talk about Past Emotions: Relations of Maternal Language and Child Gender over Time. *Cognition and Emotion, 9,* 265–283.

Kuipers, J. C. 1990. *Power in Performance: The Creation of Textual Authority in Weyewa Ritual Speech.* Philadelphia: University of Pennsylvania Press.

Kummer, H. 1995. *In Quest of the Sacred Baboon.* Princeton, NJ: Princeton University Press.

Kundera, M. 1981. *The Book of Laughter and Forgetting.* Harmondsworth: Penguin.

—— 1995. *Testaments Betrayed.* New York: Harper-Collins.

Küntay, A. 1997. Extended Discourse Skills of Turkish Preschool Children across Shifting Contexts. Ph.D. diss., University of California, Berkeley.

Küntay, A., and Ervin-Tripp, S. 1997. Narrative Structure and Conversational Circumstances. *Journal of Narrative and Life History, 7,* 113–120.

Kushner, J. 1998. These Are the Words They Don't Put in These Stories: The Negotiation of Sephardic Moral Frameworks through Narrative. Paper Presented at the American Association for Applied Linguistics, Seattle.

Labov, W. 1966. *The Social Stratification of English in New York City.* Washington, DC: Center for Applied Linguistics.

—— 1972. *Language in the Inner City: Studies in the Black English Vernacular.* Philadelphia: University of Pennsylvania Press.

—— 1982. Speech Actions and Reactions in Personal Narrative. In D. Tannen, ed., *Georgetown University Round Table on Languages and Linguistics 1981: Analyzing Discourse: Text and Talk.* Washington, DC: Georgetown University Press, pp. 219–247.

—— 1986. On Not Putting Two and Two Together: The Shallow Interpretation of Narrative. Claremont, CA: Pitzer College Invited Lecture, 10 March.

Labov, W., and Waletsky, J. 1967. Narrative Analysis: Oral Versions of Experience. In J. Helm, ed., *Essays on the Verbal and Visual Arts: Proceedings of the 1966 Annual Spring Meeting of the American Ethnological Society.* Seattle: University of Washington Press, pp. 286–338.

Langer, L. 1991. *Holocaust Testimonies: The Ruins of Memory.* New Haven: Yale University Press.

Laub, D., and Auerhahn, N. C. 1993. Knowing and Not Knowing Massive Psychic Trauma: Forms of Traumatic Memory. *International Journal of Psycho-Analysis, 74,* 297–302. Chicago: University of Chicago Press.

Leitch, T. 1986. *What Stories Are: Narrative Theory and Interpretation.* University Park: Pennsylvania State University Press.

Leont'ev, A. N. 1979. The Problem of Activity in Psychology. In J. V. Wertsch, ed., *The Concept of Activity in Soviet Psychology.* Armonk, NY: M.E. Sharpe, pp. 37–71.

Lerner, G. H. 1987. Collaborative Turn Sequences: Sentence Construction and Social Action. Ph.D. diss., University of California at Irvine.

—— 1991. On the Syntax of Sentences-in-Progress. *Language in Society, 20(3),* 441–458.

—— 1997. On the "Semi-Permeable" Character of Grammatical Units in Conversation: Conditional Entry into the Turn Space of Another Speaker. In E. Ochs, E. Schegloff, and S. Thompson, eds., *Interaction and Grammar.* New York: Cambridge University Press, pp. 238–276.

Lewis, M., and Brooks-Gunn, J. 1979. *Social Cognition and the Acquisition of Self.* New York: Plenum Press.

Lifton, R. J. 1993. *The Protean Self: Human Resilience in an Age of Fragmentation.* New York: Harper and Row.

Linde, C. 1993. *Life Stories: The Creation of Coherence.* Oxford: Oxford University Press.

Linell, P., and Jonsson, L. 1991. Suspect Stories: On Perspective-Setting in an Asymmetrical Situation. In I. Markova and K. Foppa, eds., *Asymmetries in Dialogue.* Savage, MD: Barnes and Noble, pp. 75–100.

Linenthal, E. T. 1995. *Preserving Memory: The Struggle to Create America's Holocaust Museum.* New York: Viking Press.

Lock, A. 1981. *The Guided Reinvention of Language.* London: Academic Press.

Locke, J. 1975. *An Essay Concerning Human Understanding.* Oxford: Clarendon Press.

Loftus, E. F. 1979. *Eyewitness Testimony.* Cambridge, MA: Harvard University Press.

—— 1980. *Memory.* Reading, MA: Addison-Wesley.

—— 1997. Memory for a Past that Never Was. *Psychological Science, 6,* 60–70.

Loftus, E., and Ketcham, K. 1991. *Witness for the Defense.* New York: St. Martin's Press.

Loveland, K., McEvoy, R., Tulani, B., and Kelley, M. 1990. Narrative Story Telling in Autism and Down Syndrome. *British Journal of Developmental Psychology, 8,* 9–23.

Loveland, K., and Tunali, B. 1991. Social Scripts for Conversational Interactions in Autism and Down Syndrome. *Journal of Autism and Developmental Disorders, 21(2),* 177–186.

—— 1993. Narrative Language in Autism and the Theory of Mind Hypothesis: A Wider Perspective. In S. Baron-Cohen, H. Tager-Flusberg, and D. Cohen, eds., *Understanding Other Minds: Perspectives from Autism.* Oxford: Oxford University Press, pp. 247–266.

Luckmann, T. 1991. The Constitution of Human Life in Time. In J. Bender and D. E. Wellbery, eds., *Chronotypes: The Construction of Time.* Stanford: Stanford University Press, pp. 151–166.

Lynch, M. 1985. *Art and Artefact in Laboratory Science.* London: Routledge and Kegan Paul.

Lynch, M., and Woolgar, S. 1988. *Representation in Scientific Practice.* Cambridge, MA: MIT Press.

Lynn, S. J., and Payne, D. G. 1997. Memory as the Theater of the Past: The Psychology of False Memories. *Psychological Science, 6, 55.*

MacIntyre, A. 1984. *After Virtue.* Notre Dame: University of Notre Dame Press.

Main, M. 1991. Metacognitive Knowledge, Metacognitive Monitoring, and Singular (Coherent) vs. Multiple (Incoherent) Model of Attachment: Findings and Directions for Future Research. In C. M. Parkes, J. Stevenson-Hinde, and P. Marris, eds., *Attachment across the Life Cycle.* New York: Routledge, pp. 127–159.

—— 1993. Discourse, Prediction, and Recent Studies in Attachment: Implications for Psychoanalysis. *Journal of the American Psychoanalytic Association, 41,* 209–244.

—— 1995a. Attachment: Overview, with Implications for Clinical Work. In S. Goldberg, R. Muir, and J. Kerr, eds., *Attachment Theory: Social, Developmental, and Clinical Perspectives.* Hillsdale, NJ: Analytic Press, pp. 407–474.

—— 1995b. Discourse, Prediction, and Recent Studies in Attachment: Implications for Psychoanalysis. In T. Shapiro, R. N. Emde, et al., eds., *Research in Psychoanalysis: Process, Development, Outcome.* Madison, CT: International Universities Press, pp. 209–244.

—— 1996. Introduction to the Special Section on Attachment and Psychopathology: 2. Overview of the Field of Attachment. *Journal of Consulting and Clinical Psychology, 64,* 237–243.

Mandelbaum, J. 1987a. Couples Sharing Stories. *Communication Quarterly, 35(4),* 144–170.

—— 1987b. Recipient-Driven Storytelling in Conversation. Ph.D. diss., University of Texas at Austin.

Mandler, J. H. 1979. Categorical and Schematic Organization in Memory. In C. K. Puff, ed., *Memory Organization and Structure.* New York: Academic Press.

—— 1984. Representation and Recall in Infancy. In M. Moscovitch, ed., *Infant Memory*. New York: Plenum Press.

Mandler, J. M., and Johnson, N. S. 1977. Remembrance of Things Parsed: Story Structure and Recall. *Cognitive Psychology, 9,* 111–151.

Markus, H. R. 1983. Self-Knowledge: An Expanded View. *Journal of Personality, 51,* 543–565.

—— 1997. Self-Schemata and Processing Information about the Self. *Journal of Personality and Social Psychology, 35,* 63–78.

Markus, H. R., and Herzog, A. R. 1995. The Sociocultural Self-Concept. In I. Lubek, R. van Hezewijk, G. Pheterson, and C. W. Tolman, eds., *Trends and Issues in Theoretical Psychology.* New York: Springer, pp. 39–45.

Markus, H., Kitayama, S., and VandenBos, G. R. 1996. The Mutual Interactions of Culture and Emotion. *Psychiatric Services, 47,* 225–226.

Marshack, A. 1989. Evolution of the Human Capacity: The Symbolic Evidence. *Yearbook of Physical Anthropology, 32,* 1–34.

—— 1991. *The Roots of Civilization.* Mount Kisco: Moyer Bell Limited.

Martin, N. 1999. Some Tales Are Best Left Untold. *Los Angeles Times Magazine,* October 24, 18–19.

Maslow, A. 1970. *Religions, Values, and Peak Experiences.* New York: Viking Press.

Mather, M., Henkel, L. A., and Johnson, M. K. In press. Evaluating Characteristics of False Memories: Remember/Know Judgments and Memory Characteristics Questionnaire Compared. *Memory and Cognition.*

Mattingly, C. 1998. *Healing Dramas and Clinical Plots: The Narrative Structure of Experience.* Cambridge: Cambridge University Press.

McAdams, D. 1996. Personality, Modernity, and the Storied Self. *Psychological Inquiry, 7,* 295–321.

McCabe, A. 1997. Developmental and Cross-Cultural Aspects of Children's Narration. In M. Bamberg, ed., *Narrative Development: Six Approaches.* Mahwah, NJ: L. Erlbaum, pp. 137–174.

McCabe, A., and Peterson, C. 1991a. *Developing Narrative Structure.* Hillsdale, NJ: Erlbaum.

—— 1991b. Getting the Story: A Longitudinal Study of Parental Styles in Eliciting Narratives and Developing Narrative Skill. In McCabe and Peterson, 1991a, pp. 217–253.

McClatchy, J. D. 1995. James Merrill. *New Yorker,* 27 March, 59.

Meltzoff, A. 1988. Infant Imitation and Memory: Nine-Month-Olds in Immediate and Deferred Tests. *Child Development, 59,* 217–225.

Menchú, R. 1984. *I, Rigoberta Menchú: An Indian Woman in Guatemala.* Trans. Ann Wright. London: Verso.

Meng, K. 1992. Narrating and Listening in Kindergarten. *Journal of Narrative and Life History, 2(3)*, 235–276.

Michaels, S. 1981. "Sharing Time": Children's Narrative Styles and Differential Access to Literacy. *Language in Society, 10*, 423–442.

—— 1985. Hearing the Connections in Children's Oral and Written Discourse. *Journal of Education, 167(1)*, 36–56.

—— 1991. The Dismantling of Narrative. In McCabe and Peterson, 1991a, pp. 303–351.

Middleton, D. 1997. The Social Organization of Conversational Remembering: Experience as Individual and Collective Concerns. *Mind, Culture and Activity, 4(20)*, 71–85.

Middleton, D., and Edwards, D. 1990. *Collective Remembering.* Newbury Park, CA: Sage.

Miller, P. 1982. *Amy, Wendy, and Beth: Learning Language in South Baltimore.* Austin: University of Texas Press.

—— 1986. Teasing as Language Socialization and Verbal Play in a White Working-Class Community. In B. Schieffelin and E. Ochs, eds., *Language Socialization across Cultures.* Cambridge: Cambridge University Press, pp. 199–212.

—— 1994. Narrative Practices: Their Role in Socialization and Self-Construction. In Neisser and Fivush, 1994, pp. 158–179.

—— 1996. Instantiating Culture through Discourse Practices: Some Personal Reflections on Socialization and How to Study It. In R. Jessor, A. Colby, and R. A. Shweder, eds., *Ethnography and Human Development: Context and Meaning in Social Inquiry.* Chicago: University of Chicago Press, pp. 183–204.

Miller, P., Fung, H., and Mintz, J. 1996. Self-Construction through Narrative Practices: A Chinese and American Comparison of Socialization. *Ethos, 24*, 1–44.

Miller, P., Mintz, J., Hoogstra, L., and Fung, H. 1992. The Narrated Self: Young Children's Construction of Self in Relation to Others in Conversational Stories of Personal Experience. *Merrill-Palmer Quarterly, 38(1)*, 45–67.

Miller, P., and Moore, B. B. 1989. Narrative Conjunctions of Caregiver and Child: A Comparative Perspective on Socialization through Stories. *Ethos, 17(4)*, 428–448.

Miller, P., Potts, R., Fung, H., Hoogstra, L., and Mintz, J. 1990. Narrative Practices and the Social Construction of Self in Childhood. *American Ethnologist, 17*, 292–311.

Miller, P., and Sperry, L. 1982. Early Talk about the Past. *Journal of Child Language, 15*, 293–315.

—— 1987. The Early Acquisition of Theories of Personal Experience. Paper presented at the meeting of the Society for Research in Child Development, Baltimore, April.

Miller, P., Wiley, A. R., Fung, H., and Liang, C.-H. 1997. Personal Storytelling as a Medium of Socialization in Chinese and American Families. *Child Development, 68(3)*, 557–568.

Minami, M. 1996. Japanese Preschool Children's and Adults' Narrative Discourse Competence and Narrative Structure. *Journal of Narrative and Life History, 6(4)*, 349–373.

Minami, M., and McCabe, A. 1991. Haiku as a Discourse Regulation Device: A Stanza Analysis of Japanese Children's Personal Narratives. *Language in Society, 20*, 577–599.

—— 1995. Rice Balls and Bear Hunts: Japanese and North American Family Narrative Patterns. *Journal of Child Language, 22*, 423–445.

Minuchin, S., and Fishman, C. H. 1981. *Family Therapy Techniques.* Cambridge, MA: Harvard University Press.

Mishler, E. G. 1995. Models of Narrative Analysis: A Typology. *Journal of Narrative and Life History, 5(2)*, 87–124.

Mishler, E. 1999. *Storylines: Craftartists' Narratives of Identity.* Cambridge, MA: Harvard University Press.

Mitchell-Kernan, C. 1972. Signifying and Marking: Two Afro-American Speech Acts. In J. J. Gumperz and D. Hymes, eds., *Directions in Sociolinguistics: The Ethnography of Communication.* New York: Holt, Rinehart and Winston, pp. 161–179.

Modell, A. 1993. *The Private Self.* Cambridge, MA: Harvard University Press.

Monaco, J. 1981. *How to Read a Film.* New York: Oxford University Press.

Morgan, M. 1997. Conversational Signifying: Grammar and Indirectness Among African American Women. In Ochs, Schegloff, and Thompson, 1997, pp. 405–434.

Morrison, T. 1994. *The Nobel Lecture in Literature.* New York: Knopf.

Morson, G. S. 1994. *Narrative and Freedom: The Shadows of Time.* New Haven: Yale University Press.

Muhlhausler, P., and Harré, R. 1990. *Pronouns and People: The Linguistic Construction of Social and Personal Identity.* Oxford: Basil Blackwell.

Mullen, M. K. 1994. Earliest Recollections of Childhood: A Demographic Analysis. *Cognition, 52*, 55–79.

Mullen, M. K., and Yi, S. 1993. The Cultural Context of Talk about the Past: Implications for the Development of Autobiographical Memory. *Cognitive Development, 10(3)*, 407–419.

Munn, N. D. 1992. The Cultural Anthropology of Time: A Critical Essay. In

B. J. Siegel, A. R. Beals, and S. A. Tyler, eds., *Annual Review of Anthropology*. Palo Alto: Annual Review Inc., pp. 93–123.

Musil, R. 1995. *The Man Without Qualities.* Trans. Eithne Wilkins and Ernst Kaiser. New York: Knopf.

Naddaff, R., and Tazi, N. 1989. *Fragments for a History of the Human Body.* New York: Zone Books.

Nakamura, K. 1993. Referential Structure in Japanese Children's Narratives: The Acquisition of Wa and Ga. In S. Choi, ed., *Japanese/Korean Linguistics.* Stanford: Stanford University Center for the Study of Language and Information, pp. 84–99.

Neimeyer, G. J., and Metzler, A. E. 1994. Personal Identity and Autobiographical Recall. In Neisser and Fivush, 1994, pp. 105–135.

Neisser, U. 1962. Cultural and Cognitive Discontinuity. In T. E. Gladwin and W. Sturtevant, eds., *Anthropology and Human Behavior.* Washington, DC: Anthropological Society of Washington, pp. 54–71.

—— 1988. Five Kinds of Self-Knowledge. *Philosophical Psychology, 1,* 35–59.

—— 1994. Self-Narratives: True and False. In Neisser and Fivush, 1994, pp. 1–18.

Neisser, U., and Fivush, R. 1994. *The Remembering Self: Construction and Accuracy in the Self-Narrative.* Cambridge: Cambridge University Press.

Neisser, U., and Harsch, N. 1992. Phantom Flashbulbs: False Recollection of Hearing the News about Challenger. In E. Winograd and U. Neisser, eds., *Affect and Accuracy in Recall: Studies of "Flashbulb" Memories.* Cambridge: Cambridge University Press, pp. 9–31.

Nelson, K. 1973. Structure and Strategy in Learning to Talk. *Monographs of the Society for Research in Child Development, 38* (serial no. 149).

—— 1986. *Event Knowledge: Structure and Function in Development.* Hillsdale, NJ: Erlbaum.

—— 1989a. *Narratives from the Crib.* Cambridge, MA: Harvard University Press.

—— 1989b. Monologue as Representation of Real-Life Experience. In Nelson, 1989a, pp. 27–72.

—— 1990a. The Psychological and Social Origins of Autobiographical Memory. *Psychological Science, 4(1),* 7–14.

—— 1990b. Remembering, Forgetting, and Childhood Amnesia. In R. Fivush and J. A. Hudson, eds., *Knowing and Remembering in Young Children.* New York: Cambridge University Press, pp. 301–316.

Nelson, K., and Gruendel, J. 1981. Generalized Event Representations: Basic Building Blocks of Cognitive Development. In M. E. Lamb and A. L.

Brown, eds., *Advances in Developmental Psychology*. Hillsdale, NJ: Erlbaum, pp. 131–158.

—— 1986. Children's Scripts. In Nelson, 1986, pp. 21–46.

Noble, W. and Davidson, I. 1996. *Human Evolution, Language and Mind*. Cambridge, UK: Cambridge University Press.

Norman, D. A. 1988. *The Design of Everyday Things* (originally published as *The Psychology of Everyday Things*). New York: Doubleday.

Norton, B. 1936. *The Complete Poems and Plays, 1909–1950*. London: Ridgway.

O'Brien, T. 1990. *The Things They Carried*. New York: Penguin.

Ochs, E. 1988. *Culture and Language Development: Language Acquisition and Language Socialization in a Samoan Village*. Cambridge: Cambridge University Press.

—— 1994. Stories that Step into the Future. In D. F. Biber, ed., *Perspectives on Register: Situating Register Variation within Sociolinguistics*. Oxford: Oxford University Press, pp. 106–135.

—— 1997. Narrative. In T. A. Van Dijk, ed., *Discourse as Structure and Process*. Thousand Oaks, CA: Sage, pp. 185–207.

Ochs, E., and Capps, L. 1996. Narrating the Self. *Annual Review of Anthropology*, 25, 19–43.

Ochs, E., Gonzales, P., and Jacoby, S. 1997. "When I Come Down, I'm in a Domain State." Talk, Gesture, and Graphic Representation in the Interpretive Activity of Physicists. In Ochs, Schegloff, and Thompson, 1997, pp. 328–369.

Ochs, E., and Jacoby, S. 1997. Down to the Wire: The Cultural Clock of Physicists and the Discourse of Consensus. *Language in Society*, 479–506.

Ochs, E., Jacoby, S., and Gonzales, P. 1994. Interpretive Journeys: How Physicists Talk and Travel through Graphic Space. *Configurations*, 2, 151–172.

Ochs, E., and Schieffelin, B. B. 1979. *Developmental Pragmatics*. New York: Academic Press.

—— 1984. Language Acquisition and Socialization: Three Developmental Stories. In R. A. Shweder and R. A. LeVine, eds., *Culture Theory: Essays on Mind, Self, and Emotion*. Cambridge: Cambridge University Press, pp. 276–320.

—— 1995. The Impact of Language Socialization on Grammatical Development. In P. Fletcher and B. MacWhinney, eds., *The Handbook of Child Language*. Oxford: Blackwell, pp. 73–94.

Ochs, E., Smith, R., and Taylor, C. 1989. Detective Stories at Dinnertime: Problem-Solving through Co-narration. *Cultural Dynamics*, 2, 238–257.

Ochs, E., and Taylor, C. 1992. Family Narrative as Political Activity. *Discourse and Society, 3(3)*, 301–340.

—— 1993. Mothers' Role in the Everyday Reconstruction of 'Father Knows Best'. In *Locating Power: Women and Language, Proceedings of the Berkeley Linguistics Society*. University of California, Berkeley, pp. 447–463.

Ochs, E., Taylor, C., Rudolph, D., and Smith, R. 1992. Story-telling as a Theory-building Activity. *Discourse Processes, 15(1)*, 37–72.

O'Connell, B., and Gerard, A. 1985. Scripts and Scraps: The Development of Sequential Understanding. *Child Development, 56*, 671–681.

Ornstein, P. A., Gordon, B. N., and Larus, D. M. 1992. Children's Memory for a Personally Experienced Event: Implications for Testimony. *Applied Cognitive Psychology, 6*, 49–60

Payne, D. G., Neuschatz, J. S., Lampinen, J. M., and Lynn, S. J. 1997. Compelling Memory Illusions: The Qualitative Characteristics of False Memories. *Psychological Science, 6*, 56–60.

Peters, A. M., and Boggs, S. T. 1986. Interactional Routines as Cultural Influences upon Language Acquisition. In B. B. Schieffelin, and E. Ochs, eds., *Language Socialization across Cultures*. Cambridge: Cambridge University Press, pp. 80–96.

Peterson, C., and McCabe, A. 1983. *Developmental Psycholinguistics: Three Ways of Looking at a Child's Narrative*. New York: Plenum.

—— 1991. Children's Connective Use and Narrative Macrostructure. In McCabe and Peterson, 1991a,
pp. 29–54.

—— 1992. Parental Styles of Narrative Elicitation: Effect on Children's Narrative Structure and Content. *First Language, 12*, 299–321.

Piaget, J. 1952. *The Origins of Intelligence in Children*. New York: International Universities Press.

Pirandello, L. 1929. Six Characters in Search of an Author. In E. Bently, ed., *Naked Masks: Five Plays by Luigi Pirandello*. New York: Penguin.

Plato. 1952. *Gorgias*. Trans. W. C. Helmbod. New York: Bobbs-Merrill/Library of Liberal Arts.

Polanyi, L. 1985. *Telling the American Story: A Structural and Cultural Analysis of Conversational Story-Telling*. Norwood, NJ: Ablex.

Polkinghorne, D. E. 1988. *Narrative Knowing and the Human Sciences*. Albany: State University of New York Press.

Pomerantz, A. 1984. Pursuing a Response. In J. M. Atkinson and J. Heritage, eds., *Structures of Social Action*. Cambridge: Cambridge University Press, pp. 152–164.

Pratt, M. L. 1977. *Toward A Speech Act Theory of Literary Discourse*. Bloomington: Indiana University Press.

Preece, A. 1985. The Development of Young Children's Productive Narrative Competence in Conversational Contexts: A Longitudinal Investigation. Ph.D. diss., University of Victoria.

—— 1992. Collaborators and Critics: The Nature and Effects of Peer Interaction on Children's Conversational Narratives. *Journal of Narrative and Life History, 2(3)*, 277–292.

Propp, V. 1968. *The Morphology of the Folktale*. 2nd ed. Trans. T. Scott. Austin: University of Texas Press.

Proust, M. 1981 [1913]. *Remembrance of Things Past*, vol. III. Trans. C. K. S. Moncrieff, T. Kilmartin, and A. Mayor. London: Chatto and Windus.

—— 1989 [1913]. *Swann's Way*. New York: Random House.

Putnam, F. 1989. *Diagnosis and Treatment of Multiple Personality Disorder*. New York: Guilford Press.

—— 1997. *Dissociation in Children and Adolescents: A Developmental Perspective*. New York: Guilford Press.

Pye, C. 1992. The Acquisition of K'iche Maya. In D. I. Slobin, ed., *Crosslinguistic Study of Language Acquisition*. Hillsdale, NJ: Erlbaum, pp. 221–308.

Quasthoff, U. M. 1997. An Interactive Approach to Narrative Development. In M. Bamberg, ed., *Narrative Development: Six Approaches*. Mahwah, NJ: Erlbaum, pp. 51–84.

Quirk, R., Greenbaum, S., Leech, G., and Svartvik, J. 1985. *A Comprehensive Grammar of the English Language*. New York: Longman.

Radden, J. 1996. *Divided Minds and Successive Selves: Ethical Issues in Disorders of Identity and Personality*. Cambridge, MA: MIT Press.

Radin, P. 1972. *The Trickster*. New York: Schocken Books.

Reese, E., and Fivush, R. 1993. Parental Styles of Talking about the Past. *Developmental Psychology, 29*, 596–606.

Reese, E., Haden, C. A., and Fivush, R. 1993. Mother-Child Conversations about the Past: Relationships of Style and Memory over Time. *Cognitive Development, 8*, 403–430.

Renner, T. 1988. *Development of Temporality in Children's Narratives*. Ph.D. diss., University of California, Berkeley.

Reviere, S. L. 1996. *Memory of Childhood Trauma: A Clinicians' Guide to the Literature*. New York: Guilford.

Ricoeur, P. 1981. Narrative Time. In W. J. T. Mitchell, ed., *On Narrative*. Chicago: University of Chicago.

—— 1984. *Time and Narrative*. Vol. 1. Trans. K. Blarney and D. Pellauer. Chicago: University of Chicago Press.

—— 1985. *Time and Narrative*. Vol. 2. Trans. K. Blarney and D. Pellauer. Chicago: University of Chicago Press.

—— 1988. *Time and Narrative*. Vol. 3. Trans. K. Blarney and D. Pellauer. Chicago: University of Chicago Press.

Roediger, H. L., and Craik, F. I. N. 1989. *Varieties of Memory and Consciousness: Essays in Honor of Endel Tulving.* Hillsdale, NJ: Erlbaum.

Roediger, H. L., and McDermott, K. B. 1993. Creating False Memories: Remembering Words Not Presented in Lists. *Journal of Experimental Psychology: Learning, Memory, and Cognition, 21,* 803–814.

Rogoff, B. 1990. *Apprenticeship in Thinking.* New York: Oxford University Press.

Rogoff, B., and Mistry, J. 1990. The Social and Functional Context of Children's Remembering. In R. Fivush and J. A. Hudson, eds., *Knowing and Remembering in Young Children,* Emory Symposia on Cognition. New York: Cambridge University Press, pp. 197–222.

Rosaldo, M. 1984. Toward an Anthropology of Self and Feeling. In R. Shweder and R. A. Levine, eds., *Culture Theory: Essays on Mind, Self, and Emotion.* Cambridge: Cambridge University Press, pp. 137–157.

Rosenberg, B. 1970. *The Art of the Folk Preacher.* New York: Oxford University Press.

Ross, M. 1997. Validating Memories. In N. L. Stein, P. A. Ornstein, B. Tversky, and C. Brainerd, eds., *Memory for Everyday and Emotional Events.* Mahwah, NJ: Erlbaum, pp. 49–81.

Rubin, D. C. 1995. *Remembering Our Past: Studies in Autobiographical Memory.* Cambridge: Cambridge University Press.

Rymes, B. 1996. Naming as Social Practice: The Case of Little Creeper from Diamond Street. *Language in Society, 25(2),* 237–260.

Rymes, B. R. 1997. Dropping Out and Dropping In: Discourse Genres in an Urban Charter School. Ph.D. diss., UCLA.

Sacks, H. 1972. On the Analyzability of Stories by Children. In J. J. Gumperz and D. Hymes, eds., *Directions in Sociolinguistics: The Ethnography of Communication.* New York: Holt, Rinehart and Winston, pp. 325–345.

—— 1974. An Analysis of the Course of a Joke's Telling in Conversation. In R. Bauman and J. Sherzer, eds., *Explorations in the Ethnography of Speaking.* Cambridge: Cambridge University Press, pp. 337–353.

—— 1978. Some Technical Considerations of a Dirty Joke. In J. Schenkein, ed., *Studies in the Organization of Conversational Interaction.* New York: Academic Press, pp. 249–269.

—— 1992. *Lectures on Conversation.* Cambridge: Blackwell.

Sacks, H., Schegloff, E., and Jefferson, G. 1974. A Simplest Systematics for the Organization of Turn-Taking for Conversation. *Language, 50,* 696–735.

Salovey, P., and Mayer, J. D. 1990. Emotional Intelligence. *Imagination, Cognition, and Personality, 9,* 185–211.

Sampson, B. 1982. The Sick Who Do Not Speak. In D. Parkin, ed., *Semantic Anthropology.* New York: Academic Press, pp. 183–195.

Sankoff, G. 1980. *The Social Life of Language.* Philadelphia: University of Pennsylvania Press.

Sarbin, T. 1986. *Narrative Psychology.* New York: Praeger Science.

—— 1995. A Narrative Approach to "Repressed Memories." *Journal of Narrative and Life History, 5(1),* 51–66.

Schachtel, E. G. 1982. On Memory and Childhood Amnesia. In U. Neisser, ed., *Memory Observed.* San Francisco: Freeman, pp. 201–212.

Schafer, R. 1983. *The Analytic Attitude.* New York: Basic Books.

—— 1992. *Retelling a Life: Narration and Dialogue in Psychoanalysis.* New York: Basic Books.

Schank, R. C., and Abelson, R. P. 1977. *Scripts, Plans, Goals and Understanding.* Hillsdale, NJ: Erlbaum.

Schegloff, E. A. 1982. Discourse as an Interactional Achievement: Some Uses of "Uh huh" and Other Things that Come between Sentences. In D. Tannen, ed., *Georgetown University Roundtable on Languages and Linguistics.* Washington, DC: Georgetown University Press, pp. 71–93.

—— 1986. The Routine as Achievement. *Human Studies, 9,* 111–151.

—— 1995. Discourse as an Interactional Achievement III: The Omnirelevance of Action. *Research on Language and Social Interaction, 283,* 185–211.

—— 1997a. Narrative Analysis Thirty Years Later. *Journal of Narrative and Life History, 7,* 97–106.

—— 1997b. Turn Organization: One Intersection of Grammar and Interaction. In Ochs, Schegloff, and Thompson, 1997, pp. 52–133.

Schegloff, E. A., Jefferson, G., and Sacks, H. 1977. The Preference for Self-Correction in the Organization of Repair in Conversation. *Language, 53,* 361–382.

Schegloff, E. A., and Sacks, H. 1973. Opening up closings. *Semiotica, 8,* 289–327.

Schieffelin, B. B. 1990. *The Give and Take of Everyday Life: Language Socialization of Kaluli Children.* Cambridge: Cambridge University Press.

Schieffelin, B. B., and Ochs, E. 1986. Language Socialization. In B. J. Siegel,

A. R. Beals, and S. A. Tyler, eds., *Annual Review of Anthropology.* Palo Alto: Annual Reviews, Inc., pp. 163–246.

Schieffelin, E. L. 1976. *The Sorrow of the Lonely and the Burning of the Dancers.* New York: St. Martin Press.

Schore, A. 1994. *Affect Regulation and the Origin of the Self: The Neurobiology of Emotional Development.* Hillsdale, NJ: Lawrence Erlbaum Associates.

Schreiber, F. R. 1974. *Sybil.* New York: Warner Books.

Schultz, A. 1967 [1932]. *The Phenomenology of the Social World.* Evanston: Northwestern University Press.

Scollon, R., and Scollon, S. B. K. 1981. *Narrative, Literacy, and Face in Interethnic Communication.* Norwood, NJ: Ablex.

Scollon, S. 1982. *Reality Set, Socialization and Linguistic Convergence.* Ph.D. diss., University of Hawaii.

Scribner, S., and Cole, M. 1981. *Psychology of Literacy.* Cambridge, MA: Harvard University Press.

Shapin, S. 1994. *The Social History of Truth: Civility and Science in Seventeenth-Century England.* Chicago: University of Chicago Press.

Shapin, S., and Schaffer, S. 1985. *Leviathan and the Air Pump: Hobbes, Boyle and the Experimental Life.* Princeton: Princeton University Press.

Sharff, S. 1982. *The Elements of Cinema: Toward a Theory of Cinesthetic Impact.* New York: Columbia University Press.

Shay, J. 1994. *Achilles in Vietnam: Combat Trauma and the Undoing of Character.* New York: Simon and Schuster.

Sheingold, K., and Tenney, Y. J. 1982. Memory for a Salient Childhood Event. In U. Neisser, ed., *Memory Observed.* San Francisco: Freeman, pp. 201–212.

Sherzer, J. 1983. *Kuna Ways of Speaking: An Ethnographic Perspective.* Austin: University of Texas Press.

Shobe, K. K., and Kihlstrom, J. 1997. Is Traumatic Memory Special? *Psychological Science, 6,* 70–74.

Shore, B. 1982. *Sala 'iliua: A Samoan Mystery.* New York: Columbia University Press.

Shotter, J. 1995. A "Show" of Agency is Enough. *Theory and Psychology, 5,* 383–390.

Shuman, A. 1986. *Storytelling Rights: The Uses of Oral and Written Texts by Urban Adolescents.* Cambridge: Cambridge University Press.

Siegel, D. J. 1995. Memory, Trauma, and Psychotherapy. *Journal of Psychotherapy Practice and Research, 4,* 93–119.

—— 1996a. Cognition, Memory, and Dissociation. *Child and Adolescent Psychiatric Clinics of North America, 5,* 509–536.

—— 1996b. Dissociation, Psychotherapy, and the Cognitive Sciences. In J. L. Spira and I. D. Yalom, eds., *Dissociative Identity Disorder*. San Francisco: Jossey-Bass, pp. 39–79.

Siegel, D. 1999. *The Developing Mind: Toward a Neurobiology of Interpersonal Experience*. New York: Guilford Press.

Sigman, M., and Capps, L. 1997. *Children with Autism: A Developmental Perspective*. Cambridge, MA: Harvard University Press.

Silverman, W., Cerny, J. A., Nelles, W. B., and Burke, A. E. 1988. Behavior Problems in Children of Parents with Anxiety Disorders. *Journal of the American Academy of Child and Adolescent Psychiatry, 27,* 779–784.

Slobin, D. I. 1998. Verbalized Events: A Dynamic Approach to Linguistic Relativity and Determinism. Paper presented at 'Humboldt and Whorf Revisited' Symposium, Duisburg, Germany.

Snow, C. E. 1990. Building Memories: The Ontogeny of Autobiography. In D. Cicchetti and M. Beeghly, eds., *The Self in Transition: Infancy to Childhood*. Chicago: University of Chicago Press, pp. 213–242.

Solomon, O. 1997. A New Year Wish for Joshua. Manuscript, UCLA.

—— 1999. Casting the Future: Discourse and Temporality in Russian Toast Performances. *Crossroads of Language, Interaction and Culture, 1,* 3–23.

—— 2000. *Narratives of a Different Order: Autistic Children*. Paper presented at the CLIC Conference, Los Angeles, May.

Spear, N. 1979. Experimental Analysis of Infantile Amnesia. In J. F. Kihostrom and F. J. Evans, eds., *Functional Disorders of Memory*. Hillsdale, NJ: Erlbaum, pp. 75–102.

Spence, D. 1982. *Narrative Truth and Historical Truth: Meaning and Interpretation in Psychoanalysis*. New York: Norton.

Squire, L. 1987. *Memory and Brain*. New York: Oxford University Press.

Stein, N. 1982. The Definition of a Story. *Journal of Pragmatics, 6,* 487–507.

Stein, N., and Albro, E. 1997. Building Complexity and Coherence: Children's Use of Goal-Structured Knowledge in Telling Stories. In M. Bamberg, ed., *Narrative Development: Six Approaches,* pp. 5–44.

Stein, N., and Glenn, C. 1979. An Analysis of Story Comprehension in Elementary School Children. In R. O. Freedle, ed., *New Directions in Discourse Processing*. Norwood, NJ: Ablex, pp. 53–120.

Stein, N., and Goldman, S. R. 1981. Children's Knowledge about Social Situations: From Causes to Consequences. In S. R. Asher and J. M. Gottman, eds., *The Development of Children's Friendships*. Cambridge: Cambridge University Press, pp. 297–321.

Stein, N., and Policastro, M. 1984. The Concept of a Story: A Comparison between Children's and Teacher's Viewpoints. In H. Mandl, N. Stein, and T. Trabasso, eds., *Learning and Comprehension of Text.* Hillsdale, NJ: Erlbaum, pp. 113–158.

Stein, N. L., and Salgo, D. 1984. *The Relationship between the Story Concept and the Development of Story Telling Skills.* Psychonomic Society Meetings, San Antonio, Texas.

Stern, D. 1977. *The First Relationship: Infant and Mother.* London: Fontana/ Open Books.

Sterponi, L. 1998. Narratives and Speech Activities: For a Functional Perspective on Family Dinner Storytelling. Manuscript, UCLA.

Steveron, M. T. 1995. The Mother's Role in Japanese Dinnertime Narratives. Masters thesis, University of Hawaii.

Stoll, D. 1998. *Rigoberta Menchu and the Story of All Guatemalans.* Boulder: Westview Press.

Strage, A., and Main, M. 1985. Attachment and Parent-Child Discourse Patterns. Presented at biennial meeting of the Society for Research in Child Development, Toronto, April.

Street, B. V. 1984. *Literacy in Theory and Practice.* Cambridge: Cambridge University Press.

Sugiyama, M. S. 1996. On the Origins of Narrative: Storyteller Bias as a Fitness Enhancing Strategy. *Human Nature, 7(4),* 403–425.

Swearington, C. J. 1990. The Narration of Dialogue and Narration within Dialogue: The Transition from Story to Logic. In B. K. Britton and A. Pellegrini, eds., *Narrative Thought and Narrative Language.* Hillsdale, NJ: Erlbaum, pp. 173–197.

Tager-Flusberg, H. 1993. What Language Reveals about the Understanding of Minds in Children with Autism. In S. Baron-Cohen, H. Tager-Flusberg, D. J. Cohen, eds., *Understanding Other Minds: Perspectives from Autism.* Oxford: Oxford University Press, pp. 138–157.

—— 1995. "Once Upon a Ribbit": Stories Narrated by Autistic Children. *British Journal of Developmental Psychology, 13(1),* 45–59.

Tager-Flusberg, H., and Sullivan, K. 1995. Attributing Mental States to Story Characters: A Comparison of Narratives Produced by Autistic and Mentally Retarded Individuals. *Applied Psycholinguistics, 16(3),* 241–256.

Tannen, D. 1987. Repetition in Conversation: Toward a Poetics of Talk. *Language, 63(3),* 574–605.

—— 1990. Gender Differences in Topical Coherence: Creating Involvement in Best Friends' Talk. *Discourse Processes, 13(1),* 33–72.

Taylor, C. 1989. *Sources of the Self.* Cambridge, MA: Harvard University Press.

Taylor, C. E. 1995a. *Child as Apprentice-Narrator: Socializing Voice, Face, Identity, and Self Esteem amid the Narrative Politics of Family Dinner.* Ph.D. diss., University of Southern California.

—— 1995b. "You Think It Was a Fight?" Co-Constructing (the Struggle for) Meaning, Face, and Family in Everyday Narrative Activity. *Research on Language and Social Interaction, 28(3),* 283–317.

Terasaki, A. 1976. Pre-Announcement Sequences in Conversation. Social Science Working Paper. School of Social Sciences, Irvine, CA.

Terr, L. 1994. *Unchained Memories.* New York: Basic Books.

Thigpen, C., and Cleckley, H. 1955. *The Three Faces of Eve.* Augusta, GA: Cleckley-Thigpen.

Toth, N. 1987. The First Technology. *Scientific American, 255(4),* 112–121.

Trabasso, T. 1997. Whose Memory Is It? The Social Context of Remembering. In N. L. Stein, P. A. Ornstein, B. Tversky, and C. Brainerd, eds., *Memory for Everyday and Emotional Events.* Mahwah, NJ: Erlbaum, pp. 429–444.

Trabasso, T., and Nickels, M. 1992. The Development of Goal Plans of Action in the Narration of a Picture Story. *Discourse Processes, 15,* 249–276.

Trabasso, T., Secco, T., and Van Den Broek, P. 1984. Causal Cohesion and Story Coherence. In H. Mandl, N. Stein, and T. Trabasso, eds., *Learning and Comprehension of Text.* Hillsdale, NJ: Erlbaum Associates, pp. 83–113.

Trevarthen, C. 1979. Communication and Co-operation in Early Infancy: A Description of Primary Intersubjectivity. In M. Bullowa, ed., *Before Speech.* Cambridge: Cambridge University Press, pp. 321–349.

Umiker-Sebeok, D. J. 1979. Preschool Children's Intraconversational narratives. *Journal of Child Language, 6,* 91–109.

Van der Kolk, B. A. 1994. The Body Keeps the Score: Memory and the Evolving Psychobiology of Posttraumatic Stress. *Harvard Review of Psychiatry, 1,* 253–265.

Van der Kolk, B. A., and Van der Hart, O. 1989. The Failure of Adaptation to Trauma. *American Journal of Psychiatry, 146,* 1530–1540.

Van Dijk, T. 1976. Philosophy of Action and Theory of Narrative. *Poetics, 5,* 287–338.

Van Dijk, T., and Kintsch, W. 1983. *Strategies in Discourse Comprehension.* New York: Academic Press.

Volosinov, V. N. 1971. Reported Speech. In L. Matejka and K. Pomorska, eds., *Readings in Russian Poetics: Formalist and Structuralist Views.* Cambridge, MA: MIT Press, pp. 149–175.

—— 1973 [1929]. *Marxism and the Philosophy of Language.* Trans. L. Matejka and I. R. Titunik. New York: Seminar Press.

Von Frisch, K. 1967. *The Dance Language and Orientation of Bees.* Cambridge, MA: Harvard University Press.

Watson, R. 1989. Monologue, Dialogue, and Regulation. In Nelson, 1989a, pp. 263–283.

Watson-Gegeo, K., and Gegeo, D. 1986. Calling Out and Repeating Routines in the Language Socialization of Basotho Children. In B. Schieffelin and E. Ochs, eds., *Language Socialization across Cultures.* Cambridge: Cambridge University Press, pp. 17–50.

Weber, M. 1958. *The Protestant Ethic and the Spirit of Capitalism.* New York: Charles Scribner's Sons.

Weisner, T., and Gallimore, R. 1977. My Brother's Keeper: Child and Sibling Caretaking. *Current Anthropology, 18,* 169–190.

Weissman, M. M. 1993. Family Genetic Studies of Panic Disorder. *Journal of Psychiatric Research, 27(1),* 69–78.

White, H. 1980. The Value of Narrativity in the Representation of Reality. In W. J. T. Mitchell, ed., *On Narrative.* Chicago: University of Chicago Press, pp. 1–24.

White, S. H., and Pillemer, D. B. 1979. Childhood Amnesia and the Development of a Socially Accessible Memory System. In J. F. Kihostrom and F. J. Evans, eds., *Functional Disorders of Memory.* Hillsdale, NJ: Erlbaum, pp. 29–74.

White, T. L., Lechtman, M. D., and Ceci, S. 1997. The Good, the Bad, and the Ugly: Accuracy, Inaccuracy, and Elaboration in Preschoolers' Reports about a Past Event. *Applied Cognitive Psychology, 11,* 537–554.

Whitfield, C. L. 1995. *Memory and Abuse: Remembering and Healing the Effects of Trauma.* Deerfield Beach, FL: Health Communications.

Wing, L. 1981. Language, Social, and Cognitive Impairments in Autism and Severe Mental Retardation. *Journal of Autism and Developmental Disorders, 11,* 31–44.

Woods, L. 1997. College Football: Play-by-Play Narrative Structure. Manuscript, UCLA.

Wooffitt, R. 1991. 'I Was Just Doing X . . . when Y': Some Inferential Properties of a Device in Accounts of Paranormal Experiences. *Text, 11(2),* 267–288.

Young, K. G. 1984. Ontological Puzzles about Narrative. *Poetics, 13,* 239–259.

—— 1987. *Taleworlds and Storyrealms: The Phenomenology of Narrative.* Dordrecht: Martinus Nijhoff Publishers.

Zeskind, P. S., and Collins, V. 1987. Pitch of Infant Crying and Caregiver Responses in a Natural Setting. *Infant Behavior and Development, 10,* 501–504.

INDEX

LIBRARY, UNIVERSITY OF CHESTER